mobile electronics certified professional

Powered by Consumer Technology Association™

MOBILE PRODUCT SPECIALIST

STUDY GUIDE

This Study Guide is designed to prepare Mobile Electronics Product Specialistsfor the MECP Mobile Product Specialist Exam and can also be used as a reference guide. It is based on carefully documented material and research, and every attempt has been made to relay accurate and up-to-date information. MECP and/or the Consumer Technology Association cannot be held responsible for discrepancies or inconsistencies contained in this publication.

ISBN: 978-1-58887-046-9

Consumer Technology Association™

MECP

Consumer Electronics Association
1919 S. Eads St.
Arlington, VA 22202
MECP@mecp.com

CONTRIBUTORS

Contributing Writers

Joel Anderson
Kris Bulla
Jeff Cantrell
Shawn Curlee
Pete Daley
Doug Dobson
Nicholas Frazier
Ernie Hartman
Jesse Leppanen
Shaughnessy Murley
Christopher Pearson
Kaleb Pfaff
Todd Ramsey
Doug Tessman
Aaron Thomas
Ray West

Contributing Companies

AAMP Global
Automotive Data Solutions, Inc.
Best Buy
Escort Radar
iNNovative Concepts
JC Audio
Marketing Pros
Sony
The Ramsey Consulting Group, Inc.
Techni-B
Visions Electronics

TABLE OF CONTENTS

ACKNOWLEDGEMENTS, TRADEMARKS, ETC.

INTRODUCTION

INTRODUCTION

Margin Notes

The standards for the MECP certificate are set forth as guidance by the Consumer Technology Association (CTA)™ in its capacity as a trade organization and owner of the Mobile Electronics Certification Professional program. This study guide is the cornerstone of learning the basic elements of car electronics technology and products that are sold and installed through retail channels and is intended to be a study aid for the Mobile Product Specialist exam. Detailed information is presented in an uncomplicated way, and important points are summarized through bold type and margin notes.

EXPERIENCE

There are no prerequisites for hands-on experience to take the MECP Mobile Product Specialist exam. It assesses the competency and understanding of customer-facing retail sales professionals who are either new to the trade, just starting their career or professionals working to improve their current 12 Volt industry career path. While it is not necessary to attend a training program or vocational school to take the MECP Mobile Product Specialist (MPS) Exam, it is encouraged. Doing so will enhance your ability to understand the basic concepts and ask questions of a qualified instructor in a real-time environment.

JOB DESCRIPTION – MECP MOBILE PRODUCT SPECIALIST

The MECP Mobile Product Specialist directly interfaces with end-user clientele in a retail environment. This interaction requires asking qualifying questions, evaluating the client's vehicle for fit/compatibility and recommending car electronics products and installation services that fit their needs to provide a successful outcome.

Duties and Responsibilities

Answer phone (and potentially social media or email) inquiries from prospective clientele with accurate product and installation information with the goal of bringing them in as a customer.

Greet and qualify walk-in clientele with questions about their vehicle and car electronics technology interests for providing personalized product and installation recommendations.

Inspect the client's vehicle before quoting costs on undefined scopes of installation work.

Recommend products and installation services that correlate to the client's goals after answers to qualifying questions have been established.

Ensure compatibility of aftermarket electronics with the vehicle's existing electronics and customer's portable device(s) with the use of vehicle fit guides, manufacturer technical support resources and/or verifying with in-store colleagues.

Interface with the client and installation technician(s) during installation services.

Demonstrate completed installation to client showing features, operational characteristics and locations of important components (fuses, equipment or reference pages in the user manuals).

Attend manufacturer product training or in-person events for maintaining product-specific application and knowledge.

Margin Notes

Knowledge, Skills and Ability

Knowledge of MECP-defined car electronics installation guidelines relating to safety and longevity including proper wire routing techniques, proper wire gauge for circuit current, proper circuit protection devices, MECP-recommended wire-to-wire connection methods, etc.

Knowledge and understanding of the Magnusson-Moss Warranty Act. Also, a general knowledge of safety-related and driver distraction concerns that, although may vary state-to-state (or province-to-province), provide a fundamental background on how to advise prospective clients on installation-related features, placement and configuration.

Knowledge and understanding of MECP-defined, industry-standard terminologies for products and installation details (e.g., head unit, vehicle security system, preamp-level, speaker-level, shock sensor, auxiliary input, dash kit, wiring harness, signal summing, DSP, etc.).

Knowledge and understanding of electrical terminologies and relationships (volts, ohms, amperes, watts, etc.) including the base unit and smaller or larger units (milli, micro, kilo, mega, etc.).

Knowledge and understanding of audio terminologies (amplitude, frequency, period, wavelength, frequency response, S/N ratio, channel separation, RMS, peak, octave, harmonics, decibels, etc.).

Knowledge of audio system components and what function each serves (e.g., head unit, satellite radio, HD radio, AUX input, amplifier, subwoofer, coaxial speaker, component speaker – including tweeter, midrange and midbass drivers, signal processors of all types, line output converter, active crossover, passive crossover, etc.).

Knowledge and understanding of audio signal delivery methods (e.g., FM transmitter, Bluetooth® streaming, preamp-level, speaker-level and S/PDIF) and the audio bandwidth capability of each.

Knowledge and understanding of various commercially available installation accessories such as dash kits, wiring harnesses, antenna adaptors, speaker adaptors, line output converters, steering wheel control (SWC) adaptors, specialty interfaces for OEM premium audio system replacements (OnStar, chime retention, etc.), audio signal cables, high current power/ground wiring, circuit protection devices, etc.

Understanding of series and parallel wiring configurations for multiple speakers (or voice coils).

Knowledge and understanding of aftermarket rear seat entertainment (RSE) sources, screen types/common locations and audio output (connection to

Margin Notes

speakers, use of headphones, etc.). Also, knowledge of entry-level factory-installed RSE system interfacing fundamental objectives.

Knowledge and understanding of vehicle security/convenience system terminologies (1-way, 2-way, air-interface, transponder interface, keyless entry, entry point, sensor types, common programmable features such as siren duration, driver's only or all doors unlock, etc.).

Knowledge of the differences between analog (wire to wire) and digital (data module to module) connections in vehicle security and remote starter installations.

Knowledge of the GPS satellites and how in-dash or smartphone-based navigation systems collect and process the GPS data on maps displayed to the user. Additionally, general knowledge of traffic and emergency services enabled on many navigation systems. Knowledge of the requisite navigation-related terminology (GPS, POI, latitude, longitude, elevation, destination, re-route, etc.).

Knowledge of Bluetooth wireless communication profiles (HSP, HFP, A2DP, AVRCP, HID, etc.), device pairing and interoperability.

Knowledge of wireless data delivery methods/networks for use in the vehicle (e.g., tethering a smartphone for Wi-Fi hotspot, dedicated Wi-Fi hotspot, head unit interface through the phone's data connection, 3G/4G/LTE data networks, etc.) and common applications which utilize wireless data (e.g., streaming internet radio, security/RS activation, accessing email/text/maps/social media via Apple CarPlay™, Android™ Auto or proprietary user interfaces, etc.).

Knowledge of reverse camera and viewing screen configurations for correct image viewing (e.g., standard or mirror image) as well as what integrates with existing equipment (interface to in-dash LCD screen, add a stand-alone screen, rear view mirror screen, using a factory camera with aftermarket head unit, etc.). Additionally, knowledge of reverse sensor systems and how they sense obstacles within their range.

Knowledge of Forward Collision Warning (FCW), Lane Departure Warning (LDW) and Blind Spot Detection functionalities regarding the specific purpose of each system, even if contained as a multi-use system.

Skill to use a personal computer and/or tablet, email systems, internet browser and various point-of-sale and inventory management software. In some cases, knowledge of social media platforms.

Skill to demonstrate products configured as a 'system' on a demonstration board or installed in a vehicle.

Establish priorities and work with supervision; ask for clarification when necessary.

Ability to diagnose and resolve common consumer operational errors through in-person and over-the-phone troubleshooting assistance.

Margin Notes

Credentials and Experience

No professional experience is necessary although may be expected by some employers.

Candidate should possess a minimum of a 12th grade reading and mathematics proficiency.

Candidate should have firsthand experiences with his/her own automotive and consumer electronics products.

Special Requirements

Must be able to speak/read English (MECP Mobile Product Specialist exam and study materials are currently delivered in English only).

Willing to work weekends, holidays and shift overtime as required by the employer.

MAKING THE MOST OF THIS STUDY GUIDE

The MECP Mobile Product Specialist Study Guide is not a "How To" book. The purpose of this guide is to provide a greater understanding of critical topics today's customer-facing product specialist must know. The study guide will be your basic source of information needed to pass the MECP Mobile Product Specialist exam. Hands-on training and/or in-store retail aftermarket car electronics experience in this area will also help as well.

READ AND RE-READ SECTIONS

The ability to understand and absorb information presented in this study guide is enhanced by repetition. Grasping concepts, terminology and learning the topics presented throughout the book will be easier when you re-read sections of this book. Don't underestimate the importance of repetition when learning the detail-oriented and technical aspects of the business and always ask questions of other, more experienced colleagues whenever you can.

BOLD TYPE

Important terms in the text are defined and printed in bold. Many of these terms are important to help identify context or critical parts of that topic.

ILLUSTRATIONS AND PHOTOS

Illustrations and photos are provided wherever possible to reinforce concepts introduced and described in the text. Where necessary, specific details such as acoustic concepts, measured values or electrical references are also included in the diagrams.

Margin Notes

GLOSSARY OF TERMS

A glossary of important terms is included at the end of the text. The language used in this text is intended for mobile product specialists and may not describe an application from an "absolutely textbook" electronics or physics application nor may it directly match common marketing terminology used by some manufacturers. However, the terminology is used throughout the aftermarket automotive consumer electronics industry and is common to other MECP study guides.

MARGIN AREAS

There are empty margin areas for you to make notes as you are reading. This practice will help when you review your materials as well as help refresh your memory about sections you have read. Here's how you can make the most of this information:

1. Take notes – write in the margins. You can also use highlighter pens to enhance key areas of the text you wish to review later.

2. Lean on your experience, but do not assume what you know is the "industry standard" of knowledge.

3. Ask questions to experienced professionals or instructors in training programs.

4. Study additional sources of information to round out your knowledge.

5. This is not meant to be the definitive source for brand-specific product knowledge or installation instructions. Refer to the appropriate manufacturer's publications or websites for actual installation information on specific products or to vehicle information resources for data about a specific year/make/model of vehicle.

6. Read and re-read material and your notes. Get comfortable with common numeric values that you should come to expect (such as electrical measurements or product specifications) and industry terminology to increase your absorption of what will become everyday knowledge.

7. Commit to ongoing learning and educating. There's always something more to learn!

WHAT IS AN MECP MOBILE PRODUCT SPECIALIST...AND WHAT DOES IT MEAN TO YOU?

MECP stands for the Mobile Electronics Certified Professional. It was designed and developed by the MECP Committee of the Consumer Technology Association (CTA), which is a non-profit trade organization dedicated to supporting the consumer technology industry. CTA is also the owner and producer of the premier consumer technology trade show, CES.

The MECP Mobile Product Specialist certificate is the industry's entry-level credential for customer-facing Product Specialists. The Product Specialist is often the critical interface between a customer and the installation technician and translates customer needs

Margin Notes

to the technician. MECP MPS level credential is offered by many training schools and vocational programs, and many MECP-supporting retailers require it as a prerequisite for employment. What it means to you is that you must promise what you can deliver to employers and customers and deliver on that promise.

The MECP Mobile Product Specialist (MPS) exam covers:

- Knowledge and understanding of basic electrical and audio fundamentals, including the related terminologies and units such as volts, amps, hertz, watts, etc.
- Knowledge and understanding of mobile audio and video product categories.
- Knowledge and understanding of vehicle security and convenience (including remote starter) categories.
- Knowledge and understanding of vehicle safety and driver awareness categories.
- Knowledge and understanding of installation-related considerations concerning product application or choices made at the time of the sale.
- Knowledge and understating of MECP recommended practices in the customer service arena, including before, during and after the sale.

MECP is also a learning and educational tool that allows product specialists and installation technicians of all levels – through continued study and daily experience – to grow to the next level of expertise. It is the responsibility of all MECP certified professionals to encourage other professionals employed in the industry to work at achieving their own increased levels of knowledge and experience.

Finally, MECP is a partnership that involves a network of schools, manufacturers, retailers, installation technicians, product specialists and concerned industry professionals throughout North America whose primary goal is to help make the aftermarket automotive sector of the consumer technology industry educationally sound with ongoing testing and training.

Remember that (in the 12 Volt aftermarket industry) you are in the entertainment business. It's important to make sure the customer's purchase is more entertaining, more productive and easier to use than what they had before with clear and easily identified benefits.

BOTTOM-LINE BENEFITS

Benefits of MECP Mobile Product Specialist certificate:

- Demonstrates your commitment, dedication and professionalism.
- Qualifies people within their profession.
- Qualifies the people who do the work.
- Demonstrates an "I care" attitude.
- Reinforces the quality and integrity of your operation.
- Challenges you to keep pace with the needs of the industry.
- Rewards you with the respect of customers and employers who seek a professional.
- Begins a challenge to ascend the certification ladder to other MECP levels.

Margin Notes

THE MECP MOBILE PRODUCT SPECIALIST EXAM AND HOW IT WAS DEVELOPED

The questions on the MECP Mobile Product Specialist exam are designed to test a basic (entry) level of knowledge and understanding in aftermarket automotive consumer electronics as well as installation-related considerations. The test questions are written and developed by a committee of MECP Subject Matter Experts and industry experts and are continually updated.

The exam development process is psychometrically validated by creating questions based on your knowledge of the subject, not how well you can take a test. If you truly know the information, you will be in the best position to take the Mobile Product Specialist exam. Psychometric test question development includes some of these guidelines:

- Most questions are multiple choice; however, there are some True/False questions.
- Multiple choice questions have four possible answers. There are no "All of the Above" or "None of the Above" type answers. There are no "Both A and B" type answers. Only one answer is correct in every question and there is a clearly defined choice in each answer.
- There are no "trick questions" or "hidden meanings" in the questions. Read and answer the question exactly as it is written. You will have three hours in which to complete the exam. This provides ample time to read and re-read questions.

The MECP Mobile Product Specialist Exam has 150 questions and is broken into five categories. The categories are:

- Chapter 1 – Electrical Basics and Audio/Video
- Chapter 2 – Security and Convenience
- Chapter 3 – In Vehicle Communication, Driver Safety and Awareness
- Chapter 4 – Installation and Configuration Application Knowledge
- Chapter 5 - Customer-Facing Etiquette and Recommended Practice

Each section contains various questions covering that general range of topics. For more detail about the exam content and breakdown of questions per section, please visit the MECP website at **www.MECP.com** to review the Exam Content documentation.

HOW AND WHERE TO TAKE MECP EXAMS

MECP testing can occur at one of several hundred Prometric test centers using a pre-scheduled online appointment or by testing with an approved MECP proctor. MECP tests are 100% supervised and computer-based. Ninety-eight percent of MECP exams are delivered through Prometric test centers, the path most candidates choose.

All candidates **must complete a registration at the MECP Registration Portal and specify how they wish to test**. Once registration is completed, you will be emailed confirmation of registration. In that registration confirmation email will be your unique Eligibility ID code required to either schedule at a Prometric test site, or allow a test to be delivered by an approved proctor.

Supervised, computer-based exam delivery makes MECP testing available to a wider variety of potential candidates. The hours you work or your geographical location is less of a burden for scheduling and taking an MECP exam. Whatever type of delivery method you choose, MECP has committed to uphold the highest standards of both the test participant session AND the supervision that ensures the validity of the test.

To pursue MECP registration and testing, follow these steps:

(1) First Step: *Determine How You'll Test*

Prometric Test Center Path

Candidates can make an appointment at any one of several hundred Prometric testing centers throughout the US and Canada.

- Check out the Prometric test site locations available, even before registering with MECP, by visiting **www.prometric.com/MECP** and choose "Locate a Test Center."
- Follow the prompts by inputting the State (or Province) and selecting which MECP exam the candidate wishes to take, then search locations by zip code (or postcode). Once a suitable location is identified, the candidate can check appointment availability once registration with MECP is completed.

Proctored Testing Path

Candidates also have the option of a proctored test at an industry training school, public library or community college.

- For a list of current MECP pre-approved proctors, simply fill out a request form at the MECP website or email mecp@mecp.com to request the list.
- The candidate then contacts the pre-approved proctor to verify their willingness to proctor an MECP exam before completing a registration. An Eligibility ID number is obtained via email once registration is completed.

If no pre-approved proctors are available, candidates can also seek out public libraries or community colleges to request a temporary proctor arrangement. Candidates in North America (including the US, Canada and Puerto Rico) can contact their local public library or community college to see if there is availability for supervised proctoring services for a computer-based test.

- To be able to qualify as a temporary proctor, the prospective proctor must be able to provide (or have uninterrupted access to) a computer with DSL or higher bandwidth internet access, a compatible internet browser (IE, Chrome, Firefox, Safari, etc.) and a quiet location in which to provide the exam. No special software is required to be installed on the testing computer.

Margin Notes

Margin Notes

- The responsibility of locating the library/college and making the initial contact is placed on the test participant. Both the candidate and proctor must contact MECP using the process outlined at the MECP website.
- MECP reserves the right to grant or deny any temporary proctor requests as appropriate.

Visit **http://mecp.com/Professionals/Get-Certified/Take-an-MECP-Exam.aspx** for complete information on either path of MECP testing for specific steps to follow.

(2) Second Step: *Complete a Registration*
All candidates must complete a registration at the MECP Registration Portal and specify how they wish to test.

The MECP Registration Portal is also the database where MECP exam records for all US- and Canadian-based MECP exams since 2009 are held. If you've taken a supervised, computer-based MECP exam, chances are your exam records are in the database and you already have a profile to use as the basis for beginning a registration.

MECP recommends using a personal email account as your primary email address in your certification profile. If you use an employer-supplied email address and should change employment, you may not have access to that email address in the future.

It's very important that your registered name matches what's on your government-issued ID (such as driver's license), which you'll be required to show once you arrive to test. If the registered name does not match what's on your ID, you will not be able to test.

- To register visit **www.MECP.com** and click the top right "Login" icon to begin.
- At the registration site, click "Get Started" if you do not know whether you have a current profile. You'll enter the email address last used when you previously registered or tested with MECP. You can have a password reset email sent to you for easy login to the existing record.
    - o If you no longer have access to that email address, please do not create a new profile. Instead, email mecp@mecp.com and request your records be updated with your current email address.
    - o If you have never tested with MECP before, you'll need to create a new profile. Remember to register with the same name as appears on your ID.
- Once logged into the MECP registration portal, you'll see the options of which MECP exams are available to you for registration. Click on the exam for which you wish to begin registration and follow the on-screen instructions.
- Registrants can pay for their MECP exam fees with a valid credit/debit card or use an employer-supplied voucher.
- Once registration is completed, the test taker will see an "order confirmation" screen. The test taker is then emailed confirmation of registration which contains the Eligibility ID code required to either schedule at a Prometric test site or with a pre-approved proctor.

Margin Notes

The registration confirmation email may take up to four hours to generate once a successful registration is completed. If you do not receive the registration confirmation email within 24 hours, please email mecp@mecp.com with your name and test for which you registered to get assistance.

(3) Third Step: *Scheduling*

Once you receive an Eligibility ID code, schedule your MECP exam either at a Prometric Test Site or directly with your chosen proctor. Each Eligibility ID code can only be used once.

- For Prometric Test Sites, the Eligibility ID code is required to make an online appointment. Please review the rescheduling or cancelation policy before making the appointment. If the test taker does not attend their scheduled appointment, it's considered a no-show and the test taker forfeits any paid registration fees (or voucher used). Visit **www.prometric.com/MECP** and choose "Schedule My Test."
- For proctored exams, the scheduling is directly with the chosen proctor. Contact them directly after completing the registration process and receiving an Eligibility ID code. If the proctor charges any fees for their services, it's the responsibility of the test taker to pay those fees to the proctor directly. The Eligibility ID is entered at the time of testing.

READING THE STUDY GUIDE AND PREPARING FOR THE EXAM

For some people it's reading and comprehension that's challenging. For others, it's "test anxiety." Either way, taking an important exam can be difficult. Here are some steps that can help prepare for your MECP Mobile Product Specialist exam:

- Choose a time when your mind is rested and ready to study.
- Read the Table of Contents to find the sections in which you need to focus your studies. For many people, just start at the front of the book and take it one page, one topic at a time. If you are an impatient reader, consider scanning through the appropriate sections to get a feeling for how the information is organized. This is not a substitute for learning the material, but you'll almost certainly find a topic or term that catches your attention.
- Make notes in the margins about key points you've learned. You can also benefit from highlighting sections or sentences with highlighter pens.
- Read and re-read each study guide section. Progress one section at a time by re-reading before moving on if that is more sensible for your schedule and learning style. Repetition equals retention!
- Re-read each section a few days later until you feel you know the information.
- Flag important topics or areas where you are weak.
- A week before the exam, re-read or review the chapters one more time to refresh your memory.
- In between reading the chapters, review the Glossary so you're familiar with the key terms and definitions.
- Wherever possible, seek the assistance of additional learning resources such as experienced, MECP certified colleagues who have also gone through the process and the other study materials suggested by MECP.

Margin Notes

SCHEDULING, RESCHEDULING OR CANCELLING AN MECP EXAM AT A PROMETRIC TEST SITE

To schedule an MECP exam at a Prometric test site, you must first complete a registration at the MECP Registration Portal and have an Eligibility ID code from the registration confirmation email. Once you schedule an appointment date, time and location, Prometric will send you an email confirming your appointment. That email also contains the necessary information to follow should you need to reschedule or cancel.

If you need to reschedule or cancel your MECP exam at a Prometric test site:

- Visit **www.prometric.com/MECP** click the "Reschedule/Cancel My Test" selection and follow the directions on the site necessary to reschedule or cancel your exam.
- You can also follow the "Reschedule/Cancel" links in the appointment confirmation email sent to you by Prometric after you originally scheduled.

Please note that rescheduling or canceling submissions through the online "Contact Us" form available at ***www.prometric.com*** *is not a valid method to request an appointment reschedule or cancellation.*

You can reschedule or cancel your exam up to five full calendar days (EST) before your scheduled exam appointment. There may be a fee assessed to do so in accordance with the policies. Prometric imposes and collects any rescheduling or cancelation fees, not MECP.

30 Days or More from Scheduled Appointment

If you wish to cancel your MECP exam 30 days or more from the scheduled date, you can get a full refund of your registration fees from CTA following confirmation from Prometric of the cancellation. Allow 30 business days after cancellation for confirmation to pass over to CTA for processing.
If you wish to reschedule your MECP exam 30 days or more from the scheduled test date, you may do so and will not be charged a fee from Prometric.

5-29 Days from Scheduled Appointment

If you wish to cancel your MECP exam between 5-29 days from the scheduled date, you will be charged a $35 penalty fee assessed by Prometric for the cancellation. AFTER you are confirmed to have paid the $35 cancellation fee, you can qualify for full refund of your registration fees from CTA. Allow 30 business days after cancellation for confirmation to pass over to CTA for processing. If you do not pay the $35 fee from Prometric for cancellation, you forfeit your entire MECP exam registration fee paid to CTA.

Margin Notes

If you wish to reschedule your MECP exam between 5-29 days from the scheduled test date – you are charged a $35 fee from Prometric to do so. This is a fee imposed and collected by Prometric, not MECP.

Less than 5 Days from Scheduled Appointment

Cancellation or rescheduling is not allowed if under five days from your scheduled appointment. If you do not show up to your scheduled appointment on time (defined by late 30 or more minutes), you forfeit your exam registration fee paid to CTA.

CTA Refund Policy for Scheduled MECP Exams:

- Refund of registration fees will be administered in accordance with the cancellation policy stated in this section. Please allow 30 business days for processing.

SCHEDULING, RESCHEDULING OR CANCELLING A PROCTORED MECP EXAM

If you choose to take your MECP exam directly through a proctor, library or school, please call or email the proctor to confirm the testing date once you know the test location is able to accommodate your MECP testing needs. Do not schedule anything until you have completed a registration and have obtained the necessary Eligibility ID code in the registration confirmation email. There may be a few business days to wait until the proctor is authenticated by MECP. Don't assume your appointment is firm until you receive confirmation from your proctor. If you need to reschedule or cancel for any reason, contact the proctor directly. If the proctor charges any fees for rescheduling or canceling appointments, it's the responsibility of the test participant to pay directly.

THE DAY BEFORE THE EXAM

- Do not try to "cram" for the test the day before you are scheduled to take it. This means if you haven't done any studying and cramming it all in the day prior to testing is not going to help and can make you more anxious about the test. Review each chapter and the sample questions to refresh topics and terminology.
- If you have properly read this study guide and you have the bonus of hands-on experience in a retail 12 Volt environment, the information should already be in your head and the correct answers will come to you quickly during the test.
- Review each area in which you feel you may be weak and review your notes in the margins. Ask a colleague or friend to quiz you on sample questions or other topics in the study guide.
- Get plenty of rest the night before.

Margin Notes

WHAT TO BRING THE TEST SITE

Bring the following:

- **You will need two forms of ID**. At least one form of government-issued photo identification that's current (not expired) and an additional form of ID such as a student ID, credit card, etc. It's important that **the name on your ID matches exactly the name under which you registered**, or you risk forfeiting your appointment and any exam fees paid (or the voucher used).

- Your Scheduling Confirmation (sent to you via email if you are testing at a Prometric test center). If you set up with a proctor at an alternative test site, make sure you already confirmed prior to the appointment that you have everything you need, including your Eligibility ID code.

DO NOT bring these items into the test:

- Calculators or computing devices
- Mobile phones or PDA devices
- Portable media players
- Cameras of any type
- Backpacks (a locker or safe storage is usually provided at the test location)
- Notes or study materials of any kind

AT THE TEST SITE

- Arrive at the test site 30 minutes prior to the scheduled appointment time.
- Check in at the room, front counter or designated testing area.
- Have your information available to give to the proctor (test supervisor).
- Listen carefully to the proctor's instructions. They will instruct you on how to handle any breaks if you need them.
- No smoking is allowed in the test room.

DURING THE EXAM

- Do not talk during the test.
- The appearance of cheating will immediately disqualify you from the test, so make sure you follow the proctor's directions in all areas. The testing centers have CCTV cameras monitoring the testing rooms in addition to a proctor being present.
- If you must leave the room, do so quietly, leaving all your test materials on the table. Understand that the test time still counts down while you are away. You may be limited to a short bathroom break.
- If you have a question or there is a problem with your test, raise your hand or wait for the proctor to come to you. The proctor will not be able to help you with the test content, but may be able to answer process-related questions.
- Be courteous to others taking the test as you would expect them to be with you.

HOW TO TAKE THE EXAM

Margin Notes

Here are some tips that will help you improve your performance:

- Once you begin the exam, read each question thoroughly before you look at the answers. Please check your answers carefully before marking them.
- If you come to a question that you cannot answer, flag it for review or skip it and come back to it after you finish that section. The computerized testing process allows you to easily do this.
- Remember you can review any answer before selecting "finish" with your computer-based exam.
- Take extra time to review your answers if you have additional time left in the exam. It will allow you to review any answers you flagged or were unsure about while still within the allotted three-hour time limit.

AFTER THE EXAM

When you are finished:

- Whether you passed or failed the exam will display on the screen once you confirm you are ready to finish the exam.
- Follow the final instructions on the screen for finishing the exam and take your test materials to the proctor.
- Leave the room quietly.
- If you're waiting for someone else to finish the test, wait in the lobby or somewhere away from the test room.
- If testing at a Prometric test center, you will receive your test results via email. If testing with a proctor, please have the proctor print out the on-screen results.
- If you passed, your certificate will be mailed to you in approximately three weeks. It is very important that your address and contact information are correct during registration to ensure that you receive your certificate. If necessary, log back into the MECP Registration Portal and select "Update my Information" to review and update any mailing address or other contact information.

TEST SCORE INFORMATION

Information for your MECP test scores is contained on the scoring report that you receive at the end of your MECP testing session.

- If testing at a Prometric testing center, the test score results are sent via email.
- If testing with a proctor at an approved MECP location, the test score results should be printed by the proctor after completing the exam. If the results are unable to be printed, the proctor can also print to a PDF document and email that to you if their computer supports creating PDFs.

Should there be any question of your test results, this is also proof of your testing session. Therefore, it's important to print or write down the information contained on the test score report.

Margin Notes

If you do not have a copy of your MECP exam report, you can obtain a copy from Prometric (the test service provider for all MECP exams) by calling 800-853-6769 or via their website request form at **www.prometric.com/ContactUs**. Provide your name, exam level and date and location of your Prometric test site (city/state). If it was taken at a proctored test site, state that it was an exam delivery in "TCNet" (the proctored testing system) and not in a Prometric test center location. This will help Prometric locate your test score records and differentiate between an exam taken at one of their test centers versus at a proctored location you arranged.

RECORDS TRANSFER

Generally, within a few business days your exam results are passed from the test service provider (Prometric) into the MECP Registration Portal and database. Once exam records are in the database, you can monitor your certification progress or update your vital contact information. It's important to provide a valid email address when registering for your MECP exam. Without an email address to contact you, many of the enhanced reminders and other database features are not able to find you. Aside from certificates, MECP does not generally send you any correspondence through the mail regarding your certification status.

Even if you do not pass your MECP exam, your test records are still archived in the database.

MECP DATABASE ACCESS

MECP certification records are stored in a user-accessible MECP Registration Portal and database. This database holds exam records for all US-based MECP exams and Canadian MECP exams since 2009.

Accessing the MECP Database

To access the MECP Registration Portal and Database from a secure internet browser, go to: **www.MECP.com** and click the "Login" icon in the top right corner. MECP recommends using a personal email account as your primary email address in your certification profile. If you use an employer-supplied email address and should change employment, you may not have access to that email address in the future. If you require a username or password recovery from the MECP database, it will send information to the email address on file. This is why it's recommended to use a personal (or permanent) email address for your database records.

The database sends email reminders to candidates from time to time. The most common reminders are notifications of pending expiration and updating your information. These are sent to the primary email address in your certification profile.

CERTIFICATES

If you have passed your MECP Mobile Product Specialist exam, you should receive your certificate within three to four weeks of completing the exam.

MECP Mobile Product Specialist Certificate packets contain:

- Welcome Letter
- Two MECP Mobile Product Specialist Certificates
- MECP Code of Ethics
- MECP Window Cling Decal

If you wish to order additional certificates, visit www.MECP.com and fill out the online request form or call MECP Customer Service at (866) 858-1555. Only current (non-expired) certifications qualify for additional certificate purchases. MECP does not offer duplicates of expired certificates.

CONTACTING MECP

For general MECP information and to order study guides, call MECP Customer Service at (866) 858-1555. For additional information visit www.MECP.com. The website allows you to learn about all the MECP exam levels, purchase study guides, locate a supervised Prometric testing center in your area, request the pre-approved proctor list and register for an MECP exam at the registration portal (using a credit/debit card or a valid exam voucher). The MECP website also contains FAQs, many other tips for taking exams, suggested study materials, sign up for the MECP On-The-Move e-newsletter and other up-to-date information about MECP.

For email inquiries or general questions not addressed on the MECP website, please send to mecp@MECP.com.

Margin Notes

1

BASIC ELECTRICAL TERMINOLOGY AND KNOWLEDGE

BASIC ELECTRICAL TERMINOLOGY AND KNOWLEDGE

Margin Notes

Understanding principles of electronics is an important part of being a top-notch Mobile Product Specialist. It's your job to match the right products with customers' needs and communicate the goal effectively with the installation technician. Because a basic understanding of electronics is a key element of the process, this chapter covers what you need to know to make a win-win sale.

Basic Electrical Principles

Electricity in a car moves in a "circular path." It leaves the electrical supply (such as the vehicle battery) and travels through wires, components, etc., and then returns to the opposing side of the electrical supply. This circular path is what's called an electrical circuit. The basic elements in an automotive electrical circuit are:

- The power source (also called the voltage source) such as the vehicle's battery and alternator.
- The electrical path, generally wires connecting components together.
- The circuit protection such as fuses and/or circuit breakers.
- The control of the circuit such as on/off switches or control modules.
- The loads such as lights, motors, speakers or other devices (like head units or amplifiers).
- The electrical "return" path, which are generally wires, but in automotive electrical circuits can also be the metal chassis of the vehicle itself.

It's no accident that the word "circuit" sounds a lot like "circle." Since the electrical path must have a starting and ending point at the same power source, think of it as a circle. What's moving in that circle are tiny charged particles called **electrons**. Electrons are the negatively charged particles in an atom, and these tiny charged particles do the "work" of electricity.

This section will explore the fundamentals of electronics, how electricity works within the 12 Volt environment and terminology you need to understand to speak confidently with a customer.

Voltage

An electrical circuit must have voltage present before any electrons can move. Higher values of voltage require proportionally lower values of electron "flow" to accomplish the same electrical work. A stable supply of voltage is critical to the reliable operation of any mobile electronic component. Voltage is measured or expressed in units called **volts** – sometimes simply a capital V). Smaller units of volts are expressed in millivolts (abbreviated "mV"). There are 1000 millivolts in 1 volt.

1000mV = 1 volt = 1V

Voltage is a difference of electrical potential or "charge" between two points. Electrical potential can be thought of like holding two magnets together. Depending on the polarity (or potential difference of each charge), the magnets are strongly attracted (or strongly opposed) to each other, hence the term "like charges repel and opposites attract." Larger magnets produce larger attraction or opposition because

Margin Notes

they contain more charge. With more charge (or strength), the attraction to the opposing polarity (meaning positive to negative) is what forces electrons to move. More voltage (or difference in potential between the two polarities) means more force to move electrons.

Current

Current is the movement or "flow" of free electrons through a conductor. These electrons are attracted to the opposing polarity by the voltage levels in a circuit. More voltage means more potential for attraction (or repulsion) of the free electrons. Current flow is expressed, rated or measured in units called **amperes**, or "amps" (often abbreviated with an "A" – such as 30A). Smaller units of amperes are expressed in milliamps (abbreviated "mA"). There are 1000 milliamps in 1A.

1000mA = 1 ampere = 1A

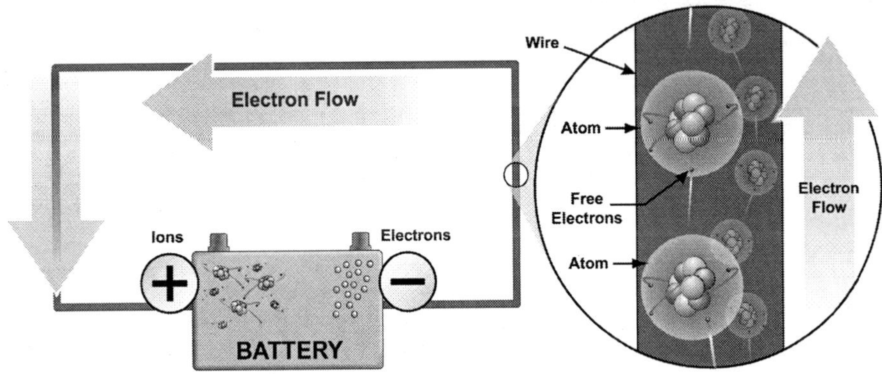

Whenever many free electrons are moving in a conductor, friction is generated. As current flow increases, so does the number of electrons flowing, and so does the friction. Higher rates of current flow need larger conductors to accommodate the electron movement, or unwanted (and unsafe) amounts of heat will result from all that friction. That is the reason a mobile audio power amplifier has a larger power wire requirement as power levels increase. A 100-watt amplifier doesn't need as large of a power and ground wire as a 1000-watt amplifier. That is also the reason that a higher power amplifier needs a larger heatsink. The larger amplifier consumes more current and produces more heat that must dissipate.

There are two types of electrical current: **AC and DC**. AC periodically reverses direction of electrons flowing (back and forth), while DC always flows in only one direction.

AC Current

AC stands for Alternating Current, which is current that alternates polarity (or its magnetic field) between positive and negative. AC has both an amplitude component (how much) and a frequency component (how often). The "how much" part of AC is the potential, measured as voltage, whereas the "how often" is called

Margin Notes

the frequency, which is measured in cycles per second, or Hertz (Hz). One cycle per second is 1Hz. Two cycles per second is 2Hz, and so on.

AC current examples in the vehicle include:

- The vehicle's alternator internal parts that create the charge (called the stator and rotor).
- Analog audio signals (such as those on speaker wires or analog preamp RCA outputs).

DC Current

DC stands for **Direct Current**, and it is current that supplies power to electronic components. DC is either positive or negative in polarity, but not both. DC has only an amplitude component called potential (again, that's the voltage) and a frequency of zero since it does not alternate back and forth.

DC current examples in the vehicle include lights like parking, head, and tail lights, power windows, and rear defroster elements."

Which Way Does DC Current Really Flow?

Which way does the current actually "flow" in a DC circuit? Does it start at the positive side of the circuit and flow through the load to the negative side or is it the other way around and start at negative flowing towards positive? There are a couple of theories on that.

- Conventional current flow theory says that current flows from positive to negative.
- Electron flow theory says that current flows from negative to positive.

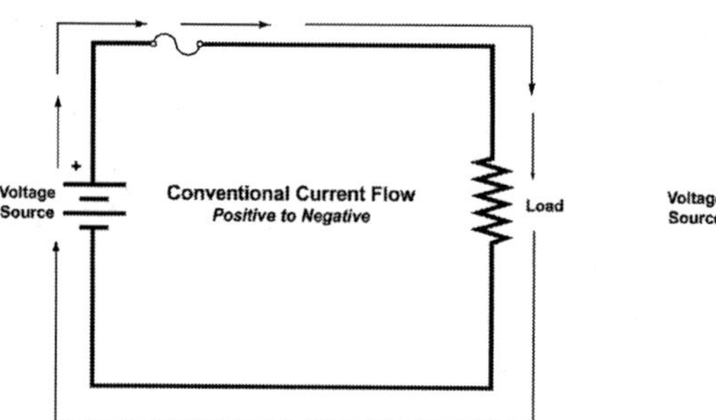

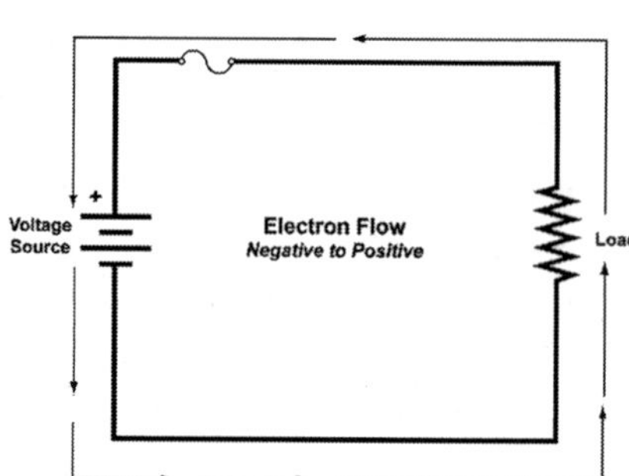

Conventional thinking of most product specialists and installation technicians, as well as the default in many automotive electronics applications (such as installation manuals), is that conventional current flow theory is the basis for in-vehicle circuits and installation practices. Many engineers designing products at the circuit board level adopt the electron flow theory. Neither is wrong; it's still a circular flow to complete the electrical path.

Margin Notes

Don't be too concerned with which way current flows, instead recognize it is a circular path and the **current capacity of the negative side of the circuit is equally as important as the positive side**. That's often why upgrading electrical grounds are so important. If the installation calls for large-gauge wiring for amplifiers or other accessories at the positive battery post and there are no upgrades or enhancements to the chassis electrical connections from the negative side, then the circuit is only as capable as its weakest link.

Resistance

People frequently use the term "ohms" throughout mobile electronics for many reasons, often related to speakers or when discussing the relative output power of an amplifier. Sometimes people lack the understanding of the relationship that electrical resistance has to voltage and current, especially in mobile audio, video, security and charging systems. That relationship of voltage, current and electrical resistance (measured in ohms) is called Ohm's Law, named after a pioneering scientist Georg Simon Ohm who did much research on the topic of electrons moving from a storage battery through a working circuit. This relationship is the fundamental of how batteries, wires, loads (i.e., light bulbs or electrical motors) and switches work in automotive electrical circuits.

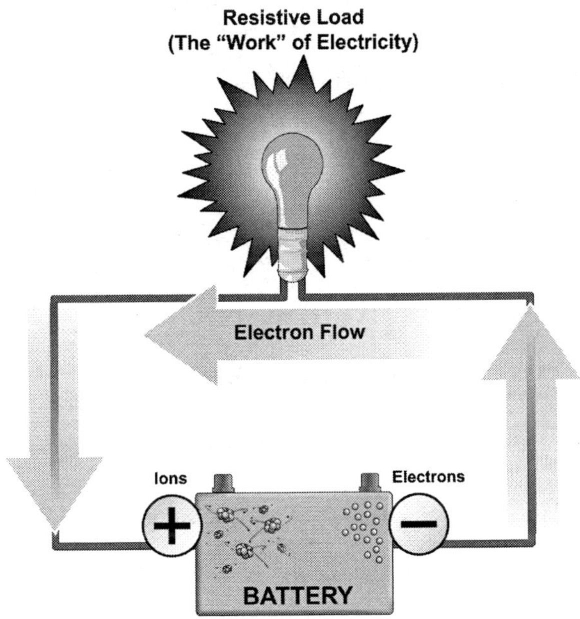

Resistance is the opposition to current flow. Greater amounts of resistance result in smaller amounts of current flow when a given amount of voltage is applied. An infinite amount of resistance would produce no current flow, which is known as an "open circuit." Likewise, smaller amounts of resistance enable much higher current flow. No resistance results in the highest possible current flow, which is known as a "short circuit." Short circuits will cause fuses to blow or equipment to fail; therefore, some amount of electrical resistance is necessary for any electrical circuit to operate safely and dependably.

Margin Notes

Many things can cause unnecessary electrical resistance in a circuit. In mobile electronics installation situations, unnecessary (unintended) resistance is typically caused by corrosion or poor connections. An efficient circuit minimizes unnecessary resistance to allow proper operation of the components.

Using an analogy of an internal combustion engine with fuel flowing into the cylinders, resistance is similar to a kink in the fuel line or a clog in the fuel pump. There's a restriction to the flow of fuel keeping it from maximum flow. Without the proper flow, the power the engine can deliver is reduced. In electrical circuits (just as in fuel lines to an engine) **there is always some resistance present**, but preferably none that is limiting the expected performance.

Electrical resistance is measured in ohms, often symbolized with the Greek symbol "omega" (Ω) when it appears in ratings such as speakers, electrical motors, lights and other electronic components. When there are large amounts of resistance beyond 1000 ohms, it's common to be expressed as kilo ohms (simply "kOhm" or kΩ).

1kOhms = 1000 ohms OR 1kΩ = 1000 Ω

OHM'S LAW

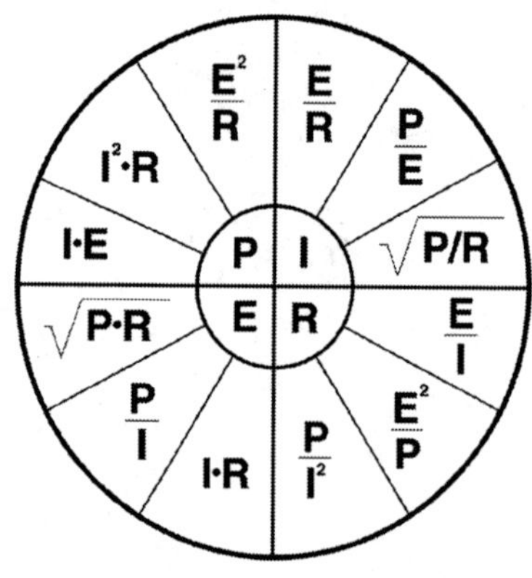

P = Watts **E = Volts**
I = Amps **R = Resistance**

Keep in mind that resistance is not the same as impedance. While the two often interchange in a conversation, resistance is the same across all frequencies whereas impedance is a value of ohms that changes with frequency, such as in speakers playing high and low notes. When a speaker's resistance is rated at a certain value (such as 4 ohms), it really means its "nominal impedance" without a reference to which frequency is specified.

Electrical Power

Electrical power is easily described as the relationship of voltage and current doing work. Power output must at least be equal to power input. In the most basic sense,

Margin Notes

power is simply the **conversion of one kind of energy into another over a period of time**. Electrical power is expressed in Standard International (SI) units of watts. In the expression of units, often multiples of 1000 will be expressed as kilowatts.

1kW = 1000 watts

If there is not enough electrical power supplied to a device to begin with, a device or the circuit can't just "magically" make more power. This over simplified phrase is often ignored to the regret of a well-meaning industry professional facing an upset customer with burned out subwoofers, an overheated amplifier or a multitude of other audio system or automotive electrical issues. For example, it's common for a 12 Volt retail shop to sell a power-hungry consumer thousands of watts in amplifier power and massive subwoofers with no thought given the electrical requirement needed to supply the power output the amplifier(s) delivers. This presents inherent problems that the customer may experience after a given installation is completed.

This common example is completely avoidable with a simple matter of respecting the electrical indicators that influence responsible audio system design, or recommendations of other products that require electrical power to operate safely and successfully in the vehicle.

Law of Conservation of Energy

It's rare to harness 100% of the electrical power consumed by a component and turn it all into one form of energy. In the process of converting electricity into light, some of the energy is wasted and the result is heat. You know this because when you touch an incandescent light bulb, it's hot.

The Law of Conservation of Energy states that energy consumed by any component cannot be destroyed or lost. The energy consumed must be converted somehow. In the case of a light bulb, the electrical energy is not 100% converted into light and some of that energy becomes heat (thermal) energy. This division of energies is known as inefficiency. Incandescent light bulbs are less efficient than LED lighting, which is why many modern vehicles use more efficient LED lighting. More efficient light bulbs produce more light and less heat for a given amount of voltage and current supplied (i.e., less power consumption for a given output result).

The same is true for other efficient electronics. Car audio amplifiers, in general, are not efficient. Some designs called "switching amplifiers" improve that problem and that's often why you'll see a smaller chassis size for those types of amplifiers when compared to a traditional amplifier of the same power rating.

If converting from one form of energy into another single form is not 100% efficient, there will be another form (typically heat) as the result of the inefficiency. Just as electrical power cannot be destroyed or lost, it cannot be magically created either. The electrical energy must first exist before it can be converted. For example, a high powered, in-dash head unit does not consume

Margin Notes

200 watts of electrical energy, there is no possible way it can output 200 watts of audio power into a speaker. Since amplifiers and high-powered head units in mobile audio systems have at least some heat present during operation, it's clear that they too are not 100% efficient at converting energy. Remember, power is not delivered out of thin air; it must come from somewhere. Power "in" has everything to do with the actual power "out."

Often mobile audio amplifiers are described in terms of their efficiency, which means how much of that electrical power consumed is required to provide a given output power. Traditional Class A/B amplifiers are 50-60% efficient, which means that for 100 watts of output, at 50% efficient a Class A/B amplifier would have to consume about 200 watts of electrical input power. In other words, 50% efficiency in an amplifier means drawing twice the energy it can output, and the remaining energy not sent to the speakers is given off as heat. In many ways this is why different amplifier topologies (like Class D switching amplifiers) with higher efficiencies are a great alternative for electrical systems with limited capacity for aftermarket electronics. Read more about specific amplifier topologies and related efficiencies in the Aftermarket Amplifiers section later in this chapter.

Why is this discussion of electrical input/output efficiency important? Factory-installed alternators generally supply between 65 and 100 amps (depending on the model and features of the vehicle), with around 150 amps total in the best case scenarios in larger or more accessory-laden vehicles. In any case, the factory charging system is designed to supply little beyond the vehicle's factory supplied electrical accessory requirements. The capacity of the vehicle's ability to supply electrical energy must always be compared with the equipment choices and their electrical needs. One general exception to this is large trucks or SUVs that are designed to tow or power heavy equipment, as these vehicles are typically equipped with either large capacity batteries or multiple batteries, and high-output alternators to recharge them.

Even if one considers that the vast majority of car audio systems will not run at full electrical energy consumption for more than short bursts for average listeners, it is easy to see that a system such as the example presented previously can easily be power starved and result in inadequate performance. Of course, the more demanding listener who plays the system at high volumes all the time will require more from the vehicle's electrical system. Eventually, there is a point where the vehicle simply can't keep up with the electrical demands of the audio system.

While an audio system is an example of vehicle electronics with a fairly robust current demand, there could be many other things that require the vehicle's electrical power to operate as intended.

Margin Notes

Electrical Topics as a Quick Reference

Voltage

- Voltage is electrical pressure.
- Voltage is measured in units called volts.
- 1000 millivolts = 1 volt.
- The higher the voltage, the higher the electrical pressure pushing electrons around in the circuit.
- Voltage is symbolized in Ohm's Law as "E" or "V."

Current

- Current is the movement of electrons.
- Current is measured in units called amperes (or amps for short).
- 1000 milliamps = 1 amp = 1A.
- Current cannot flow unless there is voltage to "push" it around in the circuit.
- Current is symbolized in Ohm's Law as "I" or "A."

Resistance

- Resistance is inherent in every electrical circuit.
- Resistance is measured in ohms.
- 1000 ohms = 1 kilo ohm (1k ohm or 1kΩ).
- 1 million ohms = 1 Megaohm.
- Excessive resistance is often the result of corrosion or poor connections.
- No resistance is a short circuit.
- Resistance is symbolized in Ohm's Law as "R."
- Resistance can also be written with the Greek letter omega (Ω).
- Resistance values are independent of frequency; however, impedance does vary with frequency.

Power

- Electrical power is simply voltage and current working over a period of time.
- Power is the conversion of energy from one form to another form.
- The Law of Conservation of Energy states power cannot be created or destroyed, only changed into some other form of energy.
- Electrically powered devices such as amplifiers, light bulbs, etc., are not 100% efficient so the by-product is heat.
- Electrical power is expressed in units of watts.
- 1000 watts = 1 kilowatt (1kW).
- Power is symbolized as "P" or "W."

Margin Notes

BASIC AUDIO TERMINOLOGY AND KNOWLEDGE

Music (audio) signals are interesting from both electrical and acoustic perspectives. Electrical audio signals are complex AC waveforms of signals called sine waves that represent low, medium and high "tones" or "pitch," also called "notes" by musicians.

Electrical audio signals move from the source unit through the signal processors (if present), which is then amplified to drive the loudspeakers. An audio signal connected to a speaker carries that electrical wave form and converts it to cause the speaker's in and out movement. The electrical audio signal connects through the speaker's voice coil and repels from or attracts to the speaker's magnet assembly. This is how the similarity to AC electrical signals correspond to speakers moving out and in (pressure and vacuum) to create sound audible by the human ear.

Either way, the audio signal contains many varied components of frequencies and amplitudes that make up the tempo and pitch of individual sounds in music. Pure tones (sometimes used in testing) in which only a single frequency is produced over and over are different than music. While test tones are just one single frequency, real music is made up of many frequencies all at the same time. This section covers those basic terminologies and how they apply to audio.

Sound waves (acoustic) and audio signals (electric) are made up of four important components:

- Amplitude (or Level)
- Frequency
- Period (or Time)
- Wavelength

Amplitude

Amplitude is the measurement of how powerful the waves are in terms of pressure (acoustically) or how powerful the signal is (electrically). Higher amplitude means higher volume in sound or higher voltage in electricity. It is measured at the peak and the valley (highest and lowest points) of the waves.

Of course with music, the amplitude varies over the course of the song. Sometimes it's high when other times it's low. With test tones the amplitude and frequency are constant at a given volume position. In those cases, when a listener raises the volume, the amplitude rises accordingly in a measured and predictable fashion. That's why test tones are often used to perform various audio system measurements. It provides a stable, constant type of audio signal, which, although useful for measurement purposes, is a bit of a misnomer since people really don't listen to test tones.

Margin Notes

To summarize, amplitude:

- Is the "How Much" of a signal or sound.
- Strength of signal or loudness of a sound.
- Typically measured in volts (if an electrical signal), though sometimes in amperes.
- Definitely measured in decibels (if a sound in air). See dB/SPL later in this section.

Frequency

The frequency of the signal refers to the number of repetitions (cycles) that are completed in one second. The more repetitions of that signal per second, the higher the pitch of the sound. The fundamental unit used to describe frequency is "cycles per second." This measurement is more commonly referred to by the term Hertz (Hz). The higher the frequency, the more of these "vibrations" are packed together in a one-second period. Frequency is directly related to the pitch of the sound humans hear. Human hearing is said to have a frequency range from 20Hz to 20,000Hz (or simply 20-20kHz). Most equipment used in audio systems have ratings at which the equipment is able to reproduce. For example, a component speaker set might have a frequency range of 40-20,000Hz. A subwoofer might only have a usable frequency range of 20-200Hz.

To summarize, frequency:

- Is the number of cycles in a signal or sound.
- *Rate of signal changing/alternating or pitch of a sound.*
- Frequency Response of Human Hearing (20Hz-20kHz).
- Music is made up of multiple frequencies simultaneously.
- Pure (test) tones are only a single frequency.

Period (Time)

Period describes the amount of time required for a single cycle of a sound wave. This is called the period of the wave. The period is expressed in seconds per cycle, usually as a fraction of a second (expressed in milliseconds). It's determined by dividing 1 by the frequency. The period is a time representation that is equal to a wavelength, one being represented in time, the other represented in distance.

Period = 1 / Frequency

Remember there are 1000 milliseconds in 1 second. Milliseconds are usually abbreviated as ms. As frequency increases, the period of the sound wave is shorter.

To summarize, period:

- Measured in seconds, usually fractions of a second (milliseconds - ms).
- 1 Second equals 1000 ms.
- Some DSP devices (like integration processors) use this unit of ms for their time delay or time correction settings rather than distance.

Margin Notes

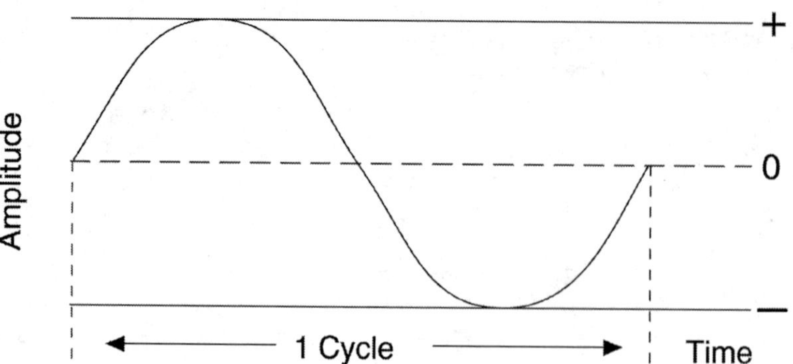

Wavelength

Wavelength refers to the length or distance to complete a full sound wave at a given frequency. The distance is determined by dividing the speed of sound by the frequency. The speed of sound depends on the density of the transmission medium and somewhat on its temperature and altitude. At 70° F or 21°C and at sea level, sound travels at 1,130 feet per second (or 344 meters per second). Other textbooks may present the speed of sound anywhere from 1128-1132 ft./sec., but for purposes of consistent learning, MECP relies on 1130 ft./second (344m per second) as the reference.

Wavelength (in Feet) = 1130ft / Frequency
Wavelength (in Meters) = 344m / Frequency

To summarize, wavelength:

- Based on the speed of sound in air (1130 ft./second or 344 meters/second) at a specific frequency.
- Measured in distance, inches/feet or centimeters/meters
- Some DSP-based signal processing devices (like OEM audio integration processors) use this unit of distance of fractions of an inch (small segments of wavelength) for their time delay or time correction settings instead of milliseconds (ms).

dB/SPL

Sound output is described as Sound Pressure Level (SPL). SPL is an acoustic measurement for the ratios of sound energy and is rated using a unit called the **decibel** or **dB/SPL**.

The ability to create louder sound requires high amounts of power. For example, if there is 100 watts of power on a speaker and the power is doubled to 200 watts, the listener will only notice a minor increase in volume (typically no more than 3 dB). For a demonstrably noticeable difference in SPL, the system power usually has to be increased considerably, perhaps four times or more of the original amount (in this example from 100 to at least 400 watts). The **decibel** is simply a way to express differences as a ratio and is used to compare ranges of measurements that are too wide and require too many zeros to work easily.

Margin Notes

Assuming no other changes in the system occur, with SPL:

- Doubling the system power equals an increase of about 3dB SPL.
- Increasing system power by 10 times equals an increase of about 10dB SPL.

Given that fact, it's often smarter to reduce any inefficiency in the audio system such as subwoofer enclosure design/placement, quality and integrity of connections, efficiency of amplifiers and correctly calibrate/adjust equipment so that critical power is not wasted. Sound damping or deadening materials are also an effective way to reduce the overall interior cabin noise levels so it's a quieter environment in which to play an audio system. **Remember, the quieter the listening space, the louder a given sound source will seem because it is not fighting other noises** (such as road, wind and mechanical noises in a vehicle cabin).

Instead of looking at overall sound pressure levels as adding more power to achieve adequate listening levels, consider how to maximize the efficiency of the power levels in a system design while also making the overall listening space quieter. Waste less power instead of trying to make more if the end result in perceived loudness to the listener is the same.

Basics of Sound Waves (Quick Review)

- Sound is pressure and vacuum (movement) of air molecules.
- Amplitude of the sound wave relates to the volume or "intensity."
- The Decibel (dB) is how Sound Pressure Level (SPL) is measured.
- Sound moves at 1130 ft. per second, regardless of how loud it is (@ Sea Level, 70 ° F) or 344m per second (@ Sea Level, 21 ° C).
- Frequency of the sound wave refers to the pitch or "note."
- Hertz (Hz) is the amount of cycles per second. 1Hz = 1 cycle/second. 2 Hz = 2 cycles/second, and so on.
- A "Cycle" is a full sound wave, both pressure and vacuum.
- Wavelength of the sound wave refers to the physical distance for that frequency to be produced by the sound source.
- Period is the elapsed time it takes for 1 complete cycle (peak to peak, or valley to valley, etc.)
- The higher the frequency, the shorter the sound wave's length.
    - o To determine a sound wave's length: 1130 ÷ Hz = Wavelength in feet (or 344 ÷ Hz = Wavelength in meters)
    - o To determine a sound wave's frequency: 1130 ÷ Wavelength (feet) = Hz (or 344 ÷ Wavelength in meters)
    - o To determine a sound wave's period: 1÷ Hz = Period (in ms)

In the subsequent sections of this chapter, the terminology of certain types of audio equipment is introduced to connect the concepts of audio fundamentals with where it applies in actual practice. Later in this chapter, each of those types of audio equipment is presented in detail and ties back to this section's terminology and examples. This should assist the reader in connecting the concept of audio fundamentals to a feature, function or solution that a particular piece of audio equipment provides.

Margin Notes

Phase and Polarity – What's the difference?

Phase is the time relationship of a sound wave to a known time reference and is measured in degrees from 0 degrees to 360 degrees (just like a circle). **Polarity**, in this context, refers to the electrical connection of a speaker reproducing those sound waves and whether or not the positive and negative speaker terminals are connected correctly.

When a loudspeaker pushes and pulls the air in front of it, it creates **waves of compressed air followed by waves of stretched air**. This is called **compression and rarefaction**, and correlates with the way a sound wave or electrical audio signal is represented. **One complete cycle of compression and rarefaction corresponds to 360 degrees**.

As the wave moves outward from the loudspeaker, it exhibits characteristics that are important to producing sound. All by itself though, **one speaker making sound doesn't really matter if it compresses first then rarefies the air because human ears still sense the compression (pressure) and rarefaction (vacuum)**. It's only a problem when there are **two or more sound sources. Then it's important they are working together** during compression and rarefaction duties otherwise they're **fighting each other**—one speaker pressurizes the air and the other rarefies (depressurizes) the air cancelling much of the sound the human ear hears.

There is a tendency among some industry professionals, particularly those in marketing, to intermingle the two terminologies. For example, a technician may state something is "out of phase" when it is actually a polarity reversal of the (+) and (-) speaker or signal leads. "Out of phase" is a matter of degrees anywhere in the cycle of "360 degrees," the movement of the speaker in and out. Polarity defines a condition that can only be 0 or 180 degrees different from the reference speaker(s) in the system.

If one were to take two wires that were connected to a speaker and reverse them (positive and negative wires switched), the resulting electrical signal would move the cone in the reverse order. In other words, the waveform would be the exact mirror image of what it should be so rather than the cone moving outwards, it would be moving inwards at that time and vise-versa. This is called a polarity reversal, and it is equal to a 180 degree phase shift. If there are two speakers next to one another and one's polarity is reversed from the other, yet they are playing the same input signal, there will be a condition where they're fighting each other called **destructive interference**. This is to be avoided and is why technicians must get connections on the speaker (and throughout the audio system) right. If two speakers are mounted beside each other and both push and pull at the same time, the speakers are considered to be **in phase** or **absolute polarity** and working together.

Phase is also important when one considers the alignment of all sound waves (short and long) across the entire frequency range in the listening position. Even if speakers are each in correct (absolute) electrical polarity, the physical position of

Margin Notes

speakers relative to one another can (and does) introduce frequency-dependent phase shifts. If two speakers are mounted side by side but one is further forward than the other (physical alignment), when the speakers are electrically wired in the correct polarity, the wave from one speaker will interfere with the other to some extent. The two waves are not starting from the same physical point, even though they are starting at the same time. The sound can be out of phase anywhere in that 360 degrees; however, a technician can't simply switch the speaker wiring around to correct the issue as that only changes it 180 degrees (which is simply reversing the speaker's movement from outward first then inward to inward first then out).

The wavelength of higher frequencies is shorter than low frequencies, so home speaker manufacturers will often build speakers that have the tweeters set back slightly from the woofer so that the voice coils are vertically aligned. This is often referred to as mechanical time alignment. Mechanical time alignment by specifically positioning the speakers on the same vertical plane compensates for the different sizes (lengths) of the wavelength each one produces.

There are many mobile audio products that also feature time alignment (more appropriately "time correction" or "delay") capabilities, but to some extent, it's part of why placing speakers in specific, complementary locations with more equal left and right path lengths to the listening position are chosen. In this way, phase shifting of left versus right speakers is minimized because of different physical locations and so is the concern of timing of signals because the differences throughout the frequency range are similar on the left and right.

The more **similar the left and right path lengths** of speakers in the vehicle are, the more **equidistant** they are said to be. Since this is an ideal scenario and not always possible in factory speaker locations, the use of signal processors with time correction and/or up-mixer capabilities is another tool to achieve more balanced sound. See the "Signal Processors" section later in this chapter for more detailed information.

Resonance

All objects have a natural tendency to vibrate at certain frequencies. This is their point of natural resonance. In a loudspeaker by itself, resonance is defined as a particular frequency where the speaker moves most easily. This parameter in a loudspeaker is called the **Free-Air Resonance**, symbolized as Fs. Another way to describe resonance of a loudspeaker is a frequency at which (once it's moving) it wants to ring out, or move on its own, until it slows and finally stops. Since there is so much natural propensity of movement on the part of the loudspeaker at this particular frequency, the amplifier to which it's connected isn't asked to work hard to play this frequency.

Other objects also have a natural resonance, defined by the materials they are made of, physical size and weight (or mass). Heavy objects take more energy to vibrate so their natural resonances are often lower than light objects.

Margin Notes

- For example, a crystal wineglass (when tapped) will vibrate air to produce a tone somewhere between 2 kHz and 6 kHz. The smaller the glass, the higher the pitch of the tone.
- Door panels, plastics and glass in the vehicle all have a natural resonance too.

If you were to play a tone at the same frequency that the glass produces, the glass would begin to vibrate on its own. This is known as sympathetic vibration or sympathetic resonance and is caused by the natural resonance of the object.

Sympathetic resonance can be a problem when things vibrate that you don't want to, such as plastic interior panels or the mounting surface of a door speaker. The speaker's job is to move air. For any signal, the speaker produces a certain amount of energy to move that air. If other panels move as a result of the moving speaker, some of the energy is wasted in moving the panels and less energy is applied to moving the air.

For more information on controlling unwanted resonance (known as "damping"), see the "Speaker Installation Considerations" section in Chapter 4.

Frequency Response – Where Audio System Design Begins

Human hearing has an accepted frequency range from 20Hz to 20,000Hz (or simply 20-20kHz). Audio equipment and frequency response of a great-sounding audio system is usually designed with at least 20Hz-20kHz in mind, although not all audio equipment is capable of covering that range (particularly speakers and some types of amplifiers). Conversely, some high resolution (Hi-Res) audio source equipment goes well beyond that range, especially in the high frequencies.

As identified earlier in the chapter, music is made up of multiple frequencies within the 20-20kHz range, each happening at the same time. This makes the job of any speaker, which is expected to **exactly** reproduce each of those frequencies simultaneously, somewhat difficult. With current speaker technology, it's simply not possible to make a cost effective, single element speaker that plays everything from the lowest bass to the highest highs accurately. To get the best performance and cost blend, speakers are traditionally produced for different frequency ranges so they can perform better without costing a lot in the process. This is the concept of separate speakers for low bass, midrange and high frequencies.

Generally, the fewer frequency-range-specific speakers that are in use, the more limited the overall range of the audio system. Most great-sounding systems use separate speakers to cover low bass (called "subwoofers"), middle ranges (called "midrange") and high frequencies (called "tweeters"). Keep in mind, however, that it is not the number of total speakers that results in better sound but **covering all the ranges effectively**. If there is a full range (or equal balance) of variety, then it's easier to expect a full range 20-20kHz (equally balanced) quality of sound from the sound system.

Margin Notes

Breaking up the 20-20kHz Reproduction

Midrange frequencies are produced well (at least at moderate volumes) in many cars because **midrange sounds are easiest for speakers to reproduce**. Human hearing is also more sensitive in the midrange area (particularly around 1-4kHz) **so humans actually hear midrange with less effort** than extreme highs or lows. Given that, the factory-installed speakers don't have to be as good for the human ear to hear sound in the middle range.

The quality (or accuracy) of the midrange from inexpensive speakers is not always realistic and can easily sound objectionable, particularly as the volume increases. Having good, balanced frequency response is important. The mark of a good audio system is to be able to reproduce 20-20kHz with a range of about +/- 3dB from frequency to frequency. This does not necessarily mean the frequency response needs to be a flat line. In order to hear a flat frequency response, the amplitude (volume) of the bass and treble regions must be boosted and a reduction in midrange to counteract what is known as the **Equal-Loudness curves** (better known as **Fletcher-Munson curves**). These curves depict the uneven frequency response of human hearing at different sound pressure levels. While the actual target frequency response will not be a flat line because listener preference and vehicle interior space is different, the capability of having 20-20kHz with a range of +/- 3dB simply means all the right frequencies have at least been considered.

Woofers (or subwoofers) and tweeters have specific jobs to do in achieving that balanced frequency response of 20-20kHz with a range of +/- 3dB, but to accomplish their respective tasks requires better materials and more costly manufacturing. This is why vehicles equipped with woofers and tweeters from the manufacturer are often in the "premium" audio system package, although even moderate level factory systems often have separate midrange and tweeters; some even have subwoofers.

While the factory premium package may be an improvement in sound over base models, **the obvious upgrade when a car has no woofers and tweeters whatsoever is to consider adding those (and other necessary related equipment such as amplification) first**. This lays the groundwork for a full range of sound from the lowest lows to the highest highs approaching 20-20kHz. An addition of a subwoofer to a factory system, for example, is a popular and effective upgrade for many vehicles lacking low frequency response.

Filtering Frequencies – Routing the Appropriate Frequencies to the Appropriate Speakers

In audio systems that use separate speakers to cover multiple frequency ranges, there are filters used to route the right signals to the correct type (range) of speaker. In doing so, the filters also block the damaging frequencies from reaching the speaker. These filters are called **crossovers (or crossover networks)**, and there are two types: passive and active.

Margin Notes

Common 3-Way System Design

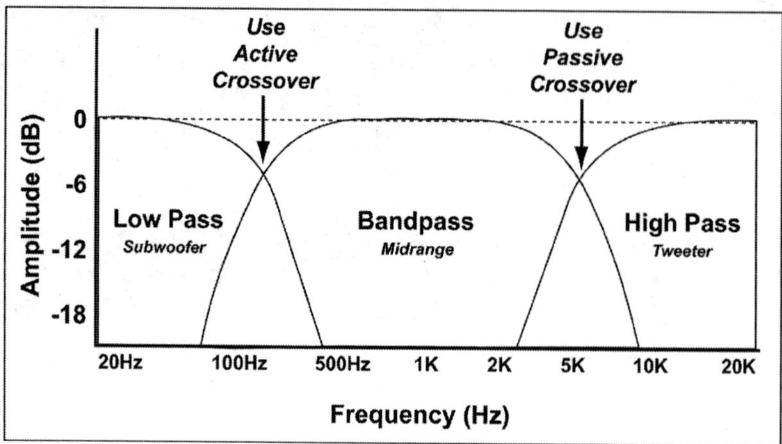

Passive crossover networks use passive electronic components including capacitors, inductors and resistors in specific combinations to help the speakers (as a group) do their best job of getting to that 20-20kHz goal. Passive crossover networks are placed in the audio signal path **AFTER** the amplifier and before the speaker. These are found with component mid/tweeter speakers as part of a complete speaker system, but they can also be custom built from those electronic components to suit just about any particular filtering need.

Advantages of Passive Crossovers:

- Often these are pre-engineered and included with a component speaker system. Just connect and make no other (or minor) adjustments.
- Their relatively small size increases installation location options (although some premium component speakers have larger than normal passive crossover networks).
- Passive crossovers can be as simple as a single non-polar capacitor (often called a "Bass Blocker") or a single inductor. Although minimalist, these examples still are better than nothing at all if the speaker is otherwise going to be subjected to distortion trying to reproduce music outside its intended range.

Disadvantages of Passive Crossovers

- They have a limited ability to change the filter set points (crossover points).
- They consume some of the power that would otherwise be delivered to the speaker because some part of the signal is filtered out. As filters get more complex (with more components), that too consumes a little more amplifier power. Sometimes it's negligible if it's a midrange or tweeter but much more concerning for subwoofers.
- Since they use one or more inductors, passive crossovers are susceptible to radiated noise if placed near other noisy vehicle wiring (particularly high current power wiring or batteries). Inductors can absorb neighboring magnetic fields with relative ease.

Margin Notes

Active crossovers filter the preamp signal chain **BEFORE** the amplifier and rely upon discrete amplifier channels to drive bandwidth-limited channels directly. In these instances, active crossovers often have more flexibility or adjustment, but rely on more amplifier channels to get the full 20-20kHz frequency range covered by the speakers. This could add cost or installation space requirements, but there are certainly fidelity advantages of making rapid adjustments to crossover frequencies (also called crossover points) when fine tuning.

Advantages of Active Crossovers:

- These usually allow for a wide range of adjustment, most of the time even while listening to the system.
- They can be implemented into another piece of equipment like an in-dash source unit or (most often) in multi-channel amplifiers.
- They allow the full power output of the amplifier to be delivered to the speaker. For subwoofers in particular, this is a distinct advantage over a passive crossover.

Disadvantages of Active Crossovers:

- They require the audio system to have discrete (independent) channels for each frequency range. This could mean four, five, six or more channels, which potentially means more equipment, as well as added costs or electrical power requirements.
- They can be complicated for a novice to adjust and set if all of the parameters that are adjustable are not understood. In some cases this can deliver poor sounding results and even allow amplifiers to deliver harmful frequencies to speakers that they are not intended to play.

Pre-engineered passive crossovers that come with component speakers often include non-standard alignments designed not only to divide the frequencies, but also to perform some **frequency response shaping**. These alignments are usually NOT available in basic active crossovers and to do the whole job, the passive crossover would have to be replaced with a complicated active crossover or an active crossover and EQ. Since that necessitates more equipment, more amplifier channels and more cost to the audio system, one can see how a highly engineered passive crossover network can balance the frequency response between that midrange and tweeter for the tradeoff of otherwise requiring additional active amplifier channels. There is more detail about the application of passive crossovers in the "Speakers" section of this chapter.

Because there's not one perfect speaker, the traditional approach is to use active or passive crossovers (or a combination of both) to direct the right signals to the right speakers.

Margin Notes

Classifications of Filters

- **Low-pass crossovers** allow low frequencies to pass through and primarily direct bass ranges to the components operating the subwoofers. Technically speaking though, the range of frequencies that "pass" below the crossover point depends on exactly where that point is set.
- **High-pass crossovers** allow only higher frequencies to pass through to high-frequency drivers. Sometimes high-pass applications include cutting the lowest bass from front speakers so that those duties are handled only by the subwoofer. Again, the range of frequencies that "pass" above the crossover point depends on exactly where that point is set.
- **Bandpass crossovers** allow a middle-range bandwidth, the "pass band," to pass through to the speaker and that bandwidth is cut off on both the high and low sides. Such applications typically apply to mid-range speakers, although in some cases, a bandpass crossover (or filter) will be used to let the entire musical band pass, but not subsonic and ultrasonic frequencies. Narrow bandwidth bandpass applications apply to dedicated midbass speakers and subwoofers with both low-pass and high-pass filters.

All of this is actually helpful to fine tune the pursuit of a true full-range 20-20kHz frequency response. With crossovers and potential speaker choices, there are many possibilities to arrive at just the right combinations to achieve a great sounding system that will not overwork the speakers.

The general rule of thumb when mixing passive and active crossovers in a common 3-way system is to utilize an active crossover between the subwoofer and midrange speaker, then a passive crossover network between a mid and tweeter. This is a tried-and-true balance where you get the most pleasing results without unnecessary cost or amplifier power requirements.

Balancing the Frequency Response

As stated earlier, audio systems commonly use multiple speakers in several frequency ranges to achieve 20-20kHz full-range response; however, there can be "too much" or "too little" in certain areas of that response. A firm understanding of the terminology and underlying principles provides an excellent foundation for the Mobile Product Specialist to approach each audio system as an improved solution, rather than just "adding or changing parts."

Octaves

An **octave** is a specific measured interval between two tones or frequencies. An octave gets its name because in music, there are eight steps, tones or "notes" within an OCT-ave. "Oct" is a prefix meaning "eight." For notes spaced an octave apart, the human ear hears them as being essentially the same. That's why, in music, notes spaced an octave apart have the same name, "A," "B," "C," etc. Looking at octaves mathematically reveals that the interval between one musical note and another that's an octave directly above or below that note is a 2:1 ratio.

Margin Notes

- For example, middle "C" or "C4" on a piano is 261.6Hz. The "C" one octave below (C3) would be 130.8Hz, and the "C" an octave above (C5) would be 523.2Hz.

Whenever frequency response limitations or characteristics are discussed, one needs a reference point from which to start and then move up or down the frequency scale in measured, predictable steps as octaves above and octaves below. Having that reference point gives you a clear direction to the next interval, in this case double or half of that starting reference frequency.

In the human hearing range of 20Hz-20kHz, there are about 10 octaves:

1) 20-40Hz
2) 40-80Hz
3) 80-160Hz
4) 160-320Hz
5) 320-640Hz
6) 640-1280Hz
7) 1280-2560Hz
8) 2560-5120Hz
9) 5120Hz-10,240Hz
10) 10,240Hz-20,480Hz

Flute - Fundamental Note - G4 (392 Hz)

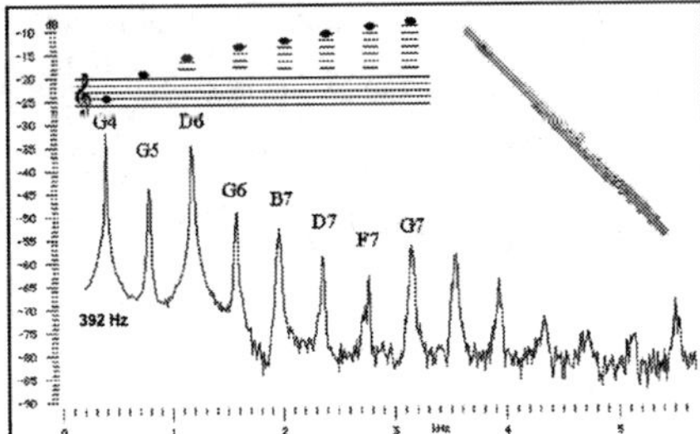

Violin - Fundamental Note - G4 (392 Hz)

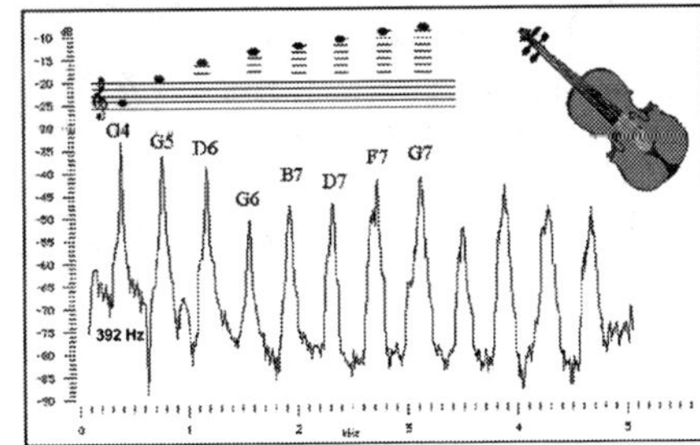

In actuality, human hearing can't extend all the way through that last octave, but it's clear to see how a range of frequencies is easier to analyze when the octave spread is the focus.

Harmonics

Unless it is an electronically produced pure tone, a person's voice, or other natural sound will have overtones, also known as **harmonics**. A harmonic is a weaker (lower amplitude or quieter) overtone of the original note (the fundamental frequency) and is responsible for the character of the sound produced by the instrument or voice that plays or sings the note. The character is like its unique signature or audio DNA. The harmonic structure of musical instruments is what makes them sound different, and the harmonic structure of someone's voice is what allows us to recognize that voice, when compared to other ones.

It's easy to see that, although the fundamental **note that's being played is precisely the same** between two instruments, **the sounds of the two instruments are different**. It's those additional harmonics that also occur when the instruments are played that give each instrument its unique "sound." **Added harmonics** are also one of the reasons that harmonic distortion in an amplifier or other sound system component is **not desirable** and can affect the way things are supposed to sound in a negative way.

Margin Notes

- Total Harmonic Distortion (THD) is a rating that is part of an amplifier's power output specification and indicates the harmonics the amplifier adds to the audio signal path. Industry-accepted practice for CTA-specified ratings is that amplifier power output can't exceed 1% THD at the rated power, which ensures the power is "listenable" and not full of distortion. Read more about THD and its relationship to amplifier power ratings in the Mobile Audio Amplifiers section of this chapter.

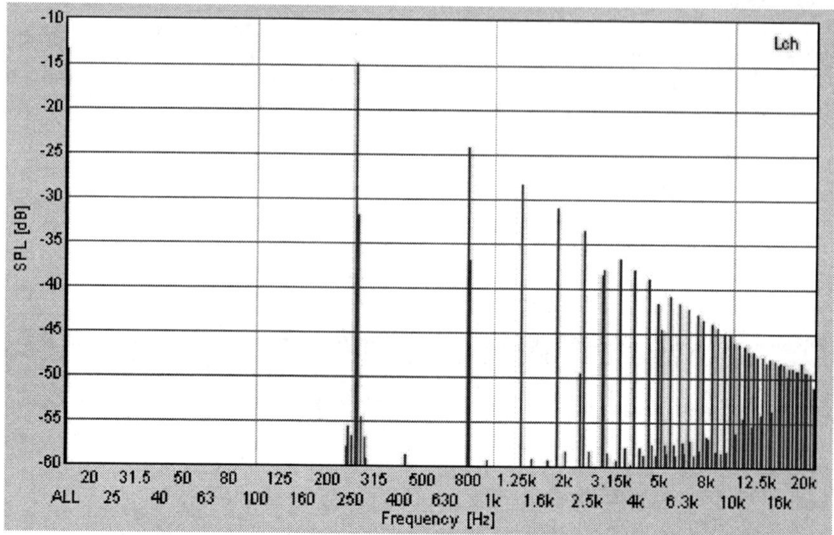

When distorting the original harmonic content or adding extra (unwanted harmonics), the unique signature of that sound is changed. Musicians use "effects boxes" to change the harmonic structure of the instrument they are playing to add interest or to make the instrument sound different. Distortion in an amplifier affects the entire signal—all the instruments and voices—and doesn't add interest to any single instrument. Rather, that distortion degrades the overall quality of the sound. With enough training, you'll know right away when something does not sound right because the harmonics are distorted from how they were originally created.

When an amplifier is driven into audible distortion (commonly known as clipping), the additional harmonics that are created occur as direct multiples of the fundamental. If an amplifier is reproducing a pure tone, say it's C4 (261.6Hz), the second harmonic is C5 (523.2Hz), one octave above. Most people would think the third harmonic would be C6, which is another octave up from C5, so double 523.2Hz or 1046.4Hz. Unfortunately that's not the way harmonic distortion works, which is why it does not register as "good sound" to the human ear.

When the amplifier produces distortion, the first harmonic is double (2x) the fundamental tone (identical to an octave above). The next step though is three times (3x) the fundamental. Since the pure tone was C4 at 261.6Hz, then three times the fundamental is (261.6Hz x 3) 784.8Hz. The odd harmonics aren't spaced at pleasant musical intervals like octaves are and add an unpleasant sound to the music. Remember that for notes spaced an octave apart, the human ear hears them as essentially the same (some listeners even prefer equipment that creates these even harmonics). When the harmonics are not spaced as octaves (**odd harmonics**), the human ear may identify it as wrong.

Margin Notes

Signal to Noise Ratio (S/N)

Signal to noise (S/N) is a ratio that indicates how much audio signal there is in relation to noise, under specific conditions. **This is generally measured in decibels (dB) and higher numbers are always better**. A musical note can be masked in a number of ways. Acoustically, the ambient noise that occurs in the vehicle – as well as the road, wind, and traffic – will combine to mask the quieter musical passages. This is referred to as the **noise floor**, and is concentrated mostly in the bass regions. Many of today's cars, particularly luxury cars, do an excellent job of lowering the noise floor by insulating the outside noises.

When applied to audio equipment, this specification describes the difference between the audio signal from the source material and any residual noise generated by the audio component itself. Again, higher numbers are always better because that indicates the component adds as little noise as possible. When lower-grade (more economical) parts are incorporated into an audio product's design, they will contribute to the thermal noise that infects the musical signal. In those cases quiet passages in the music will be covered by an audible hiss.

Dynamic Range of a Music Recording

Dynamic range (measured in dB) is the ratio of the largest to the smallest intensity of sound transmitted or reproduced by a sound system. The reference is usually a musical selection or program signal being played. A program is a structured, narrow-band signal, while noise is a random, wideband signal.

In many ways, the overall dynamic range a listener experiences in the vehicle's audio system depends on the recording of the music itself. Many modern recordings are not produced with dynamic range in mind; rather recording engineers often replace soft and loud passages with a recording that is loud most of the time. For example, computer speakers and book shelf speakers have a limited ability to produce a dynamic frequency range with the required power and cone area. Engineers may choose to make the average recording levels louder (with less dynamic range) to sound as if the smaller speakers do a better job. In cars, that reduction in dynamic range can be useful too, since it raises the level of the quietest sounds to make them louder than the noise floor of the moving car.

Often the recording of the music has a lot to do with the target audience who will listen to it. Popular music that gets a lot of radio play may not always be recorded with the best dynamic range in mind because of the variety of playback scenarios fans of that music will utilize. These days, it's also a consideration for recording engineers to think about how something will sound with a pair of ear buds on a portable device, so it's not just about traditional speakers (or lack thereof). It used

Margin Notes

to be people could say one type of music was more dynamic than another, but that assumed the recording engineers allowed as much dynamic range on the recording as was necessary to reproduce the difference between the loudest and quietest passages accurately. It takes a well-trained listener to detect small amounts of dynamic range compression applied to recordings and many listeners appreciate the overall volume increase that it provides. Too much dynamic range compression makes quick, or transient signals sound "mushy" or less impactful.

When people are disappointed with the entertainment quality of a sound system, it's sometimes because the original recording lacks enough dynamic range to be entertaining when it's played at higher volume levels. Loud music for the sake of only being loud all the time introduces listening fatigue and that's exactly the opposite of the desired effect. Preserving dynamic range as much as possible allows listeners to enjoy the music and, if the Mobile Product Specialist has done their job right in designing an audio system upgrade (and the technician has installed it with the same attention to detail), all the dynamic range included in the original recording should be preserved.

Dynamic Range of a Mobile Audio System

Since dynamic range is the range of volume, in decibels (dB) from the softest to the loudest, produced by a source of sounds, the vehicle's audio system also has a dynamic range. This is not about the recording of the music though; rather **it's about the softest to loudest ranges of sound in the vehicle**. To characterize it simply, the quietest the vehicle can be is with the volume all the way down making no sound from the audio system. There you are just dealing with ambient noises. Unlike most homes where noise can be contained, in a moving car, the audio system has to contend with various environmental and mechanical noises such as wind, the sound of tires on the road, the engine, etc. All of this ambient noise is what establishes the noise floor. That's the low (or softest) level of the dynamic range of the audio system because the system has to come up to that level and overcome that noise level before your ears ever hear any music.

On the top (or loudest) end of dynamic range in an audio system is its maximum, undistorted volume level. The maximum volume establishes the high number and when the floor noise (lowest number) is subtracted, what is left is the dynamic range. Regardless of how a higher dynamic range is achieved, the more dynamic range a system has, the louder it will seem.

This concept was presented earlier in this chapter under the topic of **decibels**. If the car is quieter to begin with, there will be less power required to achieve an identical dynamic range to a car that has a higher noise floor. This is often why premium cars with factory systems seem to sound "decent" to some people. It's not just the upgraded factory sound, but it's also that it's in a really quiet car. Read more about lowering the noise floor using sound deadening and damping materials in the Speakers section of this chapter, as well as Speaker Installation Considerations in Chapter 4.

Margin Notes

Headroom

Music signals are comprised of peaks (loud sounds) and valleys (quieter sounds) all mixed together. In music that has a "beat," those louder sounds are periodic—they happen at regular intervals—like the sound of a drum. In between those drum beats, the level of the music is often much lower. "Headroom" is an indication of the amount of power that's reserved to reproduce those peaks.

Headroom is one of those terms that are quite common in audio jargon. Consumers certainly may not understand what headroom means. Be sure to characterize any use of the term in a customer conversation accurately.

- As an amplifier specification, headroom refers to the difference between the amount of power the amplifier can produce constantly and the amount of power the amplifier can produce during an instantaneous peak in the music without distortion.
- As an informal term, "headroom" refers to the amount of electrical or acoustic output the system can produce in excess of the amount required for normal listening or for reproducing the average level of the music. Obviously, more headroom is desirable, but it comes at a cost. Amplifier power and the electrical capacity to reliably support that amplifier power simply costs money

Think of headroom with this analogy:

- Imagine jumping on a trampoline in a room with a low ceiling – the consequences could be painful if you hit your head. If you could *raise* the ceiling (add more "headroom"), then the chance of hitting your head on the ceiling would be reduced even if you aren't always jumping that high on an average (nominal) basis.

In mobile audio systems, headroom is attained by increased amplifier power. Even if the listener does not operate the audio system at full volume all the time, a quick peak of energy will be delivered more effectively with more power on tap. Some people say this headroom translates into the "emotion" a listener experiences when playing certain music that envelops them into an experience rather than simply hearing the sound or words of a song. Some might describe headroom as more closely replicating an intimate live musical performance rather than just sound through speakers. The tradeoff to achieve that emotion and listening experience with headroom is that power on tap has to be reliable and the vehicle electrical system actually has to be capable of supplying it. It's always a balance of how much headroom an audio system can have versus the cost to reliably supply that headroom.

Summary of Basic Audio Terminology and Knowledge

In this section, not only Basic Audio Terminology and Knowledge was introduced, but to help with the context, terminology of certain types of audio equipment was also introduced to connect the concepts of audio fundamentals with where it applies in actual practice. Later in this chapter, each of those types of audio equipment is presented in good detail and ties back to this section's terminology

Margin Notes

and examples. This should assist the reader in connecting the concept of audio fundamentals to a feature, function or solution that a particular piece of audio equipment provides.

Some readers may wish to read through the entire Chapter 1 and review (again) this Basic Audio Terminology and Knowledge section for even greater comprehension. Putting this fundamental audio knowledge to practice with audio equipment recommendation and selections provides the greatest value of a Mobile Product Specialist to both their customer and their MECP certified technician colleagues who are tasked with expertly installing it all.

AFTERMARKET IN-DASH HEAD UNITS

The term "head unit" is an industry-specific term, but there many names consumers use for an in-dash car stereo. It's important to understand the terminologies because consumers seldom use industry terminology when shopping for a new in-dash unit. These other terms can include:

- Radio or CD Player
- Source Unit
- In-Dash
- Deck
- Stereo
- Receiver
- Controller
- Tuner

Sizes

Aftermarket in-dash head units are typically offered in two standardized sizes: DIN (also known as Single-DIN) and Double-DIN. While there are also other configurations for special circumstances in marine, off-road and custom vehicle applications such as hideaway or water-resistant controllers, the vast majority of in-dash head units are either DIN or Double-DIN sized. The acronym DIN (Deutsches Institut für Normung) describes standardized German sizing for various production items, in this case head units. It was standardized in early Porsche, Audi, BMW® and Mercedes-Benz® vehicles.

- DIN Head Unit – approximately 2" tall x 7"wide
- Double-DIN Head Unit approximately 4" tall x 7"wide
- There is not a standard depth size for DIN or Double-DIN head units, so they can vary depending on the features and functionality.

Aside from features, selection of a DIN or Double-DIN head unit for the consumer is largely influenced by the vehicle's dashboard space and the availability of any installation accessories required. The vehicle must have an opening to accommodate the Double-DIN or installation accessories must be available to facilitate that fitment. Double-DIN Head Units have more space for larger buttons and displays or even video screens. Multimedia head units with video playback capability and touch screens are commonly Double-DIN for example, because of the additional space

Margin Notes

for physical features Double-DIN head units are typically preferred when they will fit easily. Almost all head units with GPS navigation are Double-DIN sized. Some Double-DIN multimedia head units lacking a disc player may have a Double-DIN screen attached to a Single-DIN chassis due to smaller electronics. In those cases, only the first inch or so of depth thickness at the face of the unit is the Double-DIN size to provide mounting provisions and the screen housing. There is more information on installation-related accessories for head units later in this section and in Chapter 4.

Throughout the 1990's vehicle manufacturers often used head units that were smaller than Double-DIN. Due to this, Single-DIN aftermarket head units became popular because they could be installed without major modification to the vehicle. As vehicle manufacturers focused on the multimedia offerings in their vehicles over the years, head unit openings have become larger and therefore more vehicles can accommodate a Double-DIN aftermarket head unit without needing major modifications.

Common Features and Functions

The primary function of any head unit is playback and (typically) control of source material. Sources can be any type of audio, video or information in an audible and/or visual format. This study guide lists the basics of the most common sources found in aftermarket head units.

AM/FM

Virtually all aftermarket head units include an AM/FM tuner. The head unit lacks a built-in antenna, so the vehicle must have a working AM/FM antenna to receive AM/FM radio broadcasts.

AM/FM tuner quality varies by head unit manufacturer. This determines the ability of the tuner to pull in weak or distant AM or FM radio stations. Most factory-installed head units have a high-quality tuner and many customers use that as their reference of how AM/FM radio reception should be. When customers cite poor reception with an aftermarket head unit, it is usually due to the quality of the tuner. AM/FM Tuner Sensitivity is the specification that represents the quality of the tuner's ability to receive a radio station. A higher AM/FM sensitivity number indicates that the tuner is able to pull in weak or distant radio stations better than tuners with a lower sensitivity number.

Radio Data Steam (RDS) is a feature on common on most factory installed AM/FM radios, as well as many aftermarket head units. RDS allows the radio to display metadata that is transmitted along with the radio station's audio content. This metadata shows up as text on the head unit's display. It is typically used to display the radio station's name, artist, song name and album name. If this metadata is important to the customer make sure the aftermarket head unit's tuner also has RDS built in. All AM/FM tuners receive analog audio signals from the radio station's broadcasting antenna. Due to bandwidth limitations on AM and FM radio frequencies this audio

Margin Notes

signal does not cover the full spectrum of human hearing. This means some high and low frequency audio signals will are lost. FM broadcasts range from 30Hz-15kHz and AM broadcasts range from 40Hhz to 5kHz. As referenced earlier in this chapter, human hearing and CD quality audio is typically 20Hz-20kHz. This means analog AM/FM broadcasts are not capable of reproducing full range, CD-quality sound. It's evident and most people can easily hear the difference of an analog AM/FM broadcast versus a CD-quality sound.

HD Radio

HD Radio is a digital audio signal transmitted along with the radio station's analog signal. The HD channels are transmitted on the radio stations sidebands, so stations are able to transmit multiple HD channels along with their analog signal. This is called multicasting. The compromise of multicast stations is they are not as strong as the station's analog signal. This means HD channels will not travel as far as analog channels and reception can be blocked easier in areas that experience poor reception.

Since HD is a digital signal, the frequency bandwidth is improved over analog AM and FM radio. HD channels on the FM bands *can* be close to CD quality in terms of sound quality. Both AM and FM stations can broadcast HD channels. AM stations broadcasting HD signals will typically have the sound quality of a standard analog FM station. HD radio also transmits metadata and since the signal is digital, much more information can be transmitted over HD channels. Artist, song name and album name information are transmitted on HD channels. Some radio stations use metadata to transmit traffic and weather information as well.

Multicasting allows radio stations to transmit multiple digital HD channels in addition to the standard analog signal.

HD-to-analog channel switching is an issue to be aware of with HD radios since the HD signal does not travel as far and can be blocked easier than analog signals by buildings, geographic features of the landscape, or other structures. There is no poor reception or static with HD radio, so when the HD signal is weak or lost, the tuner will switch to the station's analog signal automatically. This switching can be noticeable to the listener because the frequency response of analog radio is not as good as HD radio. If the HD signal becomes weak or is lost while listening to a multicast channel the radio will revert to the stations main analog broadcast. In some reception areas the analog and HD channels may switch back and forth as the HD signal strength changes (and that usually means the content is different between those broadcasts). Customers may perceive this switching as a defective radio, but the head unit's display should have an indication that HD to analog switching is happening to validate that it is a normal operation.

Satellite Radio

Satellite radio is another digital radio platform only available in North America. Instead of using terrestrial AM/FM radio frequencies, the signal is transmitted over microwave frequencies from satellites orbiting above North America. The satellite radio signal is broadcast by satellite, so coverage is coast to coast as long as the satellite antenna has a clear view of the sky. The satellite coverage operates within the 48 contiguous United States, the District of Columbia and Puerto Rico (with some limitations), hundreds of

Margin Notes

miles out into the Atlantic and Pacific Oceans, the Gulf of Mexico, Caribbean Sea and the Great Lakes. For urban areas where tall buildings or other obstacles could block satellite coverage, there are also ground-based repeaters to ensure consistent signal.

- Note: The signal broadcast from the satellites does not cover the U.S. s tates of Alaska and Hawaii, so if customers in those states wish to receive satellite radio content, they must stream it with an internet enabled device such as a smartphone. Traditional satellite radio tuners intended for installation with a companion aftermarket head unit won't work in Alaska and Hawaii, nor do the satellite radio tuners that come factory-installed in the vehicle.

Receiving satellite radio requires its own antenna separate of the vehicle's AM/FM antenna. This needs a clear view of the sky and is typically mounted outside of the vehicle via magnet and/or adhesive. Aftermarket head units typically do not come with built-in satellite radio tuners, although there may be an external tuner packaged with the head unit. This is because satellite radio is only available in North America and most aftermarket head units are produced on global manufacturing platforms.

If the customer has OEM satellite radio and wishes to retain it with an aftermarket head unit, they may be able to do so if proper adaptors are available, but it depends on how the satellite radio tuner is configured.

- If the satellite radio tuner was built in to the OEM head unit the antenna may be able to be reused but a new tuner will be required because the factory head unit will be removed when an aftermarket head unit is installed.
- If the OEM satellite tuner was external then in certain cases an interface module may be able to retain the OEM satellite radio tuner and antenna.

Compressed Audio Playback

Compressed audio is a term used to describe digital audio content altered from its original Compact Disc (CD) audio format into a smaller file size. CD-based audio files are large so various compression techniques have been developed to allow the audio information to be transmitted over lower bandwidth mediums (ex. satellite radio or streaming audio services) or stored on smaller-capacity media storage devices (ex. smartphone or USB drives).

Commercially recorded CDs utilize a WAV file format. For 16-bit WAV files, about 10 MB per minute of audio is required. DVD-based audio and other high resolution digital audio formats utilize 24 bits and require even more storage capacity. On the other hand, a compressed audio file uses closer to 1-2 MB per minute depending on compression type and bitrate.

Common lossy compression techniques are MP3, WMA and AAC. These are called "lossy" because in the process of compressing the file size down much smaller, some content in the file is discarded. This is sometimes regarded as content that is otherwise not noticeable to the human ear, but audiophiles with astute hearing may debate that if comparing a song using lossy compression to an uncompressed song.

Margin Notes

- MP3 is the oldest and most common compression technique and uses several different compression bitrates. These bitrates determine how large the files are and how close the audio quality will be to CD quality. Megabits per second (Mbps) are how the compression (bit rate) is rated in compressed audio formats. 64mbps, 128 mbps, 256 mbps and 320mbps are the most common bitrates for MP3 files. The higher bitrate numbers indicate larger file size and better audio quality. 64mbps will work fine for talk radio type content, but significant audio will be lost if listening to musical content.

- WMA is a compression technique developed by Microsoft. Windows Media Audio (WMA) was designed to be an improvement to MP3 in terms of file size to quality ratio. It also includes Digital Rights Management (DRM) metadata to prevent the files from being copied and shared. WMA files also have different bitrates and they follow the same rules as MP3 bitrates. Higher bitrates mean better quality, but larger file sizes. WMA files are a little more proprietary than MP3 files. There are some devices that do not support WMA playback but will support MP3. Most aftermarket head units will support WMA files.

- AAC is a compression technique developed by Apple®. It was also developed as an improvement to MP3 in terms of sound quality to file size. It also includes Digital Rights Management (DRM) metadata to prevent the files from being copied and shared. AAC files are largely supported on most devices, however DRM can be an issue depending on what type of device these files are stored on.

Several lossless compression formats have been developed such as Free Lossless Audio Codec (FLAC) and Apple Lossless (ALAC). These are called "lossless" because they use techniques similar to zipping a computer file to remove and then later unzipping to restore the original data. Many aftermarket head units or "media boxes" that connect directly to a hard drive storage system allow playback of these lossless file types. The capability of FLAC and Apple Lossless playback is fairly common, but always check the product specifications to ensure the capability if the customer is a lossless or hi-res audio listener.

Since the 1980s, CDs were the primary method to play back premium audio files. CDs are still common in aftermarket head units, but have evolved significantly past simple WAV file playback. CD-R along with compressed file playback ability can be used to hold 10 times the music that a commercial audio CD was able to. DVDs can be used to hold even more information than a CD. DVD playback is not common on standard audio-only head units, but can often be found on multimedia head units. High-fidelity formats that may be used in home theater applications such as Blu-ray or SACD have not been quick to be adopted in the vehicle with commercially available products.

For hi-res audio playback, either a 'media box' or portable players are a viable choice to use because they provide a digital output that can directly connect to a DSP-based signal processor that supports the 24 bit, hi-res format. In those cases, the traditional head unit may connect to the analog inputs of the DSP and then the hi-res player functions on the AUX digital audio input.

Aftermarket head unit audio input options

Aside from the tuner and any disc play capabilities, most aftermarket head units also have multiple options for transferring audio/video content from an external device into the head unit.

- **Front Panel Media (USB, SD card, etc.)**
  Front panel media connections allow the user to connect digital devices or digital storage media directly to the head unit. The head unit is able to transfer the data from the device or the storage media in digital format and convert the files (MP3, WMA, AAC) into an analog audio signal. It is important to understand that this conversion process takes place in the head unit, so the file format must be supported by the head unit for it to work.

  USB and SD card are the two most common digital media input types on head units. There are some differences between USB connections to be aware of, though. Some USB connections will support USB drives but do not support smartphone file playback. This is due to DRM protocols and licensing requirements.

  USB ports also have different electrical current output capacities. This will affect the USB port's ability to charge a smartphone or tablet. These current capacities are rated in milliamps or amps and can usually be found in the product's specs. Higher numbers indicate faster charge rates.

- **Front AUX Input Jacks – 3.5mm headphone-style jack**
  3.5mm auxiliary (AUX) input jacks allow analog audio signals into the head unit. These are also called a 1/8" input jacks. Typically, a 3.5mm to 3.5mm male-to-male cable is used to connect this input to an MP3 player or smartphone through the device's headphone output. When using this type of input, the volume on the device should be turned up to get the best quality audio signal into the head unit. Some smartphones may lack a 3.5mm output jack and require a special cable to utilize a front AUX input headphone jack on the head unit to be able to listen to music from the phone.

- **Rear USB Input**
  Some head units have rear USB connectors instead of or in addition to front panel USB connectors. Having the connection on the back of the head unit allows the cable to be routed to a location specified by the customer during installation. The main benefit is cosmetic, since the cable will not be hanging out of the front of the head unit. Another benefit to rear USB connections is they may be able to be integrated with factory USB ports. Usually an adaptor is required to convert the factory USB cable's connection to work on the aftermarket head unit.

Margin Notes

Margin Notes

- **Rear RCA Preamp Inputs**
  Some head units have rear RCA inputs in addition to preamp-level audio outputs. These are primarily used when integrating the head unit with an existing rear seat entertainment system. These inputs allow the audio from the rear video screens to be played through the vehicle's speakers. RCA inputs can also be used to input audio from MP3 or smartphone devices. An adaptor cable will be needed to convert the RCA connectors into a 3.5mm connector that can be plugged into the device's headphone jack or proprietary connector (such as Apple Lightning).

- **Wireless Inputs**
  Bluetooth is the most common type of wireless input. Bluetooth is commonly associated with hands-free phone calls, but can also be used for streaming audio (via A2DP profile) and other types of low-bandwidth wireless data transfers. Some aftermarket head units may use combinations of a wired USB connection along with Bluetooth for more complex connections.

  Wi-Fi is another type of wireless connection. Currently Wi-Fi is not common in aftermarket head units but may become more common as the types of data being transferred become more complex. Bluetooth's bandwidth limitations prevent it from streaming things like video. A Wi-Fi connection can handle streaming video or other more complex applications.

Sound Control Features

- **Balance/Fader**
  The balance control on a head unit allows the user to adjust how loud the left speakers are in relation to the right speakers. Adjusting the balance towards the right will decrease the volume of the left speakers and vice versa.

  The fader control is similar to balance, but it controls the front to back speaker volume relationship. Fading the system to the rear will decrease the volume of the front speakers. Fading the system to the front will decrease the volume to the rear speakers. While the fader is normally operational in a factory system, the configuration of aftermarket speaker layouts and whether or not the preamp outputs versus powered speaker outputs within the aftermarket head unit are used may determine whether the fader is able to operate in a traditional front and rear arrangement.
  For example, if the head unit only has one set of RCA preamp outputs and those are used to drive an amplifier connected to front speakers, the preamp outputs may be non-fading (meaning the position of the fader does not alter the level of the preamp outputs relative to other powered speaker outputs).

- **Tone Controls**
  Tone controls allow the user the ability to adjust the sound to match their preferences. Most head units have a minimum of bass and treble tone controls. The bass control allows the user to increase or decrease low frequencies. Most

bass controls adjust the 100Hz frequency range. Treble controls adjust the high frequencies and are typically set at 10,000Hz (10kHz). Mid-grade head units may have bass, midrange and treble controls with the added midrange control centered at about 1000Hz (1kHz). Some high end head units will allow for more precise adjustments of the tone dividing the audible spectrum to between five and 30 frequency ranges that can individually be adjusted. The specifications in the head unit's operational manual will specify the exact center frequencies and levels of cut or boost for any tone adjustments.

Margin Notes

- **Loudness**

  The Loudness circuit on aftermarket head units is typically an on/off or variable setting that increases the bass and treble of the audio signal. Human hearing is less responsive to high and low frequencies at lower volumes. This phenomenon has been well-researched and documented. For more information, reference the Fletcher-Munson (also called "Equal Loudness") curves in the glossary at the back of the study guide.

  Loudness circuits do vary by aftermarket head unit manufacturer. They are typically labelled "Loud," but some manufacturers have come up with their own names like "Extra Bass," "Bass Boost," "Bass Engine," etc.

  Some aftermarket head units have variable Loudness circuits that allow the user to adjust the amount of bass and treble boost that happens when the circuit is activated. A well-designed Loudness circuit will reduce the bass and treble boost effect as the volume is turned up. Using Loudness circuits at high volumes can overdrive speakers causing damage to them.

  Finally, loudness is generally absent on a modern factory head unit because the vehicle manufacturer can implement other forms of volume-dependent equalization that incorporates other input from vehicle speed or ambient interior cabin noise. Or the manufacturers may have preset loudness settings that have labels like "Rock," "Talk," "Pop," "Jazz," "Flat," etc.

- **Onboard Equalization**

  Digital Signal Processing (DSP) chips are found often in aftermarket head units. Historically audio signal modification (ex. bass, treble, loudness) was done by modifying the analog audio signal inside the head unit using discrete components like capacitors, resistors and transistors.
  With DSP, the audio signal is modified digitally and converted to analog before sending it to the speakers through the head unit's powered IC amp chips, or through the preamp level RCA outputs. DSP chips are cheaper and more powerful than using analog components. By using DSP, multiband equalization replaces the standard bass and treble adjustments. Advanced audio adjustments like time correction, speaker filters (crossovers) and programmable audio presets are also common on head units with DSP processing built in.

Margin Notes

- **Compressed Audio 'Sound Enhancement'**
  Compressed audio music sources such as MP3 files and streaming audio often lose some of the audio details like extended high and low frequencies and dynamic range.

  Head unit manufacturers *may* include audio modification schemes designed to restore some of the audio information that is lost during the compression process. Manufacturers all have their own names for these types of compressed audio enhancement circuits and they vary in their effectiveness. See the manufacturer's website or the documentation in the owner's manual for more details.

- **Subwoofer Output**
  A preamp level RCA subwoofer output (sub-out) allows the user to control an external subwoofer amp/speaker from the head unit. Typical adjustments available are subwoofer level, subwoofer low pass filter (crossover point) and subwoofer polarity inversion (0 or 180 degrees). A subwoofer output will typically not be affected by the fader on the head unit (sometimes called a non-fading output) and may also be a mono output that is not affected by balance either.

  Subwoofer level allows the user to adjust the volume level of the subwoofer. Subwoofer level can be adjusted as needed depending on the music.

  Low pass filter (subwoofer crossover point) adjusts what bass frequencies are sent to the subwoofer. The low pass filter point is typically set based on the size of the subwoofer.

  Subwoofer polarity (also mistakenly called "phase") simply inverts the polarity of the subwoofer signal. Inverting the polarity allows the user to possibly better match the subwoofer's output with the interior speakers in the vehicle. Even if the feature is labeled as such, to say "phase" would mistakenly indicate that the adjustment was variable anywhere in the range 0 to 180 degrees such as in home audio subwoofers. On head units, this is not usually the case – rather it's a simple polarity inversion, either 0 or 180 degrees. Like switching the positive and negative speaker wires around. Read more about the difference of phase versus polarity in the Audio Fundamentals section earlier in this chapter.

Functionality Features

- **Volume – Knob or Buttons?**
  While it's something that's engineered into the design of a given head unit, the type of volume control is worth noting when a customer has a particular preference. If the customer absolutely has a preference of a rotating knob over buttons, this is something to consider when showing them selections in aftermarket head units. Also keep in mind that vehicles with a factory steering wheel control for the volume up/down can be interfaced into aftermarket head units, so the customer may not necessarily utilize the front

Margin Notes

panel volume control on a regular basis when steering wheel controls are available.

- **Touch Screens**

  Head units with video touch screens use two different technologies to detect the users touch inputs.

  Resistive touchscreens have been around the longest and are common in the automotive environment. They use a thin, clear overlay over the screen that detects pressure when pressed. The location of the touch corresponds to a location on the overlay's grid and each location has a unique resistive value allowing the unit to know what area of the screen was pressed. Resistive screens are generally cheaper to manufacture and can remain functional if the user is wearing gloves.

  Capacitive screens are becoming more common. Smartphones and tablets both use capacitive screen technologies. The screen detects the user's finger directly without requiring pressure being applied to the screen. It does this by sensing the small amounts of electricity in human skin.

  Capacitive screens are generally more responsive, and work well on multi-touch applications like pinch to zoom and scrolling applications. The one disadvantage is they do not work well if the user is wearing gloves.

- **Programmable Illumination and dimming at night**

  Head unit displays used to rely on colored LEDs for illumination. This usually meant the display color and brightness were set by the manufacturer. Modern head unit displays are much more flexible because they are dimmable and many are capable of multi-color illumination. Dimming can typically be controlled manually or automatically. Units with automatic dimming will have a wire on the head unit that connects to the vehicle's dash light circuit. When the vehicle's dash lights are adjusted the head unit's illumination will adjust as well.

Head units with multi-color illumination allow the user to pick from a variety of pre-programmed colors. Some manufactures also allow the user to "mix" their own colors by adjusting the red, green and blue levels (RGB) going to the display. These types of displays are capable of producing millions of color combinations, so the head unit can be customized to match the vehicle's dash light color or whatever color the user prefers.

Margin Notes

HEAD UNIT ACCESSORIES

Dash Kit

Aftermarket head units are often a different size or use different mounting systems than the factory head units. To accommodate these differences a dash kit will need to be installed. Dash kits are specific to the type of vehicle into which the head unit is being installed.

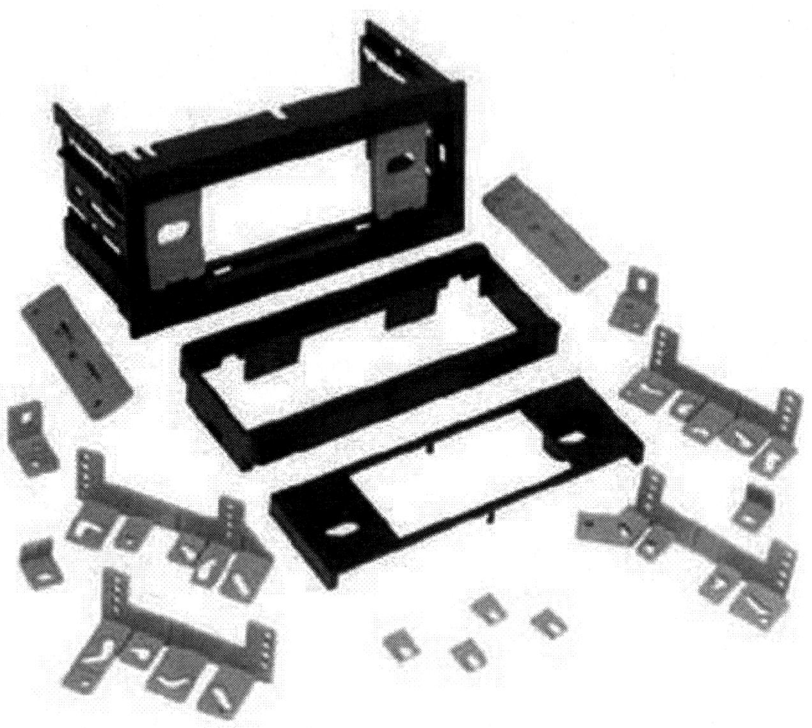

Vehicle dash kit types

- **No kit required**

  Some vehicles have standard DIN or Double-DIN opening and do not require a kit. Some examples are older Fords, Volkswagens and Hondas, as well as many early 1990s or older Mercedes-Benz®, Audi and BMW®. After removing the factory radio the opening in the dash is a standard DIN size 2" x 7". In these vehicles the mounting sleeve that comes with the aftermarket head unit can be installed into the dash opening without requiring a kit.

  Older Toyotas and Nissans have ISO-DIN or ISO-Double-DIN head unit openings. These vehicles will accommodate an aftermarket head unit using the OEM ISO-mount brackets without a need for an aftermarket kit. An OEM Double-DIN opening will accommodate an aftermarket Double DIN head unit without a kit or a Single-DIN head unit if a storage pocket is installed below the head unit.

- **Simple dash bracket kits**

  Basic dash kits are used to convert the vehicle's dash opening to the Single-DIN or Double-DIN aftermarket head unit dimensions. These kits will also include

Margin Notes

brackets to mount the kit to the factory radio mounting locations. These kits are usually made from ABS plastic and can be packaged as multi-kits that cover multiple vehicle platforms or vehicle specific covering only a specific make and model of vehicle. In some cases, the plastic kit panel can accept the factory radio's metal mounting brackets (typically 1980s to early 90s GM vehicles).

- **Replacement dash panel kits**
  On the newest makes and models of vehicles the factory radio is often part of the vehicle's dashboard configuration. Removing the factory radio means part of the vehicle's dash will be missing as well. In these vehicles the dash kit solution includes a dash replacement panel along with the typical mounting brackets that accompany simple dash kits. These types of kits are usually specific to a single make and model of vehicle, usually within a small range of production years. Often times they are color matched to the vehicle so there may be several options for a specific vehicle.

- **Dash kits with built in electronics**
  On some vehicle platforms the factory head unit is also integrated with the vehicle's heating, ventilation, and air conditioning (HVAC) system and/or other vehicle controls. On these vehicle removing the factory head unit means the HVAC controls and displays also need to be replaced with some method of controlling the HVAC or other features. Dash kits are available that replace these controls and display panels. These kits are designed to maintain the same functionality as the factory controls but may have a much different look and feel. The kit will also include the replacement dash panel and head unit mounting brackets

- **Dash kits with head unit interface adaptor**
  There is another solution for vehicles where the factory head unit and HVAC controls are combined. Rather than replacing the HVAC controls, the kit comes with a head unit interface allowing the aftermarket head unit to control the HVAC system. This type of solution is head unit-specific and vehicle-specific, meaning the head unit must have firmware built in to reproduce the HVAC controls on the unit's GUI and it must have the ability to communicate with the vehicle's data bus network to control the HVAC system. Since these kits communicate with the vehicle's CAN-Bus data network they can also display additional vehicle information like engine performance data, tire pressure monitoring, backup sensor data and other vehicle functions available on the vehicle's CAN-Bus. These additional display capabilities vary depending on the type of vehicle and type of aftermarket head unit.

Wiring Harness Adaptor

Factory installed head unit and aftermarket head unit manufacturers both use proprietary wire connectors that are not compatible with each other. This means it is not possible to plug an aftermarket head unit into a vehicle's OEM wire harness without a wire harness adaptor.

Margin Notes

There are many types of harnesses available. They are each specific to a vehicle manufacturer's platform, for example, a GM (General Motors®) wire harness will work on several models of Chevrolet®, Buick®, GMC® and Cadillac® vehicles, but will not work with other manufacturers like Ford® or Chrysler®. The OEM vehicle manufacturers also change harness configuration every few years as new technology becomes available, so there are several harness types for each vehicle manufacturer depending on the vehicle year, make and model. Using an aftermarket vehicle parts "Fit Guide" is highly recommended to determine the proper part for the vehicle platform in which the head unit is being installed. This information is widely available on the aftermarket parts manufacturer's website.

Wiring harness adaptors come in two types. The first type consists of a female connector or multiple connectors that plug into the OEM wire harness and has unterminated wires coming out that can be connected to the aftermarket head unit's wiring harness with a reliable method. The connections between the two harnesses are made by matching the wire colors/functions of each wire and using wire connectors or soldering the unterminated wires together, the aftermarket harness adaptor and aftermarket radio harness will both use EIA standardized wire colors.

Data Interface (Ignition Signal, Factory Safety Systems Retention, etc.)

The second type is a wiring harness adaptor that plugs into the factory radio and is intended to have the original vehicle wiring grafted on to unterminated wires (also by using wire connectors or soldering the unterminated wires together).

This is generally for vehicles replacing the factory radio from theft where the wiring harness was cut or damaged. It can also be used in conjunction with the first type of harness when retaining the factory radio to create a "T-harness" that allows another device to connect in between the factory radio and the vehicle wiring. A good example is an amplifier that connects its speaker outputs into the vehicle wiring behind the head unit, thereby eliminating the need to run separate wires into each of the vehicle's front and rear speaker locations with all new wire.

The second type of wire harness adaptor may also be used to add an electronic interface between the OEM plug and the unterminated wires. The black-box is required to decode digital/analog signals that are present at the OEM connector and convert them to digital/analog signals that the aftermarket head unit can understand. These signals are part of the vehicle's communication network and provide information like radio on/off, vehicle warning chimes, HVAC control, parking brake status, amplifier turn-on, steering wheel controls and other functions. Some complex vehicle specific mounting kits may include this wiring adaptor and interface device.

Margin Notes

AM/FM Antenna Adaptor

There are several different types of AM/FM antenna connectors used by vehicle manufacturers. All aftermarket head units use a standardized Motorola® connector for their antenna connector, but if the vehicle into which it is being installed does not use the Motorola standard antenna connector, an antenna adaptor will need to be installed.

Antenna adaptors have a female connector on one end that will connect to the vehicle's OEM antenna connector and a male Motorola connector on the other end that plugs into the aftermarket head unit's antenna connector.

Some antenna adaptors will also include interfaces in-line that replace powered antenna amplifier circuits that may be built into the factory head unit.

Steering Wheel Control (SWC) Adaptor

Most aftermarket head units have wired remote inputs designed to integrate with an external controller. This connection is commonly used for OEM head unit controls built into the vehicle's steering wheel. Vehicle manufacturers and aftermarket head unit manufacturers all use different communication protocols to transfer the steering wheel control commands to the head unit, so it is common to need an interface to translate the commands.

When installing an aftermarket head unit, a steering wheel adaptor is required to decode the factory steering wheel control commands and convert them into commands that the aftermarket head unit can understand. The steering wheel control adaptor is connected to the vehicle's steering wheel control wiring and the aftermarket head unit's steering wheel control input. The adaptor also needs to be programmed to know into which type of vehicle it is installed, as well as to what type of head unit it is connected. Some adaptors can learn the vehicle type when powered up, some use dip switch settings and some are connected to a computer and flash programmed. Some vehicles convert messages from analog to data commands before sending them to the radio, some adaptors may be able to use the data command signals at the radio but some require you to retrieve the analog connection closer to the steering wheel.

Some head unit interface harnesses (discussed previously) also have steering wheel adaptor controls built in, eliminating the need for a stand-alone steering wheel adaptor.

Margin Notes

Smartphone Charging/Interface Cable
Aftermarket head units have the ability to integrate with most smartphones and portable media players on the market. This integration can be done through several different methods depending on the level of integration desired.

The most basic connection is the 3.5mm AUX input (sometimes also called a 1/8" input jack). This connection only allows audio to pass from the device to the head unit. Music selection and control all need to be done from the smartphone or MP3's interface and the connection will not charge the external device.

USB connectors are common on aftermarket head units. These connectors can be used to connect USB drives or smartphones to the head unit. USB drives can be plugged directly into this port and the music files on the USB drive can be selected and played from the head unit's control system. Be sure to note the file structure format required by the aftermarket head unit to be sure the USB drive can be read. Most will accept FAT16 or FAT32, but many will not support NTFS or other formats.

Smartphones can also connect to USB inputs. The connection requires the proper phone to USB connector cable. USB-A to Apple Lightning, USB-A to micro-USB, and USB-A to USB-C are the most common types. Older Apple products require a USB to 30-pin cable. Some aftermarket head unit USB ports will only charge the smartphone and not connect to its onboard music library, but many will allow the head unit to control the smartphone from the head unit. The amount of control will vary depending on the type of phone and head unit manufacturer, though. The most basic type of control is allowing the head unit to play and control the music on the smartphone. More advanced models will allow the head unit to control apps on the phone like streaming music services. USB ports on aftermarket head units will typically have minimal current capacity (1 amp or less) and depending on the device may struggle to charge or even maintain the battery in the device.
Apple CarPlay™ and Android™ Auto also use USB connections to communicate with the head unit. Both of these services open up advanced head unit integration to the smartphone. Services like navigation, messaging and music apps can all be controlled by the head unit.

- **HDMI Connections**
  HDMI connections are somewhat common on multimedia units with video screens. These inputs allow viewing of HDMI® devices on the head unit screen. When combined with a smartphone these HDMI inputs can be used to mirror the content that is displayed on the phone. Some phone/head unit combinations also allow the phone to be controlled through the head unit's touch screen. This level of functionality often requires a Bluetooth connection in addition to the wired connection. This type of integration makes it possible to use and control smartphone apps from the head unit. A good example of this is using the smartphone's navigation app through the head unit's screen. This allows the user to take advantage of the larger head unit screen to control the smartphone navigation app. It is important to note

that because video outputs on head units are typically analog, they will not be able to play any video put into the head unit through an HDMI cable.

Margin Notes

FACTORY-INSTALLED AUDIO SYSTEMS

When seeking to upgrade a vehicle's audio system if some of the factory equipment will be retained (more appropriately described as integrating with the vehicle's infotainment system), there are two distinct approaches. It's common that some of the factory infotainment will require remaining in the vehicle and depending on what the customer wishes to achieve, along with availability of solutions for the specific year, make and model of vehicle, the approach should always seek to retain all of the vehicle's original safety and convenience functions.

The two approaches are:

1. Replace the factory head unit. This allows enhancement of in-dash features such as smartphone integration, navigation, multiple music source inputs and other possibilities like touch-screen control. This approach would not necessarily require any other equipment such as speakers, a subwoofer or amplifier(s) to be upgraded.

2. Retain the factory head unit. This is typically an upgrade path that focuses on improving the sound of the system, rather than adding features. It's also a great choice when the factory head unit's physical integration is so much a part of the dashboard that removing it would be challenging to have it appear visually appealing. Instead, adding better sound may involve a vehicle-specific interface or "after the factory amplifier" solutions that involve an OEM audio integration signal processor, one or more amplifiers and (generally) some speaker upgrades – at least front speakers and a subwoofer.

Replacement of Factory Head Units

When replacing the factory head unit in modern vehicles, it is important to take into consideration all the factory features that are built into, or routed through, the factory head unit. Many safety systems and telematics systems will be lost or disabled when the factory head unit is removed. Also, many convenience systems such as steering wheel controls (SWC), Bluetooth hands-free calling, navigation and satellite radio that are built into the factory head unit would be lost when it is removed. Some automobile manufacturers include an audio information screen in the Instrument Panel Cluster (IPC) or other areas of the dashboard where information is displayed and that display will go blank once the factory head unit is removed. Depending on the specific features that the vehicle's head unit came with, the customer will typically wish to retain some (if not all) features, but may be willing to let go of others if the new head unit will serve the same function or improve upon it. While some of these features will be replaced by the aftermarket radio (because it includes them as well), others will require extra, third-party interface devices to retain.

Margin Notes

Some of the features that may lose access or functionality by removing the factory head unit include:

- Steering wheel audio controls
- VR (Voice controls)
- Bluetooth connectivity
- Satellite radio
- Factory amplifier/DSP
- OEM telematics (i.e. OnStar®, Sync, etc.)
- USB media players
- Rear seat entertainment systems
- Safety alerts (reverse/forward sensor chimes, blind spot warning chimes, etc.)
- Reverse camera
- Navigation

Features commonly replaced by aftermarket head unit features:

- Bluetooth connectivity
- VR (Voice controls)
- USB Media Players
- Navigation
- Satellite radio (May require purchase of new satellite tuner)

Features requiring third party adapters to retain:

- Steering Wheel Controls
- OEM telematics (i.e. OnStar, Sync, etc)
- Factory amplifier/DSP
- Rear seat entertainment systems
- Safety alerts (Reverse sensor chimes)
- Reverse camera

There are several aftermarket interface companies that offer solutions to retain these features. It is important to know all the features of the vehicle, how they interact with the factory head unit, and possibly even what databus system the vehicle uses, in order to find out what parts are required to successfully plan a head unit replacement without the loss of any important factory features.

Steering wheel mounted audio controls are probably one of the most common features the customer demands to retain when upgrading the factory head unit. Steering wheel control (SWC) retention is one of the easiest features to integrate with a new head unit as many aftermarket head units include some type of steering wheel control input capability. In order to retain steering wheel control functionality, two things are required:

1. An aftermarket head unit with a steering wheel control input. The head unit part is relatively easy due to the widespread nature of this feature. When showing customers potential new head units, first ensure steering wheel

control input capabilities are available on the head unit if the customer's vehicle has steering wheel audio controls present.

2. A compatible SWC adapter. This can be a bit tricky as every vehicle's steering wheel control architecture is different. Vehicles can be equipped with a multitude of different SWC systems from analog to CAN-Bus. The best way to determine what the correct SWC adapter is for the customer is research on any number of interface manufacturer websites. All of the third-party companies that manufacture these types of interfaces have comprehensive vehicle application guides on their website that can be used to determine what the correct part is for each situation. Remember, every vehicle is different so it is important to know things about the vehicle like make, model, year, trim level, and even small things like whether or not the vehicle is equipped with Bluetooth or a factory amplifier are key to finding the right interface.

Margin Notes

In order to retain access to features like OEM telematics (OnStar, Sync) you need another type of adapter known as a Radio Replacement interface. These adapters are much more complex than steering wheel control adapters, and many of them include the ability to retain SWC functionality along with a multitude of other features. With the correct interface module, it may be possible to retain multiple features at once such as:

- Steering Wheel Controls
- OEM telematics (i.e. OnStar, Sync, etc)
- Factory amplifier/DSP
- Rear seat entertainment systems
- Safety alerts (Reverse sensor chimes)
- Reverse camera

These interface modules are designed to be plugged into the original factory harness and then connected to a compatible aftermarket head unit. The features that you retain access to will depend on a few different factors, including the type of vehicle, vehicle features, its data bus architecture, the available interface modules, and the capabilities of the aftermarket head unit that you choose.

For instance, if the vehicle is a 2012 GMC Yukon with factory navigation, then the OEM head unit included a built-in satellite radio tuner, in which case an interface module won't allow you to retain access to the factory satellite radio functionality as you are removing the satellite tuner when you remove the factory head unit. Now, if the vehicle is a 2008 GMC Yukon, then the OEM head unit was only satellite radio ready and the vehicle has an external satellite radio tuner, then an interface module will probably allow you to integrate it with the new head unit, if you select a compatible aftermarket head unit ***and*** that a compatible interface module exists in the first place.

What if the factory head unit is retained?

Having read the previous section, it's now relevant to consider the other side of the coin; retaining the factory head unit and upgrading to new technologies or

Margin Notes

features in other ways than a new head unit. In many dashboards, it's simply a difficult proposition to consider removing the factory head unit because it's highly integrated, so an upgrade that retains the factory head unit is certainly a viable option. This is most common for upgrades that are focused on improving the sound rather than adding more in-dash features.

- This can be audio-related upgrades with something as simple as adding an amplified subwoofer, or as complex as a DSP-based integration processor becoming the hub that mates the factory audio system with the aftermarket amplifiers and speakers.

- This can be safety-related by adding a backup camera to factory head unit with an existing navigation screen, or adding an interface to allow multiple camera inputs for things like side-view/blind-spot cameras or a front-facing camera with night vision capability. In this case the upgrade is not at all audio-related, but utilizes the in-dash display for view of the safety features the camera(s) provide.

- This can also be feature-related where an aftermarket satellite tuner is added to a factory radio that does not have one, or adding an auxiliary input (such as USB or 3.5mm headphone-style jack) to allow a secondary audio source to connect into the audio system. When vehicles lack factory-installed Bluetooth hands-free calling functionality, this is also a popular feature to add to a factory infotainment system. Increasingly as more and more vehicles have factory-installed features like Bluetooth, smartphone integration, AUX inputs or USB ports, the opportunities for feature-based upgrades is much more vehicle-specific where the Mobile Product Specialist identifies vehicles (even certain trim levels) that lack popular features and target those vehicles with add-on features to compliment what's already in the dash.

The challenge is that today's OEM infotainment systems are so integrated into a vehicle's electronics that it's sometimes a smarter path to upgrade the system to achieve the desired result than to try and replace the factory head unit.

Ppgraded sound (typically meaning amplifier(s) and speakers are upgraded) is one of the most popular requests from customers seeking an improvement from their factory infotainment system. The most important factor to consider when adding aftermarket audio equipment is whether the factory system is equipped with an audio amplifier. The presence of a factory amplifier presents some challenges.

Many modern audio systems with a factory amplifier communicate with the in-dash head unit via some sort of data bus connection, such as CAN-Bus or MOST. There are vehicle-specific solutions to make the retention of a factory head unit a program, plug and play exercise and that saves considerable time, plus addresses the retention of critical factory-installed features.

Vehicle-Specific OEM Audio Interface

For this category of devices, the audio input is taken from the vehicle's infotainment network, typically either CAN-Bus or MOST, using vehicle-specific wiring harnesses that simply plug the interface device into existing wiring. The interface device in this case is specifically engineered to use the vehicle's infotainment network wiring to pull in the audio signal and condition it to be compatible with the downstream devices, such as other signal processors or (most commonly) aftermarket amplifiers.

Margin Notes

In simple terms, here's how the vehicle-specific interface interacts with the factory infotainment system:

- There are two channels of dedicated audio from the factory head unit to the factory amplifier that are at maximum output all the time. When volume is adjusted on the factory head unit, it sends data commands to the factory amplifier telling it to turn up/down the volume.
- There are also usually two or more channels dedicated to warning chimes (such as "key in reminder" and reverse proximity beeps) and Telematics. All this information is sent to the factory amplifier, which is also on the infotainment network, and then redirected to the proper channels and the levels are adjusted by the factory amplifier.
- Many vehicles with factory amplifiers that are networked also get commands from the Bluetooth hands-free calling and spoken navigation system prompts. Essentially these systems allow the audio system to mute at the proper times so a hands-free call or navigation commands are audible to the driver.
- Most factory amplifiers in these highly integrated use-cases have bandwidth-limited frequency response and time-correction on each individual speaker output. The idea is to allow the factory designers to be specific and deliberate with the final tweaking of the amplifier to provide optimized signals to each speaker. This usually means that some sort of OEM integration signal processor or summing device will be required to obtain the proper signal inputs for aftermarket amplifiers if no vehicle-specific interface device is/was available to obtain the clean 2-channel audio signal from the infotainment network. This attribute alone adds significant labor compared to a program, plug and play vehicle-specific interface solution.

Fortunately, the same aftermarket companies that make factory radio replacement interfaces also manufacture factory amplifier integration interfaces to simplify this process. These devices are "flashed" or programmed to tell the interface what vehicle it's in. These interfaces communicate with the vehicle's infotainment network and use a pre-wired harness (known as a "T-harness") that plugs into the vehicle's infotainment system to acquire the audio inputs and control commands necessary to maintain operation of the vehicle's integrated features. One of the major advantages is the ability to retain volume control from the factory head unit for the entire aftermarket system and the preservation of all warning chimes and factory

Margin Notes

telematics (as well as Bluetooth hands-free and spoken navigation commands, if the vehicle is factory-equipped).

The pre-wired T-harness assembly is tapping into the factory amplified system ***before*** the factory amplifier, unlike many of the other DSP integration processor solutions which occur ***after*** the factory amplifier. This makes integration of aftermarket audio equipment easier as other factory features such as warning chimes, telematics systems and other vehicle integrated functions of the factory audio system are handled by the interface.

Vehicle-specific OEM audio interface devices often come with built-in signal processing. The device is technically an interface product but often has signal processing features such as EQ, bass restoration and correction of factory-conditioned signals so the aftermarket products are provided a "clean" audio signal free of the factory-applied signal processing.

Using a vehicle-specific interface solution is an excellent way to ensure a predictable outcome because the engineering of how to interface into the vehicle's infotainment system is pre-configured, so there's no guesswork on the part of the Mobile Product Specialist as to whether or not a mix of other "after the factory amplifier" products will work.

Other approaches to retaining the factory head unit

When a vehicle-specific interface solution is not available, there are other methods for retaining the factory head unit. The most common is the "after the factory amplifier" approach because most modern vehicles have some kind of factory amplifier. The link between the factory amplifier and the aftermarket upgrades used to be a simple **line output converter (LOC)**. This is essentially a small box with some passive electronic components that allow relatively low-power speaker-level signals to be reduced in signal voltage level for compatibility with an amplifier's preamp level inputs. Passive means the LOC is not powered with +12 volts. Rather the speaker-level audio signals run through the electronic components within a **passive LOC** (mainly **resistors and small transformers**) and the result is the reduction of signal level. LOCs are still an option for basic integration, such as when there is no factory amplifier present, although they should not be considered the "go to" item when retaining a factory head unit because there are more variables to consider.

As speaker outputs have moved from relatively low power "built in" to a head unit and are now more commonly found at the output of a factory amplifier, most LOCs are not designed for the internal resistors to accommodate the increased output power found at the factory amplifier's outputs (sometimes in excess of 20 volts AC). In many LOCs, this presents a significant problem of heat and **the higher the factory amplifier's signal voltage, the greater concern for overheating the resistors inside the LOC**.

Margin Notes

Another challenge with using LOCs is that they do not individually address each of the actively crossed over output channels that connect the factory amplifier to specific speakers. These are called bandwidth-limited channels. If there are many speakers in the car, a factory amplifier in a premium system may have 8, 10, 12 or more channels, and there's a high probability that many (if not all) of those channels are bandwidth-limited. This would require multiple LOCs for each channel and that still would possibly only address the signal voltage level. It would not address any other factory-applied audio signal effects like equalization, time-correction, bandwidth-limitations, etc.

One final concern about using only LOCs on modern factory-amplified audio systems is that the cheaper the LOC, the more likely it is to have its own frequency response limitations. Even connected to a flat 20Hz-20kHz signal, many of the low-priced LOCs will roll off the high and low frequencies so that whatever audio signal the next component is fed, it can only work with that limited frequency response. This is especially troublesome when trying to use an LOC in a simple subwoofer upgrade or addition. If the low frequency response is already diminished through the LOC, it reduces the probability of the amplifier/subwoofer combination being as effective as it could be.

All of these considerations for factory amplified systems are where the need for an OEM audio integration processor comes in. These may have narrow to broad-ranging functionality, depending on what it's designed to accommodate integration-wise. There are also cases where there is no factory amplifier, in which case the audio interface point becomes the speaker outputs of the factory head unit, although that is more the exception than the rule.

OEM audio integration processors feature **speaker-level inputs intended to get the analog audio signal input from the OEM head unit or factory audio amplifier as the source**. These integration processors are popular because they are not vehicle specific and sometimes feature preamp level inputs as well, so they can be used in just about any car audio system design plan. The most robust OEM audio integration processors provide a variety of internal signal processing features which make the interface into the vehicle's existing audio system pair well with aftermarket amplification on the output side of the integration processor. Some of those signal processing features include:

On the input side:

- Level matching of multiple input channels (essentially what multiple LOCs might accomplish but with a much wider range of input voltage capability and relatively no heat).
- Signal summing of bandwidth-limited channels.
- Un-EQ of factory-applied equalization curves.
- Volume-dependent bass restoration to compensate for the factory signal's low frequency roll off at high volumes.
- Removal of factory-applied time correction.

Margin Notes

On the output side:

- Auto-EQ or "target curve" of an output equalizer.
- Graphic and/or parametric equalization (user adjustable).
- Variable crossover filters (high-pass, low-pass and/or bandpass).
- Time correction of independent output channels.
- Phase control of independent output channels.
- Invert polarity (0 or 180 degrees) on independent output channels.
- Upmixer functionality (two stereo channels become 5.1 or 7.1 independent output channels).
- Preamp level line driver (increases preamp level signal voltage to reduce floor noise and increase dynamic range).
- Remote control of system volume, sub bass and memory presets.

These OEM audio integration processors also have **a broader input signal voltage range that** allows them to accept the speaker-level inputs that would otherwise overdrive the input of a device intended to accept only preamp level signals. Read more about the specific functionalities of these devices in the Signal Processors section of this chapter.

There are numerous methods to integrate with a vehicle's factory infotainment system and retain the in-dash head unit. The approaches discussed in this section are the most widely accepted methods to achieve a predictable outcome. Always consult with an experienced installation technician so that what is promised to the customer is be delivered.

SIGNAL PROCESSORS – AN OVERVIEW

Earlier in this chapter in the "Basics of Sound" section, certain elements of sound and, in particular, the limitations of speakers, listening spaces (like a vehicle interior) and human ears were presented. Selecting an appropriate **preamp level signal processor (after the head unit but before the amplifier)** with the functionality and features that address those limitations is a common approach for fine tuning an audio system's performance. There are high-fidelity, full digital choices that allow **a source unit with a digital output to directly connect to a DSP-based processor with a digital input**, thereby eliminating the probability for noise and other common interference related to the preamp level analog audio signal path.

What is a "Signal Processor?"

A signal processor is a device that "does something" to the audio signal. Exactly what's done to the audio signal depends on the type of signal processing. Signal processors are found in a number of forms:

- Equalizers (also called EQ) tailor the character of the sound by adjusting specific frequencies.
- Active crossovers (also called filters) limit the frequency range of the audio signal for a specific purpose, such as subwoofer, midrange or high frequency.
- Subsonic filters (also called Infrasonic filters) protects the subwoofer from damaging low frequency content that would otherwise create excessive excursion.

Margin Notes

- Bass enhancement devices (not just bass boost) enhance bass and compensates for the natural volume-based roll off in many factory audio systems.
- Noise gates mute the hiss when no music is playing between songs.
- Preamps provide level matching or a single volume control of multiple sources.
- Preamp level line driver increases preamp level signal voltage output to reduce floor noise and increase dynamic range.
- Summing devices are used specifically for OEM audio integration functions to address reassembly of multiple bandwidth-limited channels into a full-range audio signal. Summing capabilities are often built in to a more full-featured OEM audio integration processor.
- Upmixers take a two-channel stereo signal and create a surround sound-like effect with dedicated outputs to front left/center/right, rear left/right and subwoofer channels. Some might say it's like a 5.1 sound effect for regular stereo recordings and the purpose is to allow the relatively small space of a vehicle cabin to seem as if the listener is in a larger space.
- Digital signal processors (DSPs) often have many of the above features and may also add time/phase and significantly more EQ adjustments, among other adjustable features.
- Factory audio interface DSPs "un-EQ" a factory audio signal so the result is a flat 20Hz-20kHz audio output. Taking that factory interface capability further, there are also some DSPs that remove any factory-applied time correction so that any specific settings can be chosen by the technician using the built in tuning tools of the processor. Of course the ability to sum the input signals (if necessary) is also typically a feature of a factory audio interface DSP. To use a simple description, the factory audio interface DSP device allows the factory audio signal to get back to "square one" and the aftermarket audio system upgrade can be built out from there.
- Vehicle-specific OEM audio interface with signal built-in processing use a pre-wired harness (known as a "T-harness") that plugs into the vehicle's infotainment system to acquire the audio inputs and control commands necessary to maintain operation of the vehicle's integrated features like muting the audio to allow spoken navigation commands, maintaining Bluetooth hands-free calling, as well as preserving chimes and warning beeps. These devices are "flashed" or somehow programmed to tell the interface what vehicle it's in. The device is technically an interface product, but often has signal processing features such as EQ, bass restoration and correction of factory-conditioned signals so the aftermarket products are provided a "clean" audio signal free of the factory-applied signal processing.

The most common signal processors used in mobile audio applications are crossovers and equalizers and this section focuses on signal processing done at the preamp (before the amplifier) stage.

Preamp level signal processors used in the mobile audio environment have three primary objectives:

Margin Notes

1. To optimize the performance of, and to protect, the speakers in the system by allowing them to work within their specified frequency ranges.

2. To correct (or at least minimize the negative impacts) for frequency response and interior resonance/reflection issues that can alter the acoustic output result when compared to the original studio recording.

3. To tailor the final sound characteristics of a well-designed audio system the personal tastes of the listener.

The Signal Path

In the most basic sense of signal path, it is accepted practice to begin with the in-dash source unit, then move on to an equalizer, then to an active (electronic) crossover, and finally the amplifier. Some signal processors with multiple functions would handle the entirety of all signal processing functions within one single device so that order of operations is somewhat invisible, but still must occur in the correct order. All of the components that come before the amplifier, by definition, are known as "preamp level" signal processors because it's **before the amplifier** (pre-amplification).

- Any passive (unpowered) crossovers will be located after the amplifier output terminals of the amp, but before the appropriate speakers themselves. Passive filters are the only filters that provide a signal processing functions post-amplification. Passive crossovers are the most common example of a passive filter.

While it's not always necessary to have each one of the components mentioned in the preamp level signal chain (except for a source unit of some kind), these paragraphs illustrate how they would be placed to correctly function if each were a separate component. Placing an active crossover before an equalizer, for example, would limit the equalizer to only being effective at adjustments in the range of the crossover output.

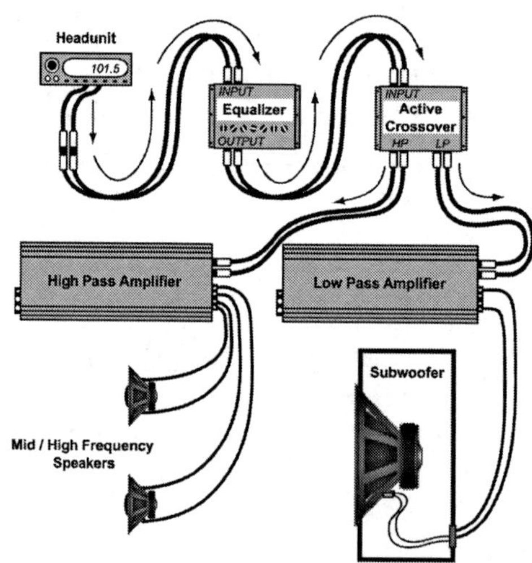

Margin Notes

Analog Audio Inputs

The audio inputs are how the electrical audio signal gets into the signal processor. The most common methods to send an audio signal into a signal processor is via **Preamp Level** analog audio inputs.

- Preamp Level (also called "low level" or "single-ended") is a standard RCA audio connection on the majority of aftermarket head units and other audio products; typically coded **red for right channel** and **white for left channel**. Using a pair of RCA audio cables allows the audio signal to transfer from the source unit to the amplifier. Preamp level is often a single-ended design, meaning a separate left and right positive (+) input. The positive signal is the center conductor of the RCA connector. At the source end, the outer shield functions as the negative (-) input (also called the audio signal ground). This negative (-) signal is shared between left and right in a single-ended design. Depending on the other preamp equipment in the system and how inputs are configured with single-ended audio signal ground reference, using these inputs can be a potential source of audio system noise commonly known as a ground loop.

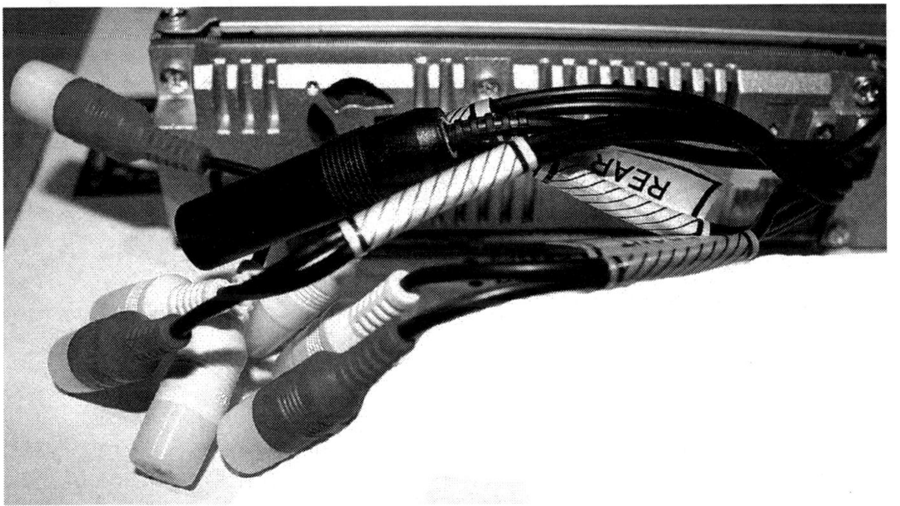

As mentioned, with signal processors that are intended to aid in an OEM audio system integration function, there are other analog audio inputs present called Speaker-Level inputs.

- Speaker-Level (also called "high-level" or "differential") is any audio signal that can directly drive a speaker. For an integration processor that utilizes speaker-level connections, the audio signal input is achieved by connecting into the speaker wires that carry the signal from the OEM source unit, or if a factory audio amplifier is present, the signals from the factory amplifier that connect directly to the speakers. The choice of whether or not to connect at the OEM head unit outputs or (if present) the factory amplifier depends on whether the outputs of the head unit are controlled by the volume knob or whether that functionality occurs in the factory audio amplifier. When the volume and other

Margin Notes

functions like Bluetooth hands free, spoken navigation commands, reverse beeps and door chimes originate in a factory amplifier, the connection for the integration processor should be done at the factory audio amplifier outputs. A Mobile Product Specialist should work together with an experienced technician to determine the best approach.

- Speaker-level inputs often yield noise-free results because each channel input has a separate positive (+) and negative (-) signal input. The audio signal grounds are not shared as in many single-ended, preamp level (RCA) audio signals. It's important that the input voltage range of the speaker-level inputs at the integration processor can accept the signal voltage level present on the OEM speaker wires. Factory audio amplifiers in some vehicles may have a signal voltage that exceeds 20 volts AC, so it's important to know that a given integration processor will accept the vehicle's speaker-level signal without overdriving the processor input.

Combo Analog Audio Input – Only RCA Jacks Present

Depending on the processor's design and features, it may only accept preamp level inputs. Signal processors that accept both preamp and speaker-level input offer greater flexibility with the installation (i.e., OEM audio integration), yet may still only exhibit RCA jacks as an audio input. The connection type on the processor does not necessarily dictate what type of audio inputs it will accept, though.

Some signal may have only RCA input connections but will have the extra installation hardware/adaptor (or capability) to accept speaker-level inputs in those RCA input jacks. For this dual-purpose audio input scheme to be possible, the RCA jacks must not be electrically common as if to be configured only for single-ended audio input. If the RCA jacks are to accept speaker level inputs, there must be two factors present for that approach to work:

1. **The RCA shields of the left and right channel inputs must not be common** (electrically connected). This typically means a high resistance between left and right channel RCA shields (the outer conductor, not the center pin) when measured with a Digital Multimeter (DMM). If these are isolated, meaning not electrically connected, the measurement should be in the range of 10k ohms or greater. This ensures there is no chance of electrical connectivity between the left and right negative signal leads in the internal signal processor circuitry. This also reduces the chance for engine noise problems.

2. **The RCA input signal voltage range must be able to accept speaker level voltages**, which may be 20 volts AC or more. This would certainly be indicated in the signal processor's technical specifications, particularly if it's suggested to be an OEM audio integration processor.

Accepting both preamp and speaker level inputs on the same input connector simplifies the construction of the amplifier due to fewer parts on the connection panel while also maintaining that installation flexibility.

Margin Notes

Digital Audio Input (S/PDIF)

Some high-fidelity signal processors feature digital audio input. This is typically part of an "all-digital" signal path in which a digital source unit features a digital audio output that can connect directly to a processor's digital input.

The digital signal itself is a series of "1s" and "0s" (or high and low voltages) packaged with the defined channel encoding called S/PDIF, which stands for Sony/Philips Digital Interface Format. In the S/PDIF format, both stereo channels are encoded in this digital bit stream along with sync bits that allow the receiving device (in this case, the amplifier) to synchronize with the signal. S/PDIF is more or less the standard digital audio format used in most digital audio products.

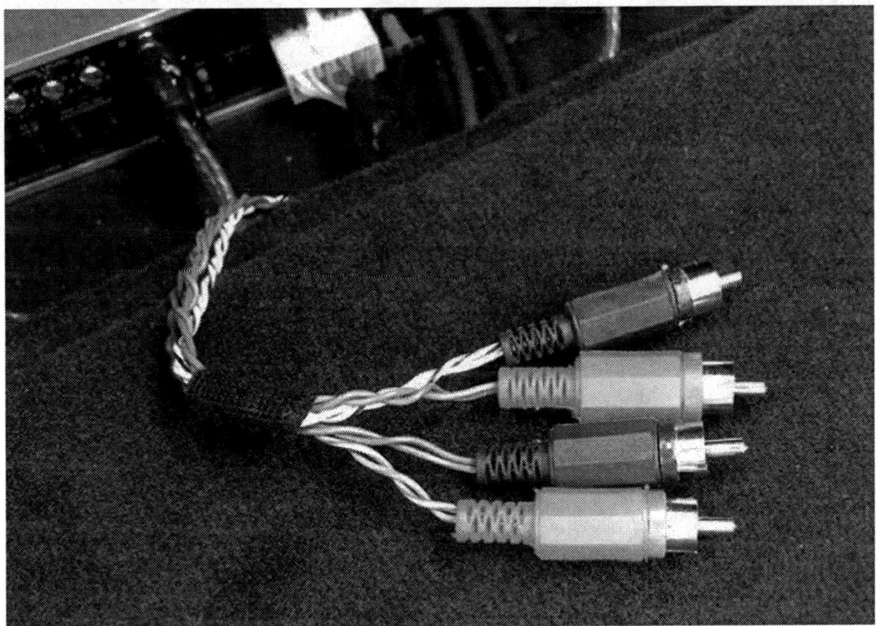

A signal processor with a digital input may also have a digital output to further the "fully digital" signal path concept all the way to the final stage of conversion from a digital signal into analog which occurs in the amplifier(s). That approach is said to preserve the highest resolution of signal quality and provide the best noise immunity for any chance of unwanted induced/radiated noises. This depends on the brand and features of the signal processor and amplifier(s).

Similar to other mobile audio products with digital inputs or outputs, there are two possible types of connections that can be present on a digital amplifier input: coaxial (copper wiring) or TosLink (optical). Either connection type still receives the S/PDIF digital bit stream format; it's simply the manufacturers' preferences for the connection type. Both have excellent noise immunity. Optical cables for a TosLink input need to ensure they are not pinched or bent to affect the transmission of light pulses between the connected devices.

Margin Notes

If a coaxial or TosLink digital input is present on a signal processor, chances are there are also analog preamp (RCA) or speaker-level inputs that allow flexibility of however the system configuration offers signal transfer from the source unit (OEM or aftermarket) or factory audio amplifier. This is because not all systems have a digital output available for use with a signal processor's digital input.

Wireless Input

While not a frequently used method for audio input into signal processors, if a processor supports wireless input capability such as Bluetooth audio streaming, this feature provides an option to use a source other than a wired head unit. A smartphone or tablet could wirelessly stream audio to a signal processor's wireless input and then the signal processor makes sound adjustments and connects to the amplifier(s) which then connect to speakers.

This input method would generally be an add-on option so that the added cost of the wireless receiver is not built into the cost of every signal processor. Rather, if supported, it could be added to the processor for system designs that utilize that functionality. Those use-cases could include powersports vehicles (SSVs, UTVs), recreational marine or VIP transportation vehicles where a passenger's carry-in source device (such as smartphone) can be easily connected. If a wireless input is not offered in a signal processor, a separate wireless receiver could be used to accept the streaming audio signal, then connect with wires (such as RCA audio cables) into the processor's wired audio inputs.

Vehicle-Specific OEM Audio Interface

For this category of devices, the audio input is taken from the vehicle's infotainment network, typically either CAN-Bus or MOST, using vehicle-specific wiring harnesses that simply plug the interface device into existing wiring. The interface device is specifically engineered to use the vehicle's infotainment network wiring to pull in the audio signal and condition it to be compatible with the downstream devices, such as other signal processors or (more commonly) aftermarket amplifiers.

TYPES OF SIGNAL PROCESSING FUNCTIONS

Preamp Equalizer

An equalizer (EQ) is essentially a tone control with other features. Equalizers accentuate (boost) or attenuate (cut) the signal at a given frequency (adjacent frequencies are also affected to some degree). In equalization, the effect to neighboring frequencies is referred to as the "Q" (quality factor).

- A stereo with simple "bass and treble" tone controls can have a two-band equalizer with fixed frequency and Q. Bass and treble are typically set at 100Hz and 10,000Hz for the fixed frequencies that allow adjustment.
- A bass, mid and treble control might be considered a three-band equalizer.

Margin Notes

The more "bands" on the equalizer, the less band width (coverage in between bands) there is on each band. By limiting bandwidth, it is easier to fine tune a system to minimize uneven frequency response at certain frequency points.

A Real Time Analyzer (RTA) with a microphone "listening" in the space where the music plays is the only way to accurately see those types of issues and to correct for them. The RTA helps visually understand where frequencies are abundant or absent so the technician can make adjustments accordingly. In most cases, if the response is ruler flat from 20Hz-20kHz, the audio system is capable of reproducing good sound.

How the overall frequency response is adjusted with an EQ is up to individual taste, but a totally flat response won't sound good in an automobile. Some additional bass output and attenuation at high frequencies are usually required for the sound to be perceived as accurate, but further adjustments may be made to accommodate listener preference. It's important to remember that proven methods and listener preference to established frequency response curves are well documented, but the customer's preference should always be considered.

The goal of system tuning with an equalizer is to eliminate the major peaks and dips in the response and to achieve good baseline performance before any fine-tuning to a listener's tastes. Equalizers can range from as few as two bands to 31 bands and more. The more bands and the more adjustment available in the equalizer, the more necessary it is to use an RTA to see what effect tuning or adjustment has on the overall frequency response of the system. It takes lots of practice to learn to tune vehicles quickly and effectively, and simply installing an EQ won't improve the sound of the system. Tuning vehicles is often the responsibility of a technician, but a good Mobile Product Specialist should have a solid understanding of audio system design and acoustics.

A tuner's ability to make the best use of the adjustment capabilities of the EQ determines the overall system performance. This is a more advanced topic that experienced technicians typically tackle as the end-of-installation process before delivering the vehicle to the customer. Most RTAs used for mobile audio tuning and adjustments are 1/3 octave, which means three measurements per octave. Since there are typically 10 octaves in the 20Hz-20kHz spectrum, a 1/3 octave works out to 31 data points. This format works out well with 1/3 octave equalizers as there's an adjustment where there's a measurement on the RTA to display registers near the frequency captured by the microphone. If the equalizer has more adjustments, the RTA should have higher resolution to display those data points (such as 1/6 octave, 1/12 octave, etc.).

There are graphic equalizers or parametric equalizers, and both can be excellent additions to an audio system. Both types of equalization offer cut or boost at the desired frequency, although a lot of boosting may indicate acoustic problems in the sound system that are better served by fixing phase differences, reflections and speaker placement issues. Remember that an equalizer is designed to enhance the sound and will not fix a poorly designed audio system.

Margin Notes

- **Graphic EQ** - Graphic equalization utilizes fixed band centers at evenly spaced frequency intervals. It's common to have octave equalizers with one adjustment per octave in the audible range of 20Hz-20kHz. Often there will be half-octave (twice as many) or third-octave (three times as many) adjustments on more serious equipment. Regardless of how many bands, what makes it a graphic EQ is that the **frequency and "Q" are fixed** and only the cut or boost in that frequency band is adjustable. Remember the Q is how much an adjustment affects the neighboring frequencies. That part is fixed in the graphic EQ.

- **Parametric EQ** - Parametric equalization typically offers an **adjustment for the frequency and "Q,"** which is why the parametric equalizer is an excellent tool for mobile audio systems that simply need a few targeted equalization points not served with a fixed band graphic style equalizer. In fact, without an RTA to look at where the adjustments are centered versus the car's frequency response, adjusting a parametric equalizer can be nothing more than a guessing game with the tuner's ears. The flexibility of the adjustment of frequency and Q allows fewer bands in a parametric EQ to be more effective if the vehicle only has a few areas that need equalization.

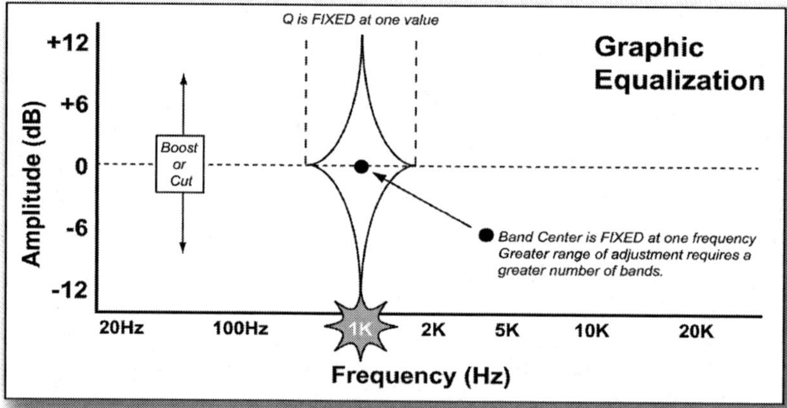

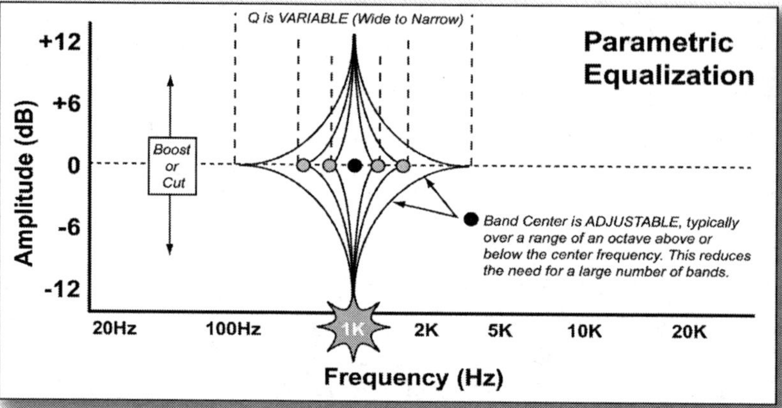

Adjusting a parametric EQ requires a well-developed understanding of acoustic

Margin Notes

principles and a lot of practice. Although parametric equalizers often include fewer bands than a 31-band graphic, they can be far more powerful because a single, well-adjusted band can do the work of several bands on a graphic EQ and can more precisely address the problem areas.

Crossovers

The purpose of a crossover is to connect each driver to a specific range of frequencies, and there are two types: passive and active. A passive crossover is basically a capacitor or coil installed on the speaker leads between an amplifier and a speaker that stops certain frequencies from reaching the speakers. An active crossover is installed between the receiver or equalizer and the amplifiers and filters and directs the frequency bands in the preamp-level signal before they reach the amplifiers.

The goal with crossovers in an audio system is to help reproduce the entire recorded frequency range as accurately as possible and limits the frequency range a given channel (ultimately connected to a speaker) will be provided. Crossovers allow a system to have an even frequency response with linear (overall equal) response across the 20Hz-20kHz range.

Most active crossovers include adjustable slopes. The **slope of a crossover is the rate of attenuation** beyond the filter's frequency. These can range anywhere from 6dB/octave to 24dB/octave and higher. A few offer as steep as 36 or 48dB/octave slopes, but between 12-24dB/octave slopes are most common. Other features in an active crossover may include bass equalization and subsonic filters (also called infrasonic filters) to further refine system performance. The most significant difference between active and passive crossovers is that the **active crossover is before the amplifier in the preamp-level signal path**.

Active crossovers are also called:

- Electronic crossovers
- Active filters

Active crossovers offer three major advantages over passive crossovers:

1. In many cases, active crossovers offer adjustable frequencies to suit the needs of a given system. Most offer adjustable frequency slopes, and other allow for customizing the system performance.

2. Since the active crossover is in the signal chain before the amplifier, it does not take any output power away from the speaker. Passive crossovers are post-amplifier and will consume some of the power coming from the amplifier in the process of filtering through various inductors, capacitors and resistors. While some passive crossovers offer limited adjustability (usually only the level of output), they have nowhere near the adjustment capabilities of an active crossover.

3. An active crossover limits the range of frequencies that the amplifier must produce. For example, an amplifier driving a pair of component speakers filtered actively at 100

Margin Notes

Hz doesn't have to produce any power at the lowest frequencies. That minimizes the potential for distortion in the amplifier's output when a big bass note occurs.

Many of today's in-dash source units include crossovers, equalizers and varying forms of digital sound processing. The same may be said of many of today's amplifiers, particularly multi-channel amplifiers intended to run an entire audio system from a single chassis amplifier. It is possible to use combinations of these signal processing features to refine system performance. For example, a low-pass crossover on an in-dash source unit can be used in combination with a high-pass crossover on an amplifier to form a bandpass crossover that is ideal for a midrange/midbass situation. The danger is using multiple signal processors in the signal chain to perform the same function (known as cascading). It's a good idea to decide which piece of equipment to use for a given signal processing task and avoid any duplications or possible conflicts between multiple signal processors doing the same job.

- Example: In a system design approach, do not plan to use the low-pass crossover in a subwoofer amplifier if the head unit's SUB OUT already utilizes its own low-pass crossover and that will be used as the sub amplifier's input source. If both are used, that would be cascading crossovers and the chances (without an RTA) of aligning both crossovers to the exact same frequency is unlikely.

Another consideration is using speakers on an active channel that has no passive crossover. When a tweeter is actively filtered, a non-polar capacitor must be used just as a measure of protection, not as a crossover. If something were to go wrong with the signal or the amplifier itself, the relatively small voice coil and diaphragm of the tweeter is easily damaged. In this instance, the capacitor would simply serve as a passive protection device adding an additional 6dB of filtering atop what the active filters are doing. The actual value of the capacitor should be determined by the nominal impedance of the tweeter and have a value that is at least one octave the active crossover point so that cascading effects are not a concern. This would typically be done at the time of installation by the technician installing the tweeter(s).

Summing Devices

Many factory amplifiers have actively crossed-over output channels that connect to specific speakers. These are called bandwidth-limited channels. It's not uncommon for a factory amplifier in a premium system to have 8, 10, 12 or more channels if there are that many speakers in the car and there's a high probability many (if not all) of those channels are bandwidth-limited. By using active filtering and even some equalization, the manufacturer can use speakers for that application, which is also an overall cost saving.

Aftermarket additions to these kinds of systems are more difficult because there's no simple place to connect the aftermarket system. A full-range (20Hz-20kHz) isn't available on any of the factory amplifier's output connectors.

When bandwidth-limited audio signals are summed, it is effectively performing the exact opposite function of a crossover. In a crossover where audio signals go to specific speakers in specific frequency ranges are split up into those bandwidth-limited ranges, summing signals means bringing those crossed over signals together to recombine into something full range.

Margin Notes

Signal Summing - Creating a Full Range Audio Signal

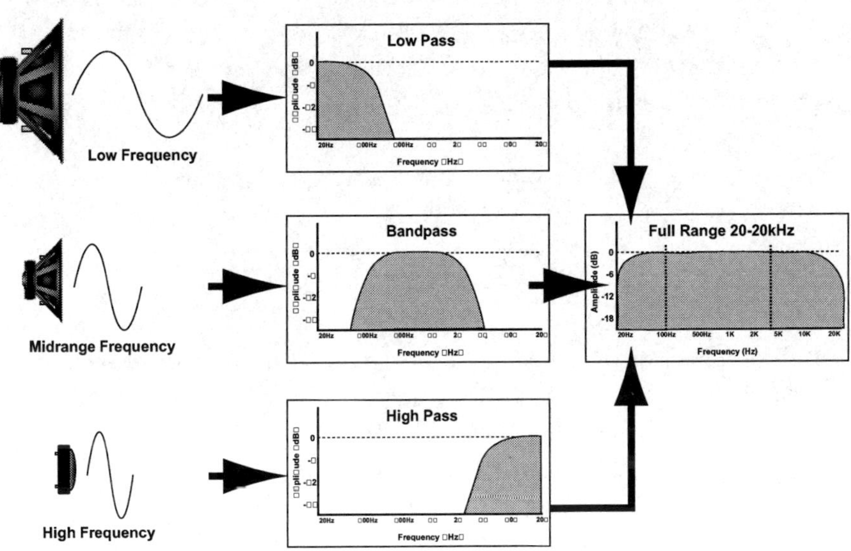

Doing this used to require multiple LOCs and Y-adaptors but is now easily done with a multi-channel summing device for that specific purpose. A summing device simply takes several signals over several different bands and combines their signals together to provide a wider bandwidth (usually full range) onto which other aftermarket components can be added. Often you can configure them to route various signals to one single output or to multiple outputs separately, so it can accommodate fader functionality or level control. A summing device may have an auxiliary input as well, making it another easy place to plug in a second source like a portable media player with simple RCA inputs.

Depending on the device, it can be a stand-alone summing device or it can be a more feature-rich processor with other functionality (such as EQ and active crossovers). The device chosen should reflect the needs of the vehicle and audio system, as well as what the customer wants.

- If only adding a subwoofer for example, the need to sum multiple channels to get a full range signal may not be necessary. Rather, the signal may only need be enough to satisfy the bandwidth that the subwoofer needs to play.

- On the other hand, if doing a big system upgrade and the factory amplifier has many channels that are all actively crossed over (i.e. bandwidth-limited channels), several channels may require summing to get a front full range output and separate rear full range output to maintain the factory fader operation.

Margin Notes

Every OEM audio integration need and system upgrade will be different. Luckily there are many choices for summing devices to accomplish those tasks.

Summing signals is not necessarily the end of the road to get an amplifier signal input. In some cases, there are channel-specific equalization curves, signal delays or phase shifts built into the factory amplifier that require more than just simple summing to get a good signal from which to build an aftermarket system. There are other devices that have those interface capabilities in which summing channels is just one of the things the device can do.

Built-in Signal Processing Considerations
Some things to consider about "built-in" signal processing features of other devices:

- Just because a device has a built-in signal processing features does not mean one of them needs to be used, or any of them for that matter. Don't make the mistake of thinking that single signal processing feature must be maxed out or tweaked to get the best sound. Understand what each built-in feature does and whether or not it has a value in your overall goals with the audio system.

- Use only one device for a particular job of signal processing (for example, do not use the low pass crossover in an in-dash source unit AND in the amplifier). Choose one component or the other to do the work. Choosing two or more things to do the same job adds complications and too many variables to set adjustments, controls, etc.

- Even though many in-dash source units have signal processing functionality, be aware of giving the customer too much access to adjustments, which can result in a poor performing audio system.

  Amplifiers that have built-in signal processing features with selectable features like crossover slope or variable frequency on which a bass boost is activated can be an excellent choice.

MOBILE AUDIO AMPLIFIERS

Amplifier Fundamentals

An amplifier's primary task is to increase the overall volume level of sound. It does this by increasing the amount of power in the audio signal connected to the speakers.

While some factory-installed mobile audio systems contain an amplifier, this section is addresses only the aftermarket mobile audio amplifier category where it would be considered upgrading (supplementing or bypassing) a factory amplifier.

Amplifiers can be broken down into fundamental sections:

- Audio Input section – how audio signal gets into the amplifier.
- Power Supply section – the engine of the amplifier.
- Audio Output section – drives the speakers' movements.

- Integrated Signal Processing – what happens to the signal after the audio input section and before the audio output section that is specific to suit the speakers connected to the specific amplifier channel(s).

Margin Notes

Analog Audio Inputs

The audio inputs are how the electrical audio signal is sent to the amplifier. The two most common are Preamp-Level and Speaker-Level.

- Preamp-level (also called low-level or single-ended) is a standard RCA audio connection on the majority of aftermarket head units and other audio products, typically coded red for right channel and white for left channel. Using a pair of RCA audio cables allows the audio signal to transfer from the source unit to the amplifier. Preamp-level is often a single-ended design. Single-ended means a separate left and right positive (+) input. The positive signal is the center conductor of the RCA connector. At the source end, amplifier end or both, the outer shield functions as the negative (-) input, also called the audio signal ground. This negative (-) signal is shared between left and right in a single-ended design. Depending on the other preamp equipment in the system and how inputs are configured with single-ended audio signal ground reference, using these inputs can be a potential source of audio system noise commonly known as a ground loop.

- Speaker-level (also called high-level or differential) is any audio signal that can directly drive a speaker. For an amplifier input using the most basic form of speaker-level connections, the audio signal input is achieved by connecting into the speaker wires that carry the signal from the source unit directly to the speakers. This is a simple input signal method when the amplifier is constructed with this option. Speaker-level inputs often yield noise-free results because each channel input has a separate positive (+) and negative (-) signal input. The audio signal grounds are not shared as in single-ended designs.Some factory audio systems often feature a separate amplifier and/or digital signal processor between the source unit and speakers, where in those cases it's the factory amplifier that powers the speakers (not the source unit). Either case is still considered a speaker-level signal. It's only important that the input voltage range of the speaker-level inputs at the amplifier can accept the signal level present on the speaker wires. Factory amplifiers in some vehicles may have a signal voltage that exceeds the speaker-level input capacity of some aftermarket amplifiers.

Combo Analog Audio Input – Only RCA Jacks Present

Depending on the amplifier's design and features, it may only accept preamp level inputs. Amplifiers that accept both preamp and speaker-level input offer greater flexibility with the installation, yet may still only exhibit RCA jacks as an audio input. The connection type on the amplifier does not necessarily dictate what type of audio inputs it will accept, though. Some amplifiers may have only RCA input connections but will have the extra installation hardware/adaptor (or capability) to

Margin Notes

accept speaker-level inputs in those RCA input jacks. For this dual-purpose audio input scheme to be possible, the RCA jacks internally must not be electrically common as if to be configured only for single-ended audio input. If the RCA jacks are to accept speaker-level inputs, there must be two factors present:

1. **The RCA shields of the left and right channel inputs must not be common** (electrically connected). This typically means a high resistance between left and right channel RCA shields (the outer conductor, not the center pin) when measured with a Digital Multimeter (DMM). If these are isolated, meaning not electrically connected, the measurement should be in the range of 10k ohms or greater. This ensures there is no chance of electrical connectivity between the left and right negative signal leads in the internal amplifier circuitry. This also reduces the chance for engine noise problems.

2. **The RCA input signal voltage range must be able to accept speaker-level voltages**, which may be 20 volts AC or more. Often there will be a switch on these amplifiers that sets the presumed signal range by designation on the switch. This could be as simple as "HI/LOW" or identify a numeric range for the acceptable signal voltage.

Accepting both preamp and speaker-level inputs on the same input connector simplifies the construction of the amplifier due to fewer parts on the connection panel while also maintaining that installation flexibility.

Digital Audio Input (S/PDIF)

While rare, select high-end mobile audio amplifiers may contain a digital audio input. This is typically part of an "all-digital" signal path in which the final stage of conversion from a digital signal into analog occurs in the amplifier. That approach is said to preserve the highest resolution of signal quality and provide the best noise immunity for any chance of unwanted induced/radiated noises.

Like other mobile audio products with digital inputs or outputs, there are two types of connections that can be present on a digital amplifier input: coaxial (copper wiring) or TosLink (optical). Both have excellent noise immunity. Optical cables for a TosLink input cannot be pinched or bent as it will affect the transmission of light pulses between the connected devices.

If a coaxial or TosLink digital input is present on an amplifier, chances are there are analog preamp (RCA) or speaker-level inputs that allow flexibility of how the system configuration offers signal transfer from the source unit or signal processor. This is simply because not all systems have a digital output available for use with an amplifier's digital input. The majority of signal connections into aftermarket mobile audio amplifiers are analog.

One additional type of digital amplifier input connection may be a proprietary connection that a manufacturer uses to specifically connect their brand of source

Margin Notes

unit and/or signal processor or OEM audio interface device to their branded amplifier as a complete system solution. In those cases, the actual connector type can be anything that supports transmission of the proprietary digital signal between that specific manufacturer's devices.

Pass-Through Outputs

Some mobile audio amplifiers provide RCA preamp level outputs called pass-through outputs. These allow additional amplifiers to be added without running multiple preamp level RCA signal cables to the front of the vehicle at the head unit. Utilizing pass-through RCA outputs makes it easy to have an additional amplifier added later without having to completely disassemble the vehicle, depending on the way that additional amplifier is utilized and if the existing amplifier is repurposed to a different use within the system.

Pass-through RCA outputs can be unaffected by the amplifier's settings (meaning pass the signal through without *any* changes or effects), or the pass-through RCA outputs may use the amplifier's onboard signal processing to apply effect for the next amplifier. An example might be an onboard crossover that has a low-pass signal for the amplifier itself, then the pass-through RCA output is high passed at that same frequency for the next amplifier which would connect to midrange/high frequency speakers.
When using pass-through RCA outputs, keep in mind that all amplifiers that use that signal path will be on the same head unit section. This means if it's run off of the front output of the head unit, the amplifiers that utilize the pass-through signal path are all affected whenever the fader is moved off of the front to the rear. This may not be a concern depending on the way the pass-through RCA output is used (if at all), but something to note in the system design process if a customer wishes to have an operational front/rear fader.

Summing Bandwidth-Limited Signals

Where factory amplifiers in multi-speaker OEM audio systems are found, the speaker-level signal to a given speaker may not be full range. Instead, the audio signal is likely bandwidth-limited to focus its range only in the frequency bands best reproduced by that specific speaker to which it connects (such as a signal only intended to drive a subwoofer, midrange or tweeter). Bandwidth-limited speaker-level signals may not be appropriate as an audio input signal if the goal is to have a full range signal coming into the amplifier. In these cases, a summing device may be required to blend multiple speaker-level signals to create a full range audio signal suitable for use as an input.

Switching Power Supply

Power ratings in various products can lead to a lot of confusion in the process of buying car audio equipment, particularly when comparing head unit power to amplifier power. Part of that confusion is the difference between a built-in "chip amp" of most head unit designs versus external amplifier with a switching power supply and why there is a need for a switching power supply.

Margin Notes

A switching power supply converts the vehicle battery's 12 volts to much higher internal voltage that amplifiers require when delivering hundreds, sometimes thousands of watts. An amplifier with increased output provides enhanced sound quality due to increased dynamic range and headroom. The confusion is not because the amplifier is physically larger. Size is not the appropriate comparison here. Although more space does allow the manufacturer more flexibility to include the necessary high current parts in an amplifier, such as a switching power supply. It's because the amplifier design using a switching power supply allows for more measurable/recognizable power output to the listener's ear when compared to a powered head unit.

- Picture a small bedroom in a house completely empty. And think of how much free space there is. Now try to picture that room after adding a bed, then a dresser and a night stand. And think of how the room got significantly smaller. Then add a computer desk or a TV stand. Where a given piece of furniture may be ideal for the room, it may not fit in the useable space. Thus, choices are more dictated by the dimensions of the room rather than what furniture design and placement may be preferred. This is a similar compromise when a head unit is built, and the manufacturer must make certain choices about what to fit into a pre-determined chassis size. Only a certain small amount of that head unit space can accommodate a powered output to drive speakers and these are typically small integrated circuit (IC) chips with specifications of output power and total harmonic distortion (THD) that are nowhere near as good as an external amplifier.

External amplifiers, for the most part, can be designed without compromise. When it comes to deciding on power supplies, output transistors, heat sink (outer chassis) and other large components that make up the amplifier, the manufacturer has a larger space with which to work when compared to a head unit. This allows for the necessary higher current-capable components in the amplifier to enable greater output power delivery. One simple way to tell an amplifier's high current capability is the wire gauge size of the power/ground connections as well as the recommended fuse size. In a head unit, it's common for fairly modest 18- or 16-gauge wire and a 10-15 amp fuse. In an amplifier of several hundred watts, the power and ground wiring might be at least 8 gauge or larger and have 25-30 amp fuse recommendations.

Some amplifiers that are specifically designed for a small footprint and to conserve current draw may use other power supply designs and focus on efficient use of energy. Comparably, premium aftermarket head unit designs may also employ technology in the power section that provides better-than-average performance over other head units. Overall though, an external amplifier is more likely to deliver greater power output than a head unit the majority of the time because it's designed to do so.

Importance of Sufficient Power and Ground Wiring

Having sufficient power and ground cabling to provide the power supply with enough current to achieve rated power is critical to amplifier performance.

Margin Notes

Not all power and ground wiring are constructed of the same materials, so the size (wire gauge) of a cable may not compare. Oxygen-free copper (OFC) is the preferred conductor material. Less preferred is copper-clad aluminum (CCA) which has less conductivity than oxygen-free copper if comparing an equally sized cable. Always choose oxygen-free copper wiring for the best performance and current-carrying capacity.

RMS vs. Peak Power Ratings

Two ratings commonly used to describe audio output (from head units, amplifiers) and power handling (of speakers) are **RMS power** and **Peak power**. Peak ratings are often prominent on a product's packaging because people assume the higher the number the better it is.

- **Peak power** indicates the power the product delivers or can handle in a burst. Peak power is often an unrealistic or unattainable number in a real-life situation when it's spread over a long period of time, such as an entire song at high listening levels. Sometimes in industry circles peak power is referred to as "ILS" power, meaning "If Lightning Strikes."

- **RMS (Root Mean Square) power** is a more realistic rating and should be used as a reference. For output devices (head units, amplifiers), an RMS rating of output power indicates the amount of power capable of being delivered continuously. When RMS power handling applies to speakers, RMS indicates the power they can handle continuously.

Amplifier Loads

Manufacturers also advertise how amplifiers are stable at different nominal impedance loads (i.e., "ohm loads"). Some consumers view those numbers and, with no other considerations, assume the lower the impedance that an amplifier is rated as "stable," the better it is. Stable is a relative term that does not guarantee ideal performance in every scenario. Decreasing the ohm load increases output power in most cases, but it's not a free ride. That increased power must come from somewhere. Potential sacrifices of using amplifiers at a low impedance are excess current draw, increased heat and compromises in sound quality. One-ohm stable is a common merchandising tactic used to help differentiate one amplifier against another. Something to consider about low impedance output loads is that the lower the resistance of a circuit the closer it is to a short. A short creates heat. Also keep in mind that as the output impedance load lessens more heat is created. This means existing form factors and circuitry has to work harder with each step in lowering the ohm load on the amplifier.

General recommendations on amplifier ohm loads:

- Greater than 4-ohm loads may not always optimize the amplifier for its best power output, but are safe and consume minimal current.
- 4-ohm loads present a comfortable operating load for amplifiers in mobile audio systems that seek longevity and reliability.

Margin Notes

- 2-ohm loads may be something to consider if there is a reasonable sized heat sink to dissipate heat and the vehicle electrical system can support increased current.
- 1-ohm or lower loads should only be used on carefully-designed systems and only if the amplifier and vehicle electrical system can support the increased current demands.

Matching Amplifier Power Output with Speaker Power Handling (CTA-2006-B and CTA-2031)

To make selecting and matching car audio equipment easier for consumers, the Consumer Technology Association (CTA) creates standards for car audio product specifications. Two of them are listed here and relate to matching amplifier power output to the power handling of a speaker.

- **CTA 2006-B (or later)** – This standard defines power output for car audio amplifiers (and in-dash head units) that have power output greater than 5 watts. CTA-2006-B provides an RMS power output rating (in watts) derived from a standardized battery voltage of 14.4, replicating vehicle voltage while the engine is running. Furthermore, the power output can't exceed 1% Total Harmonic Distortion (THD), which ensures the power is "listenable" and not full of distortion. Amplifiers and in-dash head units that meet the standard publish their CTA-2006-B ratings, making the stated 'watts' of assorted products comparable without confusion to the consumer. Remember, the RMS power rating indicates continuous power output capability, not peak or momentary power.

- **CTA-2031** – This standard defines power handling for all car audio speakers, including tweeters, midrange drivers, coaxials and subwoofers. The ratings consider RMS (continuous) power handling rather than "max" "momentary" or "peak." These ratings are the most accurate measure of a speaker's performance capability. Speakers that meet this standard publish their CTA-2031 ratings.

That standard of how to characterize amplifier power is particularly useful when consumers see a high-power number on the front panel of the head unit and assume it is the same thing as a much larger amplifier with a similar power rating. Unless both product ratings are comparing "apples with apples" in a RMS or CTA-2006-B format, any direct comparison would not be accurate. The idea is to match the amplifier's CTA-rated output power closely to the same level of a speaker's CTA-rated power handling.

If CTA ratings for amplifiers and speakers are not available, compare or use only RMS (continuous) power ratings to match subwoofers with amplifier power. Avoid using "peak" or "max" power ratings to match speakers of any type with a given amplifier output power because the compatibility is questionable at best.

MECP recommended practice for optimum performance is to match the RMS power output of the amplifier with the speaker's RMS power handling.

Margin Notes

Example 1: One 4-ohm SVC subwoofer with 200 watts RMS power handling. Match to an amplifier with 200 watts RMS power output at 4 ohms.

Example 2: One 8-ohm DVC subwoofer with 200 watts RMS power handling in each voice coil. Two 8-ohm voice coils wired in parallel is 4 ohms (doubles power handling to 400 watts). Match to an amplifier with 400 watts RMS power output at 4 ohms.

Damping Factor

Damping factor is a measurable specification for amplifiers with some importance. It's a relationship between the output impedance of the amplifier and the speaker's impedance "load" presented to the amplifier. More simply, damping factor describes the ability of the amplifier to control undesirable movement of the speaker cone. This is another consideration about running amplifiers into low impedance loads, sometimes unnecessarily.

Two things that affect the damping factor of an amplifier:

1. The amplifier's output impedance.
2. The impedance of the load connected to the amplifier.

By reducing the resistance (nominal impedance) of the load attached to the amplifier, it effectively lowers the damping factor. It can also increase the total harmonic distortion (THD) specification at the increased power level. Whether a higher damping factor with a low THD equates to better quality sound is up for debate, as e person hears things differently. However, the more the speaker cone is under control, the more accurate the audio produced by the amplifier will be,

Amplifier Classes

All amplifiers perform and operate under the same basic principles. They take a signal going in to them and amplify it. That doesn't mean they are all created equally. Amplifier topologies (the basic design of the circuitry of how it amplifies signal) are designated with classes. Each class offers pros and cons depending on the needs of the client.

- Class A – This topology is known as linear amplification. Their transistors are always "on" since the circuitry is designed to always have current moving through the output transistors regardless if the output waveform is positive, negative or zero. They are rare within the car electronics aftermarket since they consume so much power for limited output. Class A amps are usually large because of the hardware inside of them, but are often considered the best sounding amplifiers by sound quality enthusiasts.

- Class B – This topology is also a linear amplification class. However, both power output transistors in the amp are not always on like a Class A amplifier. Meaning when the audio waveform represents a positive signal, the amplifier's positive output transistor will be on and the negative output transistor will be

Margin Notes

off, and vice versa. This helps with the amplifier's efficiency when compared to Class A amps. However, this constant handoff of signals switching the positive and negative transistors of the amplifier on and off causes what's known as "crossover distortion" that is obvious to the human ear, especially at lower volumes. Because of this, there are no real "true Class B" car audio amplifiers.

- Class A/B - these amplifiers are a hybrid of class A and class B designs. Class A/B offers the best of both worlds. To keep the amplifier efficiency high when there is no signal, the output transistors will only be on minimally. When there is an audio signal waveform present, the positive and negative output transistors each stay on a bit longer than the respective positive or negative part of the waveform is present. This overlap in the output transistors remaining energized for that brief period prevents crossover distortion. Class A/B amplifiers are reasonably efficient (typically 50-60%) and provide good sound quality.

- Class D – The "D" in Class D does not stand for digital. These are a switching amplifier, meaning instead of the output transistors staying powered on, these amplifiers switch the output transistors on and off the transistors hundreds of thousands of times per second in an effort to reproduce the audio waveform. This makes Class D a highly efficient power design; however, this constant switching can introduce unwanted noise to higher frequencies. Some listeners regard Class D as having less favorable sound quality than Class A or A/B designs, and these amplifiers are smaller in size than a Class A or A/B amplifier. They can also be subject to picking up or emitting unwanted noise in a car (particularly if installed near an AM antenna). More care is needed for mounting locations and wire management when using Class D amplifiers. Finally, some multi-channel amplifiers meant to drive an entire system may use a combination of Class D on the subwoofer channels and a Class A/B, on the channels that connect to the mid and high frequency speakers for the best balance of sound quality and efficient power output.

- Class G/H - This class combines the sound quality of a Class A/B amp with the efficiency of a Class D amp. With a dynamic adjustable supply voltage, it allows the amplifier to stay efficient while still powering the outputs sufficiently. However, because of the circuit complexity, the cost of the product increases.

Amplifier Channel Configurations

How many channels an amplifier has relates to how many speakers the amp will power. However, depending on the amplifier's specifications, it can drive more than what it's labelled as. It's important that the amplifier's ohm load and wattage specifications match those of the speakers the amplifier is to power.

Some common amplifier channel configurations and uses:

- Mono channel – Used to almost exclusively for subwoofers. A mono amplifier will have one positive and one negative terminal for output connections to the speaker. Sometimes a mono amp will have two sets of output terminals to allow more flexibility with the install; however, both terminals share the same connections inside of the amp.

- 2 channels – Most commonly used to power a pair of speakers or a pair of subwoofers. Most 2-channel amplifiers are bridgeable to a single, more powerful mono channel. This allows flexibility in how the amplifier is used and is a smart option for keeping sellable inventory because it can apply to many applications.
- 4 channels – Most commonly used to power four full-range speakers, such as front and rear speakers. Similar to 2-channel amplifiers, many 4-channel models are bridgeable in channel pairs to a single, more powerful mono channel. This could be 4 stereo channels, 3 channels (2 stereo + 1 bridged channel) or 2 bridged channels and allows flexibility in how the amplifier is used, especially with audio systems that grow and change over time.
- 5 channels – Most commonly used as a "system" amplifier where four of the channels power four full-range speakers and the fifth channel powers a subwoofer.
- 6 or more channels - Since more factory systems have more than four speakers, this category allow easier integration without having to use multiple amplifiers. Another popular use is for audio systems using a digital signal processor (DSP) for active channels in each of the frequency bands to eliminate passive crossovers. In active systems, there is a channel specifically for the subwoofer, channels for the midrange and channels for the tweeters. Some component speaker systems also have a dedicated midbass driver to supplement the frequency range in between the subwoofer and midrange driver.

Margin Notes

Bridging Channels
Bridging an amplifier is a widely used option that combines the power of two individual channels into a single, more powerful channel.

For example:

- A 2-channel amplifier at 100 watts per channel (100 +100 w) into 4 ohms = total of 200 watts.
- Bridging that same (100 +100 w) amplifier into a single channel into 4 ohms = also a total of 200 watts.

Bridging the amplifier does not necessarily produce more output power; rather, it repurposes two channels of an amplifier into a single, more powerful one.

If an amplifier is bridgeable, there will be markings at the output terminals and/or configuration switches. Normally, a speaker is driven by the positive output of an amplifier while the negative output of that amplifier is a "floating ground." When two channels are combined to bridge the amplifier, the negative output of one channel powers the negative speaker terminal, and the positive output of the other channel powers the positive speaker terminal. Since the signal on the negative output is 180 degrees out of phase (inverted) when compared to the positive, they

Margin Notes

work in unison to power them, thereby combining the power of two channels into one.

Bridging is most commonly used to power subwoofers. It's a good business decision for a retailer to carry a wider selection of 2- and 4-channel amplifiers instead of mono channels to power specific subwoofers. This allows the retailer more stock flexibility and knowing they will always have a solution on hand without tying up inventory on specific mono amplifiers (which would generally only apply to subwoofers).

It's important to fully comprehend and understand the amplifier's specifications, both in 2-channel and bridged modes. Ensure the nominal impedance of the subwoofers or speakers it will be powering are configured to the amplifier's rated specification. As with all amplifier configurations (bridged or not), a steady supply of voltage and current as well as a suitable space to allow heat dissipation are fundamentally important to achieve optimum performance and reliability.

Remote Level Control

Some mobile audio amplifiers feature a port for a remotely-mounted knob to connect. This feature is known as remote level control and functions as a volume attenuator for that specific amplifier. It's most commonly used on subwoofer amplifiers, so the overall level of the subwoofer's output can be tailored to blend with the other system's speakers. Since it's an attenuator (meaning turns down overall output power), the highest level of the remote level controller is equal to the amplifier's gain setting position. The remote level controller would then reduce that amplifier's output level as it's turned down. This is different than a bass boost controller, which only controls one specific frequency rather than the overall level of the amplifier's output. Read more about bass boost in the next section.

Built-In Signal Processing Features

With built-in crossovers (high pass and low pass filters), the amplifier has control over what frequencies are reproduced on a given channel or pair of channels. Subsonic (also called "infrasonic") high pass filters, 0 or 180° polarity inversion and bass boost give more flexibility to the characteristic and tasteful blending of a subwoofer into the rest of the audio system. Sophisticated amplifiers may have a broad range of signal processing built-in, including graphic or parametric equalization, crossover filters with selectable slopes (6-24dB/octave) and even time correction (also called time delay).

Separate sound processors are often added before the amplifier(s) in the audio signal path to provide control over even more metrics, then deliver those specific attributes on to individual amplifier channels. This is particularly common for high-end digital signal processors (DSPs) used in OEM audio integration because the amount of technology found in an integration processor may be far beyond the cost constraints to build it into an amplifier.

Margin Notes

Amplifiers with full-blown DSP or other signal processing attributes are and may also have a digital input. In some of those examples where many internal signal processing attributes are present, the amplifier does not have dials or switches to tune the sound. Instead, a laptop computer or mobile device (smartphone to tablet) become a controller for tuning the audio system. Some wired tuning software connects between the amplifier and computer with a USB cable; other types connect wirelessly using 802.11-based WiFi or Bluetooth. An amplifier with wireless connectivity may have an add-on module to enable that functionality so that the cost is not 'built in' to the amplifier.

These are some standard internal signal processing features/settings found on many amplifiers.

- Crossover (also called "Filter") – This allows the amplifier channels affected by the crossover's filter to only reproduce certain frequencies. A Low Pass Filter (LPF or LP) tells the amplifier to only reproduce lower frequencies below the set filter frequency. A High Pass Filter (HPF or HP) tells the amplifier to reproduce only higher frequencies above the set filter frequency. Full Range (FR) tells the amplifier to reproduce everything in the audio signal it is sent. Some amplifiers not only switch on the filter type but allow the frequency at which the filtering begins to be set by the technician upon installation. For example, if the amplifier is configured to use the low pass filter (LPF) and the frequency of the filter is set to 100Hz, that means the amplifier begins to attenuate frequencies higher than 100Hz at whatever rate is part of the filter (6db/octave, 12db/octave, 18db/octave, 24db/octave or greater). It is most common for selectable crossovers built into an amplifier to have a rate of attenuation of 12db/octave.

- Subsonic Filter (also called "Infrasonic Filter") – Used in this application, it is a high-pass filter (HPF) for low frequencies, generally below the subwoofer's ability to reproduce effectively. Whatever frequency is set for this filter, the amplifier will only produce the frequencies above that. The purpose is to keep the subwoofer(s) from incurring damage due to low frequencies that strain the subwoofer's excursion limits. The lower the frequency, the more excursion a subwoofer requires to reproduce it at the same volume level, so at some point the cutoff offered by a subsonic filter allows the maximum usability of the subwoofer and limits the probability for damage from trying to reproduce low frequencies outside its ability. The actual limitations depend on the type of enclosure in which the subwoofer is installed. Read more about those subwoofer enclosure characteristics in the "Subwoofers" section of this chapter.

- Bass Boost – Many people who use a bass boost feature do so because their subwoofer system lacks the performance it should have to produce the desired quality and level of bass output. Bass boost features in an amplifier focus on two areas: the frequency at which the boost occurs and the amount of boost applied (expressed in dB).

Margin Notes

- o The frequency of bass boost may be fixed at one specific frequency, or it can be variable either with a range on a dial (say 40Hz-60Hz) or a switch with two or more choices of frequency.
- o The amount of boost applied is typically variable with a dial on the amplifier, such as 0-12dB or 0-18dB of boost, but may be a switch with two or more fixed positions of boost (such as 0-6-12dB settings).
- o An additional control of the boost may be a remote-mounted bass knob that allows the listener to attenuate the boost level or turn it up to whatever the maximum setting is at the amplifier. The remote-mounted knob does not add any more amount of boost than is set at the amplifier. The purpose is to make it easy for the listener to implement subtle level adjustments in the amount of bass boost to accommodate different content within a range of music that's played. Some music may already be more bass-heavy than other music, which can be attenuated with the remote-mounted bass boost knob. This is different than a remote level control where the control is over the entire amplifier's output, rather than one specific frequency associated with bass boost. On occasion, an amplifier may offer the choice of remote level control or remote bass boost depending on how the technician wishes to configure the remote-mounted knob's use.

Ideally a well-designed subwoofer system will achieve the desired results without the need for bass boost because the boost only enhances one specific frequency rather than other means of fine tuning the bass response with graphic or parametric equalization in several frequencies throughout the bass region. In addition, excessive bass boost will cause a subwoofer's suspension to suffer from over excursion and (at that one bass boost frequency) the amplifier may also be clipping and producing more heat into the subwoofer's voice coil.

MOBILE AUDIO SPEAKERS

Speakers – An Introduction

The basic function of a moving coil loudspeaker has not changed since the 1930s, but there have many been innovations in materials, construction methods, and design. Its principal function is to take electrical energy in the form of an audio signal and covert that to acoustic energy that moves the speaker cone in and out representative of the same audio signal pattern.

There are many configurations of car audio speakers, but the majority are moving coil, cone-type speakers that have common sizes in round and oval mounting frame shapes. The speaker frame designs and accompanying vehicle-specific adaptors allow a retailer to stock and sell predictable sizes that best without having to re-invent the wheel every time.

Frequency Response Limitations

No single element speaker is perfectly suited to play music across the entire human hearing range of 20Hz-20kHz with equal output energy in each frequency range. Instead, speakers are generally grouped into the range they best cover. These multiple elements may be in the same singular frame (such as a coaxial speaker) or separate elements (such as a component speaker set). The number of elements are indicated in the way the speaker is further described, such as 2-way or 3-way.

Margin Notes

Replacing Factory Speakers in Factory Locations

The most common way to replace speakers is to exchange them for similar sizes. This typically requires minimal modification of the vehicle.

Common automotive OEM speaker sizes:

- Round Sizes – 2", 2.5", 3.5", 4", 5.25"and 6.5".
- Oval Sizes – 4x6", 4x10", 5x7", 6x8", 6x9".
- Tweeters – 3/4" and 1".
- OEM subwoofers come in many different variations and often include a customized enclosure.

Commercially available speaker adaptors adapt a common aftermarket speaker size in to a different sized OEM location with minimal modification. The more popular the vehicle, the more likely an adaptor will be available from many accessory suppliers. The same companies who supply dash kits, wiring harness adaptors, etc. also offer a wide variety of commercially available speaker adaptors to fit standardized speakers into specific OEM locations. Always consult a vehicle fit guide or an experienced installation technician if unsure about what adaptor is required.

Upgraded Aftermarket Speakers

Upgraded aftermarket speakers are typically offered two configurations: component sets and coaxials.

- Component speakers encompass multiple drivers in individual housings, most often having crossovers that are separate from the individual speakers themselves. The entire system is the component speaker set.

- Coaxial speakers are made up of multiple drivers all housed in a single chassis. Typically, they are made up of a single woofer with one or more tweeters housed in the center over the top of the woofer diaphragm (cone). They will typically have a small capacitor in place as a simple passive crossover, so the tweeters only receive higher frequencies.

- 2-way, 3-way, 4-way, 5-way refers to the number of different drivers in a speaker or speaker system. A coaxial speaker will most likely have only one woofer and everything else will be considered tweeters if greater than 2-way. A component speaker is most commonly a 2-way configuration with a single woofer and a single tweeter, however higher end 3-way components may feature a midrange speaker (between 2"-4" in diameter) that carry the frequencies in between the woofer and tweeter.

What makes an aftermarket speaker "upgraded" from an OEM speaker? Typically, it's the materials, construction methods and overall engineering that yield an enhanced

Margin Notes

acoustic performance over factory speakers. Speaker size configurations for upgraded aftermarket speakers can be summarized as follows:

- Premium coaxial speakers may have frame sizes and mounting whole patterns that are similar to OEM speaker mounting patterns, making installation straightforward. Upgrading speakers is an efficient way to improve the vehicle's speakers without overly complicated installation procedures.

- Some high-end component speakers have odd frame diameter and mounting hole patterns, as well as greater mounting depths that require customized installation in order to fit in vehicles. Speaker adaptors allow component speakers to fit with a given vehicle when it's not a direct "bolt-in" application. Whether commercially available adaptors or custom fabricated, secure and rigid mounting is a must for any aftermarket upgraded speaker not directly compatible (with hole pattern, diameter or depth).

- Upgraded tweeters are usually under 2" in overall diameter, and it is common for the diaphragm of a tweeter to be 3/4"-1" with and added 1.5"-2" for housing. Even if the aftermarket tweeter is the same outer diameter as an OEM tweeter it's replacing, it will still likely require some slight modification.

- For upgraded tweeters placed in locations where no tweeter existed, many tweeters come with surface- and flush-mount installation parts to facilitate fitting the tweeter securely and visually integrated (so the tweeter does not look like an afterthought). There are times when expert fabricators create custom tweeter pods to optimize positioning of the tweeter placement.

- OEM subwoofers can rarely be swapped with aftermarket due to odd sizes and customized enclosures, power concerns and impedances. Most of the time upgrading to an aftermarket subwoofer means construction of an enclosure where the new subwoofer will reside. There are a few vehicle-specific solutions for a replacement of a factory subwoofer (speaker only) while retaining the existing enclosure. Depending on cost, often the aftermarket subwoofer solution offers better performance for the investment.

Performance specifications for speakers are beyond the scope of the Mobile Product Specialists' knowledgebase, but specifications like sensitivity and power handling can indicate how loud a speaker plays with a given amount of amplifier power or how well a speaker will tolerate extended periods of a given power level (in watts) significant without concern of damage.

More speakers does not necessarily translate to better sound. Placing more speakers in the listening space without regard to how they all interact with one another, the vehicle interior and the listening positions is not a recommended approach. The final choice of the component speaker set should have compelling reasoning behind it, whether that be value for money, high sound quality, ability to fit the desired location, power handling, product warranty or whatever else the customer needs.

Margin Notes

Speaker Adaptors

Aftermarket speakers may not fit perfectly into an OEM location even though the technician is replacing a similar size speaker. The issue may be the OEM hole is too big or small, the aftermarket speaker is too deep or something as simple as the mounting holes don't line up, and a speaker adaptor may be needed. Speaker adaptors fall into one of three categories:

- Universal speaker adaptors are readily available; however, depending on the vehicle, universal adaptors may still require additional work to get the right fit. A common universal adaptor might fit a slightly smaller speaker into the next larger size (such as fitting a 5.25" speaker into 6" or 6.5" opening). Another example is an oval speaker opening adapting to a round speaker, such as a 6.5" speaker fitting into a 6x8" opening. Some aftermarket speakers come with a universal adaptor as part of the pre-packaged installation parts.

- Vehicle-specific adaptors are often available for popular vehicle makes and models. The more popular the vehicle, the more likely there is a vehicle-specific speaker adaptor for its factory locations. These are easy to install and look the cleanest, but because they are vehicle-specific, they may need to be ordered if the shop does not stock a wide variety of adaptors.

- Custom speaker adaptors (or "pods") are fabricated by the technician. Shops with the ability to fabricate custom adaptors out of raw materials often take this approach because the type of material, as well as the thickness of the adaptor and its speaker size opening, are all controlled factors the technician chooses.

Custom speaker adaptors can be fabricated to angle the mounting plane of a speaker to aim it in a more advantageous direction toward the listener. Similarly, custom speaker pods can be fabricated to allow speakers to mount in elevated, forward locations such as the dashboard corners or A-pillar to raise the perceived location of where vocals and instruments emanate. Kick panels are another common custom location to mount speakers because of the near equidistant placement between left and right sides relative to the listener's ears. Depending on the vehicle and the complexity of the adaptor or speaker pod desired, a technician would fabricate a custom solution using ABS plastic, expanded PVC, marine-grade plywood, fiberglass or other materials for more complex adaptors or speaker pods.

Although MDF is also a common fabrication material, it's not recommended for speaker adaptors that install into locations exposed to moisture, such as a door speaker application. Over time the MDF wicks up moisture like a sponge and deforms the adaptor creating an uneven speaker mounting surface with air leaks and (often) misaligned speaker frames. A Mobile Product Specialist should always involve a technician when deciding whether a custom adaptor is required and the right choice for the expected outcome.

Margin Notes

Passive Crossover Networks

Aftermarket speakers typically use simple components to create passive crossover networks (also called filters). These are called passive because they do not connect to any DC power source; rather they use basic filter components like non-polar capacitors and inductors to accomplish the task after the amplifier, but before directing the audio signal to the speaker. Often the filter components are built on to the speaker itself in simple applications, or in the case of component speakers multiple filter components are housed in a separate box to be mounted elsewhere.

Here are some examples of passive filter networks:

- A simple non-polar capacitor is typically utilized as a high pass filter and protects the tweeter from any damaging low frequencies. An inductor (small coiled wire winding) may also be found to filter high frequencies to the woofer on a premium coaxial speaker.

- Separate passive crossovers containing capacitors, inductors and resistors typically accompany component speaker sets. The crossovers are in separate housings and may also have provision for tweeter attenuation.

- Tweeter Protection – a poly switch or light bulbs in the passive network can act as overcurrent protection for a tweeter. A poly switch is a self-repairing fuse that can temporarily cut off the flow of current to the speaker in the event it spikes too high. An incandescent light bulb can filter off any current that makes it to the circuit through distortion or clipping in the audio signal. These components are often built into passive crossovers that come with component speakers.

Active crossovers are different and apply an electronic filter to the audio signal before the amplification stage. This requires dedicated amplifier channels directed to each speaker for a given frequency range. Read more about active crossovers in the "Basic Audio Terminology and Knowledge" and "Signal Processors" sections earlier in this chapter.

Performance-Enhancing Speaker Accessories

Performance-enhancing accessories that accompany a given speaker installation help to maximize every positive attribute of the speakers, but also minimize the negative effects of installation-related challenges. The most effective way to sell these performance-enhancing speaker accessories is to have comprehensive in-store demonstrations that customers can experience for themselves. The benefits are so clearly obvious that an in-store "before" and "after" (or "without" and "with") demonstration will essentially sell the accessories itself.

Sound Deadening

Sound deadening is also known as sound damping (not "damp*EN*ing"). The act of damping means adding mass to a surface to provide a barrier of sound transmission, in part by lowering the natural resonant frequency of the surface(s) where unwanted sympathetic vibrations like rattles and buzzes from interior panels or sheet metal are significantly suppressed.

Margin Notes

Sound deadening material can enhance the overall sound in a vehicle by providing an important sound barrier that keeps exterior road, mechanical and wind noise out, reduces sympathetic panel vibrations and preserves the audio levels inside the vehicle cabin. By reducing the interior cabin noise, the dynamic range of the audio system is improved because it doesn't have to fight past other external road/wind/mechanical noises. Sound damping materials are commonly produced as an adhesive-backed sheet material that has one or more layers of damping and/or sound absorption material.

The added weight and rigidity of sound deadening materials also helps decrease vibration. Decreasing vibration is helpful to allow speakers to project music into the listening space but not necessarily identify an exact location. When there are accompanying rattles and buzzes of a panel nearby a speaker, it's easy for the human ear to identify the location of the sound (not to mention it is annoying to hear).

Luxury vehicles typically utilize sound deadening materials throughout the entire vehicle to achieve their quiet interiors. The added mass of sound damping materials is why doors that feel heavier when they close also transmit fewer outside noises from tires, wind, the engine vibration, etc.

The most common applications of sound deadening materials in the aftermarket are placed in locations that are easy access and often part of a removal process for speakers such as door panels, the door skin where a speaker baffle would attach, the interior cabin floor (including underneath floor mat and transmission tunnel carpeting), rear deck in coupes/sedans as well as the vehicle trunk.

The most effective places to add sound damping/deadening material to quiet the interior cabin noise may not be the easiest to access for speaker installations that require minimal disassembly such as floorboards, roof, and firewall; however, these places are most susceptible to transmitting road and mechanical noises into the interior cabin.

Adding sound deadening materials into areas where speakers are installed has a significant acoustic benefit because the materials allow the vehicle cabin to be quieter and, thus, enhance the effectiveness of the speakers' performance. Always consider upselling a speaker installation with the addition of sound deadening materials. Since the installation of sound damping materials are complimentary to speaker installations, there is often a labor savings for the customer if they have the technician do both speaker and sound deadening installation work at the same time rather than come back in later to have the sound damping installed.

Foam Coupling Rings (Factory or Aftermarket)

Foam coupling rings are commonly used in factory sound systems to acoustically "mate" the speaker's cone to the speaker opening in the panel so no additional sound from the speaker is lost around the adjoining panel fit. The foam coupling ring also helps to minimize vibration from the direct contact with a speaker's edge and the panel in front of it.

Margin Notes

Foam speaker coupling rings are widely available from accessory suppliers, and installation is similar to sound deadening. Foam coupling rings should always be sold with the installation rather than something to consider installing later. In most cases the foam rings have adhesive backing to easily attach to the speaker baffle.

Polymer Damping Pads (Behind the Speaker)

Polymer damping pads are waterproof speaker damping pads designed to prevent speaker cone break-up behind the speaker due to standing waves and enclosure resonance. This allows higher sound volumes with a minimum of distortion. Because of the soft, waterproof polymer material, they are ideally suited to be installed behind any midrange or midbass speaker and replace existing fiberfill or foam absorbers, which are prone to moisture absorption.

Polymer damping pads utilize a spherical, concave surface to eliminate standing waves common in the speaker's installed environment (such as a door or other captive location enclosed with metal or hard surfaces). The material deflects and fragments the speaker's back wave energy instead of converting it to heat like Dacron or fiberglass insulation. Dacron and fiberglass insulation (such as used in attics of homes) are commonly used inside home speaker cabinets to tame the rear wave of speaker vibrations. However, because those materials easily absorb moisture, they are less ideal for locations in a vehicle where midrange and midbass speakers are installed. The result is high output with greatly minimized cone distortion and break-up, and the audible benefit is greater control and increased detail.

The basic construction material of the pad is polymer-based, but these often go by brand names specific to the manufacturer such as Deflex PowerPad, DynaXorb, Magnapad, Sorbothane, Blackhole and others. Depending on the brand, there may be additional attributes such as adhesive backing, additional closed-cell foam layers or other features specific to that brand.

Recommended sizing for polymer damping pads should be roughly the same dimension (whether square or round configuration) or larger than the speaker cone. If a shop wanted to stock only one size, a 6" or 7" size would fit most midrange and midbass applications (especially in doors) without modification and could be trimmed down for smaller speakers in tighter-fit locations.

Speaker Power Handling - RMS vs Peak Ratings

Power handling of speakers (just like power output of amplifiers) can vary widely depending upon how that power is characterized. The two most common specifications in a power rating are RMS and Peak. Other names like "max power" or "momentary power" handling for speakers are unclear references that don't denote long-term power handling over time.

- RMS – Root Mean Square. This essentially means a continuous power rating.
- Peak – This is a measurement reflecting the peak power rating at one instance throughout a measurement period, but is not consistent all the time.

Margin Notes

Refer to the Glossary in the back of this guide for more clinical explanations of these terms. These definitions are simplified within the MECP Mobile Product Specialist study guide content.

Matching Speaker Power Handling with Amplifier Power (CTA-2031 and CTA-2006-B)

To make selecting and matching car audio equipment easier for consumers, the Consumer Technology Association (CTA) creates standards for car audio product specifications. Two of them are listed here and relate to matching speaker power handling with requisite amplifier power.

- **ANSI/CTA-2031** – This standard defines power handling for car audio speakers, including subwoofers. The ratings consider RMS (continuous) power handling rather than "max", "momentary" or "peak." These ratings are the most accurate measure of a speaker's performance capability. Speakers that meet this standard publish their ANSI/CTA-2031 ratings.

- **ANSI/CTA 2006-B (or later)** – This standard defines power output for car audio amplifiers (and in-dash head units) that have power output greater than 5 watts. CTA-2006-B provides an RMS power output rating (in watts) derived from a standardized battery voltage of 14.4, replicating vehicle voltage while the engine is running. Amplifiers and in-dash head units that meet the standard publish their ANSI/CTA-2006-B ratings, making the stated 'watts' of assorted products comparable without confusion to the consumer.

These standards are particularly useful when consumers see a high number on the front panel of the head unit and assume it's comparable to a much larger amplifier with a similar power rating. Unless both product ratings are comparing "apples with apples" in a RMS or CTA-2006-B format, any direct comparison would not be accurate.

If there are no CTA ratings for amplifiers and speakers available, compare or use only RMS (continuous) power ratings to match subwoofers with amplifier power. Avoid using "peak" or "max" power ratings to match speakers of any type with a given amplifier output power because the compatibility is questionable at best.

What blows up speakers?

A speaker doesn't actually "blow up" when it fails. Failure can cause a speaker to tear itself apart or possibly produce smoke, but this is rare. A blown speaker is actually a burned or melted voice coil due to too much power over time.

An audio signal connected to a speaker carries an electrical wave form that corresponds to the speaker's in and out movement. When the audio signal gets louder and hits its limits, it distorts (known as "clipping"). When clipping occurs, the peak or valley of the audio signal momentarily goes flat. The electrical current from a clipped audio output has more energy (in heat) than a clean, unclipped audio signal. If the heat is too much relative to the speaker's power handling and goes for too much time, the result is speaker failure.

Margin Notes

It's important that both the amount of power and the distortion status of the audio signal connected to the speaker (clipped or unclipped) are considered in terms of risk/probability that a speaker could fail from too much power over time. Here are two examples to consider:

- An unclipped audio signal can easily burn up a speaker if it's simply too powerful for the speaker's RMS power handling and causes the speaker to fail. Imagine a speaker with 50 watts of continuous power handling connected to an amplifier putting 1000 watts of unclipped power. Even without clipping, over time the amount of power is far greater than the speaker's continuous power handling and could eventually fail.

- A clipped audio signal that is relatively low power compared to a speaker with a robust power handling may never fail. Imagine an in-dash head unit with 10 watts of power output clipping and creating distortion at its highest volume but connected to a speaker with 250 watts of continuous power handling. It's unlikely that scenario would cause the speaker to fail because, even clipped, the amount of power is only a fraction of the speaker's power handling.

It's not just the clipping of an audio signal alone and it's not just the power handling capability of the speaker alone. Rather it's how the two attributes influence a speaker's tolerance for power (meaning heat) over time. An increase in the clipped (distorted) audio signal only increases the heat that the speaker must tolerate and can shorten the amount of time for that tolerance relative to the speaker's RMS power handling capability.

The audio signal quality connected to any aftermarket speaker is influenced by the amplification to which it's connected. Speakers directly connected to a head unit (no power amplifier) may experience clipping well before reaching maximum volume level on the head unit. That's easily audible as a distorted sound as the volume is turned up to high levels. Many factory audio systems suffer from similar limitations. For speakers connected to a power amplifier in an aftermarket system, correctly matching the amplifier's RMS power output to the speaker's RMS power handling, as well as the calibration of the amplifier levels upon installation, provides the best prospect for ideal matching of speakers to a clean, unclipped audio signal that sound great and last a long time.

SUBWOOFERS

Subwoofer Drivers (an Introductory Section and Overview)

A subwoofer driver is a speaker that reproduces low frequencies, typically 100Hz and below. It can be any size and can vary widely in materials from which it's manufactured. Subwoofers produces the most prevalent and efficient bass in a vehicle when implemented properly in a system design, driven with appropriate amplifier power and installed in a preferred environment (meaning a suitable enclosure). Subwoofer types commonly sold for use in for car audio systems include:

- **Subwoofer Drivers** – Subwoofer drivers are individual speakers intended specifically for low frequency reproduction, not inclusive of any enclosure or

Margin Notes

power amplifier (just the subwoofer itself). Subwoofer drivers are typically round, but can be oval (such as a 6x9" shape) or square. Typical round subwoofers range from 6.5" (165mm) to 15" (380mm) with 10" (250mm) and the popular 12" (300mm). Subwoofer drivers need an optimized enclosure and amplifier power. Manufacturers generally specify the type of enclosure that's recommended and the power handling of the subwoofer once in an optimized enclosure. For this reason, custom building subwoofer enclosures to a manufacturer's recommendation is important to achieve the intended results.

- **Loaded Enclosures** – Loaded enclosures are a pre-fabricated, finished enclosure with one or more subwoofer drivers wired and installed. The loaded enclosure is commonly constructed of medium density fiberboard (MDF) or particleboard and finished with durable carpeting or some type of painted finish depending on the intended use. Loaded enclosures are conveniently wired with terminals to easily attach wiring from an amplifier. The remaining component and accessories required is a suitable amplifier, power/ground wiring and audio cables. Loaded enclosures are a great solution for reasonable bass response and are easier to install then fabricated custom enclosures.

- **Powered Subwoofers** – Also called amplified subwoofers, powered subwoofers include a subwoofer driver, the enclosure, and a built-in amplifier. The built in amplifier is matched to the subwoofer driver's power handling characteristics, and the enclosure's characteristics are optimized to yield good overall low frequency performance. Powered subwoofers generally accept speaker-level or preamp-level RCA inputs which are ideal for either OEM audio system upgrades or for use in an aftermarket audio system. Powered subwoofers typically include all the necessary mounting hardware but may require selling additional power/ground wiring and audio signal inputs (either speaker wire or RCA audio cables) to complete the installation. Powered subwoofers are an excellent solution for keeping a modest subwoofer upgrade simple. Since the built-in amplifier is engineered to match the subwoofer and enclosure type, this provide a predictable outcome for customers who want a relatively straightforward solution.

How Subwoofers Work – A Simple Overview

Like all moving coil loudspeakers, subwoofers rely on the magnetic force of power going through the voice coil to "push" or "pull" away from the magnet. The subwoofer's voice coil connects to the diaphragm, which is commonly called the speaker cone. When the speaker cone moves in and out, that produces sound waves. The voice coil allows electrical energy from the audio signal to convert to mechanical energy to push and pull the cone and create those sound waves. Since these sound waves are low frequency, the subwoofer typically has a further potential distance of travel than other mid and high frequency speakers.

Voice Coil Configurations

Subwoofers have single voice coils (SVC) or dual voice coils (DVC). The voice coil converts the electrical power from the amplifier into energy that attracts to (or repels from) the subwoofer's magnet causing the subwoofer's diaphragm (cone) to move in and out.

Margin Notes

A voice coil's rating is known as its **nominal impedance** in units of **ohms**. Nominal impedance values of voice coils vary, as do the number of voice coils in the subwoofer driver– either SVC or DVC. For example, a shop may sell single 2-ohm, single 4-ohm, single 8-ohm, dual 2-ohm, dual 4-ohm and dual 8-ohm subwoofer drivers, all in a 10" size.

Nominal impedance is representative of the workload the subwoofer presents to an amplifier. A lower nominal impedance value requires an amplifier to output more power. In the effort to output more power, an amplifier consumes more current from the vehicle's electrical system. A principal element of a Mobile Product Specialist's duties when recommending a specific model and configuration of subwoofer(s) is to determine appropriate nominal impedance voice coils once connected to the amplifier. This includes the wiring configuration and how many subwoofers, as well as the optimum workload (4 ohms, 2 ohms, etc.) for an amplifier.

Wiring configurations for a single voice coil on a single amplifier channel are straightforward. Simply match the nominal impedance to the optimized output of the amplifier channel (i.e., if the amplifier calls for a 4-ohm load, use a 4-ohm single voice coil subwoofer).

Wiring configurations for more than one voice coil are more complex. These configurations include series, parallel or series-parallel with multiple voice coils. Each wiring design allows for a different configuration of voice coils (whether one DVC subwoofer or multiple SVC/DVC subwoofers) to the intended amplifier channels. In a DVC subwoofer, both coils must be connected.

- *If you've ever heard that DVC subwoofers have two voice coils so that one can be connected while the other is a "spare" in case the first one fails, this is false. Always consider the nominal impedance of both voice coils depending on the wiring configuration.*

MECP-recommended practice is that subwoofers perform with the most reliability and longevity when the amplifier load is optimized to **comfortably power them without excess heat on the amplifier**. When the amplifier load is below (less than) the optimized ohm load, excess current draw on the vehicle's electrical system is required make more amplifier power. Conditions such as headlamps or interior lighting dimming with bass notes is an example of this. Assuming the amplifier itself has an adequate power and ground supply, optimizing the subwoofer load simply allows the whole audio system to provide a pleasing experience without creating electrical system problems from current-hungry amplifiers in the process.

Quick Reference Subwoofer Wiring Configuration Chart

A quick reference chart is available in the Appendix of this study guide to allow for a Mobile Product Specialist to easily determine the possible configuration(s) of wiring multiple voice coils so that the correct subwoofer model is sold to the customer. A knowledgeable technician is still required to execute the complex wiring during installation, but the reference chart allows for quick decision making. Additional wiring resources for multiple SVC or DVC subwoofers are also available on manufacturers' websites.

Margin Notes

Subwoofer Enclosure Types (The Basics – Brief Overview)

The reasons a subwoofer needs to be enclosed are simple. Have you ever hooked up two subwoofers that share the same air space (same box) out of polarity from one another? While one is trying to push, the other is trying to pull. They move substantially less air, creating a much lower volume and essentially fight each other. This is the same theory as if there were no enclosure at all. The rear sound waves would be out of sync with the front sound waves, therefore cancelling each other out.

There are many types of enclosures used in vehicles, from infinite baffle that uses a vehicle's trunk for the enclosure, to common sealed and vented (aka bass reflex or ported) designs. In any case, great subwoofer performance begins with a solid mounting surface and isolation of the front and rear pressure waves. A subwoofer in an enclosure is the accepted way to accomplish this and tailor the performance in bass response with the type of enclosure used.

Subwoofer enclosures are commonly constructed from medium density fiberboard (MDF). Baltic Burch, marine-grade plywood is also a viable material; however, it is slightly more difficult to cut than MDF and is also more expensive. MDF cuts and sands easily, has a wide availability and costs less than other materials.

Composite materials, such as fiberglass, blend multiple materials and are often used in custom subwoofer enclosures. Fiberglass is extremely rigid, completely air tight, and able to take on almost any shape imaginable. Fiberglass is much stronger at a given thickness when it has a curve.

Composite construction is an advanced technique that combines two materials to yield excellent enclosures. A composite is stronger and better damped than a wall of the same thickness constructed from only one material. MDF glued to marine grade plywood is one example of a composite wall. A layer of fiberglass over MDF is another common composite. In addition to the added rigidity and damping, the adhesive joining the layers further seals the surface of the enclosure. While their complexity adds extra time to the construction process, composite enclosures offer amazing performance. MDF "rings" suspended within stretched forming materials on custom enclosures are an example of using composite construction to achieve unique shapes of a subwoofer enclosure. Internally bracing the enclosure is vital to maximize the output of a subwoofer.

Infinite Baffle

An infinite baffle subwoofer system is also known as a "free-air" subwoofer system. A subwoofer (or any speaker, technically) in an infinite baffle relies solely on its suspension for the restoring force required to return the cone to rest and to protect the speaker from over excursion.

Margin Notes

A baffle is the surface on which a speaker mounts. Its principal function is to provide a rigid mounting surface for the speaker so energy from the speaker's movement is transferred to acoustic energy and not vibration of the surrounding surfaces. Another principal function is to separate the front-wave energy from the back-wave energy so the speaker's in and out movements do not cancel each other out. Common baffle materials for subwoofers in a vehicle environment are medium density fiberboard (MDF) and Baltic Burch, marine-grade plywood.

In a typical speaker enclosure, the restoring force of airspace normally inside the enclosure functions like an air spring for the speaker. Since that air spring is largely absent in an infinite baffle design, the resulting sound is determined entirely by the speaker's parameters, and there is no acoustic method to alter it during installation because there is essentially no specifically constructed enclosure — just a baffle that separates the front and rear waves from cancellation.

It is imperative that the front wave be completely isolated from the back wave of the speaker. For this reason, rigid baffles must be installed under the package tray and behind the rear seat. Remember that an infinite baffle in a car is really a large sealed enclosure and any leak between the trunk and interior will result in a loss of sound output.

The main advantage of an infinite baffle application in a car is that little to no useable trunk space is lost. However, the disadvantage is that this type of enclosure cannot be acoustically "tuned" to adjust the system frequency response or the power handling. If the customer wants more flexibility in sound contouring, consider other enclosure types such as sealed, vented or bandpass designs. The best results for infinite baffle designs are with multiple large diameter subwoofers in a trunk (two 12" or 15" subwoofers, perhaps a single 18" subwoofer as an example).

- **Benefits of Infinite Baffle Designs** — Savings of trunk space. Good low to medium output. Generally good sound quality that is linear (even) across the low frequency range.

- **Drawbacks of Infinite Baffle Designs** — Low power handling compared to an enclosed design. Bass response below Fs is lower than many sealed or vented designs. Not possible in a hatchback, truck, etc. Typically, as much labor (if not more) than constructing a sealed enclosure.

Sealed (Acoustic-Suspension)

Sealed enclosures are also referred to as air-suspension or acoustic-suspension. This is the easiest type of enclosure to design and build and a good all-around design if the subwoofer is suited for a sealed enclosure environment. The idea behind a sealed enclosure design is that the air trapped inside the box will assist the speaker's suspension (air-suspension). As the speaker moves outward, the air behind it is pulled with it, creating a decrease in pressure inside the box. This acts like a vacuum and pulls the speaker back inward. Similarly, when the speaker moves in, the air that is compressed pushes out on the speaker. Logically, the more the speaker moves in or out, the greater these forces are. Subwoofers designed with a loose suspension and a long excursion used in a sealed enclosure can provide smooth bass response, since the stiffer air pressure within the enclosure would control speaker excursions. Subwoofers with a tight suspension and less excursion may require more power to make them move and achieve full excursion sooner than long excursion designs. Manufacturers of subwoofers indicate whether or not a given model of subwoofer is better suited for a sealed enclosure, or another type of subwoofer enclosure design.

Margin Notes

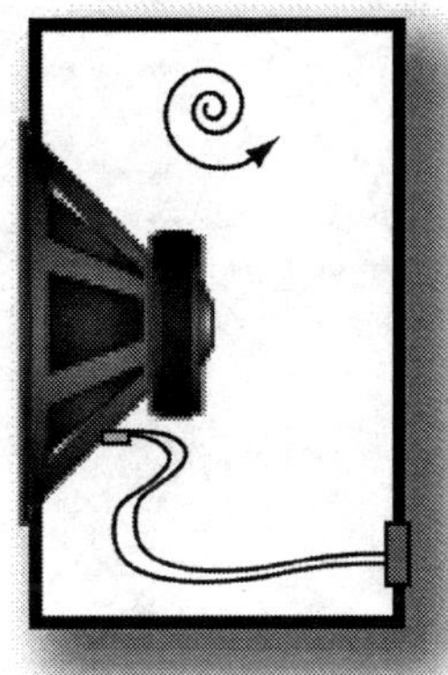

"Acoustic Suspension"

- **Benefits of Sealed Enclosure Designs** – Enclosure volume is small in comparison to other enclosure types. Good output for all music types. Easy for even moderately skilled technicians to build and tolerant of small errors in calculation of volume or if the designer forgets to subtract volume for a brace, etc. Many well-built pre-fabricated sealed enclosures available offer reliable results.

- **Drawbacks of Sealed Enclosure Designs** – Poor response below 30 Hz when compared with a vented enclosure. Low-end response gets worse as enclosure size decreases. Typically requires more power for a given output when compared to a vented enclosure.

Vented (Bass Reflex/Ported)

Vented enclosures are also called ported enclosures or bass-reflex enclosures. Instead of a completely sealed enclosure, a vent through which air resonates in tune with the speaker at the enclosure's resonant frequency is added, effectively increasing the acoustic output. You can hear the principle of vented box design at work by simply blowing air across the opening of a filled soda bottle. The tuning hole is fixed, but changing the length of the vent is accomplished by taking a drink. Blowing air again, a lower pitch is heard. If the size of the bottle opening could be altered or a different size bottle altogether is used, the pitch would also change.

Vented enclosures are more complicated to design than sealed enclosures. There is a delicate relationship between the enclosure size (box volume), port size (both the opening and length) and the speaker's parameters. By changing any one of those

Margin Notes

parameters, the performance of the subwoofer system is altered. One of the possible advantages of a vented box over a sealed box is output. For a given box size, a vented box will have additional output capabilities over most of the usable sub bass range. This additional output is compliments of the port. The port has usable output only over a narrow range of frequencies. At the frequency where the port plays, the woofer's output is minimized—the port plays and the woofer doesn't. In the vented subwoofer design, the human ear hears the combination of the output of the port and the output of the woofer as two different sources, just as if they were two different speakers. Below that tuned frequency, the box provides no additional help to the speaker's suspension, so it's as if there is no enclosure at all at low frequencies. The woofer is free to move and, if given too much power far below the tuned frequency, may be damaged.

"Ported" or
"Bass Reflex"

- **Benefits of Vented Enclosure Designs** – Usually provide enhanced low-bass response compared to a sealed enclosure. Great power handling at and above the tuned frequency. Even moderately powered subs can play loud when matched to the correct vented enclosure.

- **Drawbacks of Vented Enclosure Designs** – More complicated to build. Less tolerant of errors in design or construction. Possible to damage the woofer with excessive "bass boost" far below the tuned frequency, unless a subsonic filter is used to lessen that possibility.

Bandpass Enclosure Characteristics

Bandpass enclosures have been around since the 1930s, and the term bandpass comes from the unique characteristic of these enclosures. In addition to affecting the low frequency of the speaker, these enclosures affect the higher frequencies as well. Bandpass enclosures are usually constructed with dual chambers and share the following design criteria:

A bandpass enclosure has a woofer in a sealed or vented primary chamber that fires into a secondary chamber that is vented. The woofer in a bandpass enclosure is enclosed on BOTH sides and, depending on the type of bandpass design, at least one of those enclosed sides vents output to the outside.

Margin Notes

Bandpass designs allow only a certain band of frequencies to pass through the enclosure. In bandpass enclosures, the woofer no longer plays directly into the listening area. Instead a port or ports channel all of the output into the listening area.

Bandpass enclosures are complicated for technicians to design and build, and a computer-based enclosure design program should always be used as a guide. There are two common types:

- **Single Reflex Bandpass** - In a single reflex bandpass enclosure, the subwoofer is mounted in a sealed chamber and fires into a ported chamber. By altering the size of the chambers, and the area and length of the port, its performance characteristics are altered. The sealed section will determine the low frequency limit of the system while the ported side determines the amount of gain or loss and the shape of the response. The port needs to be tuned to the resonant frequency of the sealed box to ensure a centered (symmetric) response shape.

- **Dual Reflex Bandpass** - These enclosures are similar to a Single Reflex Bandpass except that both chambers are vented. This has both the benefits of the vented side for the low pass acoustic filter (front chamber) as well as the boost in the low end from the vented rear chamber. Note that with the Dual Reflex Bandpass design, the driver mounted inside has no connection to the outside listening area. The driver is merely a piston causing the two vents (pistons) to produce sound in much the same way as a speaker does. It doesn't matter if the driver mounts with its cone facing out or in. It is important to note that the two vented cabinets are 180 degrees out of polarity from each other. Vents must be tuned at least an octave apart to reduce cancellation.

Single reflex bandpass designs are easier to design than dual reflex bandpass designs, yet both types are considered "tricky." Making a mistake with a bandpass box can have dramatic results on enclosure performance, usually for the worse. Designing is outside the skill set for many technicians who lack fabrication and deep enclosure design experience. However, there are many pre-fabricated designs available from subwoofer manufacturers.

In either type of bandpass enclosure, a speaker can literally distort itself "to death," and it is virtually inaudible from the front seat of the car. Avoid excessive bass boosting opportunities in the signal chain because additional damaging distortion may go unnoticed until the speaker simply quits working. Turning up the bass knob or sliding up the bass EQ is an example of how bandpass systems can be harmed without knowing it until it is too late.

Bandpass enclosures are often described by order (such as 5th order, 6th order, 7th order, etc.). However, the description can be somewhat misleading because of the acoustic and electrical responses combined, the crossovers used for the signal and the enclosure's frequency response itself. For that reason, MECP recommends sticking to the terms of single and dual reflex bandpass designs so as not to confuse

Margin Notes

yourself or others. Although outside the scope of the Mobile Product Specialist level, if you wish to get a more technical overview of bandpass subwoofer enclosures, refer to the MECP Advanced Installation Technician study guide.

A summary of benefits and drawbacks of bandpass enclosure designs to consider:

- **Benefits of the Single Reflex Bandpass Enclosure Design** — Great bass from reasonable sized enclosures. Single driver systems work well to reduce costs. A lot of "bang for the buck" if the enclosure design is correctly executed.

- **Drawbacks of the Single Reflex Bandpass Enclosure Design** — Much harder to build. Speaker distortion is difficult to hear and damage to the speaker can easily occur without notice.

- **Benefits of the Dual Reflex Bandpass Enclosure Design** — Amazing bass from even small drivers, assuming the enclosure design is correctly executed.

- **Drawbacks of the Dual Reflex Bandpass Enclosure Design** — Difficult to design and build correctly. Not as accurate sound quality because of the many vents through which sound must travel and because of small enclosure sizes. Vents of a decent diameter (3-4") can be difficult to actually fit inside the enclosure. Speaker distortion is difficult to hear and damage to the speaker can occur without notice. Must use an infrasonic (subsonic) filter to limit low frequencies from damaging the woofer.

RMS vs Peak Ratings

Power handling of speakers (just like power output of amplifiers) can vary widely depending upon how that power is characterized. The two most common specifications in a power rating are RMS and Peak. Other names like "max power" or "momentary power" handling for speakers, particularly subwoofers, are unclear references that don't denote long-term power handling over time.

- **RMS** – Root Mean Square (i.e., a continuous power rating).
- **Peak** – A measurement reflecting the peak power rating at one instance throughout a measurement period, but not consistent all of the time.

Refer to the Glossary in the back of this guide for more clinical explanations of these terms.

Power Handling Ratings, Recommendations and Misconceptions

If not using a powered subwoofer, a pre-loaded or custom subwoofer enclosure must have an amplifier powering it. This section provides some guidance as to how to determine a good match between a subwoofer enclosure (with one or more subwoofers) and the power delivered by an amplifier.

Additionally, the rated power handling of a subwoofer assumes it's in a recommended enclosure and not just sitting wide open, unenclosed. The enclosure

Margin Notes

is part of how the subwoofer can handle a relatively high amount of power because the enclosure provides some air spring and restoring force to control the cone movement from overworking and underperforming.

RMS power ratings are recommended because they represent continuous power (or power handling) which makes a reliable basis for matching and comparison. MECP recommended practice for optimum performance is to match the subwoofer enclosure's RMS power handling with the RMS power output of the amplifier.

Example 1: One 4-ohm SVC subwoofer with 200 watts RMS power handling. Match to an amplifier with 200 watts RMS power output at 4 ohms.

Example 2: One 8-ohm DVC subwoofer with 200 watts RMS power handling in each voice coil. Two 8-ohm voice coils wired in parallel is 4 ohms (doubles power handling to 400 watts). Match to an amplifier with 400 watts RMS power output at 4 ohms.

Matching RMS power handling with the RMS power output the amplifier driving the subwoofer(s) ensures there is enough power to exercise the diaphragm (cone) to move air and produce bass from the enclosure without over powering or under powering the subwoofer(s). Sealed enclosures require slightly more power than a vented enclosure to deliver the same sound pressure levels (SPL) because of the tighter air spring effect (all other conditions being equal). Manufacturers may present more specific power handling and suggested amplifier power pairings based on the specific enclosure type (sealed, vented, etc.), the enclosure volume (in cubic feet or liters), nominal impedance load on the amplifier and filters used, such as an infrasonic/subsonic filter.

Matching Subwoofer Power Handling with Amplifier Power (ANSI/CTA-2031 and ANSI/CTA-2006-B)

To make selecting and matching car audio equipment easier for consumers, the Consumer Technology Association (CTA) creates standards for car audio product specifications. Two of them are listed here and relate to matching speaker power handling with requisite amplifier power.

- **ANSI/CTA-2031** – This standard defines power handling for car audio speakers, including subwoofers. The ratings consider RMS (continuous) power handling rather than "max" "momentary" or "peak." These ratings are the most accurate measure of a speaker's performance capability. Speakers that meet this standard publish their ANSI/CTA-2031 ratings.

- **ANSI/CTA 2006-B *(or later)*** – This standard defines power output for car audio amplifiers (and in-dash head units) that have power output greater than 5 watts. ANSI/CTA-2006-B provides an RMS power output rating (in watts) derived from a standardized battery voltage of 14.4, replicating vehicle voltage while the engine is running. Amplifiers and in-dash head units that meet the standard

Margin Notes

publish their ANSI/CTA-2006-B ratings, making the stated 'watts' of different products comparable without confusion to the consumer.

That standard of how to characterize amplifier power is particularly useful when consumers see a high power number on the front panel of the head unit and assume it is the same thing as a much larger amplifier with a similar power rating. Unless both product ratings are comparing "apples with apples" in a RMS or CTA-2006-B format, any direct comparison would not be inaccurate.

If there are no CTA ratings for amplifiers and speakers available, compare or use only RMS (continuous) power ratings to match subwoofers with amplifier power. Avoid using "peak" or "max" power ratings to match speakers of any type with a given amplifier output power because the compatibility is questionable at best.

Why Subwoofers Fail

Most subwoofer failures are as a result of a burned or melted voice coil. Why does the voice coil melt? Too much power over time.

This information is essentially a review of the same considerations as coaxial and component speaker failures, but since subwoofers are generally connected to significantly more amplifier power than component or coaxial speakers, the need to have calibrated, unclipped power becomes even more important.

An audio signal connected to a speaker carries an electrical wave form that corresponds to the subwoofer's in and out movement. When the audio signal gets louder and hits its limits, it distorts (clipping). When clipping occurs, the peak or valley of the audio signal momentarily goes flat. The electrical current from a clipped audio output has more energy (in heat) than a clean, unclipped audio signal. If the heat is too much relative to the subwoofer's power handling in its recommended enclosure and the heat proceeds for too much time, the result is a subwoofer failure from a burned or melted voice coil.

A burned or melted voice coil can fail as shorted (where the coil is so melted it directly shorts positive and negative leads of the amplifier output) or open (where it physically breaks somewhere in the winding and fails to have the electromotive force to attract or repel the cone from the magnet). Either way, overheating the voice coil in a subwoofer is bad. The good news is that it can be controlled and minimized when the amplifier to which it's connected is properly calibrated to minimize the probability of clipping.

Review of Power and Clipping

It's important that both the amount of power and the distortion status of the audio signal connected to the subwoofer (clipped or unclipped) are considered in terms of risk/probability that a subwoofer could fail from too much power over time. Here are two examples to consider:

- An unclipped audio signal can easily burn up a subwoofer if it's simply too powerful for its RMS power handling over a period of time and causes the

Margin Notes

subwoofer to fail. For example, an entry level 10" subwoofer with a 2.5" voice coil may have a 150 watt rating for continuous power handling. If that were connected to an amplifier producing 1000 watts of unclipped power, this may lead to the subwoofer's failure. Even without clipping, if the amount of power is far greater than the subwoofer's continuous power handling, this could eventually lead to failure. The amount of time it takes to fail depends on the listening habits of the customer. The louder and more bass-heavy they prefer it, the sooner the subwoofer will fail.

- A clipped audio signal that is relatively low power compared to a subwoofer with a robust power handling may never fail. Imagine a small 100 watt amplifier with severe clipping and creating distortion at its highest volume, but connected to a 12" subwoofer with 1200 watts of continuous power handling and a 4" voice coil with a vented magnet. It's unlikely that scenario would cause the subwoofer to fail because, even clipped, the amount of power is only a fraction of the subwoofer's power handling and the component parts of the subwoofer (such as a large voice coil and vented magnet assembly) are well engineered to dissipate heat.

It's not clipping alone or power handling capability alone, rather it's how the two attributes influence a subwoofer's tolerance for power (meaning tolerating heat) over time. An increase in the clipped (distorted) audio signal only increases the heat that the subwoofer must tolerate and can shorten the amount of time for that tolerance relative to the subwoofer's RMS power handling capability.

Review more about clipping and the importance of proper amplifier output level calibration in Chapter 4 under the "Amplifier Installation Considerations" section.

Why not just select a subwoofer with the highest power handling available regardless of how much amplifier output power is delivered? The problem with that logic is that high power handling subwoofers not only handle more power, they also require more power to move the cone (and move air) to create bass. The higher the power handling, the greater the cost. Thus, a subwoofer as described in the second example (1200 watt power handling and 4" voice coil connected to a 100 watt amplifier) would be unlikely to fail, but also unlikely to produce much bass because the 100 watts won't move the cone significantly enough to produce excellent bass response.

GENERAL MOBILE VIDEO INSTALLATION KNOWLEDGE

Overview of In-Dash Video vs. Rear Seat Entertainment

The use of in-vehicle video screens has come a long way since GM introduced a 9-inch touchscreen cathode ray tube (CRT) screen into the Buick Riviera in 1986. Video touchscreens are common in today's vehicles, and there is a wide range of entertainment and safety applications that go well beyond watching movies.

Rear seat entertainment systems are excellent for keeping kids (or other passengers) occupied during the drive. In-dash video is often only partially about entertainment with digital media video playback capability. The bigger picture is the large screen

Margin Notes

of an in-dash video unit with easy to read text, icons, and possibly touchscreen capability, is often an added benefit on its own for the driver for day-to-day operation when used properly.

Rear Seat Entertainment

Rear seat entertainment systems are intended solely for the use and enjoyment of rear seated passengers, though peace and quiet for the front seat passengers is an added benefit. Since the aim of rear seat entertainment is often to keep kids entertained, it may not always be necessary to connect these systems with the existing audio systems since the passengers can use headphones to hear the audio. Some head units will have an audio input that can be used with the output of the rear seat entertainment systems while others may require the use of an FM transmitter if the customer wants to play it through the existing audio system. This should be discussed before starting the work to avoid unnecessary extra charges or having to disassemble the vehicle again to add it later.

Overhead Monitors

A popular item for rear entertainment is the use of overhead or drop-down monitors, which can range from as little as 5.6 inches to as big as 22 inches diagonally. Many units are available with a built-in DVD player and/or video game system to make the installation process easier and quicker. Most units support CD/DVD/DVD-R playback or connections like USB, composite A/V, or media cards. Mobile video systems have been slow to adopt HD video formats, but an overhead video monitor may include an HDMI input.

When recommending placement of the overhead monitor(s), the viewing angle must be considered to achieve an optimum line of sight for all persons that are watching. A central location is usually recommended; however, it may not achieve the best views for all. Some units have a swiveling screen feature to optimize the viewing angle if only one passenger is viewing the screen and not seated directly in front of it.

It is important to speak with the installation technician when deciding where to mount the overhead screen. The ability to utilize or add structure above the headliner as well as avoid obstructions is important when deciding a location. Existing dome lights or controls may need to be removed or relocated. Overhead monitor housings sometimes have built-in lighting to replace any dome lighting that needs to be removed. Central placement in vehicles with sunroofs may be challenging given the sunroof mechanisms. Always consult the installation technician before finalizing the placement.

Headrest/Seat Back

Headrest or seat back mounted screens are another alternative and allow each person sitting in the rear to have their own monitor for viewing and may be able to play different sources at the same time as well. These screens are also the only alternative in certain vehicles due to installation restrictions such as overhead climate controls, vents, low clearance retractable sunroofs, and convertibles.

Headrest and seat back monitors typically ranging from 6 inches to 8 inches diagonally, and sometimes slightly larger. The limitation on the size is really the physical dimension of the headrest itself when the screen is mounted in the headrest. If it's a seat back mounted monitor, the sizes can be even larger given the placement.

Several manufacturers offer factory-like headrests with screens pre-mounted in them and feature materials to exactly match the vehicle's existing interior. Due to the ease and popularity of pre-fabricated headrest screens, most shops are not custom mounting screens into the headrest anymore because an out-of-the-box solution for most popular vehicles already exists.

As with an overhead, rear seat passengers can watch movies through the DVD player (if built in) or use the auxiliary/USB/memory card inputs to view external media sources. The advantage comes in the form of having two independent screens. For example, one can play a movie, and the other can show a video game. The installation is easy in most of these pre-fabricated headrest packages. A significant benefit is that the installation can be reversed and the original headrests put back into place should the vehicle be sold or traded in and the customer wants to return it to stock condition.

Active Headrests

Headrest monitors are typically not an option in vehicles with active headrests. Active headrests operate similarly to airbags, and in the event of a crash, quickly move into a position to better prevent neck injury. Active headrests are a safety feature that cannot be removed without incurring major liability. Several mobile video manufacturers have mounting options that position the monitor just behind the headrest which is one option for vehicles with active headrests.

Wireless Headphones

Vehicles with a rear seat entertainment system may not have any connection to the existing audio system. These systems can easily operate independently of one another so that rear seat passengers can enjoy a completely different source than those seated in the front. Rear seat entertainment systems usually have provisions for wired headphones, wireless headphones or both. Wireless headphones can be used virtually anywhere in the vehicle and receive the audio broadcast for the corresponding video displayed on the screen(s) in the rear seat entertainment system.

Wireless headphones specific to mobile video systems operate by two basic methods: radio frequency (RF) and infrared (IR).

- The main difference between RF and IR is that IR requires a "line of sight" between the transmitter and the headphones. The line of sight in IR headphones is typically not an issue in a traditional vehicle, but motor homes and buses may have limitations. Many video devices intended for installation in the headliner or the headrest provide an integrated IR transmitter to enhance the coverage of the infrared line of sight. Whenever installing a stand-alone IR transmitter, always locate it in an overhead location, such as the headliner

Margin Notes

Margin Notes

or overhead console, so that it transmits the best possible line of sight to the headphones.

- RF-based headphones do not have the line of sight limitations of IR headphones, but like anything operating on radio frequencies there is always the possibility of RF interference. Mobile phones, AM/FM tuners, satellite radio tuners, FM transmitters, LAN devices and even audio switching amplifiers (such as Class D) may present interference. The newest RF headphone technologies offer broadcast in high bands to minimize RF interference in many new products. Since the FCC imposes limitations of RF transmitters as used in these applications, RF-based wireless headphones are also limited on the amount of power they can transmit so they do not cause interference with other devices.

In-Dash or Driver-Viewed Video

A head unit with a built-in video monitor is typically referred to as an in-dash or driver-viewed video head unit, which can include traditional head unit sources (AM/FM, satellite radio, etc.) along with navigation, DVD/digital media playback and smartphone connectivity. Many aftermarket multimedia head unit models include multiple external inputs such as auxiliary audio/video inputs used for external DVD/digital media players, video game consoles, video cameras, phones with video outputs, even portable media players such as MP3 players. Aftermarket head units with built-in navigation can automatically mute the music playback when navigational prompts are spoken, and some provide increased accuracy using vehicle speed sensor connections instead of just GPS.

Besides the built-in entertainment sources, other safety-based video sources available to the driver may also be considered. Rear-mounted backup cameras provide a full view of the rear of the vehicle while it is in reverse gear. Additional cameras mounted to the front or sides of the vehicles can provide additional views around the car to help with parking or viewing blind spots.

Satellite video is also a potential video source that is available through special satellite antennas; however, this is mainly used in recreational vehicles. It is not a common feature in everyday passenger cars and trucks.

In-Dash or "Driver Viewed" Monitors

A stand-alone monitor can be placed almost anywhere the driver can view the LCD whereas the video-capable in-dash head units usually replace the factory installed radio. Any multimedia head units or video screens in view of the driver will typically have safety features so the monitor is not operational for video entertainment while the vehicle is in motion (i.e., can't view a DVD movie while the emergency brake is off).

When determining whether content should be able to be viewed by the driver while the vehicle is in motion, it is important to take in to account whether there is legitimate need to view the content while in motion and what type of content is allowed to be viewed by law. Safety while driving and limiting driver distractions are always a primary concern of recommending any video screen option. Know the specific laws of your state/province and local municipality.

Most aftermarket manufacturers have provisions in place to limit the use of a video screen while in motion. This typically incorporates the use of a parking brake in the car and may also utilize other circuits to determine if the car is in park or neutral and sometimes even limit the possibility of bypassing the safety circuits.

Some automotive manufacturers utilize a "dual view" screen on an in-dash LCD. Dual view screen watching is used with two separate sources. For example, the driver can only see the navigation system on their viewing angle while at the same time the front seat passenger watches a DVD movie on their viewing angle. This is done with pixel directions. One set is for the right side and one for the left side.

Touchscreen tablets can be integrated into a dashboard with the skills of a fabricator. The tablet can provide video content, whether stored locally on the device or from a streaming source if the tablet is connected to the Internet. This application could be considered a concern for driver distraction, and the configuration of app icons on a tablet screen should have only certain apps available on the main screen so that a driver is less distracted by searching multiple app icons.

There are also stand-alone screens that can be used for specific tasks that provide a solution where it might otherwise require removal of a factory component to accommodate a screen in the dash.

- Stand-alone video screens can be safely used by employing one of a variety of mounting solutions like mobile phone mounts. These screens, typically 4-7 inches in diagonal screen size, can be used in commercial applications to display navigation routes or other information specific to the driver's job.

- Rear view mirror screens are a common solution for use with backup cameras or other safety camera uses such as a "baby cam" that monitors children in the rear seats. The rear view mirror has a screen embedded behind the mirror and, when active, displays a video signal. These are factory equipment in some vehicles (particularly where backup cameras were first introduced), but they are also an easy add-on to almost any vehicle as aftermarket equipment. The advantage of a rear view mirror screen is that it does not require any modification to the dashboard electronics, which for many modern vehicles is a legitimate concern. Always keep in mind that not all dashboards with a factory screen have the ability to add additional video sources (such as a camera), so the rear view mirror screen presents an easy alternative.

Margin Notes

Driver Distraction Concerns

It is the Consumer Technology Association's (CTA)™ driver distraction policy (and law in many US States) that all drivers should not watch any type of movie or video

Margin Notes

It is the Consumer Technology Association's (CTA)™ driver distraction policy (and law in many U.S. States) that all drivers should not watch any type of movie or video entertainment while the car is in motion.

entertainment while the car is in motion. Only navigation systems are allowed because the driver's eyes are not fixed on a map all the time. Passengers can certainly enjoy video entertainment, but screens in view of the driver should be disabled from displaying that type of content. It is MECP recommended practice to enable all safety measures on aftermarket in-dash video products that prevent any distractions from video entertainment playing on screens in view of the driver while the car is in motion.

National Highway Traffic Safety Administration (NHTSA)

The National Highway Traffic Safety Administration (NHTSA), under the U.S. Department of Transportation, sets and enforces safety performance standards for motor vehicles and motor vehicle equipment. The most evident influence of NHTSA in mobile electronics is the research it conducts on driver behavior and traffic safety. NHTSA often takes on the topic of driver distraction from cell phones and video, as well as issues regarding the safety of occupants considering non-OEM installed equipment. NHTSA suggestions and laws can result in business for the mobile electronics industry, as in the case of rearview camera and other vehicle and pedestrian safety device requirements.

The NHTSA website (www.nhtsa.gov) is a helpful resource to locate safety-related published studies. 12 Volt retailers can use NHTSA data to support a position of quality and responsible installation to their retail customer base. The website also publishes safety defects and factory recalls, as well as information about the Federal Motor Vehicle Safety Standard (FMVSS) rules, many of which apply to the aftermarket products sold and installed at 12 Volt retailers.

Here are some FMVSS examples related to video screens, driver distraction, occupant safety and interior materials (such as in video headrests):

**Note: The following examples do not represent the FMVSS rules in their entirety. The full rules can be accessed on the NHTSA website (www.nhtsa.gov).*

- FMVSS 101 (Controls and Displays) - This standard requires that essential controls are located within reach of the driver when the driver is restrained by a lap belt and upper torso restraint, and that certain controls mounted on the instrument panel be identified, either by words or illuminated symbols. Technicians making dash modifications must consider these safety guidelines if relocation of HVAC or other controls is required (such as for a custom tablet installation in the dash). For instance, relocation of HVAC controls to the glove box may not be an adequate solution given the requirement of 'within reach' of the driver wearing a seat belt.

- FMVSS 111 (Rear Visibility) - This standard specifies requirements for the performance and location of inside and outside rearview mirrors. Its purpose is to reduce the number of deaths and injuries that occur when the driver of a motor vehicle does not have a clear and reasonably unobstructed view to the rear. Any aftermarket rear view mirror installations must comply with this standard unless exempt under modification for handicapped-equipped vehicles.

Margin Notes

- FMVSS 201 (Occupant Protection in Interior Impact) - This standard covers many of the interior components regarding protecting the occupant (rather than adding to injury) in the passenger compartment. This covers everything from sun visors, armrests, seats, console armrests, and even the glove box door. The automotive manufacturer has already complied with this safety standard, so it is important that any aftermarket modifications do not create the potential to cause unnecessary harm to the occupants because of the modification.

  Changing or altering the latch on the glove box or center-console storage compartment so that it can come open in an accident is one example. Another example is altering the head restraints so that they come loose or have parts that come loose (such as a video screen) in an accident. Changing or altering the armrest on a door panel so that it does not absorb energy in the event of a crash is yet another example. When considering interior modification of any kind, it is important to use a factory-like approach about the occupant protection outlined in FMVSS 201.

- FMVSS 202 (Head Restraints) - This standard specifies requirements for head restraints to reduce the frequency and severity of neck injury in rear-end and other collisions. It regulates the ability of a headrest to provide sufficient restraint for the occupant's head in the event of a crash. For shops producing their own custom headrest video-screen installations or using full-replacement solutions from other companies, it is still important to make sure the headrests are within compliance. For this reason, many seat back rear seat entertainment options are available (particularly for high-end European sedans or vehicles with active headrests) that don't alter the factory head restraint whatsoever.

- FMVSS 302 (Flammability of Interior Materials) - This standard establishes burn resistance requirements in the occupant compartments of motor vehicles. Besides obvious materials like plastic, leather, vinyl and carpeting, this standard also covers damping, and absorption materials behind the panels and underneath the carpeting. Headrests with video screens should comply with FMVSS 302 specifications so customers know their aftermarket rear seat entertainment system is compliant with US safety regulations for interior flammability.

These FMVSS rules are just an example of areas in which the mobile electronics and accessories retailers may have cause to exercise caution. While the idea of someone placing the entire liability on the shop or installation technician is not common, it can happen. There is simply no substitute for staying informed about issues that can place the product specialist, the technician or the employer at risk. Taking a good look at various FMVSS rules will not only limit liability but adds an inherent sense of professionalism and value for the Mobile Product Specialist and their shop.

VEHICLE SECURITY AND CONVENIENCE SYSTEMS

VEHICLE SECURITY SYSTEMS

Margin Notes

Functions of a Vehicle Security System

An aftermarket vehicle security system protects a vehicle from theft by appealing to a basic risk-reward scenario; that is, the risk of attempting to break into the vehicle and getting caught is not worth the potential reward. An aftermarket security system should increase the risk and act as a deterrent.

Aftermarket vehicle security systems offer different levels of defense. Visual indicators such as LEDs and window stickers let anyone outside the vehicle know that the vehicle is protected by an aftermarket security system. If the individual is not deterred by the visual indicators, the second level of defense is auditory response at all entry points (or "zones"): hood, doors, windows and trunk. If any of these entry points are opened or broken, the security system should trigger a loud siren that draws attention to the vehicle and scares the thief away. Finally, the security system should alert the owner that the security system has been triggered. This is increasingly important as sometimes security system sirens are ignored due to improperly installed systems that frequently experience a false alarm.

Parts of the Security System

A security system is primarily made up of the following components:

1. The control unit operates the entire system, monitoring the input triggers and sensors, and provides outputs to a siren(s), LED, door locks and/or other peripherals.
2. A data interface connects to the vehicle to communicate back and forth and perform commands over data.
3. Radio frequency (RF) key fob transmitters to control the system.

The Control Unit (Brain)

The control unit, also known as the "brain" or "controller," controls all the output functions and monitors all the input functions and sensors of the security system. The control unit also has programmable features to customize the functionality of the unit; therefore, it is important that you learn the available features of the brands and specific models of security systems your shop uses so you may properly suggest and sell features that fit your customers' needs.

Useful features in an effective vehicle security system include battery backups, starter kills, passive arming, auto relock and expandable features by auxiliary channels.

- A battery backup provides an extra layer of reliability if a thief gains access to the vehicle's battery and attempts to disconnect power going to the brain. The battery backup allows the siren to continue to sound when power is cut and/or allows the owner to get an alert and locate the vehicle if equipped with a telematics (tracking) device. Battery backups come in three variations:

Margin Notes

1. First is a universal battery backup that connects in-line to the security system's main power, allowing power to remain active on the control unit even if the vehicle battery is disconnected. Some models are not isolated from the rest of vehicle's electrical system, which means the universal battery backup will draw down faster than models that are isolated from the vehicle electrical system.

2. Second is a backup battery siren that has both a backup battery and a second siren in one unit. This further protects the vehicle in the event the security system's main siren wire is cut. The backup battery siren is typically only disarmed by reconnecting the vehicle's main battery power or by a key switch on the unit itself.

3. Third is a control unit-specific battery backup that plugs into the control unit itself. The control unit has circuitry that detects when the main power has been cut and switches to the backup battery power allowing power to remain active on the control unit. This type of system is isolated from the vehicle's electrical system and provides all its capacity to power the security system.

A starter interrupt (also called "starter disable" or "starter kill") disables the vehicle's starter by interrupting a wire(s) automatically when the security system is triggered. The user can also activate, with additional wiring, the starter interrupt remotely by an RF transmitter or telematics device. Interrupting the starter (rather than the vehicle's ignition circuits) is considered safer. Ignition or fuel pump interrupts are not recommended because these devices can affect the operation of the vehicle if there is a failure. If the starter interrupt fails, the worst that can happen is the car won't start. A starter interrupt requires a relay that can be onboard the security system's brain or (more commonly) an external relay.

The **starter interrupt** relay can either be wired normally open or normally closed.

- o Normally open: the wire or wires interrupted are disconnected and are only reconnected when the security system is disarmed allowing, the vehicle to start.
- o Normally closed: the wire or wires interrupted are only disconnected when the security system is armed and/or triggered, preventing the vehicle from starting.

Starter kills are less common today due to the prevalence of factory immobilizer systems, which require a key paired to the vehicle or other informational input to enable the vehicle to start.

- **Passive arming** automatically locks and arms the vehicle after the last zone has been closed. Typically, there will be a predetermined time that must elapse after the last zone is shut to give the user an opportunity to get back into the vehicle before it locks itself. This feature is particularly useful for clients who prefer a more automated approach, especially with the growing number of smart keys that unlock the vehicle when the driver is in close proximity.

- **Auto relock** is similar to passive arming in that it will automatically lock the doors and arm the vehicle. However, auto relock differs in that it applies when

Margin Notes

an unlock command is sent to the vehicle and the user fails to open a zone within a defined time period. If the user does not open a zone within that time, the system will automatically relock itself under the assumption that the unlock command was in error or the user changed his/her mind.

- **Auxiliary channels** are flexible add-on features that can be used for almost anything: rolling up and down windows (some vehicles require an additional integration device to properly control the window motors without risk of damaging something in the vehicle); activating auxiliary lights such as LED light bars; turning on the dome light when the vehicle is unlocked/disarmed; turning on the headlights when the vehicle is turned off and/or locked/armed, etc.

Trigger Inputs

Every security system has individual (zone) inputs for entry points, such as the doors, trunk and hood. If any of these entry points are opened or broken, the control unit receives an electrical signal that triggers the security system to alert of a potential break-in. The ability to separately monitor individual entry points allows the installation technician to divide the vehicle into separate zones for easier system management and troubleshooting. Some systems with multiple trigger inputs include a method sometimes called diagnostics to individually monitor and verify each trigger. This aids the technician or product specialist in isolating a trigger-related problem and lets the customer know the area (zone) that was tampered with upon returning to his or her vehicle.

Nearly every vehicle has existing door, hood and trunk switches to trigger lights when that entry point is opened. This is the same way the vehicle security system is triggered. If the vehicle has a light that turns on when a door is opened, there's an existing trigger already (electrically) there. The same is true for the trunk or hood. If an entry point in a vehicle does not have a factory trigger, an aftermarket trigger switch can be added. There are many types of triggers in the form of switches available depending on the entry point.

- **Pin Switch:** A pin switch is a push-style trigger that typically provides a negative trigger when the switch is depressed (or the zone is opened). These can be used for any entry point where the entry point and the surface it meets have a joining flat surface. This switch type is typically used on doors, the trunk or hood.

- **Magnetic Switch:** A magnetic switch has two contacts that use a magnetic field to allow electricity to flow, or not, when the contacts are near. A magnetic switch can be either normally open (completing the circuit when a magnetic field is present) or normally closed (opening the circuit when a magnetic field is present). This switch type is typically used when a pin switch cannot be used due to a lack of mounting surface, such as in a trailer door or truck bed tool storage container.

- **Ball-Bearing Switch:** A ball-bearing switch has a pair of contacts on one end of the switch. When the switch is tilted, a ball-bearing connects the two contacts completing the circuit and providing an input to the security system. This switch type is typically used for a trunk or hood trigger.

Margin Notes

Sensors

Vehicle security systems rely upon various sensors to trigger the alarm beyond opening a door, hood, trunk or turning the ignition key. Sensors monitor different environmental conditions within or outside the vehicle to determine if the security system should trigger. There are many types of sensors designed to detect breaking glass, jacking the vehicle up, reaching into an open window or impact to the body of the vehicle. These can be internal (built into the brain) or external and intended to mount separately.

A Mobile Product Specialist must identify a customer's security needs and expectations before adding sensors to a security system. **Sensors set too sensitively have a very high probability for false alarms**, which defeats the purpose of having the sensors in the first place. Choose the most appropriate sensor for a particular job and if multiple sensors are used, make sure sensitivity is set appropriately so wind blowing or a cat jumping on the hood won't trigger the alarm If you're uncertain, consult an experienced installation technician in your shop.

Commonly used sensors in vehicle security systems include:

- **Impact Sensor:** The most common and effective single sensor is an impact sensor (also called shock sensor). This is generally the default sensor that comes with most security systems. An impact sensor monitors the vehicle for shock or impact, rather than movement such as wind blowing. Most impact sensors have varying levels of intensity that can be set to trigger the security system on impact.

  A dual threshold impact sensor (often called a "2-stage") offers two levels of sensitivity. The first level provides a warn-away function that will activate the siren and parking lights momentarily to scare off the thief. The second level provides an instant trigger and sounds the security system immediately. This sensor is appropriate for every security system because it covers such a wide variety of possible theft or vandalism conditions. For an external sensor, the center of the vehicle is the preferred location to ensure even and full coverage around the vehicle.

- **Field Disturbance Sensor:** Sometimes called interior motion, interior spatial, radar, microwave radar or proximity sensors, field disturbance sensors are one of the most important vehicle-specific sensors and sense any movement in a predetermined space. Ideal for convertibles, open vehicles, even truck beds, these sensors work similarly to radar systems by sending out a high frequency signal and then based on the reflection back to the unit (called the Doppler Effect), the sensor can determine if something such as a hand or arm has been

Margin Notes

"introduced" into the space. Coverage area is adjustable and the sensors work through plastic, glass, etc., but not through metal. Like the impact sensors, proximity sensors can also be dual zone (or 2-stage) which means movement sensed outside the boundaries of the vehicle would trigger a short warning whereas movement into the vehicle would cause a full-scale trigger.

- **Tilt Sensor:** A tilt sensor monitors the vehicle's degree of tilt when the vehicle is armed and if the vehicle is tilted in either direction by a predetermined degree, the security system will be triggered. This sensor is appropriate for every security system, especially if the customer has upgraded wheels. With factory immobilizer systems and starter kills available, stealing a vehicle and driving away with it is becoming increasingly difficult. Tilt sensors are quite useful for protecting the vehicle against car thieves with tow trucks.

- **Auditory or Glass Break Sensor:** Once calibrated, an auditory sensor is designed to sense the sound of glass breaking. The auditory sensor used in conjunction with the impact sensor will trigger the alarm if the thief attempts to enter the vehicle by force. While the impact sensor will typically sound if enough force is generated to break a window, if the thief uses an object specifically designed to break glass with little force, the impact sensor may not be enough.

Basic summary of sensors:

- Senses some kind of action (glass breaking, impact, tilt, movement, etc.).
- Impact or shock sensors are the most common sensor.
- Overly sensitive sensors are the primary cause of false alarms.
- Field disturbance (interior spatial) sensors detect objects moving within the coverage area.
- Some "2-stage" impact and field disturbance sensors give a warning chirp before fully triggering the system.

Margin Notes

Valet Switch

Most security systems can be overridden by using the valet switch **in addition to using the key in the ignition** before the system is disarmed. This is useful in the event a remote transmitter is lost, damaged or has dead batteries. A valet switch is also known as an auxiliary disarm switch. The reason it's called a valet switch is that it also allows the security system to be temporarily bypassed in a valet mode so that it does not respond to arm/disarm commands. This is useful for leaving a vehicle with a valet, mechanic or other service where the customer may not wish to complicate the service provider's interaction with their vehicle. Often the transmitter can still control lock/unlock and auxiliary remote functions, but the arming/disarming of the security system is bypassed while in valet mode.

Most security system manufacturers' default for this function is one pulse. Some systems also allow you to hook this to an existing switch in the vehicle and program the system to react to this existing switch rather than a standard valet switch. This is often referred to as a ghost switch.

While this switch can be separately installed, some security systems incorporate the valet button on the RF antenna to be mounted inside the vehicle, usually behind (or near) the rear-view mirror on the inside of the windshield.

Control Unit Outputs

The security system's control unit will also provide outputs to control or activate certain functions within the vehicle. One of the main functions the security system will control is the door locks. It's important that the system properly lock and unlock the vehicle when the system is armed and disarmed respectively.

If the vehicle does not have power locks from the factory (i.e., the user cannot press a button in the vehicle or on the factory transmitter to lock and unlock the vehicle), the control unit can operate aftermarket door lock actuators. If the need for aftermarket door lock actuators arises, be sure to consult with the installation technician about specific parts needed to do the job. For instance, some vehicles have rod-style door lock linkage which, in most cases, are easier to interface. Other vehicles have cable-style door lock linkage that may require more installation parts to accomplish the task. Each style has specific kits made to add door lock actuators, and regardless of the kit, the installation technician must run wires and perform work in each door for which an actuator is required.

Commonly utilized control unit outputs in vehicle security systems include:

- **Siren:** The siren provides a loud and audible noise to alert anyone around the vehicle of a possible break-in or theft.

  The siren also offers confirmation of commands. When the vehicle is locked/armed, the siren on most systems will chirp one time (1x) under normal conditions, meaning all zones closed and at rest. If any of the zones are open, most systems will chirp a certain number of times to indicate that the zone

Margin Notes

is open and what zone that is. The sequence is specific to each different manufacturer and system. The siren on most systems will also chirp two times (2x) when an unlock/disarm command is sent. Finally, most vehicle security systems will provide additional chirps if the security system is triggered and indicate what caused the security system to trigger by number of chirps.

There are also different styles of sirens, and most offer some adjustability in tone and/or length of sounding, either by cutting a wire at the siren itself or with a programming change in the control unit. The most typical siren is a six-tone siren; less common or available as an accessory are single-tone sirens or European-style sirens that produce more of a beep than a chirp.

Another style of siren is the piezo siren. Extremely loud and used in the interior of the vehicle, the piezo siren makes any extended stay inside the vehicle unbearable. These sirens are small and can be hidden in many places in the interior of the vehicle.

Consider local law regarding the sounding devices on a vehicle security system. Investigate and understand any ordinances that prohibit reoccurring sounding devices on triggered vehicle security systems or that specify a particular decibel level when activated. While a shop that sells security systems should already be aware of these laws (where applicable), it certainly does not hurt to be aware for yourself and your customer.

- **Flashing park lights:** The most common method of implementing a visual deterrent, this feature must be interfaced into the vehicle's parking light circuits.

  Strobes or alternative "attention getting" lighting products could be used by a flashing park light output as well. The primary concern with any highly visual lighting like strobes is that the color may be limited (so as not to be mistaken for an emergency vehicle) and their use may have local law restrictions. As with sounding devices, check the local laws in your area before installing any strobes or highly visible external security lighting.

- **Status LED:** The status LED serves provides a steady and bright flash when the system is armed and serves as a visual deterrent. The LED is small and should be mounted in a visible location. Most systems also provide security system "diagnostics" via the LED. This will indicate if the security system was triggered since the ignition was last turned on and, if the security system was triggered, what triggered the security system by the number of sequential LED flashes.

  When helping the customer choose a location for the LED, suggest a location that is visible from all sides of the vehicle, such as a central dash or console locations. A blank switch knockout panel or other panel that is low cost to replace is a good choice should the system ever be removed and the car returned to original condition. Regardless of the location, be sure the customer

Margin Notes

agrees to avoid having to replace a panel due to a miscommunication. While the status LED is typically a separately installed item, some security systems incorporate the status LED on the RF antenna to be mounted inside the vehicle, usually behind (or near) the rear-view mirror on the inside of the windshield.

- **Factory security arm and disarm:** Vehicle security systems typically have outputs to control a factory security system so that when the aftermarket system arms and disarms, it controls the factory system to perform the same functions. These outputs can typically be programmed by the installation technician in various ways to allow seamless integration with the factory security system. Some security systems have settings for arm/disarm pulses and the timing of the pulse.

- **Auxiliary channels:** Auxiliary output channels are important for add-on features, and a creative installation technician can utilize auxiliary output channels to control just about any electronic vehicle function by remote. Think of this as the creative side of a vehicle security system that allows customers to choose remote-controlled features. The ability to upsell these unique features and gain additional labor dollars is a fantastic way to utilize a technician's skill and a product specialist's expertise in helping customers tailor a security system and remote-controlled functionality to their individual taste.

REMOTE START SYSTEMS

Functions of a Remote Start System

A remote start system starts the vehicle without the user and/or key and can also warm up or cool down the vehicle prior to the user entering. Popular in warm and cold climates, "remote start season" typically begins when the temperatures start getting uncomfortably cold or hot. It's a good idea to offer remote start systems year-round to have a continuous flow of remote start systems and to minimize the wait times during the peak remote start season.

When a remote start system is installed and the customer wants to activate heating and air conditioning (HVAC), the HVAC controls, including fan speed, must be in the "on" position when exiting the vehicle. This allows the vehicle to either heat or cool when the remote starter is activated. Some vehicles have the ability to set the HVAC remotely, turn on the heat or air conditioning and/or heated seats based on interior or exterior temperature.

Remote starter systems can be broken into two primary categories: modular and all-in-one systems.

- **Modular Systems:** A modular system has multiple parts work together to perform remote start functionality. A modular system has a control unit (brain) that controls the remote start functions but requires an external or docking-style data interface to properly communicate with the vehicle's data bus and

Margin Notes

immobilizer system. A modular system is designed to be universal; it can be used with or without a data interface and typically has customizable features to meet the needs of the vehicle.

- **All-in-One Systems:** An all-in-one system consists of the remote starter system and data interface in one product. Most all-in-one systems can use T-harnesses that make the majority of the installation plug-and-play.

Remote Start and Security System Combination Units

While a security system and a remote starter system can coexist in a vehicle, controlled by separate brains, a combination unit makes functionality more fluid and integration easier. Combination units have more customizable features and expandability and typically feature the same options, accessories, and add-ons of a stand-alone security system with the added benefit of a remote start system.

PARTS OF THE REMOTE STARTER SYSTEM

The Control Unit (Brain)

The control unit, also known as the "brain" or "controller," controls the output functions and monitors the input functions of the remote starter system. Like a security system, one important function of the remote start system is door lock and factory security system control. Interfacing with the factory security system is equally important in a remote start system as it is in a security system. One very important function is the factory alarm disarm. When the vehicle remote starts, the vehicle must be disarmed beforehand. If the vehicle is not disarmed prior to the vehicle starting, one of two things will happen:

1. The factory alarm will sound when the vehicle starts.

2. The factory alarm *prevents* the vehicle from starting despite everything else in the system being installed properly.

How to Test for a Factory Security System

Testing for the presence of a factory security system is simple. Unroll the driver window and lock the vehicle with the factory transmitter then wait for approximately one minute. Once the minute has elapsed reach in and manually unlock the vehicle and open the door. If the horn starts to honk and/or the lights start to flash, there's a factory alarm and the installation technician must interface with it properly. If the horn does not honk or lights flash, there's no factory alarm for which to interface.

If the vehicle you are testing has a factory smart key (i.e., the ability to enter the vehicle by simply touching or pulling on the door handle that are typically seen in push-to-start vehicles), make sure the factory transmitter is far away from the vehicle so it doesn't unlock and disarm the factory alarm. Remote start systems can also add door lock actuators in situations where the vehicle is not equipped with power locks in the same manner as a security system.

The control unit typically has programmable features to customize the functionality of the unit for your customer's needs. Again, it's important to learn what the available features of the brands and specific models of security systems your shop uses so a Mobile Product Specialist can properly suggest and sell the ideal remote starter and interface.

Margin Notes

Some key features of a remote starter include selectable runtime, secure takeover, turbo timer, hot and/or cold starting, timed starting, low battery starting, temperature controlled accessories and manual transmission compatibility.

- **Selectable Runtime:** Allows the runtime to be adjusted up or down and is the amount of time in which the remote starter will keep the vehicle running before shutting it down (if the vehicle has not been securely taken over).

- **Secure Takeover:** Allows the user to get in while the vehicle is remote started, take control of the vehicle and drive off without shutting down and restarting the vehicle. Not all vehicles have secure takeover, however. If the vehicle does not offer secure takeover, be upfront with the customer to ensure their expectations are met.

- **Turbo Timer:** Keeps the vehicle running for a predetermined period after the user shuts off and leaves the vehicle to cool the engine down.

- **Hot and/or Cold Starting:** Allows the customer to choose a temperature, sometimes predetermined by the manufacturer, in which the vehicle will automatically start if the temperature threshold is reached. This feature typically requires the user to activate it after every ignition cycle.

- **Timed Starting:** Allows the vehicle to automatically start at a timed interval (every three hours for instance). This feature typically resets once the ignition is turned on and requires the user to activate it after every ignition cycle.

- **Low Battery Starting:** Allows the vehicle to automatically start if the battery reaches a certain voltage threshold. This feature is useful for customers who may leave their car for an extended period and cannot access it remotely.

- **Temperature Controlled Accessories:** Automatically turns on an accessory or accessories in the vehicle based on a temperature threshold when the vehicle is remote started. These accessories include but are not limited to rear defrost, mirror defrost and heated/cooled seats. The remote start system may not be able to turn these features on in all vehicles as they may be controlled by the vehicle's data bus. Consult with your installation technician to determine if these features can be turned on and what additional parts, if any, are needed.

- **Manual Transmission Compatibility:** The installation of a remote start system on a manual transmission vehicle should **only** be done if the remote start

Margin Notes

system supports manual transmission starting. This is *extremely* important for the safety of the customer, the customer's vehicle and the public. A remote start system that is compatible with a manual transmission vehicle will require additional connections within the vehicle (these can be provided over data with a data interface) to ensure that the vehicle was in neutral when the user last left the vehicle. Some manufacturers also require an additional safety measure by measuring the vehicle's movement during the remote start process and disengaging the remote start if the vehicle moves.

Safety Measures

Remote starters employ many safety measures. It is crucial that all safety measures are adhered to which means integrating into these systems without bypassing or eliminating any safety features or systems. Bypassing or disconnecting safety connections may cause injury as well as property damage. The product specialist, technician and employer could all be held legally responsible for injuries or property damage caused by a faulty or improper installation that bypassed any factory-installed or aftermarket safety features.

Typical remote starter safety features include but are not limited to:

Neutral safety switch

- Prevents the vehicle's starter from cranking while in gear or not in park position.
- Prevents the remote start from activating on manual transmission vehicles.

Parking brake connection

- Can prevent the remote starter from activating if not engaged (especially for any manual transmission applications – double safeguard).
- A parking brake connection can add additional safety features of in-dash audio/video displays on aftermarket devices (although that is independent of installing a remote starter).

Hood pin switch

- The hood pin switch is a required accessory when installing a remote start system. Some vehicles come equipped with a factory hood pin switch that can be used for this purpose, or one can be added.
- The hood pin switch tells the control unit whether the hood is open or shut. If it is open, the remote start will shut off (if running) or prevent the remote start from activating all together.
- The purpose of this safety measure is to ensure that the remote start system will not be accidentally activated while someone has their hands in or around the engine.

Brake pedal shut down

- Prevents the remote start from operating while the footbrake is pressed, preventing the car itself from shifting out of the park position.

Margin Notes

Applications and Requirements for Remote Starters

Remote starters, much like security systems, always have an open-ended variable—the vehicle. Today's vehicles are more sophisticated than ever, but there are also some basics that are assumed when installing remote starters to help level the playing field.

The following are the requirements for remote starters in most vehicles that do not require special consideration beyond these points:

- Automatic Transmission
- Fuel Injection (can be gasoline or diesel fuel)
- A battery in good condition
- No mechanical starting or idling issues
- In some cases, a spare key may also be necessary if the vehicle has a transponder based factory anti-theft system

As presented earlier in this chapter, manual transmission applications have the obvious question of safety. What if the transmission is left in gear and the vehicle is remote-started? This issue can be addressed by monitoring a number of different customized inputs, but there is always a danger to life and property, making this a potential liability. Some manufacturers build systems for both automatic and manual transmission vehicles, but there are some retailers who avoid the liability entirely by declining to do remote starter installations on manual transmission vehicles altogether. This will ultimately be up to your shop's manager or owner.

Here are some additional safety considerations for manual transmission remote starter applications:

Door or rear hatch pin switches (manual transmission)

- When selling/installing a remote starter for a vehicle with a manual transmission, it is crucial to have working pin switches in all areas of the vehicle. These are used to prevent the remote start from operating if someone has entered the vehicle and possibly bumped the gear shifter. Most of these systems will have a sequence that must be followed before exiting the vehicle, often called "Reservation Mode." If the sequence is not followed, the remote start will not operate.

Tachometer hook up (manual transmission)

- The remote start must see the vehicle operating while setting reservation mode on manual transmission vehicles.

Clutch switch integration (manual transmission)

- If the vehicle is a manual transmission, it's important that the installation technician integrates into the clutch switch whether by wired connection or a data interface signal. This ensures the vehicle will crank only when needed.

Margin Notes

Diesel applications have some considerations for remote starter system compatibility. These considerations are a simple matter of programming handled by the technician at the time of installation, such as an extended engine crank time or a "wait to start light" input that monitors the glow plugs.

Data Interfaces for Functional Integration

Modern vehicles have a data bus communication system which the vehicle uses to communicate or pass messages between the various control modules in the vehicle. When a security system is being installed, a data interface isn't necessarily required to perform the installation. However, with remote starters, most vehicles sold in the U.S. and all vehicles sold in Canada will have a vehicle immobilizer system that needs to be integrated in order to allow the vehicle to start remotely.

A vehicle with an immobilizer feature disables the vehicle from starting or running if a theft is attempted. In these systems, generally a specially coded key (called a transponder key) or key fob is required so the vehicle knows it's being started by an authorized user. If the proper key or key fob is not used, the vehicle will disable itself by preventing the starter from cranking, shutting off the fuel injectors, preventing the coil or coils from igniting or all of these things. To remote start the vehicle, the same key or key fob information needs to be presented to the vehicle prior to activating the ignition circuits.

There are primarily three forms of data interface modules: transponder integration only, convenience integration only and a combination integration module that does both.

- **Transponder Integration:** This interface will integrate the immobilizer system to provide valid key information to the vehicle allowing the vehicle to start without the actual key present. This method is available for most cars; however, some vehicles require the customer to give up a key to integrate the immobilizer system.

- **Convenience Integration:** This interface will integrate the convenience features; that is the input triggers such as the doors, trunk, hood, foot brake, e-brake, tachometer, etc. and the output controls such as door locks and trunk release.

- **Combination Integration Module:** This interface type offers both the transponder integration as well as all the convenience integration functionality in one module.

These data interfaces make the installation simpler by limiting the number of connections required and reduce the time needed for installation. In most situations, this saves the customer from having to relinquish a key (or key fob) or purchase another key from the dealership which can cost hundreds of dollars.

Control Methods for Security and Remote Starter Systems

A security and/or remote start system can be controlled by a radio-frequency (RF) transmitter, a smartphone or the factory remote.

An **RF transmitter** has a few key points to consider: transmitter style, battery style, range, communication and lifestyle.

- **Transmitter Style:** Most transmitters break down into two categories: non-LCD and LCD. Non-LCD transmitters typically have just a small light to indicate a button push while LCD transmitters have a screen to indicate a button was pushed; the LCD transmitters also provide vehicle status via some form of graphic or display.

- **Battery Style:** It's important to discuss the battery style and life of the transmitters. The transmitters come in either a replaceable or rechargeable battery. The replaceable batteries tend to have a longer single-charge lifespan due to their limited use in 2-way transmitters (which use more battery power to communicate back and forth). Rechargeable battery transmitters may not last as long as the replaceable battery transmitters but there's the added convenience of simply plugging in your remote to recharge instead of having to keep a stash of batteries on hand.

- **Range:** The ranges of an RF transmitter varies with environmental conditions. An RF transmitter will state an "up to" range, which in most situations is the maximum range possible when environmental conditions are at their best for RF transmission. The real-world range of most transmitters is going to be less than the advertised range so it's important to set the customer's expectations from the outset. While the distance is the over-arching consideration when talking about range, be sure to mention that longer range remotes typically have better resistance to interference. By far the single largest reduction of range is due to an aging (or low) battery in the remote. When a customer notices that they must be closer to their vehicle to operate it using the RF transmitter, it is time to change the battery or (if a rechargeable model) recharge the transmitter. If not, the customer runs the risk that they will be unable to disarm the security system or unlock the doors (if equipped with keyless entry functionality).

- **Communication:** The transmitter has two types of communication: 1-way and 2-way. One-way communication means the transmitter will send the signal to the vehicle and the transmitter will not indicate as to whether the desired command was performed. Conversely, a 2-way transmitter will send the signal to the vehicle, and the transmitter will indicate whether the desired command was performed by an auditory and/or visual response. Some manufacturers have what's called half-mode 2-way and full-mode 2-way. Half-mode 2-way simply means that the transmitter will provide 2-way confirmation with lock, unlock, remote start, trunk release, auxiliary commands, etc., but will not provide alerts on the remote if the alarm system is triggered (if so equipped). Full-mode 2-way means that every function of the remote start and/or security system will provide 2-way confirmation including alerts if the security system is triggered.

Margin Notes

Margin Notes

Two-way functionality is increasingly important with the more factory-installed remote start systems. Most factory-installed systems are 1-way and, even the few 2-way options available have short range, poor performance and are typically not that pleasing to the eyes.

- **Lifestyle Considerations:** Many manufacturers have RF transmitters that hold up better to everyday use of the transmitter and varying lifestyles. For instance, some remotes will feature a water-resistant or water-proof casing (including IPX7 rated cases) and shock-resistant and shock-proof casing (including the ability to be run-over without harm).

Smartphone integration is also popular. Using a smartphone to control a security system and/or remote start system has key advantages over the RF transmitter counterpart. Smartphone or computer-control allows the user to control or view the status or location of the vehicle from practically anywhere. If the user can access the internet and the telematics device in the vehicle has service, they can control or get the status or location of the vehicle. Smartphone integration allows for full 2-way communication including the ability to set geofencing alerts, speed alerts and service reminders. This means the user will be notified if their alarm is going off, if the vehicle entered or left a defined area, and if someone driving the vehicle is speeding. Smartphone integration requires a monthly or yearly service fee as a telematics device is required and a service fee is required to pay for the data transmission.

Factory Transmitter Integration is also an option when using a security system or remote start system. The factory transmitter is a convenient option that does not require the customer to carry any additional fobs. However, using the factory transmitter has drawbacks. The range is limited to 50 to 100 feet in most cases. The factory transmitter does not provide 2-way communication; the customer will need to see the vehicle to determine whether the command was sent, received and performed.

To use a factory transmitter to arm, disarm or remote start the vehicle, the brain must support that feature either over data with a data interface or via analog inputs into the brain. Not all manufacturers support this feature so make sure this feature is supported before offering it to a customer. If the feature is supported over data with a data interface, the most the installation technician will have to do is enable the feature when configuring the brain. Most shops charge for solutions, regardless of the complexity to implement.

If the feature is not supported over data and the brain supports the feature via an analog input, additional wiring and parts may be required. Some vehicles may even require the technician to run wires into the door to get the appropriate wires in which to interface. In either situation, the customer can hit lock or unlock on the factory transmitter and arm and disarm the aftermarket security system. This gives the convenience of only needing one transmitter while giving the added security of an aftermarket system. To remote start the vehicle, the customer will simply hit the lock button three times to activate or deactivate the remote start system.

IN VEHICLE COMMUNICATION, DRIVER SAFETY AND AWARENESS

IN VEHICLE COMMUNICATION, DRIVER SAFETY AND AWARENESS

Margin Notes

GPS NAVIGATION

GPS/GLONASS Satellite Basics

The Global Positioning System (GPS) is a network of 24 satellites around Earth that was developed by the United States Department of Defense (DOD) and the National Institute of Standards and Technology (NIST). GPS satellites relay precise information to receivers on the land, sea, and in the air to precisely determine velocity (speed), location and time of day. A receiver must receive information from at least three of these satellites to properly triangulate latitude and longitude for the device. A minimum of four satellites is required to accurately calculate latitude, longitude and elevation. Most GPS receivers can track as many as six to eight satellites. The more satellites the receiver obtains information from, the more precise the location and speed calculations.

The GLObal Navigation Satellite System (GLONASS) is a separate network of 24 satellites developed and maintained by the Russian Federal Space Agency. These satellites relay similar information to receivers in a similar method.

A navigation receiver or device sold in North America will have GPS compatibility, but some include GLONASS compatibility as well. This effectively doubles the number of satellites from which the receiver can obtain information, which can speed up geolocation acquisition and improve reception in areas with tall buildings or signal-inhibiting geographic features.

All antennas used for GPS or GPS/GLONASS receivers rely on line-of-sight communication with satellites overhead. The mounting location of the antenna(s) will greatly impact the accuracy and reception of the device. Here are some factors that can prohibit good reception of the satellite signals:

- Mounting the antenna at an angle or upside down.
- Mounting the antenna under metal or under a body panel or component that has metal braces, structure or heavy metallic paint.
- Placing the antenna under glass that has metal content on it or in it.
  - Metallic window film on the window.
  - Defroster grids or metallic film in the glass to remove ice, snow and fog.

Here are some environmental or geographic instances where the signals could be inhibited or intermittent:

- Large cities with tall buildings.
- Tunnels, parking garages, underground parking.
- Heavy tree coverage in forests.
- Deep valleys or mountain ranges.
- Inside any type of building.

In-Dash Navigation

Maps provided for in-dash navigation head units are provided by TomTom, Garmin, Navigo, and Tele Atlas, just to name a few. With few exceptions, most map data providers offer similar data because all of them regularly update their data to stay competitive and to provide a better customer experience.

Aftermarket head units that offer Apple CarPlay or Android Auto functionality can utilize the phone's navigation app(s) and display it on the screen. Apple Maps and Google Maps™ both offer excellent routing information and are always up to date but require a data plan for the connected Apple® or Android™ smartphone, which must be connected either with a cable, or wirelessly to the head unit while the navigation app is being used.

Points of interest are important for the user of the device as it makes finding relevant local data or locations quick and easy. Some examples of points of interest included in most map providers are:

- Gas stations
- Restaurants
- Landmarks
- Hotels
- Parks and schools
- Popular shopping locations

Local traffic conditions or real-time traffic is data that is delivered to an in-dash head unit or Portable Navigation Device (PND) via an FM frequency and/or satellite signal. Some aftermarket devices require you to subscribe to a service to receive the broadcast, but some offer the service for free. In the United States, the data is typically provided by either Tele Atlas or HERE.

There is an assortment of extra features available in in-dash and portable navigation products including:

- Free updates for in-dash navigation head units.
- Route-planning with the ability to create route with multiple destinations.
- Economy data based on speed, distance and your fuel consumption.
- Street view of the destination as you arrive.

Add-On Navigation to Factory Systems/Screens

Navigation functionality can be added to a factory head unit in multiple ways. Some aftermarket companies have a module or box with specific harnesses that plug into the factory radio and the vehicle harnesses to apply a navigation controller to the factory head unit. The size of these modules may vary but can be tucked behind the radio, behind a glove box or under a center console in most cases. There is typically very little set-up, as these modules either replicate factory controls right on the screen, or activate the built-in factory controls for use.

Other types of modules might require opening the factory radio to plug in a small harness, replace a circuit board or replace the screen. Some might require a touchscreen overlay be applied to the factory screen to impose extra non-original buttons or icons onto the pre-existing equipment. In either case, be sure to verify

Margin Notes

Margin Notes

the process and the risk with the customer before the project is started to provide awareness and protect the store from claims of damage.

Portable Navigation on Mobile Devices

The navigation on a PND is similar to using navigation apps on a smartphone; however, the user may have to perform manual software or map data updates, mount the PND for safe use in the vehicle and power the device separately using another power socket in the vehicle. Despite these drawbacks. These devices are popular for:

- Travelers who rent cars or those who have multiple vehicles and cannot permanently mount or install an in-dash unit in one vehicle.
- Drivers who only take occasional trips to areas where they require navigation assistance.
- Users who need a larger screen than their phone but cannot install an in-dash unit in their vehicle.
- Those who want reliable navigation assistance in rural areas where a cellular signal may not be present for phone navigation app use or they do not want to use large amounts of data on their cellular plan, and they cannot install an in-dash unit.

GPS TRACKING

Installed devices

Commonly used by fleet managers, permanently installed GPS tracking devices not only provide mapping but can also pinpoint vehicle assets on a back-end software package to monitor fleet efficiency, safety and provide real-time status updates. More robust units can integrate with vehicle computers to monitor vehicle health, door and cargo status and even driver fatigue. These extra features help companies save money and time, and also provide data that can minimize risks associated with tired drivers and alert managers to non-productive time in the vehicle.

Plug-In devices

These temporary or semi-permanent installed devices offer quick set-up and easy transport between vehicles. They may plug into the vehicle's OBD-II port, for example. Always consult with the user or fleet manager on how they prefer to install it as portable devices can easily be stolen or lost. These offer quick, short-term success and are excellent for small companies like locksmiths that have only one or just a few vehicles on the road.

WHAT IS BLUETOOTH?

Bluetooth is a wireless communications protocol that allows connected devices in close range to communicate. The type of communication exchanged between devices depends upon the device's intended use and the assigned profile(s). In the automotive environment, Bluetooth is best known for hands-free calling or audio streaming, but there are many other uses by different products where a wireless connection is present.

Margin Notes

Many municipalities in North America have laws that prohibit drivers from directly talking on their mobile phone (by either holding it to the ear or using the built-in speaker). In these cases, having a good understanding of Bluetooth hands-free options and whatever other Bluetooth features might be included in an aftermarket solution, such as audio streaming, will help a Mobile Product Specialist provide customers with both compliance and added conveniences.

Bluetooth Radio Frequency Spectrum and Coverage Range

All Bluetooth communication takes place on the 2.4GHz spectrum and is meant for wireless communication with nearby, compatible devices. There are three different classes of chipsets in Bluetooth products:

- **Class 1** – These devices use the most power and have the longest range at around 100 meters (328 Feet). Devices that use these types of chips are laptop computers, home audio receivers and some Bluetooth speakers. Some devices have a hybrid Class 1/Class 2 chip that will use Class 1 when plugged in with adequate power but will revert to Class 2 when on battery power.
- **Class 2** – These devices use a medium amount of power and offer range of slightly over 10 meters (33 Feet). Most cellular phones, smaller Bluetooth speakers, headsets and keyboards use Class 2.
- **Class 3** – These devices use the least amount of power and are meant to have an effective range of less than 10 meters (up to 33 Feet). These can include personal accessories like smart watches and personal care products. Capable of operating for months or even years on a single charge or battery, these devices commonly use the Bluetooth Low Energy (BTLE) profile designation.

BT Profiles

There are several types of Bluetooth profiles, and occasionally some are added to accommodate advances in technology or new product designs. Here are the common profiles and what they mean:

- **A2DP (Advanced Audio Distribution Profile)** – This is a two-channel bi-direction capable stream of audio from one device to another. It can support many types of audio codecs, including aptX and SBC.
- **AVRCP (Audio/Video Remote Control Profile)** – This allows remote control of a device (play, pause, track up/down, etc.).
- **HSP (Headset Profile)** – This allows for audio to be played to a device such as a headset for simple call and volume control ability. Some head units may use this profile for minimal Bluetooth connectivity to simply place or end a call and adjust volume. Other features associated with the phone's status and contacts access are absent in this profile.
- **HFP (Hands-Free Profile)** – This is similar to HSP but has a more robust control set with additional features like last number redial and reporting the battery and signal level to a device. This profile is present on a head unit if the battery level of the phone or its cellular signal strength is visible on the display. It also features wideband voice and compatibility with several popular codecs.
- **MAP (Message Access Profile)** – This allows for the exchange of messages between two devices and is used for voice-to-text capability in vehicle applications.

Margin Notes

- **PBAP or PBA (Phone Book Access Profile)** – This allows a device to share contacts with another device and resides in head units where the user can see a contact and initiate a call by selecting the contact, or on a head unit that shows the caller ID on the display when it rings.
- **SPP (Serial Port Profile)** – Allows the wireless connection of two Bluetooth devices.
- **SIM (SIM Access Profile)** – Allows a head unit or other device to use the SIM card in a phone so all charges and usage are attributed to the SIM card, rather than having a separate one for the vehicle or installed device.

BLUETOOTH HANDS-FREE (HF)

Stand-Alone Bluetooth Hands-Free Kits

While most new cars have at least the option for Bluetooth hands-free calling, older cars may not have this capability. Car kits, such as devices from companies like Parrot, can be installed in the vehicle with a microphone and a control panel, as well as either RF or direct-wire audio integration to an existing factory audio system. Prices for these devices vary, but a higher price typically means better hardware in terms of reliability and usability.

Bluetooth Hands-Free Calling Built Into Head Unit

Many new vehicles have Bluetooth hands-free capability contained within the factory head unit. Most aftermarket head units not only have hands-free calling, but other upgraded Bluetooth functionality (such as A2DP audio streaming) at reasonable costs. Replacing a factory head unit that does not have Bluetooth hands-free capability with an aftermarket head until that does is one of the most common reasons for an upgrade.

Bluetooth Hands-Free Integration Add-Ons

Many aftermarket companies offer modules that can either plug directly into the factory head unit to add Bluetooth hands-free functionality, or that add it via a control box and a wireless FM transmitter signal to the head unit. While a little more cumbersome to use, they are a viable option for someone who cannot replace the factory head unit in their vehicle. When properly installed, these offer good call quality, similar to a Bluetooth headset, and some flexibility on both installation and price.

SAFETY CAMERAS AND SENSORS

Rear View Camera Systems

A Rear View Camera system (also called a "backup camera" or "reverse camera") allows the driver of a vehicle to view, in real-time, the area directly behind the vehicle's rear bumper for the purpose of safely maneuvering in tight spaces and avoiding a collision with people or property. The system consists of the camera and some method to view the image, either on a dedicated screen or one already installed in the vehicle.

The design of the backup camera itself is different from other cameras **as the image** is horizontally flipped so that the output is presented as a mirror image. Using a mirrored image makes the orientation of the display consistent with the physical mirrors installed on the vehicle. Since there are also non-mirror image cameras available for "front view" applications, be sure to identify one for use in a rear view application as a mirror image camera. Some cameras have the ability to provide a standard or reverse image, and some LCD monitors allow a standard camera to flip the image to be displayed as a reverse camera, but you can't always count on that. It's best to choose the right camera for the application.

Most early and many high-end rear view cameras were Charged Coupling Devices (more commonly called **CCD Cameras**). These types of cameras convert the available light picked up by the sensor directly on the attached chip, which provides very little possible noise ("grain" effect) and a higher quality image.

Most modern rear view cameras use Complimentary Metal Oxide Semiconductor technology (known as **CMOS Cameras**). This style of camera uses a transistor for each pixel which utilizes a more common manufacturing process for making microchips. Since this manufacturing practice is more common, the cost of the sensors and camera is lower. Although the lower cost makes these attractive for a variety of consumers, the image quality is often lower than CCD cameras, and there is a higher potential for noise ("grain" effect).

The backup camera typically has a wide-angle or fisheye lens (about 120 degrees of viewing area). This type of lens spoils the camera's ability to see objects far away but it allows the camera to see an uninterrupted horizontal path from one side of the vehicle to the other. The camera is typically pointed on a downward angle to view potential obstacles on the ground as well as the position of approaching walls and obstacles, rather than straight back.

Resolution is a key specification that should be considered when choosing a camera. The higher the resolution, the more detail, which can aid the driver backing up into a low-light area or a garage where there are numerous items in the background. Higher resolution means a clearer picture, and this will ultimately be more pleasing to the consumer who sees the image every time they put the vehicle in reverse. Find a balance between the cost of the camera and an acceptable quality for the image presented.

Many cameras apply lines on the image it produces to help guide the user while parking. Some of these cameras provide a wire to cut or some way to defeat this feature to utilize a grid-line system on the screen for which it is being displayed. This is advised when some adjustment is needed of the lines to match the width of the vehicle or the depth of field for the grid in relation to the vehicle.

Some cameras have infrared (IR) illumination that comes on as the camera is powered to help brighten a low-light parking space. This is especially useful in parking garages, when parking at night, backing up to loading docks and for garages and other tight spaces. Cameras with a low-lux rating are superior, especially when paired with IR illumination capabilities in these situations.

Margin Notes

A camera with a one lux rating can produce an image of the object by the light of a candle three feet away from it. Cameras with .75, .5, or even 0 lux ratings are becoming more common.

Margin Notes

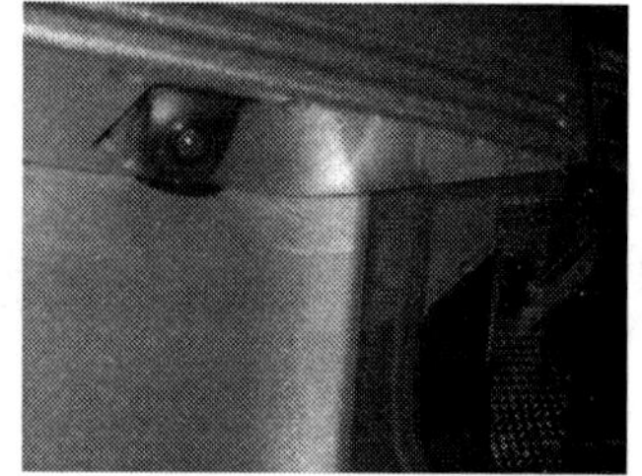

Camera Styles

In many applications, the camera is only activated when the vehicle is placed in reverse. The system detects reverse gear when 12 volts is applied to the reverse light or another signal at a control module that controls power train operation in the vehicle. The simplest designs have a camera with two wires that connect to the two wires at the reverse light on the vehicle and then transmit the video signal wirelessly to the screen. More complicated systems require running dedicated wires to the rear of the vehicle to control the unit and feed a video signal back to the front.

Rear view safety camera systems require a viewing screen to allow the driver to see the video signal from the camera, regardless of how elaborate or simple the system is. This can be applied to existing LCD screens in some vehicles by using an aftermarket integration device or a signal can be fed to a new screen that is installed in the vehicle. These screens can range from dedicated units that are included with the system that snap over, mount onto or replace the rear view mirror, to aftermarket head units with LCD screens that have a video input from external devices, or small screens that mount to the dashboard independently.

When choosing a rear view camera, remember that, on average, vehicles have a blind zone behind them that measures approximately seven to eight feet wide and 10 to 20 feet long. An area of that dimension is certainly not a just blind "spot," so blind zone is a more accurate description. To properly view the **blind zone**, make sure the camera has a wide enough viewing angle to cover the blind zone area.

For surface-mounted cameras, find a sheltered location, such as near the license plate light. This keeps the camera lens cleaner by sheltering it from the elements. Surface-mount cameras generally come with a small mounting bracket and can be easily attached with a couple of stainless steel screws. For flush-mount cameras, shelter is less of a concern, but it should be positioned where there is a good view of the blind zone. Also consider a license plate frame camera that allows installation of a rear view camera without any permanent vehicle modifications. Factory-fit cameras are available from multiple aftermarket companies and may replace a trim panel, third brake light housing or other removable feature to allow the installation. The cameras in these units may even mimic the factory camera mounting position on higher trim level vehicles. In most cases, these provide the best result as they benefit from any cover, the viewing location and the perspective as originally designed by the vehicle manufacturer.

Care should be taken on vehicles where the camera cannot be placed in the center of the vehicle, as this will affect how the image is interpreted on the screen and how the image should be utilized when backing up the vehicle. Find a centered mounting position and adjust the image and any associated grid lines to accommodate for the off center location. Be sure to educate the consumer on viewing it and accommodating for it appropriately.

Margin Notes

A 360-degree camera system (also called "bird's eye view") uses a combination of cameras placed around the vehicle and a processing unit that can combine or "stitch" the image together for display as a panoramic or overhead view of the vehicle. These systems are labor intensive as they typically require installing at least four cameras, a control module (the processing unit) and a display screen (which could also be on the OEM or aftermarket head unit in the vehicle). Most of these systems also require calibration as a last step in the installation to properly set the system up for use.

Reverse Sensor Systems
These systems are different than rear view camera systems as there is no real-time video signal to be displayed for the driver. The driver navigates using the standard mirrors and methods, and feedback about the distance between the vehicle and any obstruction behind the vehicle is relayed via beeping tones or a small display with lighting cues. These displays and sound modules can be mounted near the driver on the dashboard or the rear view mirror.

The most common technology used in these systems is Echolocation or Sonar. This is the same type of technology naval submarines utilize to avoid collisions underwater but at much lower power and with a much simpler interface. Small ultrasonic sound waves are pulsed out from the sensors when the system is on, and the echoes that are bounced off obstacles behind the vehicle are received by the sensors which allow the system to calculate the distance and alert the driver to an impending collision.

Very intuitive for the driver, the audible alert is generally a series of beeps that get faster or louder as the object is closer and then remain steady at a close distance. Some factory and aftermarket systems provide a screen with visual indicators that

Margin Notes

may show distance or bars (like signal strength, only designating distance). There are even some systems that overlay a visual indicator on to a rear view camera screen and may even combine a beeping warning system as well.

Many newer cars now have the systems on the front of the vehicle as well. Applying this technology to both the front and rear of the vehicle gives the driver confidence in parallel parking and other close-quarters maneuvering. You'll often see that the audible beeps come out of the speaker corresponding to that corner of the car near the obstacle. This is another reason to consider integration with existing audio systems if upgrading the sound instead of removing important factory components and losing that functionality.

Several aftermarket companies offer front parking sensors, also called approach sensors, that operate differently than reverse parking sensors. For instance, reverse parking sensors only come on when the vehicle is in reverse. Approach sensors, on the other hand, are always active and will only provide warning if the vehicle is under a certain speed, if the vehicle is within a certain distance of an object, or a combination of both.

FRONT VIEW CAMERA SYSTEMS

Front facing cameras can be used for a variety of reasons, such as determining the distance to the vehicle in front of you with a visual confirmation during parallel parking, pulling into a garage or parking space or even as an approach angle camera on off road vehicles.

These need to provide only a standard image but may be more advanced with water resistance or waterproofing for protection during driving. These cameras may also trade a wide viewing angle for a more distant view for certain purposes. Be sure to select cameras designed for this purpose so the resulting image is what is expected.

Infrared Cameras

Although not a common occurrence, some customers are interested in cameras that show a front view of the road ahead for a totally different reason than they'd want back up cameras. They may want to enhance their visibility of the road and any potential hazards when driving at night with a high-technology "night vision" camera system.

So, what kind of technology can enhance the view of the road at night or in inclement weather? It's called **Forward Looking Infrared Radar (FLIR)**, and it's the same technology used by the US military. FLIR has been an integral part of defense and commercial applications since the 1960s. "Thermal" or "infrared" imaging enables the viewer to see light in the infrared (IR) portion of the spectrum. Infrared means "below red," as infrared light has less energy than red light. Light energy is typically described in terms of wavelength, and as the energy of light decreases, its wavelength gets longer. Infrared light, having less energy than visible light, has a correspondingly longer wavelength.

Infrared light is invisible to the unaided eye but can be felt as heat on your skin. Warm objects emit infrared light. This IR glow enables you to see an animal or a person in a deep forest in total darkness. Infrared light can penetrate smoke and fog better than visible light, revealing objects that are normally obscured. Infrared camera technology has advanced features that enable the use of IR cameras in many applications like a passenger cars or RVs.

Margin Notes

Dash/DVR Cameras

Dash cameras, or 'dash cams,' and DVR technology provides a wide variety of customer solutions to an aftermarket retailer. Dash cams provide a sense of security for rideshare drivers who may need a record of an accident, as a deterrent to poor behavior by riders inside the vehicle, and many other instances.

DVR systems will record video, and some will record events for use on company driver monitoring or for review should a traffic accident occur. These DVRs may be part of a windshield mounted dash cam, as part of an aftermarket head unit, or as part of a rear view mirror. Some use microSD, SD or other memory cards. Others may need to be removed from the vehicle and plugged into a computer to review video.
Be sure to understand whether the video files are readily viewable from the memory card or device, or if a proprietary viewer software is required for process or export. It may also be important to the driver (or the company) that the unit or its memory card cannot easily be removed to prevent manipulation of stored files. Try to understand all aspects of how the system will be used and monitored by the purchaser so the correct solution can be sold.

Some advanced dash cams provide connectivity to a smartphone or via cellular data connection to expedite image and video data export, but may also provide real-time viewing.

INTELLIGENT WARNING AND DETECTION SYSTEMS

Driver safety is a rapidly growing portion of OEM vehicle design, and aftermarket companies are finding new ways to heighten awareness and inhibit inattentiveness behind the wheel via add-on or supplementary devices that can be installed in most vehicles. These technologies, more commonly referred to as Advanced Driver Assistance Systems (ADAS), are designed to enhance driver awareness around the vehicle and increase safety while driving. When designed with a safe and intuitive interface, they should effectively increase safety behind the wheel overall road safety.

Mobile Product Specialists should understand how to identify vehicles with OEM ADAS-based warning and detection systems and be able to explain to customers how aftermarket products offer similar features for those wishing to add those new car features to their existing vehicle. Once customers see that these advanced warning and detection systems can be added to their vehicles, many become interested in those options to create a safer driving situation. Whether for commuters in day-to-day traffic, teen or elderly drivers, those driving in neighborhoods with a lot of pedestrian traffic or as a method of reducing auto

Margin Notes

insurance costs, aftermarket warning and detection systems for safer driving are in a significantly growing category.

The best way to show these features to customers is an in-vehicle demonstration while driving. In-store videos and sales kiosks also help convey the range of safety features in these systems.

Lane Departure Warning Systems

In early 2000, automotive OEMs began offering lane departure warning systems on select vehicles. The aftermarket soon followed. Now there are many options available to the consumer in both OEM and aftermarket. By keeping drivers aware of their position in the lane, many accidents caused by inattentiveness or fatigue can be avoided.

The two types of lane departure warning systems are:

- Driver Warning (also called "LDW" or "Lane Monitoring")
- Driver Warning with Corrective Action (also called "Lane Keeping")

Because of the inherent complexity and possible liabilities managing lane keeping control of the car with corrective steering, braking, etc., normal functionality of an OEM lane departure warning (LDW) system goes beyond what the aftermarket can safely do. Sophisticated counter steering torque or a tactile shake of the steering wheel is often necessary in an OEM Lane Keeping system to keep the driver from 'jerking' the wheel in cars that self-correct the lane position.

Regardless of the system, most OEM lane departure technology uses sophisticated optical and/or high frequency sensors to detect the position of the vehicle within the lane. Optical sensors (also called video sensors) are commonly located high up on the dash with broad forward and front side coverage. They may also be integrated into the vehicle's rear view mirror. Laser and infrared high frequency sensors mount on the front of the vehicle and use distance-based calculation to help determine if the car has moved out of the lane.

The sensors all rely on road markings (such as painted lines or reflectors) to identify when it will (or has) departed the lane. Inclement weather (such as severe rain or snow covered roads) can hinder the sensor operation in some systems. Also, older roads with faded or no markings may hamper the effectiveness of some lane departure warning systems.

Like OEM systems, aftermarket lane departure warning products also use optics (video sensors) and sophisticated processing to provide audible and visual alerts to allow the driver time to react. In some aftermarket products, the analysis may be an earlier warning because the driver still requires two to three seconds to react to avoid the lane departure and other forward obstacles. Many aftermarket suppliers of lane departure warning products also have a companion smartphone app to provide supplemental visual and audible warnings that may also negate the need to install a separate warning screen.

Margin Notes

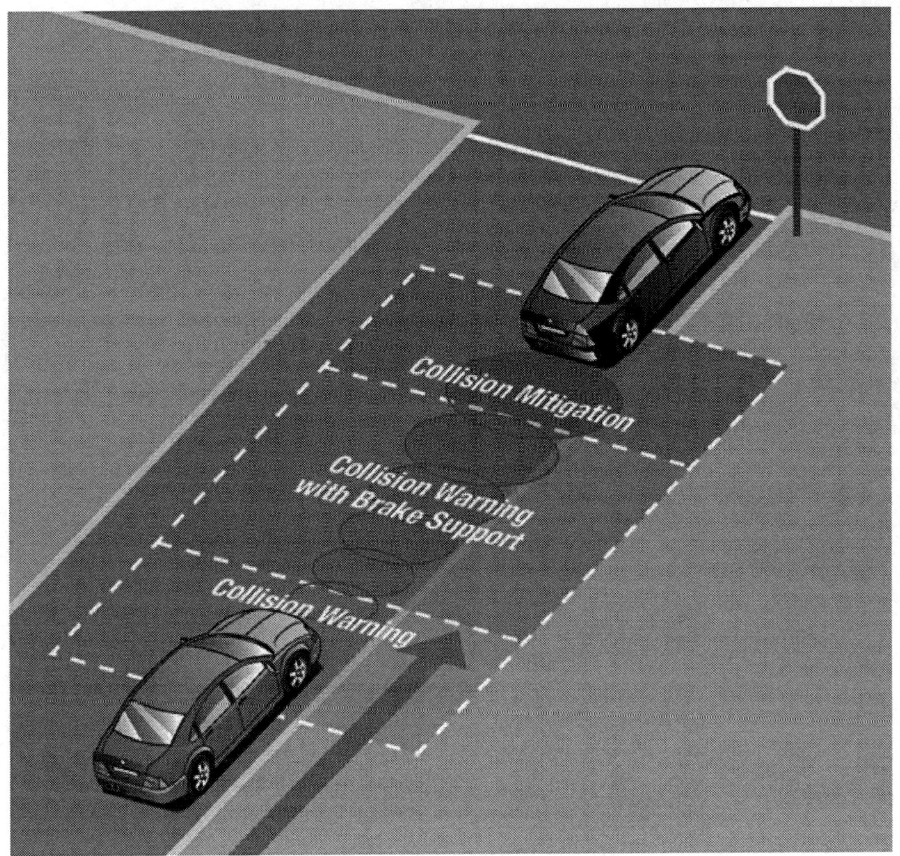

Forward Collision or Crash Avoidance Warning Systems

The ability of a safety system to gather data and predictively warn of a potential crash is somewhat more sophisticated than lane departure because the sensors must recognize pedestrians, other cars (or motorcycles), and any other non-lane obstacles in the road. This means the most sophisticated Forward Collision Warning (FCW) or "Crash Avoidance" systems use a combination of cameras, advanced algorithms and possible other sensors to accomplish the various monitoring.

Similar to the limitations of integrating an aftermarket Lane Departure Warning system, an OEM FCW system often has control and influence over many systems in the vehicle. All this is intended to reduce the likelihood of a collision and limit passenger injury with features like pre-tensioning of seat belts, automatic sunroof or window closure and adjustment of seats or head restraints.

Some OEM FCW and Lane Keeping systems also implement adaptive cruise control to detect hazards in front of the car when the cruise control is engaged. Although they may be marketed more as a convenience aspect, the adaptation of the cruise control to automatically slow the vehicle down or maintain a safe traffic gap can also be a safety benefit.

Because these highly integrated systems in an OEM application are all working at split second timing, installation of aftermarket FCW systems is often limited to

Margin Notes

audible and visual displays. With robust audible and visual warnings, aftermarket FCW systems can easily provide enough warning to limit the probability of forward collisions and may qualify for discounted insurance rates, which is why many taxi cabs and fleet vehicles are ideal clientele for FCW (and Lane Departure) systems.

Safety-Based DVR Technology

Some aftermarket LDW and FCW systems also incorporate safety-based Digital Video Recorders (DVRs) to record activity in the event of a crash or situation of potential liability. This feature provides added peace of mind for drivers and stakeholders (such as parents of teens, caregivers of independent elderly drivers and employers who have many employees on the road in company vehicles).

DVR capability may also be implemented in stand-alone DVR devices and aftermarket rear view mirrors. Typical configurations of safety-based DVR device are on-board storage that captures video in real time storing the last several seconds of video while erasing previously stored video. The stored video can be downloaded to a computer for viewing, typically via USB or memory card (such as SD, microSD, etc.). Some DVR based systems will save an "event," such as an impact that triggers an inertia sensor, which may store video for some time before and also some time after the event is detected. These devices typically save these events as a separate file and will not be overwritten as the recording continues, allowing for review of the event and possible use of the video footage to support an insurance claim or defense.

Blind Spot Detection Systems

Whereas lane departure and crash avoidance systems focus on monitoring the front of the vehicle, a Blind Spot Detection system (also called "Blind Spot Warning") typically uses sensors to monitor the sides of the vehicle for approaching vehicles

Margin Notes

that may be in the driver's blind spot. The high frequency ultrasonic sensors themselves are typically installed in the lower rear side panel or rear bumper cover (for two sensors) and in the lower front bumper corners (for four sensor systems).

Some aftermarket Blind Spot Detection systems use cameras on either side of the vehicle, typically positioned on the underside of the rear view side mirrors.

The alert to the driver is often a visual indicator in the side view mirror where another vehicle has entered the blind spot. Indicators may also be in the A-pillar, sail panel at the top of the door or instrument panel cluster.

Additional warnings typically alert the driver when they've put on their turn signal to indicate a lane change. Audible warnings will alert the driver of the obstacle in their blind spot. A feature of OEM blind spot detection systems that may not be available on some aftermarket systems is the ability to change the warning timing (or deactivate it) with low vehicle speed. Typically, if an aftermarket system is able to ignore blind spot warnings at a given speed, it will incorporate some kind of GPS reception to allow the system to understand relative vehicle speed.

ADDITIONAL IMPORTANT PRODUCT CATEGORIES

Included in this section is information about many additional and important product categories that offer retailers added opportunities for new customers. New customer opportunities may not be traditional audio, rear seat entertainment or security/remote starter customers. Rather, they may express needs or interest in one or more of the categories in this section. The information in this section is not testable on the MECP Mobile Product Specialist exam due to state (or provincial) regulatory variances but is presented for knowledge of the categories and as study material for other category-specific exams or credentials.

RADAR/LASER SPEED DETECTION DEFENSE SYSTEMS

Radar and Laser Detectors

This content covers the finer points of radar and laser detectors used in vehicles to alert the driver of law enforcement's speed detection device use. **This section about radar and laser detectors is not tested on the Mobile Product Specialist exam** because of regional limitations in some US states and Canadian provinces, but it is intended to be informational to help Mobile Product Specialists understand and utilize the category to enhance the sales and installation opportunities.

This section presents realistic expectations regarding various aftermarket speed detection devices and what types best suit customer driving styles and geographic location.

Topic covered in this section:

- Radar speed detection technology and how it operates.
- Laser speed detection technology and how it operates.

Margin Notes

- What are the terms "POP" and "LIDAR."
- Aftermarket devices to detect these technologies.
- Realistic expectations of the detection devices.

What is Radar?

Most people know the term "radar" as what police use to catch speeders while they are hiding in the trees or just over the peak of a hill. In fact, radar is a tried-and-true technology used in a variety of applications to determine both distance and speed. Radar technology is used in everything from automotive to aircraft to marine applications and has been available to law enforcement since the 1950s. The official term radar comes from "RAdio Detection And Ranging."

How Radar Works

A radar speed detection device used by law enforcement sends out high frequency waves and measures the reflection back from the vehicle in a specified time to determine vehicle speed. The reflection of the frequency is called "Doppler shift." These radar signals operate in various ranges called "bands." Common radar bands used are X, K, and Ka.

- **X Band** – 10.5 to 10.55 GHz
- **K Band** – 24.05 to 24.24 GHz
- **Ka Band** -34.2 to 35.2 GHz (covers Ka, Ka Wide-Band, and Ka Super Wide-Band)

Disregard bands like S Band (now obsolete) and Ku Band (used only in Europe for this application).

POP Radar Mode

Police radar has a fast on/off feature known as "POP mode" speed detection. In POP mode, the police radar emits only a short burst of energy and quickly estimates the vehicle's speed. The radar then goes immediately into standby. The POP mode police radar will be effectively off even though it still displays the obtained speed for a couple of seconds. The entire measurement happens so quickly that older in-vehicle radar detectors often miss the radar signal to alert the driver because the POP mode burst lasts only between 67 milliseconds or as little as 16 milliseconds. Most modern radar detectors feature POP detection modes.

POP mode radar only obtains an estimate of a vehicle's speed, so it is not 100 percent accurate. Most law enforcement must still switch to normal mode to obtain the exact speed, which can take 2-3 seconds. Generally, law enforcement will require another form of speed verification in order to write a citation. Many radar detector manufacturers believe that the POP radar mode is not utilized as often as people may think.

Laser (LIDAR) Speed Detection

Besides radar, there are other technologies of speed detection employed by law enforcement agencies utilizing laser light detection. This assists law enforcement

Margin Notes

in documenting speeders and writing more accurate speeding tickets. This is often called simply "laser detection" but is also called LIDAR ("LIght Detection and Ranging"). Essentially as far as the technology of speed detection Laser and LIDAR mean the same thing.

- **Laser** – 904 nanometer, 33MHz bandwidth

When law enforcement uses laser speed detection, the officer has already made a predetermination of the offending vehicle. They aim the laser toward vehicle much like a sniper with a rifle and scope. The laser is a highly focused beam that makes detection very difficult at close range. Since the laser speed detection devices can be utilized at a considerable distance from a hidden location and many feature a "stealth mode," which makes the accuracy of detection even harder, LIDAR can be the toughest speed detection method to accurately detect.

Laser speed detection devices have some drawbacks for the officer who uses it. It can't be used while in motion and must be operated from a parked car (or motorcycle). It also does not do well when behind glass, so it's less likely to see laser used in places with frequent inclement weather. Lasers are also less accurate (and therefore less likely to be used) on steep incline or declines. Furthermore, the accuracy of aiming the laser requires a fixed mount or a very steady hand from the officer pointing it.

Differences between Radar and Laser

The easiest way to characterize the difference between radar and laser is:

- Radar operates using radio frequency waves which are very high, inaudible frequencies. These frequencies move at **the speed of sound** – 1130 feet/second or 334 meters/second.
- Laser operates using multiple paths of infrared light. These paths of light move at **the speed of light** – 186,000 miles/second or approximately 300,000 kilometers/second.

Each system has a range of coverage and when an object passes through the path of the radio waves or light paths, the speed at which the energy is reflected back to the speed detection device can establish the object's speed with relative accuracy by determining both range and velocity. **The main difference is the speed at which they are reflected**. Radar is processed at the speed of sound whereas laser is processed at the much faster speed of light. Since radar performs under a wider variety of weather conditions and locations than laser, both are used in law enforcement.

If these systems are not against the law to have in a US state or Canadian province, they provide a reasonable and practical method of helping to reduce incidents caused by speeding.

Margin Notes

For reference, regional legalities as of 2018 according to AAA:

- US States:
  - o VA and Washington, DC prohibit radar detectors of any kind in passenger cars. Radar detectors are also illegal on all U.S. military bases.
  - o CA, UT, CO, TX, OK, MN, IL, TN and SC prohibit only radar or laser shifters in passenger cars, but detectors are okay.
  - o All US states prohibit radar detectors use in commercial vehicles.
- Canadian Provinces:
  - o Manitoba, Ontario, Quebec, New Brunswick, Nova Scotia, Prince Edward Island, Newfoundland, and all northern territories prohibit radar detectors of any kind in all vehicles, passenger or commercial.
  - o British Columbia, and Alberta ALLOW use and ownership of radar detectors
  - o Saskatchewan ALLOWS use and ownership of radar detectors ONLY in passenger vehicles. Commercial vehicles are prohibited to use radar detectors in Saskatchewan.

The Hardware of Radar Detectors

There are two hardware formats of radar detectors: dash-mounted and remote-mounted. This hardware section describes only the physical attributes. Operational features (of both types) are covered in a subsequent part of this overall topic.

Dash-Mounted Radar Detectors

These are self-contained units that are intended to face out the vehicle's front window to send and receive radar (and, if equipped, laser) detection signals. These typically appeal to Do-it-Yourself (DIY) customers because the units come with easy-to-use brackets and a cigarette lighter power plug to facilitate installation. Some companies call these "plug and play" detectors to signal the ability for self-installation to the consumer. Dash-Mounted detectors should not be confused with Windshield-Mounted devices. In states such as California and Minnesota, it is illegal to mount anything on the windshield of a vehicle as it may obstruct the driver's vision.

Remote-Mounted Radar Detectors

Very high-end radar detectors called "remote-mounted" or "custom install" are configured in multiple pieces and are very different (and profitable) compared to dash-mounted radar detectors. The major consideration for customers is these require professional installation and are not suitable for a DIY person. Some companies call these "installed" detectors to signal the need for installation to the consumer right off the bat.

- Remotely mounted sensors require expert placement in the front and rear bumpers (or that general area) by skilled installation technicians. The sensors are separate for radar and laser detection and require placement in both front and rear (total of four sensors, laser and radar for the front, then a second set for the rear).

- Inside the vehicle, there is a display and/or control panel installed somewhere in the dash or other location where creativity of the custom installation is really limited only to the consumer's imagination and technician's abilities.

- Some remote-mounted systems integrate wireless Bluetooth communication with their app which runs on your smartphone. System changes and alert data can then be interacted with via the smartphone instead of the detector's control panel.

- Depending on the brand and model of remote-mounted radar detector, interface companies may manufacture even more creative ways to display radar detector data – such as readout in the instrument panel cluster where other messages normally appear or with the display built into a rear view mirror.

Remote-mounted radar detectors and the associated installation cost thousands of dollars because of the disassembly of the vehicle's front and rear body panels. It's a lot of labor and requires skilled, carefully completed work. As a result, remote-mounted detector systems are generally found only in very high dollar or enthusiast vehicles where insurance cost is high, so speeding tickets and increased insurance rates are part of the reason why these systems are attractive to potential clientele.

Remote-mounted radar detector systems offer a more hidden installation. It's important for your customers to know that those kinds of installations, while stealthy, don't necessarily offer a significant degree of coverage or accuracy over the dash-mounted units with the same feature sets.

The clear benefits of remote-mounted systems are:

- Eliminating theft concerns.
- Discrete installation (out of sight).
- No obstructions on the windshield.
- No performance concerns of projecting through window tint.
- Ability to add laser shifters (if not already included).

Adding Laser Shifters

Remote-mounted radar/laser detector systems can have add-on features to increase their effectiveness and these features are not available in dash-mounted radar detectors. Remote-mount systems which incorporate laser shifters or laser jammers do offer a significant advantage over only having laser detectors installed. Laser shifters/jammers are at least intended to be installed in the front of the vehicle but can be added to the rear by adding additional sensors. Some complete remote-mounted systems may come with everything, meaning radar/laser detection and laser shifters/jammers. Laser shifters may also be called laser transceivers or diffusers by some manufacturers. In fact, any of those terms except "jammer" is best used for customer presentations. Here's why:

- The terms "laser shifting" or "laser diffusing" are easily misunderstood. These features do not "jam" a law enforcement's laser speed detection device using a radio frequency (how real radar jammers, which are illegal, operate). Instead, an effective laser shifter or diffuser detects the law enforcement's laser signal and light pulse rate, then responds by transmitting a similar light pulse at the same rate.

Margin Notes

Margin Notes

It should be noted that all laser detection used by law enforcement may not be detectable. In addition, laser shifters and jammers are illegal in several U.S. states and the District of Columbia. Always be aware of the local and state (or provincial) laws regarding laser shifters/diffusers so you may accurately present customers with a speed detection system that's legal where they drive.

The installation of these laser shifters/diffusers on par with the other components in a remote-mounted system, so installation at the time of bumper/fascia removal may be advantageous to a customer, cost-wise. Read more about the installation considerations of these in Chapter 4.

Radar Detector Features and Functionality

A fair statement is to say that radar detectors are only as effective as their ability to detect. If the radar detector is positioned in the vehicle so that its coverage path faces forward, and the model only provides front coverage, then it's fair to assume that particular radar detector will not protect from behind the vehicle with speed detection devices. If your customer expects rear coverage as well, ensure the model they are considering has that feature.

What about false alerts? There are radar detectors that seem to falsely trigger around grocery stores and other retail stores with radar controlled entry doors (usually in the X band), it means that overly sensitive coverage can bring the occasional false alert along with validated radar detection warnings.

Most false warnings are due to radar rather than laser. It is unusual to get false laser warnings. Some vehicle electronics and other portable electronics contain RF interference that may cause a false laser alert when certain devices are used. Although rare, using the horn, windshield wipers or accelerating, can generate RF interference in some vehicles that will trigger a false laser alert. New generation mobile phones, vehicles with laser adaptive cruise control and equipment at some major airports can also cause false laser alerts.

Generally, false alerts are 95% in the radar bands and most of those are X band alerts. X band is used less and less (as the newer speed detection equipment is mostly K or Ka band), but US states of Ohio, Indiana, North Carolina and New Jersey still utilize X band equipment.

With false alerts, drivers often become conditioned to ignore the first few "beeps" or warning signals until they become more constant or the visual indicator of signal strength becomes greater and then they slow down. Based on this behavior, what is important in selecting a radar detector for an individual is getting them to understand what features best benefit their driving style and how quickly they heed the warnings.

Some models include GPS chipsets that store fixed location false alerts such as door openers and security systems. The higher-end detectors will automatically learn and store these false alerts as you drive with no input from the driver.

Margin Notes

Another source of false alerts is modern vehicles with collision avoidance systems, lane departure warning or other radar-based vehicle safety systems. These systems often use radar signals to know the proximity of other vehicles, which a radar detector can confuse with police radar causing a false alert. The higher end detectors will better be able to distinguish these signals and reject them with no alert. The best detectors will add the capability to update these filters through an onboard USB port.

With different radar detectors, there are various indicators that can tell the driver that there is a speed detection device in range. Some radar detectors with greater feature sets will show the driver whether it's coming from the front or the rear of the car, the signal strength of the radar signal itself and some even differentiate between various radar bands or even laser detection.

Main Features

Most radar detectors cover the three radar bands (X, K, Ka) and some also cover laser detection as well. The coverage is perhaps one of the first things that will stand out between one device and another. Besides that, the method by which the warnings are delivered is standard to be audible with some visual indicator as well. The device could have a small display with alpha-numeric capabilities or simply just a series of lights that indicate what type of speed detection signal and how far it is away. Detectors with front and rear detection may use lighted arrows or separate indicators that point towards the direction of the detected radar signal.

Power cords and basic mounting hardware are also included. Beyond that, the individual features of the units begin to become more specific to the needs of the user.

Other Features

Many radar detectors have special or specific features that will help further differentiate the choices that appeal to the needs of a given customer.

- **Safety Warning System** – This feature allows the radar detector to make a unique audible warning when safety related issues are present such as hazardous road conditions, highway construction, accidents, railroad crossings, etc. The SWS messages operate on K band radar so a detector without this feature may just show a normal K band alert instead of identifying it as an SWS message.

- **Emergency Vehicle Warning** – This feature allows the radar detector to make a unique audible or visual warning when emergency vehicles (fire, medical, etc.) are approaching.

- **City/Auto/Highway Modes** – Generally this feature reduces the sensitivity of the X band mode where most "false alerts" occur. City mode would make X band less sensitive whereas Highway mode would allow more sensitivity. Auto is a balance between City and Highway automatically changing sensitivity based on certain factors such as vehicle speed.

Margin Notes

- **Voice Alerts** – Many radar detectors offer the option of spoken warnings rather than audible beeps and buzzers. Higher end models incorporate multiple spoken languages.

- **Automated Volume** – While most radar detectors have a volume adjustment, some offer an environment compensated volume based on the ambient noise in the vehicle. This is useful then the audio system is playing loudly and the unit displays a warning.

- **Bluetooth integration/app compatibility** – Some radar detectors incorporate Bluetooth to interface the radar detector with their app on a compatible smartphone. The app offers the ability to change detector settings while others add crowd-sourced alerts and speed limit data to be displayed and interacted with directly through the detector.

- **GPS or Accelerometer Logic** – Some premium radar detectors can mute or disable audible warnings during the time when the vehicle is not moving or moving below a selected speed. This can be done with a GPS receiver chip or with an accelerometer.

- **GPS-based False Signal Rejection** – Some premium models offer the ability to have a physical location identified when a false warning occurs so that the user teaches the unit once and (based on GPS location) thereafter the signals it picks up are ignored. This is great when X and K band provide false alerts around radar (proximity) operated entry doors in many retail stores or near airports. Higher end radar detectors will automatically learn, store and ignore these false alerts as the vehicle is driven with no input required from the driver.

Other Influential Factors to Consider

Excessive speed is both unsafe and impractical for accurate and repeatable detection. By the time someone is speeding excessively, traffic cameras and/or aircraft traffic monitoring is likely to have identified the offender anyway. The key is prevention of excessive speed in the first place and then understanding the capability of the device.

Beyond those precautions, accuracy in placement of the detection device is critical depending on how the device is intended to be installed. Please review the installation considerations of radar and laser detectors in Chapter 4 for more details on installation-related information.

Once again, radar detectors are not legal for use in passenger vehicles in the US state of Virginia or in Washington, DC. Furthermore, commercial vehicles in the US (exceeding 10,000 pounds GVWR) are not permitted to use of radar detectors of any kind. Much of Canada (except BC, AB and SK) also prohibits use of radar detectors.

Margin Notes

Helping Customers Choose

By now it's clear that all radar detectors are not created equally, and certain features will clearly appeal to drivers based on the frequency of regular routes they drive as well as the type of speed detection equipment used in their area.

The General Questions

In general, customers should be asked the following questions to help determine what radar detector device/features best fit their needs and preferences:

- **Do you prefer the warnings to be noises, lights, spoken words or alpha readout?** While most detectors do more than one, make sure the customer's preference is addressed. A volume control or smart volume features often help the effectiveness of any audible warnings and can promote a safer driving experience because it won't startle the driver.

- **Does the customer prefer the device be removable, or will it be staying in that car most of the time?** This indicates whether a hard wired custom installation for the power connections may be in order. If it's removed all the time, the power cord for the cigarette lighter will suffice, but if it's staying put, who wants all that unnecessary wiring hanging all over the dash? Any time the customer parks their car in an unknown area, they should unplug the unit and lock it in the glove box or console or take it with them. This is also a helpful question to address customers who want to use their dash-mount radar detector in more than one vehicle.

- **Where is most of the customer's driving done?** This qualifier helps determine if the customer is prone to X and K band false alerts in city driving. If so, a radar detector that has GPS based false alert rejection and City/Auto/Highway modes or some other abatement of X and K band false alerts will help them appreciate their purchase more. Highway driving will necessitate a radar/laser detector to cover the law enforcement that sits on (or behind) freeway overpasses waiting to catch speeders. In US states where legal, adding laser shifting/jamming can add additional peace of mind. Some freeway speed cameras also use laser to trigger the camera, so adding the possibility of warning only helps.

More Specific Questions

Some of these sales points will help indicate which features will mean the most to a customer.

- Obviously with the amount of X band radar still in use in the US states of NC, NJ, OH, and IN, any radar detector that has false alert elimination features is attractive for those customers, either who live or travel there. Since they will knowingly have false alerts around retail stores and airports, they don't want to be caught off guard by ignoring valid X band radar warnings from law enforcement.

Margin Notes

- Any time a customer has rear windows tinted, they should look for a dash-mounted radar detector that has 360-degree coverage, so they can get the best possible coverage without making modifications to the window film. Any windshield that has tint also restricts placement for effective detecting of signals. Remote-mounted detectors with front and rear coverage would essentially eliminate the concern of tinted windows on a vehicle altogether because the sensors are installed in the bumper, grille or license-plate area.
- Customers who drive high-end or enthusiast vehicles that have a high insurance cost may be ideal candidates for remote-mounted radar/laser detection systems that require custom installation.

Other Installed Safety Devices

There are many niche products marketed as vehicle safety devices that target specific audiences or needs. Some of them are user-installed and connect to a cigarette lighter or OBD-II port, but others may require professional installation. Depending on the device and clientele, these may be an added opportunity to capture a customer base outside of traditional audio or remote starters.

Breath Alcohol Ignition Interlock Device (BAIID)

A Breath Alcohol Ignition Interlock Device (BAIID) is a device that prevents a vehicle from starting if the driver's blood alcohol content (BAC) exceeds a pre-determined level. The driver must blow into the device to measure an acceptable limit which will provide a pass or fail outcome. Passing will allow the car to start. Failing keeps the vehicle from starting, typically by interrupting the same starter circuit(s) that a vehicle security system does. The legal BAC limit is any number below .08 in all US states; however, the steps of impairment by which a BAIID will enable or disable starting, as well as other caveats (such as BAC that applies to commercial driver's license holders), vary by state-to-state laws and the BAIID calibration.

Added BAIID safety features or functionality may include an on-board camera that captures an image of the person doing the breath test (to validate identity) and many require periodic retesting while the car is driving to validate the driver has not had a change of BAC status during the trip. All this data is captured in the BAIID's memory for later download and analysis.

Since a BAIID requires installation, many 12 Volt installation shops may take on this as an additional service as a supplement to traditional car audio or remote starter business. The equipment is typically provided to the installing shop by the BAIID manufacturer and 'leased' or 'rented' to the vehicle owner for the period in which their court mandated requirement of the device is in effect. On a periodic basis (typically every 30 days), the driver returns to the point of installation for a checkup where the use history of the device is downloaded and cataloged in the driver's electronic file. That electronic file is often sent to the manufacturer, motor vehicle department and/or courts to provide a progress report on the driver.

Margin Notes

Specific descriptions of ignition interlock laws in the US on a state-by-state basis can be found at the National Conference of State Legislatures (NCSL) website: ncsl.org/research/transportation/state-ignition-interlock-laws.aspx

Some Canadian provinces including Ontario and Quebec require an ignition interlock device for a specified period of time, depending on the number of prior driving while intoxicated offenses. Visit the government website in a given province for specific details.

The installation shop typically gathers revenue for the initial installation of the BAIID and for each periodic BAIID checkup. With required BAIID use durations of 6-18 months or more, this can be a steady stream of new customers visiting the store who may not otherwise have visited. Treat BAIID customers with respect and dignity. Since those new customers will visit the store many times over a period of months, many have a probability of becoming customers in the shop's other categories such as audio, security, remote starters or safety devices (like backup cameras or sensors).

Distracted Driving Smartphone "Blockers"

With the increase of driver distraction from mobile devices like smartphones and tablets, there are devices that can inhibit texting and other smartphone functionality while the vehicle is running and in motion. While there are simply apps for most smartphones that can inhibit specific functionality by recognizing the phone's built-in accelerometer movement, installed devices can extend the limited functionality to user-specified apps or even disabling use of the handset to take a call (encouraging the use of a hands-free device instead).

The installed devices range from hideaway boxes with hard-wired power/ground connections to direct OBD-II plug-in configurations. Most all of the devices have a companion app that installs on the smartphone to interact with the devices over Bluetooth wireless communication, so the phone knows when the vehicle is moving and which functionality to disable.

Retailers have an opportunity to offer these types of devices to retail customers such as parents of teen drivers or for businesses that have employees driving vehicles on-the-job. Each instance is a potential liability that could be mitigated with the use of an installed blocking device. Installation is relatively easy for an experienced installation professional if hard-wiring and module placement is required, and this may bring a new customer to the store who may not otherwise have visited for traditional categories like audio, rear seat entertainment or a remote starter.

Usage Based Insurance (UBI) Devices

Many insurance companies offer the prospect of discounted rates if the policy holder and insured drivers agree to have an in-vehicle event recorder to catalog their driving habits. The information these Usage Based Insurance (UBI) devices may gather is:

- Time of Day Start/End Travel

Margin Notes

- Average and Maximum Speed in Travel
- Braking Force during Travel
- Location(s) of Travel
- Vehicle Diagnostic Information via OBD-II Data
- Dashboard Video
- In-Cabin Audio

Depending on the arrangement and application, some or all of those features may help the insurance company determine rates that best suit that specific vehicle and driver. Commercial vehicles often use UBI information sharing to ensure compliance of their drivers as well as achieve more favorable rates. Consumers often agree to UBI devices simply to save money, particularly where they drive less often and fewer distances than their regional average. Many people who work from home, for example, may choose to utilize UBI devices to help reduce car insurance costs.

The devices themselves may or may not require professional installation. Some UBI devices are easily installed into the vehicle's OBD-II diagnostic port whereas others may require hard-wired connections, a separate GPS antenna and (depending on the functionality) other communication antennas to report usage over wireless networks.

A shop that installs UBI devices that require more than 'plugging in' can benefit from new relationships with commercial clients with a fleet of vehicles (such as service companies, delivery companies, rental vehicles, municipalities, etc.). Often referrals from insurance companies or local area brokers bring new customers into the retail store where they may not have been a traditional audio or remote starter customer.

4

INSTALLATION AND CONFIGURATION APPLICATION KNOWLEDGE

INSTALLATION AND CONFIGURATION APPLICATION KNOWLEDGE

Margin Notes

IMPORTANT INSTALLATION BAY SAFETY CONSIDERATIONS

The primary workspace for a Mobile Product Specialist is a showroom, demonstration area or product display area. There may be times, however, when you'll be in the installation bay, perhaps to give a tour to clients to present the professionalism and cleanliness of the shop. Keep in mind that customers should not enter the installation bay when work is taking place. This is due to the numerous hazards that exist within the area. Such hazards range from vehicles being pulled in and out of the bay, potentially slick floors from water or fluids, tripping hazards, flying debris, caustic chemicals and high decibel levels that could damage hearing. Most business insurance policies will specifically state customers are not to be in the installation area, and having customers present when an accident occurs may mean the shop can be held directly liable.

Ideally, customers will be able to see the installation area, either through viewing windows or from a safe distance in a marked off waiting area, so there is little chance of customers entering the workspace unexpectedly.

Personal Safety

All safety standards should be followed when you're in the installation bay. The Occupational Safety and Health Administration (OSHA) is the government agency that regulates on-the-job safety and requires that all employers maintain a safe and healthy work environment. The Code of Federal Regulations (CFRs) lists safety and health standards, and employers face stiff fines and penalties if these standards are not followed. While the shop owner can ultimately be responsible for accidents, safety begins with the individual. Therefore, a proper attitude is the most important "tool" to help promote shop safety. Sometimes safety involves the use of OSHA approved or recommended Personal Protection Equipment (PPE).

- **Eyes** – Eye protection is not just for the technician or fabricator using a power tool but rather for anyone near a potential hazard. These hazards extend from the obvious power tools, to grinders, various chemical mixtures such as polyester resin for fiberglass, cyanoacrylate adhesive (CA glue), automotive paints and solvents. If you think safety glasses are "un-cool," cool does little good if you're permanently blinded. In addition to the appropriate eye protection, the shop should have an emergency eye wash station in case a foreign substance does get into someone's eyes. This is often a simple wall mounted item that holds one or more bottles of eye wash and should be easily accessible.

Margin Notes

- **Ears** – The installation bay and fabrication areas can be noisy places. OSHA has specific regulations for hearing protection. According to OSHA, exposure to sounds measured at 100dBA SPL for two hours will start to cause hearing damage. If exposure to high-decibel sound for an extended period is a concern, wear earplugs or some type of OSHA-approved hearing protection. In the business of aftermarket mobile electronics, a functioning set of ears are a vital tool used on the job. If you are ever unsure if you should be wearing hearing protection, then you probably should be. Once your hearing is damaged, it's damaged for good.

- **Hands** – While typically a Mobile Product Specialist should have little need for hand protection, certain situations may arise where it is needed. For instance, an MPS may be asked to help clean the installation bay. This cleaning could consist of paints, primers, fiberglass, polyester resin and various other chemicals. In this case, plastic or latex disposable gloves should be used (use nitrile if you have a latex allergy).

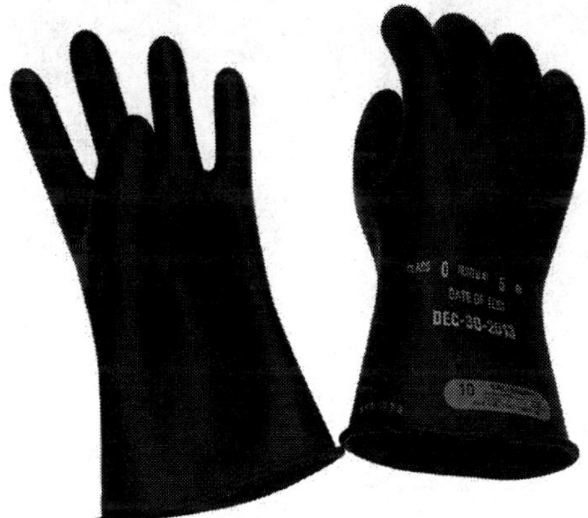

- **Respiratory** – There may be times when a technician is working with various chemicals, or plastics, woods or other composites (cutting/grinding/sanding/shaping). These chemicals and airborne materials can linger for hours. Even short exposure can be harmful. Always err on the side of caution and wear a respirator. A simple dust mask may be suitable for airborne wood dust, but an organic vapor (OV) respirator that utilizes a charcoal filter should be used if any chemicals are present in the air.

Fire Safety Concerns

Every shop should be prepared for the unexpected fire. It is important you know the locations of all fire extinguishers (more than one) along with emergency exits. These emergency exits should be clearly labeled. In the event of a fire, the first step should be to determine the size of the blaze.

- Know and review your company's specific policies on fires.
- If a larger and unmanageable fire is present, the building should be immediately evacuated and 911 called.
- In the case of a smaller, manageable fire, most shops should have a "multi-class" fire extinguisher that covers several types of fires in one device.

Margin Notes

For NFPA (National Fire Protection Association) compliance, refer to NFPA 10, which is the standard on Portable Fire Extinguishers. Otherwise, here are some tips on the operation of a fire extinguisher and the classes of fires to which they apply.

Operation-think P-A-S-S

- **P**ull the pin
- **A**im at the base of the fire
- **S**queeze the handle (valve)
- **S**weep from side to side

Start from upwind, at a safe distance and work inward. When backing out, never turn your back on the fire. Once and extinguisher has been emptied, lay it on its side (universal sign extinguisher out of service).

There are five classes of fire:

- **Class A** – Ordinary combustibles, paper, wood or cloth.
- **Class B** – Flammable and combustible liquids and gases, gasoline, oil, paint, thinners and alcohols.
- **Class C** – Energized electrical equipment. Note: De-energized equipment is no longer class C.
- **Class D** – Combustible metals that end in "ium," Aluminum, Magnesium, Sodium, etc.
- **Class K** – Kitchen fires. This class was added to the NFPA portable extinguishers Standard 10 in 1998.

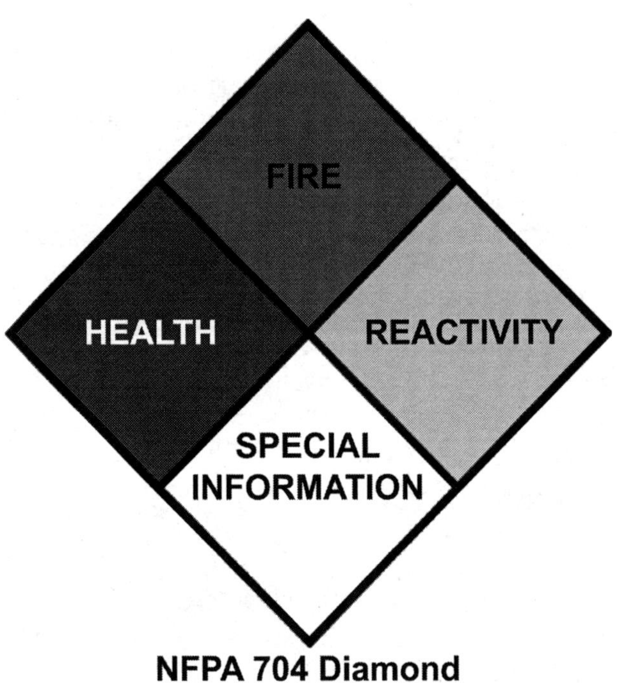

NFPA 704 Diamond

Margin Notes

Choosing "Proper Class" Extinguishers:

- **Class A fires** – Use pressurized water, foam or multi-purpose (ABC-rated). Dry chemical extinguishers. DO NOT USE carbon dioxide or ordinary (BC-rated) dry chemical extinguishers on Class A fires.
- **Class B fires** – Foam, carbon dioxide, ordinary (BC-rated) dry chemical, multipurpose dry chemical and Halon extinguishers may be used to fight Class B fires.
- **Class C fires** – Carbon dioxide, ordinary (BC-rated) dry chemical, multipurpose dry chemical and HALON* fire extinguishers may be used to fight Class C fires. DO NOT USE water extinguishers on energized electrical equipment.
- **Class D fires** – Extinguish combustible metals such as magnesium, titanium, potassium and sodium with dry powder extinguishing agents specially designated for the material involved.
- **Class K fires** – Protection contains a potassium acetate based, low pH agent that was originally developed for use in pre-engineered cooking equipment fire extinguishing systems. The Class K extinguishers are tested on commercial deep fat fryers using the same type of fire test as UL300 pre-engineered restraint fire extinguishing systems. The agent discharges as a fine mist that helps prevent grease splash and fire re-flash while cooling the appliance. The Class K extinguisher is the ideal choice for use on all cooking appliances including solid fuel char broilers.

The install bay will likely have one or more multi-class fire extinguishers typically being a low-cost NFPA-compliant extinguisher such as a Kidde that will work on Class A, Class B and Class C fires (Model PRO460-21005785 or equivalent). This Kidde model is ideal for the mobile electronics retail and installation environments and is small, lightweight and portable. The ABC fire extinguishers contain ammonium phosphate. Additionally, there are two other fire extinguishers that may be found in the install bay.

Co2 Fire Extinguishers:

- Co2 (liquefied compressed gas)
- Fire Class B & C rated only
- Non-corrosive with no mess compared to dry chemical extinguishers
- Do not have a gauge on them
- A modern replacement of Halon extinguishers for electrical equipment

Halon Fire extinguishers:

- Halon 1211 (bromochlorodifluoromethane, CF2ClBr)
- 1211 used in portable extinguishers, discharge as a clear liquid, turns into a gas
- Fire class A, B & C Rated
- Fire Stream Reach = 8-18ft
- Discharge Time = 8-18 seconds
- Have been replaced by Co2 extinguishers for Class B & C fire applications.

Margin Notes

Chemical Storage (MSDS) and Spill Concerns

On occasion, a Mobile Product Specialist may be asked to help clean the bay, deliver materials or pass through the shop with some frequency. It is important that best practices are followed for both chemical storage and safety, along with a chemical spill incident.

Chemical Storage:

- Know and review your company's specific policies on chemical use and storage.
- Always wear appropriate protective equipment and apparel (safety goggles, gloves, OV respirator, etc.) when handling or using chemical products.
- Familiarize yourself with location of the fire extinguishers, spill clean-up kit, first aid supplies and eye wash stations.
- Make sure adequate ventilation is available in the work area.
- Do not use a chemical product without reading the directions and MSDS.
- All hazardous/flammable chemicals must be stored in the safety storage cabinet.
- All empty chemical containers must be disposed of properly in the hazardous materials storage barrel.
- Store oily rags in a metal container with a lid.
- Notify the installation supervisor (or services manager) when the hazardous materials storage barrel is full.

Chemical Spill Procedures:

- Know and review your company's specific policies on chemical spills. Company policies beyond small spills may be to call the local HAZMAT team from a fire department to handle it.
- Immediately alert the installation supervisor (or services manager) and other people around of the potential risk.
- If the situation is potentially volatile or flammable, evacuate the area immediately, ventilate the space and attempt to suppress or control the potential ignition source.
- In the case of a major spill (like a 55-gallon drum), call the local fire department's HAZMAT team.
- Wear safety goggles, gloves and use a spill kit (spill socks and/or loose absorbent material) to treat the entire spill area, starting from the outside and circling to the inside.
- After spill materials have been absorbed, use the brush and scoop to place the materials in a polypropylene bag.
- Label the bag with a hazardous materials sticker identifying the material as "spill debris" involving the specific chemical.
- Clean the area where the spill occurred with a mild detergent and water.
- Properly dispose of your personal protection equipment used to clean up the spill and decontaminate yourself using wash stations.

VEHICLE ELECTRICAL COMPONENTS

Margin Notes

The Alternator

The alternator is the source for all electrical energy in an internal combustion engine vehicle while the engine is running. **When the vehicle is running, it's the alternator – not the battery – that is the source for the combustion engine vehicle's electrical energy.**

- It's important to specify an internal combustion engine vehicle because hybrid gas-electric vehicles utilize several energy sources (depending on the conditions). They have a traditional gas (internal combustion) engine as well as a high-voltage electric motor/generator.

Part of the function of the alternator is also to recharge the battery from any depletion that occurs in starting or having supplied energy to electrical accessories while the engine was not running. The alternator is an important foundation of the vehicle electrical system. It is important that a Mobile Product Specialist understand its function in the automobile. If you are selling a customer a powerful high-end audio system, you need to make sure that the vehicle's alternator can handle the demands of the newly installed equipment.

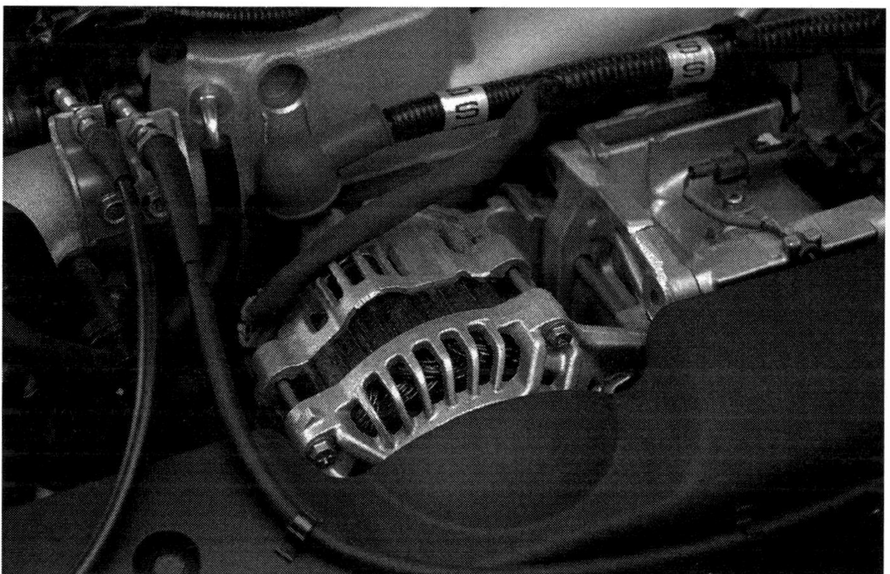

Alternator Output

The output of an alternator is expressed in amperes (abbreviated with the letter A), which is a measurement for of the amount of current that the unit can provide to all the equipment that's connected to the electrical system. A common OEM alternator in a passenger car or light truck may have a manufacturer rating somewhere between 60-120A, although there is a lot of variation from one vehicle to another. Vehicles with a higher electrical demand from additional electronics, infotainment and creature comforts require a factory alternator that has a high enough output

Margin Notes

rating to meet those needs. Vehicles with fewer electrical accessories and demands can tolerate a smaller alternator output. The vehicle's alternator output capability should meet the electrical requirements of the vehicle.

It's worth noting that the "rated" amperage output of an alternator refers to its output at engine speeds of 2,500-3,000 RPM or above where normal roadway speeds occur. Therefore, an alternator rated at 100A may only put out 40A or 50A at engine idle speeds when parked or in slower street traffic.

Why wouldn't a vehicle manufacturer just put as big an alternator in a vehicle as possible? Besides the obvious concern of increased cost, there is also a mechanical penalty for increased amperage output in an alternator. More output amperage creates more of a magnetic drag for the engine to overcome, energy that can ultimately affect fuel economy or acceleration. Thus, vehicle manufacturers balance an electrical supply need with the best achievable engine performance at a parts cost that meets mass production requirements.

The factory-rated alternator output is an important figure since OEM alternators are typically ill-equipped to handle additional loads from aftermarket equipment and upgrades. When that happens, and the vehicle's alternator output is unable to fully meet the needs of the electrical system, problems from dimming headlights to severe drivability issues can result. If left unchecked, this problem will eventually lead to the alternator failing altogether.

Since there's a difference between an alternator's rated output current and the actual amount of current that it can provide at idle speeds, it's important to have a full understanding of how to read alternator output ratings. For sound system upgrades with a lot of power-hungry aftermarket equipment, it becomes even more important to consider those differences. While the output rating of an alternator gives you an idea of what it's designed to put out, the only way to see what an alternator is capable of is to test it. This way, the actual output of an alternator is measured under a simulated load, which allows a result of what it can put out in real-world conditions.

- Measuring alternator output is part of a Standard State of Health (SOH) vehicle electrical system testing process covered in the *MECP Advanced Installation Technician Guide*. While it may be outside the scope of a Mobile Product Specialist's duties, you should be aware that such a test should be conducted by a technician before making significant audio system design plans that entail high power (current hungry) amplifiers.

The term "alternator output" refers to two distinct, yet related, concepts. The first is the alternator output rating, which is the amount of current that a unit can produce at a specific rotational speed. For instance, a 100A alternator has a "rated" output of 100A, which means that it can provide 100A when the alternator shaft is rotating at 6,000 RPM (about 2,500-3,000 engine RPM depending on the alternator's pulley

Margin Notes

diameter). The alternator output can also refer to the amount of current that it produces at any given time, which is a function of the physical capabilities of the alternator, the rotational speed of the input shaft and the momentary demands of the electrical system.

When an alternator "has 100A output," it can have a variety of interpretations depending on where the information originated. The only time that single number rating is meaningful is when an alternator manufacturer or (rebuilder) uses the term "rating" in its intended capacity.

- Standardized alternator output specifications in the automotive world are defined by international standards documents like ISO8854:2012 and SAE J56-1999. In both of these documents, alternator testing and labeling standards indicate that the "rated output" of an alternator is the amount of current that it can produce when the alternator shaft is rotating at 6,000 RPM. Each standard also indicates a range of other speeds at which an alternator needs to be tested and defines "idle output" and "maximum output" in addition to "rated output."

Although alternator manufacturers, rebuilders and suppliers typically refer to the rated output in promotional materials, both the ISO and the SAE require a format of "IL /IRA VTV," where:

- **IL** is the low, or idle, amperage output.
- **IR** is the rated amperage output.
- **VT** is the test voltage, with the last "V" identifying the units of volts.

This information results in ratings that look like "50/120A 13.5V," which are typically printed or stamped on the housing of an alternator. Check the vehicle's alternator specification guide or contact the alternator manufacturer, if there is no visible label or engraving with this number on it. Or cross reference the year, make and model of the vehicle with the factory alternator part number to see if an auto parts database provides detailed specifications.

Consider this example of a specified alternator rating:

- **50/120A 13.5V**

Since it's known that both ISO and SAE standards call for a format of "IL /IRA VTV", it's easy to interpret this rating.

1. First, consider the IL specification. In this example, it is 50. That means this alternator is capable of a 50A output current at the "low" test speed, which is either 1,500 RPM or "the idle speed of the engine," depending on which standard is referenced.

2. Next, consider the IR specification. In this example, it is 120. That means this alternator output at the "rated" test speed is capable of a 120A output when

Margin Notes

the alternator shaft is rotating at 6,000 RPM (about 2,500-3,000 engine RPM depending on the alternator's pulley diameter). Since this is the "rated" test speed, this number is usually used for the alternator's rated output.

3. Finally, consider the VTV specification. In this example, it is 13.5V. That means 13.5 volts is voltage at which the alternator was held at during the test. Since an alternator's output can vary both up and down from 13.5V in real world situations, its actual output limits will vary from the idle and rated numbers.

With all of that in mind, it's important to understand that the output of an alternator is directly related to the demands of the vehicle electrical system in addition to its inherent capabilities and the speed that its input shaft is rotating at any given moment. While maximum alternator output is dependent on the rotational speed of the input shaft, the ***actual output*** is load-dependent. This essentially means that an alternator will never generate more current than is called for by the momentary demands of the electrical system. While an underpowered alternator can cause problems by not meeting the needs of a vehicle's electrical system, a substantially overpowered alternator represents a lot of wasted potential.

- For instance, a high-output alternator might be capable of putting out upwards of 300A, but it won't actually provide more amperage than a stock 80A unit if that's all the electrical system ever tries to draw.

Refer to the *MECP Basic Installation Technician Study Guide's* Ohm's Law section for more information on the relationship of electrical capability and demand.

Does the Customer Need a Higher Output Alternator?

In most cases, no. Alternators are usually only replaced due to normal wear and tear. Internal components wear out, so the best course of action is to replace it with a new or rebuilt unit that conforms to the same output ratings. However, there are also cases where an alternator may burn out due to excessive electrical demands over a prolonged period. This usually doesn't apply to vehicles that have factory installed (OEM) audio systems or simple head unit upgrades, but it can quickly come into play as more power-hungry aftermarket equipment is added. Car audio amplifiers, off-road winches, and incandescent off-road lighting are among the most power-demanding 12v accessories.

To prevent imminent alternator failure when adding multiple high-powered accessories, an upgraded alternator with higher output capacity is a must. An alternator upgrade will ensure that the customer gets the best performance out of their new sound system and doesn't encounter any problems later with alternator failure.

Charging

A common misconception about alternators is that they will fully charge dead batteries effectively. Alternators adjust their charging load based on the battery's levels (by way of a voltage regulator), and when a battery is completely dead, the

Margin Notes

alternator is charging in a very "high current" mode. This shocks the battery and provides short term relief but does not necessarily create a sustainable charge.

Some amount of the alternator's output is allocated to maintain a normal state of charge for the vehicle battery. The more depleted the battery, the more current delivered to try and maintain that state of charge. A fundamental misconception about power reserves is that adding batteries is a good idea to supplement an underperforming alternator. Since an alternator allocates a certain amount of output to maintain a single battery's state of charge, that increases with every added battery. This means the available energy for the vehicle's electrical accessories is less – not more – than if using only a single battery.

Another misconception is that while the car is running, the battery always receives a consistent rate of charge from the alternator. In most cases, the alternator produces a very low current rate of charge at idle and does not begin charging or delivering high current until the engine reaches about 2,000+ RPM. As such, it's possible for a car to sit in traffic or at idle with a very powerful sound system and consume more current than is being created by the alternator. This deficiency in electrical demand reverts to the vehicle battery to pick up the slack. That's why running the car at actual road speed is important for balancing electrical demands with electrical supply.

Turning AC into DC

Though the alternator internally generates alternating current (AC), it must not be connected directly to the vehicle battery, which is a DC storage device. AC is turned into DC by a series of diodes known as a **rectifier bridge**. Most simple OEM rectifier bridges are built right into the back of the alternator. Most rectifiers consist of six diodes (three positive, three negative), though larger high output aftermarket alternators sometimes use groups of six to increase the heat distribution from higher levels of output current. High output alternators may have 12 or 18 diodes in the rectifier bridge to further distribute the output current (or "heat") among the group of diodes rather than just one pair per phase.

AC-to-DC conversion is covered more in depth in the *MECP Basic and Advanced Installation Technician Study Guides*. As a Mobile Product Specialist, it's important to know there is a conversion from AC into DC, which in some cases can introduce unwanted noise into the audio system.

The Battery

The common 12 Volt lead-acid automotive battery is primarily a starting battery. Its principal use is to start the engine. However, batteries also allow users of the vehicle to enjoy the electronic features and functions of the vehicle when the engine is not running. This applies to power windows, 12v power sockets, power seats, power trunk release, audio/video system, etc. When the engine is not running, the energy stored in the vehicle battery maintains the electrical functions of the vehicle. Once the vehicle is started, however, the alternator takes over and the

Margin Notes

battery becomes another electrical load on it. While the engine is running, the battery filters AC ripple from the alternator's output.

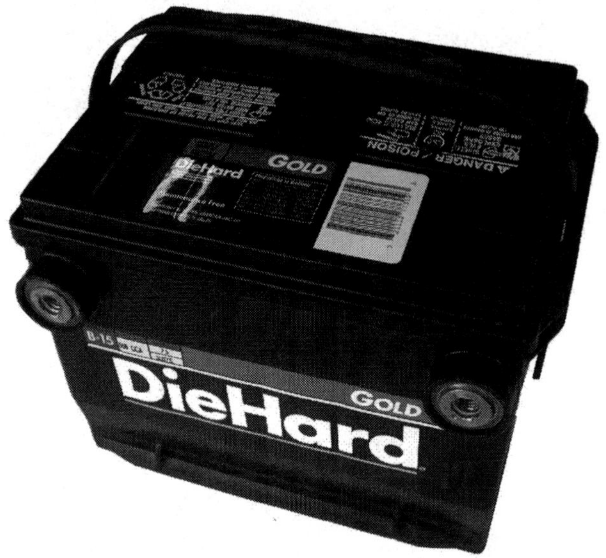

There are many types of automotive batteries (lead-acid are the most common and least expensive), though all starting batteries serve the same purpose. In many newer vehicles, absorbed glass mat (AGM) style starting batteries are used as standard equipment, particularly European and Asian vehicles. AGM batteries are costlier, but are better suited for the stressful automotive environments and the ever-growing power demands of vehicle electrical systems. A high-quality AGM battery will have a very low Equivalent Series Resistance (ESR) averaging around 4 milli-ohm. A typical lead acid battery is around 40 milli-ohm. Because of this low ESR, AGM batteries can be recharged at a much faster rate. This high rate also allows for better recovery from a deep discharge or being left in a discharged state and still be recoverable. Standard lead acid batteries with their low ESR cannot be charged quickly; they must be slow charged.

Note: When using a battery charger to recharge/recover a starting battery outside the vehicle, lead-acid batteries have a different charging recommendation than AGM batteries, so the charger used should support the battery type it's intended to charge.

A vehicle battery serves two functions:

- **Primary Function** – Provide enough high current and stable voltage **to start the engine**. Batteries with a high **Cold Cranking Amperage (CCA)** rating typically sustain a longer period of cranking the engine but consume more electrical energy from the alternator to maintain a charge once the engine has started. Depending on battery construction and its intended application, it may or may not be beneficial to "supersize" a replacement battery for the sake of assuming there

Margin Notes

is extra power for electrical accessories like an aftermarket audio/video system.

- **Secondary Function** – Provide a **filter** mechanism for any leftover AC ripple from the alternator. **An alternator or charging system that's overworked or showing premature failure can cause excessive AC ripple**. Excessive AC ripple can present many problems (especially with an aftermarket system) in the form of an annoying whine in the audio system or annoying lines on a video screen. In addition, higher-output alternators and charging systems are likely to have more AC ripple than factory installed alternators; therefore, a good battery that can filter that ripple becomes even more important.

Cautions of Haphazardly Adding Batteries

There are many things to consider when determining whether the vehicle needs an additional battery. A Mobile Product Specialist, sometimes with the help of an experienced technician, must understand what problem (or potential problem) is to be solved by the addition of a battery. When extra batteries are added to a vehicle's electrical system, there are definite precautions that need to be taken:

- First, determine if the vehicle needs an additional battery. Collaborating with an experienced technician can help arrive at a realistic conclusion based on measurements and facts, not just an opinion. Additional batteries are generally recommended only when the vehicle needs more "key off" listening time or if there is some reason the car does not drive most of the time when the audio system is being played with high current demands (such as show and demo vehicles). Otherwise, for cars that drive daily, especially cars that have factory installed alternators, adding additional batteries presents a load on the electrical system that often outweighs the benefits while the vehicle is normally running and driving.
- Second, always take into consideration the vehicle's alternator output, particularly if it's a factory-installed alternator. One may find that for power hungry aftermarket systems in demand of electrical current far beyond the capacity of the existing alternator, a high output alternator may be necessary if the intent is to supply the electrical power required to feed large amplifiers. If large amplifiers present too much of a load on the electrical system, adding extra batteries to the alternator's workload won't necessarily improve conditions for the alternator.
- If you do decide that an additional battery is needed, be sure to use some type of isolation device to separate the batteries while they are not being charged and the vehicle is not running. This will allow the complete discharge of the secondary battery without discharging the primary engine starting battery. High current relays like the PAC-200 or PAC-500 are ideal for this situation
- **Lead-Acid batteries should never be used inside of a vehicle's passenger compartment.** During charging, they produce very flammable hydrogen and oxygen gases. They are also known to emit poisonous gases such as Arsine and Stibine. For interior applications, an AGM battery is recommended. It should be vented to the outside of the vehicle.
- It's also highly recommended that batteries be the same age, type, size, etc., if they are going to charge from the same source and will be connected in parallel during

Margin Notes

charging. Each of the six cells in a battery is an independent 2.11v battery linked with others to produce the required voltage (6 x 2.11 = 12.66 volts). When connecting two or more batteries together, they essentially become one large battery. Even in a single battery, each cell is slightly different, and they will all try to equalize to a common voltage. This becomes problematic with dissimilar batteries, different size batteries, and batteries of different ages. **Always avoid using an old, factory battery for the starting battery and a new, large capacity battery (of any kind) as the auxiliary battery.** Don't mix a deep-cycle or AGM battery with a lead-acid starting battery. All these factors can and will lead to premature failure of one or both batteries, plus (very likely) an alternator. It's worth the extra cost to have everything new, fresh and matching as it will avoid future costly charging system failures or leaving the starting battery inoperable unexpectedly.

The Fuse Panel

Every vehicle has an intermediary location called a fuse panel where the high current power from the battery is split up to some of the individual high current circuit devices or routed to other sub-assemblies such as the ignition system, interior electronics, engine control, etc. There are often more than one of these fuse panels that are placed where a technician can access them with relative ease. Generally, there's one located somewhere near the vehicle battery (whether that's under the hood or in the trunk) and there is also usually one located in or around the dashboard area that specifically covers the circuits located in (or controlled by) the switches and devices in the dashboard.

The fuse panel is one of the first places a technician might check to identify why a specific function or feature (such as interior lighting, 12 Volt power socket, factory radio, etc.) is not working. If a fuse in the panel for that specific circuit blows, the power for that circuit is interrupted.

It's important to note that any fuse panel must remain original and intact. It's not recommended that a technician shove wires into fuses and push them into the fuse location to "tap" power. It's also not recommended to drill any holes into fuse panels to bring wires in, such as tapping power under the hood in a covered fuse panel. You (or the installation technician) must always consider that a mechanic or auto repair technician may need to access these fuse panels to diagnose vehicle problems and the last thing a customer needs is a roadblock installed in their vehicle in a way that leads a mechanic to blame the aftermarket installation or technician's work.

Never replace a fuse in the vehicle's fuse panel with a fuse rating higher than the original specification. If a 10A fuse is blown and, upon inserting another 10A fuse, blows again, have a technician investigate for a short circuit or component problem rather than trying a higher rated fuse. This can result in component damage or, depending on the disparity of rated fuse size versus (actual) oversized fuse used, an electrical fire hazard.

The Ignition Switch

An ignition switch is a switch in the control system of an internal-combustion engine vehicle, which activates the main electrical systems for the vehicle. The ignition switch wiring is generally accessible under the steering column of most vehicles. It is usually designated as ignition switch wiring by its larger gauge, generally 12-14 gauge in diameter, whereas most other vehicle wiring in the vicinity is much smaller. However, a growing number of vehicles have smaller diameter wiring that controls a relay bank or Electronic Control Module (ECM) somewhere else in the vehicle, and that piece is what starts the vehicle. It is possible for an ignition switch to control either (+) positive or (-) negative polarity.

Some ignition switches on the newer vehicles operate by varying the voltage to between 0 and +12 to operate different functions based on the voltage present. These ignition switches may also have a specific function result from voltage present on two wires, but one wire has voltage removed in one of the key switch sequences (common in vehicles with no dedicated "start" wire).

Low-Current Ignition Circuits

Low-current ignition circuits are found on many newer vehicles. These ignition circuits are called one of several names depending on the reference or manufacturer (if there's an aftermarket product such as an interface device or remote starter intended to connect into this circuit). Those names are:

- MUX Wiring
- Multiplex Wiring
- Variable Voltage

These circuits are used in conjunction with, or as a replacement to, the dedicated starter wire that signals the vehicle starter to engage and crank over the engine. With a low-current ignition system, the vehicle manufacturer can use fewer and thinner gauge wires, reducing the weight of the vehicle and thus increasing fuel economy and reducing cost. This type of system also allows for added security, making it more difficult to steal or "hot wire" a vehicle.

On a standard ignition system common in pre-2000 model year vehicles, there is a high-current, heavier-gauge power wire that provides 12 volts + from the key switch to the starter solenoid wire to turn the starter, whereas the low-current ignition system tells the vehicle's computer what to do (and when). The advantage is, for example, virtually eliminating grinding the starter if the engine is already running, or channeling any extra vehicle electrical power to the starter for assisting starting in cold weather. Think of a low-current ignition system as a "Smart Ignition/Starting System."

A multiplex (MUX) wire is a common wire that changes circuit resistance with the movement of the key cylinder. It will change resistance between two measured points depending on the position of the ignition key cylinder. The key cylinders on these systems have built-in resistors. The ECM/BCM/PCM sees this change

Margin Notes

Margin Notes

(electrically) and then engages the starter solenoid to allow the starter to turn over the engine. The MUX wire can generally be found at (or near) the ignition switch, and the operation should ALWAYS be verified by a technician using a digital multimeter (DMM).

Data-Bus Networks and Their Architecture

Most (if not all) modern cars are equipped with multiple data-bus networks that carry info throughout the vehicle's electronic components. These networks can be CAN-Bus (HS, MS or LSFT), D2B, IE Bus, J1850 (Class II), LIN, LAN or MOST, and are transmitted on a variety of wiring setups from single wire, dual wire, twisted pair or fiber optic cables. It's important to be able to identify what system a vehicle uses before choosing aftermarket accessories.

The main influences for the development and implementation of vehicle network technology have been the advances made in the electronics industry in general, and government regulations imposed (especially in the United States) to make the automobiles more environmentally friendly. At one time, a car radio was likely the only "creature comfort" electronic device in an automobile (aside from required components like lights, windshield wipers and HVAC systems). Now almost every component of the vehicle has some electronic feature to enhance the drivability, comfort, safety or convenience. Typical electronic modules on modern vehicles include the Engine Control Unit (ECU), the Transmission Control Unit (TCU), the Anti-lock Braking System (ABS) and body control modules (BCM).

All vehicles 2008 model year or newer have a High-Speed CAN (HS-CAN) network that controls the engine's electrical components/control modules. This network is always accessible through the On-Board Diagnostic (OBD-II) connector and is regulated by federal laws. It is usually only accessed by mobile electronics professionals when installing products like remote starts, or on occasion, a newer factory head unit replacement (to gain signals like vehicle speed sensing and reverse gear position).

The aftermarket automotive electronics industry is primarily concerned with the "Infotainment Network", which is the secondary network that connects things inside the vehicle that have to do with Information and Entertainment. These include the Body Control Module (BCM), Instrument Cluster, Head Unit/Radio, Rear Seat Entertainment systems and vehicle chime modules that can be found on the Infotainment Network. This network is not regulated by any federal laws and can differ greatly between vehicle manufacturers or even model years under one manufacturer. It is usually accessed by tapping into it at one of the modules listed, often at a location behind the factory head unit. Some manufacturers allow access to this network through the OBD II connector (e.g., Chrysler®), but not all do as it is not required by law.

The two most popular forms of vehicle infotainment data infrastructure are:

- Controller Area Network (CAN) - CAN is a vehicle data-bus standard designed to allow microcontrollers and devices to communicate with each other in applications, without a host computer. It is a message-based protocol, designed originally for multiplex electrical wiring within automobiles to save on copper. A CAN network can run on a variety of speeds:

- o **ISO 11898-2**, also called High Speed CAN (HS-CAN) or even Medium Speed CAN (MS-CAN)
- o **ISO 11898-3**, also called Low-Speed, Fault Tolerant CAN (LSFT-CAN)

- Media Oriented Systems Transport (MOST) – MOST is a high-speed multimedia network technology optimized by the automotive industry. The serial MOST bus uses a daisy-chain topology or ring topology and synchronous data communication to transport audio, video, voice and data signals via plastic optical fiber (POF) as used in MOST25 and MOST150 or electrical conductor using twisted copper wiring as used in MOST50 or MOST150 over copper physical layers. MOST technology is used in almost every car brand worldwide, including Audi, BMW®, General Motors®, Hyundai, Jaguar®, Land Rover, Mercedes-Benz®, Porsche, Toyota, Volkswagen® and Volvo®.

Recommended practice for connecting into these networks is to use a plug and play T-harness that is supplied by the manufacturer of the part being installed (especially for MOST). However, if a T-harness is not available, it is always recommended for the technician to cut (if filtering data) and solder into these wires. If the interface is only "listening" to the network and not filtering, the technician can solder directly into the network wiring with no cutting required. Keep in mind that any installation requiring access to a MOST fiber network must absolutely use some sort of T-harness as you cannot splice/solder aftermarket copper wiring into a vehicle's fiber optic cables. Thoroughly research the vehicle and its network(s) before attempting any installation of an aftermarket product.

Margin Notes

Engine, Powertrain and Body Controllers

The powertrain control module (PCM) is an electrical automotive component used on modern vehicles. It is generally made up of multiple control units, consisting of the engine control unit (ECU) and the transmission control unit (TCU). On some cars, such as many Chryslers, there are multiple computers: the PCM, the TCU, and the Body Control Module (BCM). These automotive computers must be reliable as they commonly control over more than 100 factors in the vehicle.

Instrument Panel Cluster

The instrument panel cluster (IPC) has become a critical part of the modern vehicle's infotainment system. Where the vehicle's IPC originally included a small array of simple controls and analog gauges to show speed, fuel level, oil pressure, etc., modern IPCs accommodate a broad array of digital gauges and controls, as well as infotainment information such as climate control info, entertainment system info, or navigation system information. This information is usually displayed in a central location within the IPC on a small LCD screen commonly referred to as the Driver

Margin Notes

Information Center (DIC), or Multi-Function Display (MFD). Some high-end vehicles use only an LCD screen (no other dial-type gauges) as the entire IPC and can make what's displayed customizable.

Informational features of the modern IPC may also include indicators for low fuel, low oil pressure, low tire pressure, faults in the airbag (safety restraint system/SRS) or other of indicators that are important to the driver. It's important to consider these factors and how they can be affected when adding aftermarket electronics.

Interior and Exterior Lighting

Understanding vehicle lighting is also important as a 12v product specialist. Let's start with the types of vehicle lighting:

Halogen Lighting

Halogen bulbs have been traditionally used in automobiles and are similar to incandescent bulbs. In a halogen bulb though, a thin wire filament housed inside a chamber of halogen gas (either iodine or bromine) is heated up until it begins to brightly glow, giving off light.

The light from halogen bulbs is yellowish in color rather than purely white. This means that it does not produce as much visibility as white LEDs and high-intensity discharge (HID) bulbs. In addition, halogen (and all incandescent) bulbs are the least durable option available. The filament inside the bulb is quite fragile and runs the risk of shattering if the vehicle is driving over rugged terrain. While halogen bulbs are still used in automotive lighting, more durable and energy-efficient technologies have become common.

High Intensity Discharge (HID) Lighting

High Intensity Discharge (HID) lighting was the second significant type of automotive lighting to evolve, debuting high-end luxury vehicle headlights. Now common in many vehicles, HID bulbs create light by striking an ultra-bright arc between two electrodes that are housed inside the bulb, which has a chamber of xenon gas and evaporated metal salts. A separate box housing the ballast creates and stabilizes the high voltage necessary to produce the arc between the two electrodes and connects directly to the bulbs. The ballast is powered by the vehicle electrical system, then converts the voltage to the high voltage necessary for the ultra-bright arc.

The light produced by this process is a bright, white light that allows for much more visibility than halogen bulbs. Since there are no fragile filaments, HID bulbs are much more durable. While they are incredibly bright and durable, HID bulbs do have a few key flaws:

- HID lighting systems are difficult and expensive to maintain because of the bulb and ballast.
- It can take HID lighting several seconds to achieve maximum brightness.
- They can blind oncoming traffic.

Margin Notes

When selling aftermarket HID bulbs, it is important to remember that they also need an approved HID housing/headlamp. A retrofit an HID bulb cannot safely be fitted into a halogen headlamp and maintain the same intended light projection path. When a halogen headlamp is retrofitted with an HID bulb, light distribution and output are altered. In the United States, vehicle lighting that does not conform to the Federal Motor Vehicle Safety Standard (FMVSS) 108 is not street legal. Glare is produced, invalidating the headlamp's type approval or certification and making it no longer street-legal in most of the U.S.

Light Emitting Diode (LED) Lighting

Light Emitting Diode (LED) automotive lighting is the most popular choice for most modern vehicles. An LED bulb works by lowering the energy state of electrons inside of a semiconductor, causing them to give off light. The light produced is a high-intensity, bright white light, which rivals that of HID bulbs. LED bulbs have a low current draw, making them very energy efficient.

LEDs also have a much longer average lifespan, lasting on average anywhere between 30,000 to 50,000 hours of use (compared to just 2,000 hours for HID bulbs). Since they operate on an entirely solid state, LEDs are quite durable and usually can handle rough terrain.

Interior lighting upgrades have become more popular with LED lighting advancements. Smaller and brighter bulbs make it easier to add lighting anywhere in or on the vehicle. Most cars have at least one "dome light" (or "courtesy light") located in or near the ceiling of the passenger compartment that can be upgraded. LED light sources increasingly appear as interior convenience lights in various locations, such as finely focused lighting on console control surfaces and in cabin storage areas. Map lights are aimed at specific passenger positions and allow for reading without glare distraction to the driver. Some vehicles have "approach lighting" or "puddle lights" in the exterior mirrors or lower edges of the doors, as well as interior lighting activated via the factory key fob. Many cars have lights in the trunk, in the engine compartment and in the glove box and other storage compartments. Modern pickup trucks usually have one or more white cargo lights that illuminate the bed of the truck, often controlled in conjunction with the interior dome lighting. All of these lights can be upgraded.

LED light bars are also a popular choice not only for vehicle owners, but also for power sports, off-road, and recreational marine enthusiasts too. Given the potential audience and sales opportunities, it is important that an MECP Mobile Product Specialist understand LED light bars and their applications.

Beam Pattern of LED Light Bars

Determining which type of light beam a customer needs from an LED light bar is another important decision to help them make. You will need to help them choose between spotlight beams, floodlight beams, or a combination of both.
The difference between the two is a question of depth versus width.

Margin Notes

- **Spot** – Spotlight beams are much more focused and narrow, producing a light beam that illuminates objects that are longer distances away, with less side illumination. Generally, spotlight beam patterns are preferred for on-road driving.

- **Flood** – Floodlight beams have a much wider angle of illumination but lack the ability to illuminate far-away objects. Floodlights are usually the better choice for lighting a worksite or for off-roading where brightly illuminating hazards on the side of the road is crucial.

- **Combination** – If you aren't sure which beam pattern is the best for a customer, or if they are going to be in situations where both are preferred, consider an LED light bar which offers both bulbs. Having both spot and flood beams gives customers full illumination of forward objects at a distance as well as objects that are off to the side, making combination light bars a highly popular choice.

LED light bars that are used primarily in off-road driving or marine applications need to have bulbs with either a floodlight beam pattern or at least a combination of both spotlight and floodlight bulbs. The reason for this is that when driving off road or navigating the waters with a boat, it is important to illuminate the sides of the vehicle or (vessel) just as much as it is the pathway ahead. Off-road scenarios, such as poorly maintained roads and trails, are likely to have obstructions such as rocks and fallen trees. There is also an increased risk of deer and other animals crossing the road or path. To fully illuminate these hazards, sell off-road LED lights that have a wide beam pattern that fully illuminates the sides of the road. Since off road driving involves slower speeds, illuminating far down the road is less important, so you can safely sacrifice a little distance for wider illumination.

With off-road lighting comes off-road use, which means the customer may use it with the engine off. A dead battery is never fun, especially on back roads, miles away from anyone or anything. For smaller lights (such as LED interior/courtesy lighting), there is little concern. If the customer is using a massive off-road light bar with the engine off, there is an increased concern of draining the vehicle battery, depending on what other electrical accessories are running at the same time (for example, the radio, headlights, phone charger, etc.). Some lights, especially those equipped with highly energy efficient LED bulbs, have a much lower current draw. Selecting the absolute lowest current draw LED light isn't necessary as long as the overall intended use of the lighting is taken into consideration. An LED light bar or bulb with a lower amp draw gives the customer a little peace of mind if the engine is off frequently and the battery is relied upon to power the lighting.

Off-road driving is also nothing like traveling down a smooth, paved highway. There are jarring bumps and deep potholes, pools of mud and branches slapping at the vehicle. To survive these conditions, the LED light bar needs to be built as durably as possible. One way to judge a light's durability is to look at the quality

Margin Notes

of the materials that have been used in its construction. Choosing to sell from a reputable, well-reviewed brand is also a good step to take.

LED light bars used in recreational marine applications have much the same considerations regarding energy when powered only by the battery. The light bar should not be so power hungry that it affects starting the engine later. Water-resistance is also a key factor in recreational marine use, so look for LED lighting that is IPX rated for water/moisture intrusion resistance.

INSTALLATION CONSIDERATIONS OF AFTERMARKET HEAD UNITS

Many manufacturers create parts which adapt to aftermarket equipment. Using the correct parts allows the customer to have not only an aesthetic installation but also one that doesn't sacrifice any features available with the factory equipment.

The vehicle fitment and application guides available on many parts-manufacturer websites are great resources. These will list factory specifications along with the manufacturer's model numbers for the parts needed to integrate into the selected vehicle. Most of these manufacturers also offer apps for mobile devices to access the information as well.

Common Installation Parts Required

Common parts needed to adapt an aftermarket head unit into a vehicle are dash kits, wiring harness adaptors, AM/FM antenna adaptors, USB port retention harnesses and satellite radio antenna retention harnesses. Depending on the amount of factory features, a steering wheel control (SWC) adaptor, auxiliary integration or data interface may also be needed to retain important functionality and safety features original to the vehicle. Here are some examples:

- **Dash Kits** – These are the formed plastic mounting parts needed to adapt a DIN or Double-DIN head unit into the factory dash provisions. They are typically merchandised in two fashions: multi kits and vehicle-specific kits. Multi kits are a single part number that work for multiple vehicles. In a multi kit, at the time of installation, the technician may have to remove a couple tabs or attach extra parts to fit it for the specific make and model of vehicle it is being installed. Alternatively, there are vehicle-specific kits. These are intended for only one make and model of vehicle, typically because of a unique factory dash panel or to incorporate OEM buttons or other features within the part to retain as many of these features as possible. Sometimes these kits move these controls (HVAC, hazards, vehicle info, etc.) to different spots on the dash bezel to provide the aftermarket head unit more depth for installation.

- **Wiring Harness Adaptor** – This is a wiring harness and plug that directly fits into the factory plug(s) removed from the factory head unit. It allows technicians to integrate into the factory circuits for power, ground and speaker wires, or into the factory amplifier. These harnesses will have CTA standard wire colors that match those used by the aftermarket head unit manufacturers.

Margin Notes

Since each vehicle manufacturer has its own wiring codes, this makes an install of a head unit as simple as matching colors the aftermarket head unit harness to the wiring harness adaptor, then making proper connections. It also allows the technician to keep the integrity of the vehicle's wiring, so that the factory head unit could be reinstalled by plugging it back in should the customer have a leased vehicle or wish to keep their head unit for another vehicle.

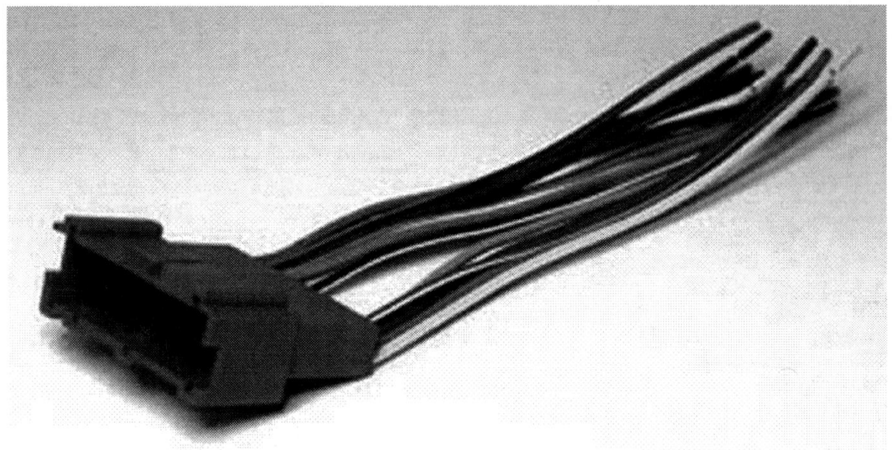

If the vehicle's factory wiring harness is missing, there are several options. If there is enough wire left on the factory plug, a technician can solder it back with the factory wires. If not, a factory "reverse wire harness" is often available from aftermarket part manufacturers. It is wired into the vehicle to bring it back to factory integrity. Other times, "hardwiring" the aftermarket harness into the vehicle's harness can be a solution when parts are not available or having the factory connectors is not of value to the client. This involves the technician using vehicle wiring database information and circuit testing tools to identify the wires in the vehicle. The circuit testing is critically important to get right since the wire colors in the vehicle harness are different than the standard CTA standard colors found in aftermarket wiring harness adaptors.

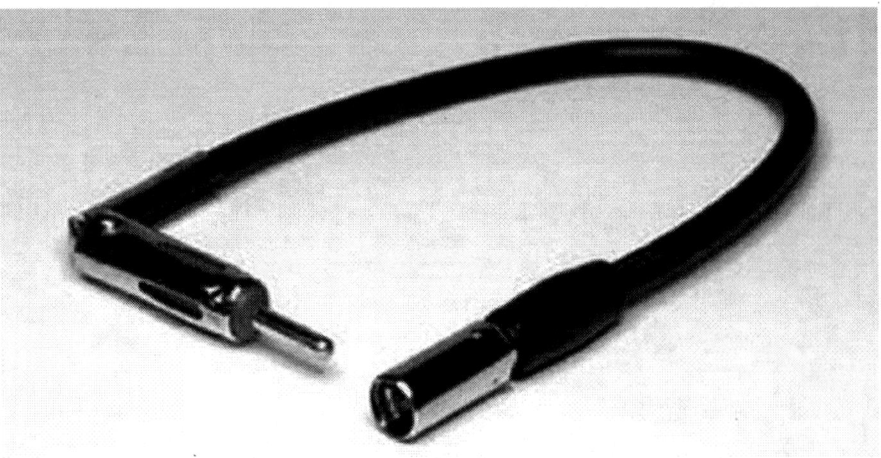

Margin Notes

- **Antenna Adaptor** – The aftermarket standard antenna connection is known as a Motorola connector, and for many years this type of connector was used by vehicle manufacturers as well. Over the years, more vehicle manufacturers have begun using proprietary designs for their antenna connectors to accommodate amplification, to save space on component design or a combination of things. When installing an aftermarket head unit, you may need an antenna adaptor, so the vehicle's proprietary end can be made into the universal Motorola end that aftermarket head units typically use.

- **Auxiliary (Aux) Integration Harnesses** – USB, 3.5mm mini-jack, HDMI and other input connections are more prevalent in modern vehicles. Most of the time these circuits can be integrated without vehicle-specific parts. However, integration parts are sometimes available for these Aux input connections to reside on a single panel in the vehicle for easier user access. The availability of these parts allows for not only a quicker install, but a cleaner one, and one that can retain OEM functionality.

- **Steering Wheel Control (SWC) Adaptors** – Steering wheel controls are simply wired switches that send commands to the head unit. Depending on the vehicle, these controls are done through data or resistance-based wiring. Most aftermarket head units need an SWC adaptor to pick up the data signals or resistance-based signals being sent when a button is pressed and translated to a signal the aftermarket head unit can understand.

  Some head units have this hardware built in. It will allow the head unit to read simple resistance-based SWC systems. There will typically be two or three wires coming off the back of the head unit harness that connect to the vehicle's steering wheel wires. Once connected, programming is done through the head unit.

  More advanced data interfaces for head unit installations can read steering wheel controls as well. They offer integrating into the vehicle's steering wheel circuit along with others as a more complete solution for data intensive vehicles. In some cases, advanced data interfaces that accommodate SWC functionality can be programmed to remap the SWC buttons or have two functions programmed – a press/release and a press/hold function, to allow adding new functionality to the existing controls to take advantage of advanced features some aftermarket head units may have.

- **Data Interfaces** – With more circuits living on a vehicle's networks and the head unit becoming more of a central part of the vehicle's comfort and convenience system, a data interface is needed to facilitate an aftermarket head unit installation. A data interface can be summed up as a wiring harness to connect to the vehicle's proprietary plugs along with a circuit board to integrate with the vehicle's data network. In other words, a data interface acts like a translator between the new head unit and the vehicle to allow communication and flawless integration into an abundance of the vehicle's

Margin Notes

circuits. Instances where a data interface would be needed are:

- Data Initiated Turn-on – Meaning no accessory power is located at the head unit. It turns on when the data bus system wakes up, thus the data interface would need to provide an output to the aftermarket head unit's accessory wire.
- OnStar – Since OnStar audio is played through the factory head unit; the data interface allows the vehicle to keep this feature with an aftermarket head unit.
- Warning Chimes – These chimes help alert the driver of the current state of their vehicle and, in many modern vehicles, the chimes commands route through the head unit to the vehicle speakers. Oil level, check engine, key in cylinder, backup sensor warnings or leaving the headlights on are some examples of warning chimes that can play through the vehicle's speakers.

There are even data interfaces that allow integration to display gauges, vehicle info, climate control and parking assist cameras and sensors on an aftermarket head unit screen. The aftermarket head unit must be capable accepting this communication from the interface module, though. Typically, a simple RS-232 style connection is made between the two to allow communication between them. The integration module then acts as a bridge of communication between the vehicle and the head unit. This allows the customer the ability to display and control vehicle-specific circuits through an aftermarket head unit.

In the past, in-dash screens would often have a separate tuner or brain. The screen would be mounted in the place of the factory head unit and then a proprietary bus cable would be used to connect it to the separate tuner box that would be mounted elsewhere. The mounting locations were limited to the length of the bus cable but would be decided using MECP-recommended practices, factoring for temperature, moving parts and water.

New vehicles with complex dashboard electronic layouts and screens make it more challenging than ever to integrate aftermarket head units. In some vehicles the dash of the vehicle is built to house just a raw screen with the tuner mounted elsewhere. Sometimes the sub dash can be modified to house a Double-DIN head unit. When that can't be done, aftermarket manufacturers often make vehicle specific kits that allow replacement of the factory screen and tuner with aftermarket components that sometimes offer bigger screens and more integration capabilities.

Audio/Video Double-DIN head units will have the same power and speaker connections common in the aftermarket Single-DIN applications. Dependent on the hardware though, there will be additional wires to integrate with more of the vehicle circuits.

- **Reverse Wire** – This wire is an input wire that, based on the head unit, can sense either, or both, negative and positive polarity signals. It allows the head unit to know when the vehicle transmission is in Reverse. This is primarily used for reverse camera integration to automatically switch the video source of the screen when the vehicle is in reverse gear.

Margin Notes

- **Parking Brake** – This wire is an input wire to allow the screen to know when the parking brake in the vehicle is applied. This is primarily used for safety reasons to allow the screen to know it is safe to display video entertainment (such as DVD or AUX Video Input) on its screen while the vehicle is parked. Some head units will also use this connection to access some head unit menus, or to access navigation information entry.

- **Vehicle Speed Sensor (VSS)** – This is also an input wire for mostly in-dash navigation units. This circuit allows the head unit to know the vehicle's speed. Not every in-dash navigation unit will have this wire and is not always necessary to make it work. However, it allows for a more accurate navigation experience. Aftermarket head units can rely on an active GPS satellite data to compare against the data pre-loaded maps. However, if the head unit ever loses a GPS signal (mountain range or tunnels) it can use the VSS circuit as an alternate way to navigate the user. Read more about the VSS connection in the GPS Installation Considerations section of this chapter.

- **GPS Antenna** – This is an antenna used to receive signals from GPS satellites. They are made to be mounted inside the vehicle and give the head unit the necessary data needed to know speed, elevation and location. Vehicles equipped with factory navigation packages will already have these connections, and it is recommended to use the antenna that comes with the in-dash screen since it is designed to work with it properly. Read about the more GPS antenna placement guidelines in the GPS Installation Considerations in this chapter.

- **Satellite Radio Antenna** – Since many vehicles come with satellite radio technology preloaded, they typically have these antennas preinstalled and will commonly have a manufacturer specific FAKRA type connection. These can be reused when installing aftermarket units with FAKRA adapters, which is a timesaver. Reuse of the factory satellite antenna may also provide more dependability against the elements. If no factory satellite radio antenna is available, the considerations for installation are similar to the GPS antenna because they both operate using line-of-sight for the intended satellite signal.

UPGRADING THE SOUND AND RETAINING THE FACTORY HEAD UNIT

OEM Audio Integration Initial Considerations

A Mobile Product Specialist must review many installation-related details when the customer is retaining the factory head unit. The considerations are complex. It's advised that any head unit retention job should include consulting with an experienced installation technician where improving the overall sound is the goal. The reason is there are so many variables that could point to selling the customer a certain vehicle-specific solution or guiding them towards à la carte products that, with professional installation, will also handle the task.

Margin Notes

The first step in discussing any details of an upgrade should always begin with listening to the customer's existing factory system and discussing with them what they do and don't like about it. Understand where they want to make improvements so that any upgraded audio installation will have a high probability of delivering what's expected. Document those comments so that there is a reference point after the upgrade is finished. It should not just be different sounding; it should be better sounding.

Some general things to consider:

- Does the factory head unit have modern technology features like satellite radio, auxiliary input (USB and/or 3.5mm mini-jack), smartphone media playback, Bluetooth, CarPlay® or Android Auto™? If so, retaining the head unit makes a lot of sense because there is a reasonable degree of technology already in the dash. Unless there are specific features an aftermarket head unit offers that are important to the customer that are not part of the factory head unit, and the customer wishes to have those additional features, the factory head unit – in some cases – is a completely viable option to retain.

- Does the vehicle have a factory amplifier or are the speakers connected directly to the head unit? If the vehicle lacks a factory amplifier, the prospect of retaining the factory head unit and upgrading the sound is less complicated – even if intending to add aftermarket amplifiers with upgraded speakers. Some factory head units roll the low frequencies off to certain speakers as the volume increases, but there are advanced LOC-type interface devices available to compensate for that volume-dependent roll-off so it can be addressed. In most cases, adding an amplifier and subwoofer (even if the other speakers are not all upgraded) will yield excellent results for systems that only have a factory head unit, but lack a factory amplifier.

- When a factory amplifier is present, what is offered as a solution for upgrading the audio depends heavily on the year/make/model of vehicle and what configuration and integrated signal processing exists in the factory audio system. For example, does it have a premium-branded system such as Bose®, Sony, Bang & Olufsen, Burmester, Mark Levinson, Fender, etc. that may contain an upmixer or time-corrected channels? This can influence whether there is a suitable easy solution with vehicle-specific interface devices, or whether an à la carte solution for one or more integration devices is the better approach. The details of what influences each decision factor are complex – such as whether summing bandwidth limited channels together is recommended or correction of the factory frequency response curve, but this section summarizes some elements to consider in the process of selecting equipment to do the job.

- Know the brands of integration devices and other car audio products with integration features that are sold in the shop. Know what items are stocked regularly and which ones are special order. This is important to develop

Margin Notes

a range of the solutions that a customer is offered to approach that OEM audio upgrade.

Whenever a vehicle has some form of OEM audio integration installation, the Mobile Product Specialist should allocate a portion of the overall budget for the appropriate interface device(s), as well as the labor associated with the installation and configuration of these devices, such as programming, running the initial measurement and correction process, or initial tuning.

At the start of any planning, it's helpful to draw the system design out on a worksheet so that the circles, squares and rectangles (representing speakers and electronic equipment) with lines for signal or speaker wiring connecting everything are visually represented to both the sales person and the customer. This can also help when a technician is brought in to assist with any technical questions about the suitability of an equipment choice and where/how it's intended to connect. For example, this can identify if the audio inputs to a given integration device are going to be preamp level, speaker level or a data-bus connection (or a combination of those).

An OEM audio integration installation that retains a factory head unit can have a customer perception challenge. Customers may assume that if a factory component is retained, the overall cost of installation is less than a complete aftermarket system. Drawing out an audio system design with the included parts helps identify the parts that may later be hidden away but are of prime importance. The reality is that approaching OEM integration the right way — using the appropriate interface techniques and devices — typically **costs at least as much, sometimes more than just a part for part replacement**, so it's best to have a visual way to represent that investment to a customer.

Vehicle-Specific Solutions

Depending on the vehicle year/make/model/trim level and options, a vehicle-specific integration device that plugs directly in to the vehicle wiring and/or fiber optic harness may be available. New vehicle-specific solutions can also be influenced by vehicles where the alternative with external summing and correction devices is much costlier, such as in the case of many Mercedes, BMW, Audi, or other MOST applications). These integration devices are generally built for one vehicle application to start and as the integration device is tested with other models it might work for others in that brand family to expand coverage.

If the vehicle has an upmixer, time-corrected channels, factory-implemented EQ, preset factory crossover points (meaning not a 'full-range' channel) and/or any other signal processing challenges to correct, a vehicle-specific integration device is a considerable savings of time or trial-and-error when one is available. Often vehicle-specific integration device requires an aftermarket signal processor and/or amplifier(s) to complete the solution. Manufacturers of these vehicle-specific integration devices have robust application guides on their websites, so doing some research to at least rule out whether one is available is one of the first things a Mobile Product Specialist should do.

Margin Notes

Of course, if a vehicle-specific integration device is both available and used, the system design worksheet gets a lot easier to draw out compared to "after the amplifier" à la carte integration processors and the installation/configuration is more predictable as far as the intended outcome.

À la carte Solutions

Where there is no plug and play vehicle-specific integration solution that provides preamp level outputs to easily add aftermarket amplifiers and speakers, there are still methods using the signal processing/integration devices described in Chapter 1 to acquire signals at the output of a factory head unit or (more likely) factory amplifier. It would connect to an integration processor and ultimately provide inputs to one or more aftermarket amplifiers; however, this requires expertise often outside the realm of a Mobile Product Specialist. Still, it's important to understand that integrating great sound with a factory-installed head unit is possible in almost every single car. This is where consulting with an experienced technician on the discussion of solutions with the customer is recommended. Read about additional considerations specific to signal processors that perform OEM audio integration functions in the Signal Processor Installation Considerations section of this chapter.

Other General Considerations (about the vehicle)

Beyond the devices available in the aftermarket to steer a Mobile Product Specialist toward a solution-based approach for an OEM audio integration job, there may be other things about the vehicle itself that require additional modification or settings to work with the aftermarket equipment. This is a case- by-case basis, so going to have a good look at the vehicle and understand its existing features is important.

- Vehicles with 'active road noise cancellation' as part of the audio system can be a concern. In these cases, there is a microphone (sometimes two) sampling some of the interior noise and attempts to counteract the noise with an equal and opposite signal to 'cancel out' the effect of the road noise audible in the interior. When adding aftermarket subwoofers, this can present an issue. Often the recommended result is to disable the interior microphone — either by unplugging it at the head unit or active noise cancellation (ANC) module, or by modifying the microphone itself if there are more than one microphone transducers present (as in the cases where the factory Bluetooth microphone is also alongside in the same mounting plate).

- Vehicles that produce engine sounds through the audio system to give a more powerful sounding driving impression, or to supplement or 'tune' the engine sounds for a more performance-oriented experience. These can be common in sports cars, trucks, and SUVs with 4- or 6-cylinder engines to give the impression of a larger 8-cylinder engine. Some vehicles allow this to be turned off in a menu, but others either require the technician to remove a signal from the Powertrain Control Module (PCM) that is supplied to the audio source unit or use an aftermarket module to remove or reduce the effect.

- Be sure to check for any navigation prompts, hands-free calling, reverse sensor beeps or other features that use the factory speakers to convey those sounds. Often a center speaker in cars so equipped may only be used for some navigation or hands-free calling purposes and then plays audio only when a DSP or 'surround' mode is engaged. That's important to know for the vehicle evaluation purposes since the interface methodology may or may not use that center speaker. You may elect to leave it as is for retaining all that original functionality.

- Other examples of speakers conveying hands-free or voice prompt information are dual voice coil speakers where one coil is used for the purpose of the prompt after the audio signal on the other coil is muted from the sound system. Always be sure to check (or have the technician check) this when inspecting channels, wiring and factory speakers upon disassembly.

No single, easy solution applies in all cases of OEM audio integration, and there can be a heightened level of complexity and cost. Even with the same vehicle and same integration challenges, the desired outcome may be different. One customer may be adding a powered   to work along with existing factory speakers, whereas another customer needs a DSP-based integration processor that sums channels, de-equalizes the factory signal and removes all factory time correction to provide a flat full-range signal that will be handled by the internal crossovers in the DSP.

Seek Experienced Guidance

The installation work of doing OEM audio integration is intended for Advanced or Master level MECP technicians. Wherever possible, pull a qualified technician into a customer discussion about retaining their factory head unit so that the technician can leverage that experience to help the sales person and customer arrive at a confident solution for the expected outcome. Teamwork benefits the customer and when there are great outcomes, that also benefits the professionalism of the industry.

If a vehicle-specific solution is not available (or chosen), the installation technician handling the work should be looking at the factory audio signals with measurement tools like a polarity detector, RTA and oscilloscope to determine the following attributes:

- **Speaker Polarity** (which wire is + and which is -)
- **Channel Bandwidth** (if not full range, what is the effective range)
- **Signal Voltage Levels** (what kind of signal voltage is present and how far can the factory volume go before clipping)

The technician would then be able to decide how many of the factory audio output channels need to be used and what integration strategy is needed to facilitate the equipment chosen as well as the outcome desired by the customer.

Margin Notes

Margin Notes

Document Results

Whenever an audio upgrade installation retaining a factory head unit is completed, document the results of the outcome. Listen to the system, document what was improved (over the factory system) and keep those notes in a file that you can access later should you want to follow the same path or make incremental improvements.

SIGNAL PROCESSOR INSTALLATION CONSIDERATIONS

The Signal Path

A signal processor is intended to be in the signal path before amplification. Typically, this would be:

- The output of a source unit feeds the input to a signal processor.
- Then the processor's outputs feed either another (different function) of processor or into an amplifier's inputs.
- Then the amplifier ultimately connects to the speakers it's intended to power.

A signal processor is anything inserted into the audio signal path with the capability and intent to "do something" to the signal, presumably to enhance it. In the case of OEM audio integration duties, it may be fixing or undoing something with the audio signal so that the audio signal is compatible with the downstream aftermarket amplifiers (or other processors, then amplifiers). In the case of a complete aftermarket system, it could be adding equalization to contour the sound with more adjustment and adding crossovers to better protect speakers intended only to operate in a specific range, such as subwoofers, midrange or tweeters.

More and more devices contain built-in signal processing, such as aftermarket head units and multi-channel mobile audio amplifiers. These built-in features, as well as dedicated signal processors, such as DSP-based integration processors, were referenced in Chapter 1 of this study guide in their respective sections. For a review of those specific features and variables, refer to those sections.

In concept, implementing a signal processor is a simple thought process; head unit to signal processor to amplifier to speaker. In actual practice, it can be more complicated when devices with their own built-in features are utilized along with dedicated (outboard) signal processors. An example of this could be a mix of electronics in a head unit, and a signal processor and amplifier that have duplicated signal processing features such as active crossovers.

Not every signal processing feature needs be utilized just because it's there. Sometimes it's okay to have features that go unused in a head unit's built-in equalization or crossover settings because there is a more robust equalization and crossover functionality in another device, such as the dedicated signal processor or multi-channel "system" amplifier. Even a factory head unit or factory audio amplifier has its own built-in features intended for that specific vehicle, some of which can be useful and others which the goal may be to 'strip away' from the audio signal path or minimize by defeating or turning off.

Margin Notes

What Is the Source?

The first question is what is the source of the audio signal?

- Is it an aftermarket source unit or portable media player that provides the audio signal? If so, chances are that it will connect to a signal processor using preamp level (RCA) audio cables or – if present in the source unit and signal processor – a digital audio connection, either optical or copper.

- Is it an OEM source unit or factory amplifier that provides the audio signal? If so, it's almost always necessary that the signal processor have speaker-level inputs to be able to accept the audio input signal, including its signal ground reference and signal voltage.

The first answer helps a Mobile Product Specialist identify what kind of basic features must be in the signal processor chosen so that it will be compatible with the source of audio, particularly on the method(s) of accepting an audio input.

The second question is what is the goal of the signal processing that will be utilized?

- If the source is an aftermarket head unit using either preamp (RCA) or digital outputs to the signal processor's inputs, the goal is typically to have tuning features such as equalization, adjustable crossover points for all the outputs, and time-correction of each channel. Other desired features may be auxiliary input for another source unit (such as a smartphone or Hi-Res audio player) and some presets for different listening profiles. This is a common approach for audio systems where an aftermarket head unit is the source. The easy way to think about this approach of signal processing is that the system starts from 'square one' without any prior audio signal complications that are common when integrating with a factory system (retaining an OEM head unit and/or amplifier).

- If the source is an OEM head unit and there is no factory amplifier present, the signal processor is going to need speaker-level inputs to function as an LOC-type device where it can provide a preamp level RCA output that is compatible with aftermarket amplifiers. Some factory head units roll the low frequencies off to certain speakers as the volume increases, but there are advanced LOC-type interface devices available to compensate for that volume-dependent bass roll-off, so it can be addressed. Addressing any bass roll-off is an example of simple signal processing where the customer may wish to add a simple subwoofer upgrade and keep the factory speakers intact. Of course, a more complex signal processor approach could also be utilized in these cases, but the complexity is far less when a factory amplifier is not present.

Margin Notes

- If vehicle has an amplifier present, there are a few more considerations depending on what kind of integration device will be used and what the overall goal of signal processing is to be. This could be looked at in two distinct parts of the process:

    - o First, the factory audio signal must have a way to get into the integration device or signal processor. As covered in the previous section about retaining the factory head unit, the choices are vehicle-specific integration devices or à la carte signal processors with integration features and functionality. The integration part of the signal processing here generally includes some degree of 'correcting' the factory audio signal by level matching the inputs, corrective equalization, possibly summing bandwidth limited channels and possibly removing factory-applied time correction of specific channels.
    - o Second, once the integration part of the signal processing does its thing, then what else does the integration device or processor need to have feature-wise to fulfill the remaining sound quality goals? This may be the same set of tuning features that the aftermarket head unit system desires, such as equalization, variable crossover points, time-correction, presets, etc. The presumption is that the fine-tuning features on this second part of the equation are only going to be effective if the first part of integration with the factory signal has correctly been addressed.

In the case of OEM audio integration where a factory amplifier is present, the important part is that a signal processor must EITHER address the factory signal first, or the 'corrected' factory signal second. Or, it could be an integration processor that does all those things in one package, but does those things in the right order.

The à la carte integration processor solution that is NOT vehicle specific must have speaker-level inputs to allow connection to the factory amplifier's speaker output wiring. The vehicle-specific solution may offer a pre-wired harness that utilizes the vehicle's infotainment network as the source of audio input to get a compatible signal that can then be utilized with aftermarket signal processing (or a vehicle-specific solution may have some of that processing built-in). It is important to know the features of a signal processor and whether or not it has the intended use as an OEM audio integration device.

Setup and Tuning

Perhaps the most time-consuming element of installing a signal processor is the setup and tuning process. One thing a Mobile Product Specialist should know when quoting labor for signal processor installations is they are not 'ready to go' out of the box in most cases. Most require setup, initial tuning settings and, in some cases, more in-depth system tuning.

Some signal processors have switches and dials for settings that are accessible to the technician during installation. This used to be the case with most analog signal

Margin Notes

processors, but more digital signal processing (DSP) has become part of most signal processor devices. Many DSP-based signal processors and vehicle-specific interface devices require setup with an internet-enabled computer or mobile device that includes updating to the latest firmware. These processors and devices may have a USB port or make a wireless connection to allow setup/programming.

Once setup of a signal processor is complete (which includes doing any OEM integration signal correction, if applicable), there is the matter of making the basic tuning settings such as crossover points, matching individual output channel levels and usually some initial settings with the equalizer while observing a real time analyzer (RTA) with a microphone to view the system's frequency response. At this time is when the amplifiers are also setup and calibrated so the signal path is ideally unclipped all the way through from the source unit, through the signal processor to the amplifier inputs.

More in-depth tuning can often be the Achilles heel to a technician if they are not following a repeatable process that maximizes the sound quality outcome without losing labor revenue for unbillable hours.

Signal Processors and Avoiding Unwanted Noise

Perhaps one of the greatest installation concerns when it comes to signal processors is that many technicians experience unwanted or unintended noise problems when they're adding in a signal processor to a system. Some of the fundamental things to observe include feeding the processor a clean audio signal (do not clip or distort the inputs) and do not add excessive boost as that can raise the noise floor and reveal any hiss or other noises that might be present.

Preamp Level RCA Input Considerations

The input configuration of the signal grounding in the preamp level audio path of signal processors is an important consideration since many signal processors are not designed to know to which head unit upstream or amplifiers downstream it'll be connected. Each of those could have different preamp level audio signal grounding schemes and the insertion of a preamp level processor in the signal path is where those differences might meet — and unwanted noise could be the result.

The best signal processors for rejecting unwanted noise on the preamp level inputs have a **high input impedance** and **do not share a signal ground path to the power supply's chassis ground** (or if they do, it's through very high resistance in kilohms or megohms). Many signal processors offer the option of adjusting this input impedance compatibility, either with jumpers or switches, usually on the circuit board so as not to be accidentally switched by the consumer. This can help installation technicians to reduce or eliminate unexpected noise issues by listening to the effect of each position "on the fly" in real time.

Margin Notes

Other tips for reducing the probability of noise in a signal processor using preamp-level inputs:

- When planning the signal cable wire run, avoid plans to route the RCA audio cables right next to high-current power wiring, either the aftermarket wiring for the amplifier power or any factory battery cables present in trunk-mounted batteries. Keeping preamp-level audio cables separated from high-current wiring is the MECP-recommended practice. This reduces the probability of radiated noise.

- The higher the analog preamp signal voltage from the head unit or signal source, the better. A one-volt output from the head unit is certainly not great. If using a portable media player or smartphone as a preamp output source, those too are often limited to a one-volt signal analog output. Two volts is better. Four or five volts (or more) of analog preamp level audio signal is even better. The higher the signal voltage into the processor, the better the "signal" in the signal-to-noise ratio of the preamp level RCA cable run. Here's an opportunity to step up customers to high-voltage RCA preamp outputs when there will be a preamp-level signal processor used in the system.

Speaker-Level Input Considerations

Noise from signal ground incompatibilities is generally not an issue when using speaker-level inputs on signal processors equipped with such inputs (such as for OEM audio integration purposes). This is because the inputs that drive speakers are already "floating" from any connection to chassis ground. Sometimes if the signal processor is not adjustable on the preamp-level (RCA) signal ground input isolation, an easy solution for the installation technician to eliminate the noise may be to **utilize speaker-level inputs (using the head unit's speaker outputs)** if it's equipped as such. Since the speaker level signal voltage is often higher than preamp level signal voltages, using this method gains the ability to reject other radiated noises as well, all while allowing amplifier(s) after the signal processor to have input gains set lower (resulting in lower floor noise or hiss).

The caution with using speaker-level inputs to a signal processor would be to ensure the technician verified **at what position on the head unit the signal clips and what is the signal voltage level at that point** so as not to clip or overdrive the signal processor's speaker-level inputs. In most cases, signal processors with speaker-level inputs can handle 20 volts or greater of audio signal, but some OEM audio amplifiers with switching power supplies can exceed that level, so therefore it's important for the technician to know the signal voltage level AND what position on the head unit, whether numeric or position of the dial, that the audio signal clips.

Digital Input Considerations

Digital audio inputs don't suffer from any major concerns of radiated noises or electro-magnetic interference (EMI). The majority of digital audio outputs and inputs are S/PDIF format, whether Toslink optical or copper (digital RCA). S/PDIF is covered in Chapter 1 for both signal processors and amplifiers with digital inputs.

One of the obvious things to consider is that the source unit's digital output connector type (Toslink or digital RCA) is available on the digital input of the signal processor.

Another, less-obvious concern for a digital signal transfer is that the sampling rate and bit depth is compatible from the digital source unit's output to the signal processor's input.

These are common examples of bit depth and sampling rates:

- **Bit Depth** – 16, 24, 32 or 48 bits. 16 is common. Many signal sources and Hi-Res digital audio file formats offer 24 bit. Sometimes a processor will say it's capable of accepting up to 48-bit depth indicating it's 'future-ready' but integrates with the lower bit rates if that's what's in the digital signal.

- **Sampling Rate** – 44.1kHz, 48kHz, 96kHz and 192kHz are the common sampling rates in digital audio formats. CD quality is 44.1kHz. Many professional mixing consoles and digital recording devices use 48 kHz sampling. 96kHz and 192kHz sampling is used by DVD-Audio (multi-channel @ 96kHz, two-channel @ 192kHz), HD-DVD and Blu-ray disc formats. Most of the Hi-Res digital audio file formats such as Free Lossless Audio Codec (FLAC) also use 96kHz or 192kHz sampling rates.

The S/PDIF format of digital audio can support up to 192kHz of audio, but similar to the bit depth, the device(s) may not support that high of sampling. For mobile audio source units and signal processors with digital audio inputs/outputs, it's most common to see 48kHz or 96kHz sampling.

Note: *Sony's Direct Stream Digital (DSD) recording format is a different structure than other, multi-bit digital audio formats. DSD is based on 1-bit depth with an extremely high sample rate. Most commercially available DSD recordings are 1-bit with a sample rate of 2.8224MHz to 5.6448Mhz, though music at sample rates up to 22.5792Mhz are starting to become available to consumers. A DSD file with a sample rate of 22.5792Mhz has 512 times the amount of sampling information as a CD music file. It's simply a necessary piece of detail to ensure the playback device can support the DSD format(s) and operational characteristics. If so, the device(s) will usually indicate that fact.*

The takeaway for digital signal compatibility is to be sure to look at BOTH the source unit and signal processor's technical specifications. Ensure a digital input/output connection will be compatible and support the file formats used for audio source files. When in any doubt, consult an experienced technician or someone who is well-versed in the digital audio signal path and playback file formats.

Other than the compatibility with an S/PDIF sampling rate between source unit and signal processor input, the only other major concern with digital audio signal paths

Margin Notes

MECP-recommended practice is to install a fuse or circuit breaker no more than 18 inches (45.7cm) away from the point of power connection.

Margin Notes

are with optical cables using the Toslink connector. The type of optical cables used in a car audio system would be Plastic Optical Fiber (POF), and it can be installation-friendly as long as the bends, especially near the connector, are not severe. Severe bends in the optical cable can affect the transmission of the light pulses, so ensure the installation technician's planned digital cable routing path allows for 'sweeping, gradual bends' rather than sharp 90 (or more) degree bends.

INSTALLATION CONSIDERATIONS OF AMPLIFIERS

Meeting expected performance of an amplifier installation requires the technician to follow many important recommended practices. It's critical for the Mobile Product Specialist to understand the basis of why these practices are necessary so that they can communicate this to clients when describing the detail of an amplifier installation, including why specific installation accessories (such as an amplifier wiring kit of appropriate wire gauge) are necessary to ensure optimized performance.

In addition, knowledge about some commonly used configurations in which mobile audio amplifiers can be utilized will help determine if some of the built-in features can be used or if other components (or functionality within another component (such as a head unit, signal processor or multi-voice coil subwoofers) are necessary.

Accessing Power at the Battery

When an amplifier installation takes place, it's necessary to sell high-current power wire and the related connectors, fuse blocks, etc. or, more likely, sell a pre-packaged amplifier power wiring kit that fits the requirements for the installation. External power amplifiers require a direct connection to the vehicle battery to provide an unobstructed, clear path for current flow to the amplifier. This connection should be circuit protected within practical limits so that the minimum amount of wire is unprotected. The power wire itself needs to support the amount of current required for the amplifier(s), considering the length required between the battery positive connection and amplifier power (+) input, as well as considering the chassis ground connection to the amplifier's ground (-) input.

- **Circuit Protection** – MECP-recommended practice is to **install a fuse or circuit breaker no more than 18 inches (45.7cm) away from the point of power connection**, but the closer the better. The fuse or circuit breaker should be placed where access for resetting or replacement is convenient. The purpose of the main fuse or circuit breaker near the battery is to protect the wire itself as well as the rest of the vehicle from any short circuit or fire hazard that might occur should the power wire become shorted to chassis ground somewhere along the way to the amplifiers.

If several amplifiers are connected to one main power wire connection, it is traditional to electrically distribute the power connection to each amplifier with its own form of circuit protection. Using power distribution blocks makes the wiring neater and provides a safe connection point for high current wire to be broken off into smaller circuit branches for each amplifier (or even for other audio system components).

Keep this in mind when selling amplifier wiring kits for more than one amplifier because if a power distribution/fuse block is not part of the kit, it should be added to the overall amplifier installation accessories being sold to complete the installation.

Margin Notes

- **Using Grommets** – When the main power wire travels through any metal holes such as the firewall, MECP-recommend practice is to **always use a rubber or plastic grommet to insulate the metal from contacting the wire**, whether a factory installed grommet or one the technician installs after drilling the appropriate hole. MECP recommended practice is to never run a wire to an amplifier through metal openings without using the proper grommet. It is also advised to use a silicone like sealer or "strip caulk" to seal around the wires to prevent any water intrusion from the new opening in the firewall.

- **Choosing Power Wiring** – Selecting the right gauge and type of power wire to run from the battery is important to the performance of any high current circuit, particularly with amplifiers. If the wire is too small or too long for a given amount of current demand, resistance increases. As resistance increases, the power cable will start to overheat, and the current delivered to the device(s) connected will drop. When this occurs, the amplifier's efficiency and power output will decrease. In more severe instances a fuse could blow, the amplifier could overheat and shut down, or the heat caused from the voltage drop will melt the cabling and fuse holder. If there is ever a question on the gauge of wire needed, consult an American Wire Gauge (AWG) reference chart.

The specific amount of resistance per foot of American Wire Gauge sizes (AWG) is available from most cable manufacturers and specifies the resistance and temperature, per foot, of a specific wire gauge rated in the AWG format. **The AWG format ensures it complies with the American Wire Gauge standards.** CTA has a "Mobile Electronics Cabling Standard" called ANSI/CTA-2015 in which the

A comparison with OFC wire (left) and CCA wire (right) shows that CCA wire often has much more insulation which many technicians mistakenly assume means it has more current capability. Remember it's the cross sectional area of the wire (not the insulation) and the conductivity of the metal that determine the real current carrying capacity.

Margin Notes

recommended cable sizes are described along with the power it would support based on CTA-2006 amplifier power measurement standards. Instead of going by the current requirement that could be assumed is needed by the amplifier, the CTA-2015 approach is to consider total system power, rated using CTA-2006 measurements. It's an easy process to match the CTA-2006 rated power on a product to the gauge of cable required to support that power over whatever length is needed the installation. The CTA-2015 wire gauge chart is provided.

While many manufacturers have similar gauge cables, the strand count differs greatly, particularly if they do not use AWG standards. A cable labeled as "4 gauge" is not necessarily the same thing as #4 AWG multi-strand, oxygen-free 100% copper wiring. The oxygen-free component keeps the copper wiring from corroding. The number of wire gauge indicates the overall thickness (diameter) of the wire. The lower the number, the larger the wire. For example, #10 AWG wire is smaller than #4 AWG wire.

Sometimes wire manufacturers present an entire packaged amplifier wiring kit as "Up to X number of watts" and don't necessarily list the wire gauge. Aluminum or Copper Clad Aluminum (CCA) wiring is common to find as a low-cost alternative for amplifier wiring kits. This is not copper wiring. It's aluminum wire that has "copper cladding" and it's not nearly as conductive as the 100% multi-strand, oxygen-free copper wiring. That means the material from which the wiring is made plays a big part in considering what size amplifier power and ground cables are ultimately selected in an aftermarket installation to deliver adequate current capacity to the amplifier.

When making amplifier power and ground cable selections, it's essential to understand what kind of wire will be used. Multi-strand, oxygen-free copper wiring is preferable. If CCA wire is used instead of 100 percent copper wire for power/ ground cables, **MECP-recommended practice is to select the next larger commercially available gauge than what's called for in copper wiring**. For example, if the recommendation is #4 AWG copper wire and CCA wire is used, the next larger gauge, #2 AWG, would be the safe choice.

Many amplifiers have external fuses designed to blow if the power cable shorts ground, if the ground cable shorts to power, or the current capacity of the circuit is exceeded. These fuses can also be used to determine the maximum amount of current the amp can draw from the battery (in the intended configuration with that fuse). If the amplifier has a 20 ampere fuse, then it's clear that the amplifier will not draw much more than 20 amperes for any sustained length of time through the power or ground wire in the circuit path.

The chart on the next page can be used to quickly determine 100 percent copper wire size based off the amplifier's fuse size. **This chart assumes the power wire is no longer than 19 feet (4.83m)f**, which is common for most trunk mounted amplifier installations that have a battery in the front engine compartment. For shorter lengths, the recommended size is adequate; however, longer power wires should use the next size larger wire. Copper wire and CCA wire are indicated with their own charts for comparison.

Margin Notes

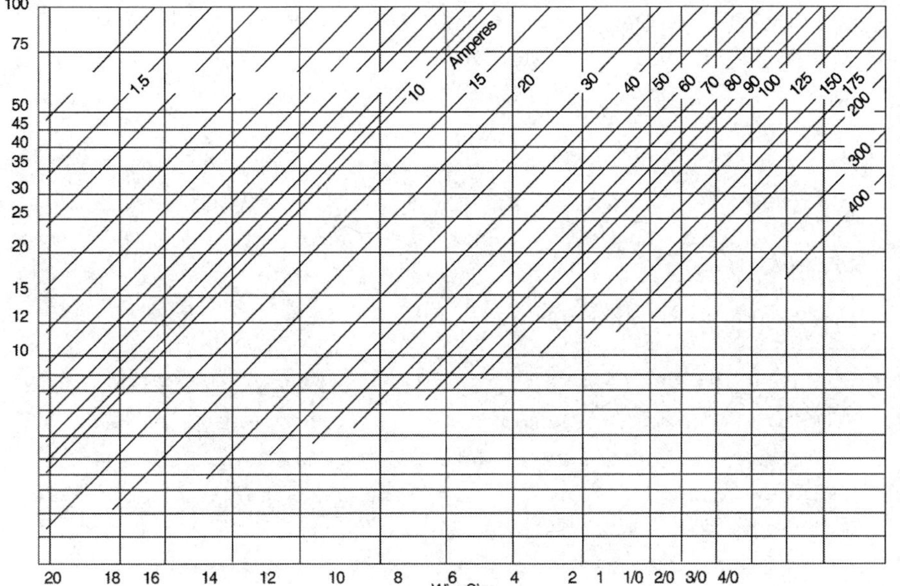

Wire Gauge Chart for OFC wire. The majority of wire gauge charts for recommended uses assume OFC wire so be sure you go up at least one size larger if using CCA wire.

- **A Healthy Battery** – Just as the wiring and components being installed are important, so is the battery. Without a good power source, the new equipment cannot perform as intended. Even worse, adding current draw to an already depleted battery will strain the vehicle's charging system, potentially damaging it. The vehicle may have difficulty starting if the voltage drops low enough. A quick test for a technician to perform is to let the vehicle sit (not running) for a few minutes, then test the battery using a digital multimeter (DMM) at the battery terminals to validate that it is resting at 12.6 volts. A better, more comprehensive test is to have the technician conduct a **State of Health (SOH) battery and charging system test** as outlined in the MECP Advanced Installation Technician study guide. This should be part of a comprehensive vehicle check-in process before beginning the installation. Experienced installation technicians should know how to perform a SOH test.

Amplifier Turn on Methods

- The most common type of amplifier turn on method is the "Remote Turn On." This is where a dedicated +12v turn on signal is sent from the head unit to the amplifier whenever the head unit is on. While aftermarket head units typically have a remote out lead, many factory head units do not. Especially with the adaptation of CAN networks in newer cars, it is getting more and more difficult to find an accessory wire that turns the factory radio on. With any remote turn-on wire, keep in mind that the source unit may have current limitations and more than one or two amplifiers may require a relay be sold/installed so the technician can ensure all the amplifiers turn on.

- The "Signal Sensing Method" relies on the presence of an audio signal or voltage surges from the alternator to turn the amplifier on. It is important to note that

Margin Notes

not all signals sensing turn on circuits use the same method to know when to provide a remote turn on.

- o The "DC Offset Method" Turns the amplifier on when a +6v signal is sensed from a speaker-level input using the chassis ground as a reference.
- o The "AC Voltage Method" of signal sense turns the amplifier on when an audio signal is sensed on the amplifier's inputs.
- o The "Voltage Surge Method" of signal sense turns the amplifier on when the battery voltage goes from a resting 12.6 volts to 14.4 volts.

While signal sense may be a huge time saver in newer vehicles that don't have an easily accessible switched power source or "remote turn on," there are some potential issues to keep in mind. You may see that when using either signal sense method, the turn on might "time out." For instance, during a non-Bluetooth call or a long lull in between music tracks, the signal threshold for turn-on may go dormant, thus creating a delay in the amplifier turning back on when signal is "sensed" once again.

- Alternative amplifier turn-on methods are those of using "switched power." While these are less preferred methods, they are still options. A physical switch can be used from a constant power source to turn an amp on and off. This is the least professional method, as it requires the customer to manually turn their equipment on and off and increases the chances of the amplifier being left on and draining the battery. A better solution is to find an accessory or retained accessory power source in the vehicle to use to turn the amplifier on and off. The benefit of this accessory power is that the customer will not have to worry about their amplifier staying on and draining the battery, as it will turn on and off with the vehicle key. However, there is the potential issue that if the radio is turned off the amplifier will still be on and any induced noise would be more prevalent.

Amplifier Signal Inputs

Many of the audio signal input formats were discussed in the Mobile Audio Amplifiers section of Chapter 1. These include:

- Preamp Level (RCA) Inputs (sometimes called "low-level inputs")
- Speaker-Level Inputs (sometimes called "high-level inputs")
- Combo Inputs (both preamp and speaker-level accepted in one connector)
- Digital Inputs – Coaxial and/or Toslink
- Bluetooth/Wireless Inputs
- Proprietary Inputs from Vehicle-Specific Integration Devices (CAN-Bus, MOST, etc.)

Of these input types, preamp-level (RCA) inputs are most susceptible to noise and interference depending on how/where those audio cables are routed in comparison to the location(s) of amplifier power wiring and how much current is carried in that power wiring to be a potential noise source. MECP-recommended practice

Margin Notes

is to keep preamp level audio cables (such as RCA audio cables) away from the power cable on its path between the battery and the power amplifier(s). The actual distance of this separation depends upon three things:

1. The amount of current flowing in the amplifier power cable.
2. The signal levels contained within the preamp-level (RCA) audio cables.
3. The ability of the component's input circuitry to reject radiated noise. This property is called Common Mode Rejection or CMMR.

Rather than guessing, MECP recommends that technicians keep these cables separate (prevent them from running alongside each other) over long distances. You should account for this in any installation labor estimate so that the technician has adequate time to correctly route signal and power cables properly. If the cables must be run near one another, MECP-recommended practice is to cross them at a 90-degree angle to minimize the chance of radiated noise problems.

Preamp-level (RCA) audio cables with twisted pair construction and proper insulation are best for preventing radiated-noise interference from power wiring.

Other types of amplifier inputs are far less susceptible to radiated noise problems, but separating audio signals from power cabling is still recommended. When planning, be sure to budget adequate time and materials for proper installation techniques.

Using Built-in Signal Processing

If no external, dedicated signal processor (such as a DSP-based processor) is used in the audio system, consider how best to utilize the amplifier's built in signal processing features whenever possible. The remainder of this topic of using built-in signal processing assumes there is no other dedicated signal processor, so the recommendations are based on that assumption.

Use the amplifier's active crossover networks, as they will be more efficient than using an external passive crossover. Depending on whether it is a multi-channel or mono/two channel amplifier different crossovers will come into play.

- A mono or two-channel amplifier intended for a subwoofer will typically have a low-pass filter (LPF). This is a crossover that allows low frequencies to pass through the amplifier but attenuates frequencies above the set point. Along with this the LPF, subwoofer amplifiers may utilize a "subsonic" filter as well. This is essentially a low frequency range high pass filter (HPF) where the job is to allow frequencies above a certain point to pass, typically 15-30 Hz. Frequencies below the subwoofer's lower limits are attenuated by the subsonic filter. The subsonic filter is also an effective tool to protect the subwoofer in a vented enclosure from damage trying to reproduce frequencies below the enclosure's tuning frequency.

- A multi-channel amplifier will typically have a high pass filter (HPF) or allow that to be selected as the filter choice. This crossover allows high frequency sounds

Margin Notes

to pass through the amplifier and will attenuate frequencies below the set point. Higher-end multi-channel amplifiers will often also have band-pass filters which allow frequencies within a set range freely pass through while attenuating those above and below the set points. Some multi-channel amplifiers that have a 3- or 5-channel configuration may also have a LPF and subsonic filter because they are intended to be used with one of the channels powering a subwoofer. This provides the greatest flexibility of use cases so that the amplifier can be easily utilized or reconfigured if the audio system expands later.

- Bass boost, or single-band equalization, should be used with caution. Bass boost is a specific centered frequency and its slope (called "Q"), which relates to how neighboring frequencies are affected, is typically fixed. When the center frequency is boosted, the intent is to enhance low frequency output (as outlined in Chapter 1). This feature is not intended to fix poorly designed and built subwoofer systems; rather, it's an enhancement of the original signal. If the subwoofer system is not satisfactory, adding more bass boost at the amplifier is not going to help.

Impedance Loads

For most amplifiers being produced, it's common to see that the lower the impedance (or "load") on the amplifier, the more power it will be rated to produce. Choosing an amplifier with the lowest impedance load possible isn't always best, and sometimes comes at a cost. Amplifiers run at 4 ohms in car audio most of the time, except for subwoofer applications. Depending on the number of subwoofers and voice coils on an amplifier channel, the impedance load can vary from 8 or more ohms to less than 1 ohm. When running at lower impedance, for example 2 ohms, an amplifier will produce more heat, making it less efficient and requiring larger gauge power and ground cables. Low-impedance operation also means the amplifier has less "control" over the speaker (known as damping factor). Conversely, an amplifier running at higher impedance (such as 4 ohms) will generally be more efficient, have more control over the speaker, and introduce less distortion. When choosing which speakers connect to an amplifier to determine the impedance load, refer to the Amplifiers and Subwoofers sections in Chapter 1 and in the appendix.

Proper Level Setting (Calibration)

Proper gain level setting is done by the technician to improve many aspects of sound quality in the system. This is necessary to match the amplifier's input stage to the signal levels to which it's connected. In home audio, preamp levels are standardized, allowing you to connect one component to another (such as a Blu-ray player to a home theater processor, then to a multi-channel amplifier) by plugging in the correct outputs to inputs. This is not the case for mobile audio amplifiers, which need to be calibrated to achieve their maximum output power without adding any unnecessary distortion or floor noise (hiss). An amplifier's gain setting (also called "level control") is not a volume control; rather, it is intended to have one correct setting, which is determined only after the system is up and running using test tones and measurement equipment (preferably an oscilloscope or distortion

Margin Notes

detector tool) to properly match the input level to the amplifier's maximum, undistorted output. This process is called "amplifier calibration."

Technicians should complete this calibration at the end of an amplifier installation. Be sure to explain to customers that when calibration is completed, their amplifier is configured to output its maximum, undistorted power. When calibration is done correctly, sound quality is improved, distortion is minimized, listening fatigue is greatly reduced, impact is more pronounced, and transient response is greatly improved. The audio system is more exciting to listen to if the distortion is minimized and sound quality is preserved. Also, by limiting clipping, you reduce the possibility of damaging speakers over time when the signal level is near or above the speakers' rated power handling.

MECP-recommended level setting processes are described in the *MECP Basic Installation Technician Study Guide* (using a DMM) and the *MECP Advanced Installation Technician Study Guide* (using an oscilloscope). It is not necessary for the Mobile Product Specialist to know the detailed calibration process. Rather, it's important that the process is recognized and completed by a qualified technician to ensure peak amplifier performance.

SPEAKER INSTALLATION CONSIDERATIONS

Just like any other component in an audio system, proper, high-quality installation of speakers is important to ensure great sound performance. This section provides some tips that Mobile Product Specialists should consider when matching a speaker choice with the vehicle, including what additional installation steps (and labor time/cost allocation) should be discussed with the customer. The overall idea is to limit surprises and ensure optimized performance of the speaker in its location if all other guidelines of powering the speaker with a head unit or external amplifier have been followed.

Factory Speaker Locations

Replacing factory speakers with a comparable-size (direct-fit) aftermarket speaker(s) seems fairly straightforward, yet there are important installation-related factors to consider to ensure optimum performance. These factors influence the amount of labor necessary to complete a speaker installation in cases where the technician will replace the factory speakers. Discussing these factors with a customer helps a Mobile Product Specialist communicate necessary installation-related details, such as the requirement of a speaker adapter, sound damping material, or whether the factory speakers can be reinstalled.

- Will the technician need to make or utilize a mounting bracket for the new speaker to fit?
- Is there enough depth for the aftermarket speaker, including clearance for windows or other moving parts to continue operating without affecting the functionality of OEM components or features?
- Is there a good seal from the speaker frame to the baffle, or panel to which the speaker is being mounted?

Margin Notes

- Is moisture or dirt from the exterior of the vehicle or from openings in the compartment where the speaker is being mounted a concern, particularly for speakers installed into doors?
- Is vibration a concern? Damping material is recommended to be part of the sale on a speaker installation to significantly reduce any chances for unwanted vibrations.
- Will the technician need to alter the OEM location, and will it affect the ability to reinstall the OEM speaker? Keep in mind if the OEM speakers are already damaged and the replacement is to address "blown" factory speakers, the customer wouldn't be likely to reinstall those factory speakers later. Reinstallation could be a concern for customers with high-end and/or leased vehicles.
- If the factory speaker is used as part of spoken navigation commands or as part of the hands-free Bluetooth calling system, will those features remain operational with the replacement of the new speaker? In most cases, the answer is yes if the factory speaker wiring is used for the speaker replacement's connections, but some factory speakers may have two voice coils--one for the audio system, when muted, and another voice coil that handles spoken directions or the Bluetooth hands-free calling. Some vehicles also utilize warning beeps or chimes through the factory speaker. This, too, is usually preserved with a direct speaker replacement. Always verify with the technician that the existing functionality of any systems that use the factory speakers will remain functional after the speaker replacement.

A salesperson or technician may not have all the answers to these questions before the technician begins the installation. It is still important to answer as much of that detail as possible to identify what additional installation steps or accessories are necessary to include in the quote for parts and labor.

In some cases where a speaker size is not a direct-fit replacement, it might be necessary to first remove the OEM speaker and test fit the aftermarket speaker to determine exactly what will be required. It is important to have the answers to these questions before modifying the vehicle in a way that cannot be returned to OEM if necessary. Direct-fit speaker replacement sizes and use of pre-packaged speaker adapters often address most speaker mounting questions. Higher-end speakers with proprietary mounting patterns and speaker frames mean the use of a custom adapter and is sometimes recommended to better ensure a good speaker-to-baffle seal and to mount it properly.

Replacing factory component speakers may require a couple of extra considerations when it comes to wiring.

- If the factory speakers have components to filter frequency (inductors and/or capacitors) built on to the speaker itself or in the wiring harness, it can be treated like a standard coaxial replacement. If the component speakers share a channel at the source unit, the crossover components will be a part of, or in-line with, the speaker.

- If the factory speakers are crossed over in a device like the factory amplifier or head unit, they might not have a full range signal. This poses several problems when replacing speakers if the intent is to have a full-range signal, such as a full-range aftermarket coaxial.

Adding a full-range speaker to a channel that is already filtered at the source unit or factory amplifier will leave the speaker under-utilized. In most cases this is acceptable unless the component that is reproducing the other frequencies is no longer in place (i.e., if the factory tweeters were removed and not replaced by another aftermarket tweeter).

Aftermarket component speakers are typically intended to take a full-range signal when they are used with a passive crossover network. Sending a filtered signal from the OEM head unit or factory amplifier into the aftermarket passive crossover may yield undesired results. Conversely, leaving the aftermarket crossover out of the install may also not be acceptable as the OEM crossover points were not set with the aftermarket speakers in mind. In a case where multiple channels are discretely filtered inside the factory amplifier or head unit, a summing device could be used to create full-range channels. This would also require the addition of aftermarket amplifiers, which may be beyond the scope of replacing factory speakers.

NON-FACTORY SPEAKER LOCATIONS

When mounting speakers in locations that didn't originally hold an OEM speaker, all the considerations of adding them to factory locations exists, and should also include:

- Will adding speakers or a structure to mount speakers in this new location impede any functional aspects of the vehicle, or obstruct any safety features or sensors designed to protect occupants within the vehicle? Any such changes should be discussed in-depth with the customer before any work is started. Any safety features that are changed or affected may violate laws in your state, so be sure to check this before proceeding.
- Will adding speakers or a structure to mount the speakers in this new location impact the serviceability or usability of the vehicle? Any changes should be discussed with the customer before work is started, and there should be documented awareness of the changes by the customer on file for future reference.
- Will the placement of the speaker be able to provide an optimal sound stage?
- What type of materials will the technician have to alter/add to be able to successfully position the speaker (plastic, fabric, vinyl, leather, metal, fiberglass)?
- Will the mounting location provide good baffle for the speaker as well as provide adequate airspace based on the speaker's parameters?

Adding more speakers than originally intended from the manufacturer will require a fair amount of planning, which will require involving both the technician and customer. It's therefore best to use a system planning worksheet to draw out what equipment goes where, including how individual speakers will be powered and what range of frequencies they will play. Following those planning steps identifies

Margin Notes

Margin Notes

if a speaker will have a full-range signal or be filtered from the amplifier or signal processor.

SUBWOOFER ENCLOSURE INSTALLATION CONSIDERATIONS

The Subwoofers section in Chapter 1 described the common subwoofer enclosure types in detail, such as infinite baffle, sealed, vented and band-pass derivatives.

Regardless of the enclosure type, there are several things to consider about the installation:

- Will multiple subwoofers be used and, if so, will they share the same air space?
- Will multiple voice coils be connected to the same amplifier channel?
- Will the enclosure's internal volume supply the recommended air space for each subwoofer?
- Will the enclosure be traditionally shaped (square/rectangle/wedge – "six-sided") or custom shaped for a specific location in a specific vehicle?
- Where will the enclosure be placed in the vehicle and in what orientation (subwoofers and/or vents facing forward, backward, down or up)?
- How it will mount (for safety)?

Ultimately the outcome of the subwoofer enclosure installation relies on the expertise of the installation technician, but this section should help a Mobile Product Specialist understand some of the variables while estimating installation and labor costs.

Installation Considerations for Multiple Subwoofers or Voice Coils

When it comes to selecting multiple subwoofers in a single enclosure, consider whether the subwoofers share a common airspace inside an enclosure. If they will share a common airspace, a mono amplifier is recommended (or a bridged 2-channel amplifier to ensure that all subwoofers are driven from the same output and move in and out identically).

Example:

- A sealed (acoustic suspension) enclosure with two 12" 8-ohm subwoofers will be designed and constructed. The subwoofers will be driven from a mono amplifier and wired in parallel to present a 4-ohm load to the amplifier. The subwoofers will share a common air space. If each subwoofer requires a given amount of air space – say one cubic foot each (28.32 liters) – then this example enclosure must have two cubic feet of internal airspace to meet the recommended performance specifications.

If using separate amplifier channels on each separate subwoofer in the same enclosure, make sure there is a dividing wall between each chamber so that each subwoofer's airspace is unaffected by the other subwoofer(s). Observing this tip ensures that no subwoofer prematurely fails from overdriving or mismatched channel levels.

Margin Notes

Example:

- As in the previous example, a sealed (acoustic suspension) enclosure with two 12" subwoofers will be designed and constructed. Since the subwoofers will be driven by separate amplifier channels intended for 4-ohm loads, 4-ohm subwoofers are chosen instead of 8-ohm because they will each be wired individually to an amplifier channel. This will present a 4-ohm load to each amplifier channel. The subwoofers will each have an individual chamber of air space with an internal divider wall separating them. If each subwoofer requires a given amount of air space – say one cubic foot each (28.32 liters) – then this example enclosure must have one cubic foot of internal airspace on each side of the divider wall to meet the recommended performance specifications. For experienced fabricators, this is an easy addition. For pre-fabricated subwoofer enclosures, many already come with divider walls, so an enclosure that meets the recommended air space specifications for the subwoofers should be selected.

Adding or utilizing an internal divider walls is also an effective way to provide internal bracing for the subwoofer enclosure so that the panels remain rigid and do not flex. Since any internal bracing and divider walls take up internal volume, be sure any custom-built enclosure takes those internal volumes into account when the fabricator takes the outside measurements. It's better to build a little larger than necessary for the air space and take up volume with braces and dividers when the outside dimensions can accommodate. As mentioned, many pre-fabricated subwoofer enclosures come with divider walls, making them an excellent choice if custom fabrication is either not possible or too costly for the client's budget.

Before choosing multiple subwoofers, consider how the voice coils will be wired to ensure the nominal impedance load on the amplifier is not below the published stable impedance load. Most amplifiers perform well (with low heat and high reliability) when connected to a 4- or 2-ohm load of subwoofers. Subwoofer manufacturers' websites provide subwoofer wiring calculators to determine the correct subwoofer voice coil configuration (Single Voice Coil or Dual Voice Coil) and what nominal impedance is best. There is a chart for multiple subwoofer/voice coil connections in the Appendix section of this study guide for general reference about which nominal impedance subwoofers connected in either series or parallel end up presenting what nominal impedance load to an amplifier channel.

Once the nominal impedance of the subwoofer(s) is determined and optimized with the amplifier's rated loading, be sure the subwoofers are going to have adequate power. If necessary, review the guidelines in Chapter 1 for both amplifiers and subwoofers for matching CTA-2031 rated subwoofer power handling to CTA-2006 rated amplifier power output. If those CTA ratings do not exist with the product specifications, try to ensure the RMS power handling of the subwoofer is not less than the RMS output of the amplifier.

Margin Notes

Meeting Recommended Airspace Requirements

For every subwoofer placed into a custom or pre-fabricated enclosure, there is a manufacturer recommended air space requirement that the enclosure must have to meet the performance expectation of the subwoofer. When selling a subwoofer (or multiple subwoofers) and determining the enclosure type (sealed, vented, etc.), it's important to ensure that there will be adequate air space for each subwoofer. Otherwise, the subwoofer can severely underperform in low-bass response, power handling, or both.

Manufacturers offer recommended enclosure internal air space volumes and enclosure types (sealed, vented, etc.) for each of their subwoofers. This information may be inside the subwoofer's packaging, on the manufacturer's website, in their printed literature or all of those. You don't want to sell a subwoofer that will never have enough air space in which to operate as intended. Too large an air space can be circumvented by adding extra bracing and other internal panels that take up space to get closer to the recommended volume. Too little available air space will result in poor low bass response and other potential issues.

Always confirm the recommended air space requirement of a subwoofer and the type of enclosure the subwoofer performs well in (sealed, vented, etc.) so that anything you ultimately sell to the customer has the best probability of performing as expected. An experienced installation technician or fabricator should be able to give a volume estimate by taking measurements of the trunk or other space to determine if the subwoofer is a suitable match.

Some companies publish their recommended enclosure volumes in cubic feet while others publish in liters (a metric measurement of volume). Converting between the two is easy. 28.32 liters (L) is equal to one cubic foot (ft3). Simply follow these conversions:

- To convert cubic feet (ft3) into liters (L), multiply:
  28.32 x Enclosure Air Space Requirement (ft3) = (L)

- To convert liters (L) into cubic feet (ft3), divide:
  Enclosure Air Space Requirement in (L) ÷ 28.32 = (ft3)

Subwoofer Enclosure Placement

Where a subwoofer enclosure can be placed has a lot to do with what type and size of enclosure will work for the expected outcome. Vehicle-specific enclosures, whether pre-manufactured or custom fabricated in the shop, will have an intended location that typically uses otherwise empty or underutilized space such as a rear side panel, empty storage well under the trunk floor or even below center consoles in large trucks and SUVs.

The variable for subwoofer enclosure placement comes when a more traditional six-sided enclosure, either pre-manufactured or custom fabricated, is to be used.

Margin Notes

At that point, a Mobile Product Specialist needs to consider where placement can both accommodate the subwoofer(s) chosen by meeting the internal air space requirements, plus how much of the available storage space the enclosure will consume in the vehicle (or how it affects accessibility – such as to a spare tire). Depending on enclosure's physical dimensions, the depth of the subwoofer driver to fit inside the intended enclosure may also be a significant consideration affecting placement.

- **Trunk or Hatchback Vehicles** – In most coupes and sedans with a trunk, as well as in hatchback vehicles, the subwoofer enclosure is installed somewhere in the rear cargo area. If it's a custom, vehicle-specific enclosure, it may be installed in a side panel. A more traditional six-sided enclosure would be placed where space allows with flat surface beneath it. In certain vehicles, the subwoofer output may be louder and seem to play lower bass if the subwoofer faces the trunk/hatch instead of the rear seat. This allows the subwoofer to load off the trunk's edges and extend the bass notes into the cabin with fewer obstacles. Always include protective grilles over the subwoofer(s) installed in a rear cargo area to avoid damage, especially if the subwoofers face the trunk/hatch area.

- **Trucks** – Single cab trucks may only have adequate space for a subwoofer enclosure behind the seat. Ensure that when the seats are in their normal position there is enough spa-ce/depth available for the subwoofer enclosure, including the subwoofer driver itself. A popular solution for trucks is to utilize a 'thin' or 'shallow-mount' subwoofer, as they require limited installation depth. Crew Cab or Extra Cab trucks with rear seats may have room underneath the rear seats for subwoofers depending on the arrangement and function of the rear seats. There are many high-performance, vehicle-specific subwoofer enclosures for trucks, and custom fabricators with the ability to work with fiberglass can create many unique solutions that fit these limited spaces. Care should be taken to ensure the seats in a single-cab truck can operate correctly and that the driver can safely and comfortably sit in the seat once the enclosure is installed.

- **Sport Utility Vehicles (SUVs) or Vans** – In SUVs or other large passenger vehicles, the rear cargo area is the most popular location for the subwoofer enclosure. Be sure to consider how much a subwoofer enclosure would encroach upon the cargo area when, for example, using a third row of seats. Always include protective grilles over the subwoofer(s) installed in a cargo area to avoid damage from cargo or other passengers. Vehicle-specific SUV subwoofer solutions often utilize alternatives to the cargo area to maintain functionality. These may use locations such as the center console, under a seat or behind a rear side panel.

When final placement is determined in any vehicle, focus on how the enclosure will be mounted to ensure it does not move around once it's installed. An unmounted subwoofer enclosure is a liability in an accident or when stopping suddenly as it can easily move around and injure passengers (particularly in hatchbacks and SUVs) or cargo and other nearby audio equipment (in all

Margin Notes

vehicles). This may require the assistance of an experienced technician who can recommend mounting points that take advantage of existing vehicle structure so that few, if any, new holes would need to be drilled into the vehicle sheet metal. When selecting mounting options, be sure to avoid fuel tanks or wiring harnesses so either is not compromised.

Importance of Mounting Enclosure and Subwoofer Drivers

Although the task of mounting the subwoofer(s) into the enclosure and the enclosure itself into the vehicle belongs to the installation technician, it's important that the Mobile Product Specialist understand why these considerations are important.

Mounting the subwoofer driver into the enclosure requires the subwoofer frame be well sealed in the opening so that there are no air leaks around the outer edges. This ensures the only air moving is from the movement of the subwoofer cone (and vent if in an applicable enclosure). This seal is typically achieved by using compressed foam gasket material that forms a seal once the subwoofer driver is attached to the baffle. MECP recommends avoiding the use of silicone or caulking material as a seal. Once dry, it's nearly impossible to remove the subwoofer driver without damaging the driver or enclosure (or both). The subwoofer driver must be serviceable should failure occur.

Mounting the enclosure itself is also a very important consideration for safety and performance. Safety of the vehicle occupants is the primary reason to ensure solid subwoofer enclosure mounting. If a subwoofer enclosure is not mounted, it can easily become a projectile in a sudden stop or an accident. The sheer weight of a subwoofer in an enclosure (even a small one) can be deadly if airborne.

MECP recommends using methods of mounting that can utilize anchor points from existing factory hardware and bracketing. This reduces the number of additional holes drilled in the vehicle body or trim panels, plus allows the subwoofer to be removed with more ease should the vehicle be sold or returned to original condition. Also consider how the mounting method can be favorable for serviceability should the subwoofer enclosure need to be removed, either for refinishing or for other vehicle repairs that would require access blocked by the subwoofer enclosure. Solid mounting improves performance because the subwoofer enclosure's energy of moving air is transferred directly to the interior cabin air and not vibrating the enclosure on the trunk or hatch floor.

Concerns of Mounting Electronics to the Enclosure

MECP does not recommend mounting amplifiers or other electronics directly to an enclosure wall due to the high probability of vibration-induced failures. The Mobile Product Specialist should consider the following:

- Mount amplifier(s) or other electronics to a separate location not on (or vibrated by) the subwoofer enclosure.
- Air circulation for adequate heat dissipation is also an important consideration when selecting the mounting location an amplifier.

- If the amplifier(s) or other electronics must be mounted to the enclosure, double the thickness of the enclosure side so that it is more rigid and vibrates less. Ideally an integrated mounting panel would not be part of the subwoofer enclosure wall and have some spacing between the subwoofer panel and electronics mounting panel. Spacing the panels an inch or two apart greatly reduces vibration transfer but also allows for running wiring behind the electronics for a cleaner look.

Margin Notes

Powered Subwoofers

Powered subwoofers are an excellent addition to an aftermarket audio system where the head unit powers the front and rear speakers. The powered subwoofer can perform the straightforward task of adding bass to the audio system without too much guesswork.

1. **Where will the powered subwoofer be installed?** This will be influenced by its size (if not vehicle-specific) and what space is available in the vehicle. Powered subwoofers are a good compromise of size for the expected performance. Always try to select a location that does not hinder the normal use of the vehicle – such as cargo space, third-row seats (in SUVs or mini-vans) or seat movement if it's suitable for an under-seat location.

2. **How will the powered subwoofer mount?** Check to see if mounting hardware is included with the powered subwoofer. This determines what additional parts or labor will be necessary if custom brackets/fabrication will be required to safely mount the powered subwoofer. If hardware is included, ensure the intended location will work with the provided hardware. A quick consult with the installation technician may help any final decisions on how (and where) secure mounting will take place.

3. **What kind of power and ground wiring is needed?** Since the subwoofer is powered, power and ground wiring need to be routed to the onboard amplifier. Generally, #8 or #10 AWG copper wiring will be appropriate for many powered subwoofers, but verify the manufacturer's requirements to be sure. Sell an amplifier wiring kit if the powered subwoofer does not come with its own power wiring. The subwoofer will also have a traditional +12v turn-on input, which will be wired to the head unit's 'amp turn-on' output. The wiring for the turn-on is low current, so typically 18 AWG wiring is either provided in an amplifier wiring kit or used from bulk wire in the shop's install bay.

4. **How will the powered subwoofer get its audio input signal?** If upgrading an OEM audio system, ensure the powered subwoofer has speaker-level inputs. If it's used with an all-aftermarket system, the head unit most likely has a preamp-level RCA output, perhaps even one designated as the "SUB OUT" which will provide level control from the head unit. If using the preamp level RCA input, be sure the amplifier wiring kit includes an appropriate length of RCA audio cable (or add that separately). Many powered subwoofers also provide signal

Margin Notes

sensing for turn-on so that a separate remote-turn on wire is not needed, which is particularly useful when used in an OEM audio integration application.

5. **What on-board signal processing is present?** If the subwoofer has a variety of on-board signal processing features such as a low-pass crossover, phase control and parametric bass EQ, follow the same recommended practices as outlined in the signal processors section (do not cascade similar filters/features). For example, if using the low-pass crossover on the SUB OUT of the head unit, do not use the low-pass crossover on the powered subwoofer, or vise-versa.

MOBILE VIDEO INSTALLATION CONSIDERATIONS

Depending on the specific type of mobile video system, be sure to discuss with clients the placement, operational aspects, and the ability to return the vehicle to original condition.

Rear Seat Entertainment Installation Considerations

As the video system in rear seat entertainment (RSE) application is completely behind the driver, the major concerns for installation are secure mounting, where the video source originates, and how the audio will be heard by the rear seat passengers.

Consider how the video signal will be sent to the screen(s)

The following considerations describe how the video signal for a rear seat entertainment system is delivered to the screen(s):

- The RSE could use a built-in source, such as SD card, DVD, USB (for thumb drive), etc.
- The RSE could use a source from a head unit or external DVD player. If a head unit is the video source, does it have dual-zone functionality and is that important to the customer? Dual-zone functionality allows the video signal to route to the RSE while the front seat passengers can experience a second source, such as AM/FM/Satellite Radio, streaming Bluetooth, etc.
- Having the right interconnect to carry the video signal is import, not only for compatibility but for picture quality as well. Common wired video connections are composite video (analog) and HDMI (digital).
- If a portable device is the video source, consider how that device will connect to the RSE (either wired and/or wirelessly).

Consider how users will listen to the RSE system

The following considerations describe how the audio signal for a rear seat entertainment system is heard, which can include playing through the vehicle's speakers or dedicated headphones (or both):

- The customer may choose to use headphones. These could be wired, infrared (IR) or radio frequency (RF). Wireless IR headphones are most common and are sometimes included with certain RSE systems. If the video source is built in or directly input to the RSE, a headphone jack and/or wireless headphone transmitter is often built in. If video is being sourced from the head unit (such as an in-dash DVD player), then a separate audio cable will need to run to the RSE along with the video cable.

- The customer could use the vehicle's speakers, either through a dedicated auxiliary input at the head unit or a FM transmitter/modulator (if the video source is built in or directly input to the RSE). Or if video is being sourced from the head unit (such as an in-dash DVD player), then it will directly out put audio to vehicle's speakers.

Margin Notes

Installation Considerations for Overhead "Flip Down" Mobile Video Screens (OHMV)

The following considerations describe installation considerations and potential obstacles in an overhead-mounted rear seat entertainment system/screen.:

- Sunroofs may limit where the OHMV can be placed.
- If the vehicle has a rear seat HVAC control, it may have to be deleted or relocated depending on where the OHMV is installed.
- In many vehicles, the dome light will be removed, and the OHMV will serve as the vehicle's new dome light. Some customers may choose to retain the OEM dome light, affecting where the OHMV can be mounted.
- Most SUVs, vans and trucks will have a brace the OHMV can be attached to. This bracing is above the headliner and will only be visible by removal of the dome light, or gently pulling down the headliner near the rear door opening and looking at the vehicles roof's interior. Frequently cars will not have such bracing and may require removal of the head liner for custom bracing to be installed.
- Customers may want a large screen size. Bigger may not always be better, as a large screen can block the rear view of the driver, not to mention weight concerns.
- If the headliner is not flat, the OHMV will not set flush. It may be necessary to contour the OHMV mounting shroud to the headliner or even make a custom shroud.

Installation Considerations for Factory Replacement-Style Headrest Screens

The following considerations describe installation considerations and potential obstacles in a headrest-mounted rear seat entertainment system/screen:

- It is very important that the headrest monitor fit securely in the seat; a loose headrest could become a projectile in a collision, or fail to provide adequate support to the customer's head and neck.
- Some newer vehicles may have active headrests. There are two primary designs. One is an explosive charge inside the headrest that, upon a collision, will deploy sending the headrest forward to prevent whiplash. The second is a rocker design. When pressure is applied to the back of the seat, it forces the headrest forward providing support. With vehicles containing both types of headrest, a universal aftermarket replacement headrest should not be installed as doing so would disable an OEM safety feature.
- If the headrest screen is being installed in second-row seating, are the second-row seats removable or folding? This may affect wire routing, or a disconnection point may be needed.

Margin Notes

- Review the FMVSS safety requirements for headrests and interior materials flammability in Chapter 1.

Connecting an aftermarket head unit to an OEM RSE system

Installation of an aftermarket rear seat entertainment system is often more straightforward than an existing (factory-installed) RSE system. An aftermarket RSE system has compatible connector types with other aftermarket A/V equipment and can be turned on/off with no command from the head unit. Factory-installed RSE systems have a broader variety of installation considerations because they are not engineered to be "open" systems like a TV at home where it has standardized connections to easily integrate with other equipment. Here are some considerations:

- Vehicles with analog A/V signal and RSE turn on typically have wiring that can be found in the OEM Radio head unit harness in the dash. There may be a retention harness available or it could be hard wired (provided the installation technician possesses the knowledge and skill to do a hard-wired interface).
- Occasionally vehicles have a separate OEM DVD player or rear seat control panel to consider for its own installation requirements. In these cases, the audio and video signal wires are not usually found in the harness at the head unit location. Instead, these signal wires often reside at the OEM DVD player or RSE controller. This process requires additional disassembly and extending wiring from the aftermarket head unit, which warrants added labor costs.
- Vehicles with RSE utilizing a digital turn-on circuit (such as Toyota) that lack a dedicated +12 Volt trigger for the screens and other RSE components require one of two solutions when utilizing an aftermarket in-dash head unit. One solution is an integration harness for retention of RSE, which means additional parts and labor costs. The other solution is to relocate the OEM head unit and keep it connected in order to generate the data turn-on signal. The second option is more labor intensive and increases installation costs.
- Vehicles with Media Oriented System Transport (MOST) infotainment systems using plastic optical fiber (POF) to transmit data, turn-on and other important commands require vehicle-specific interface devices if a factory rear seat entertainment system is intended for use with an aftermarket head unit installation. Specifically, this applies to vehicles with MOST-25 and MOST-150 infotainment systems.

Rear View Mirror screens

The following considerations describe installation considerations when utilizing a video screen embedded in a rear view mirror:

- When replacing the OEM rear view mirror, ensure that it does not contain any peripheral devices, such as a Bluetooth microphone, rain-sensing wiper sensor, compass, or telematics services (OnStar, etc.). These features would be lost with its removal and should be discussed with the customer prior to installation. It is not recommended to pursue installations where factory functionality, particularly safety-related systems, would become inoperable.
- Rear view mirrors with screens in them are always visible to the driver. As such, the video signals displayed should only be for navigation or a reverse camera

image when the vehicle is in motion.
- How the aftermarket rear view mirror is mounted is crucial. This will vary by vehicle and mirror type. Some mirrors use a simple clamp on design over the OEM mirror. Other designs replace the OEM mirror altogether. Full replacement rear view mirrors often require special mounts that depend on the OEM mirror mount type (cam lock, small foot, big foot, etc.).
- Regardless of mount and design, it's important that the mirror is securely in place so that it does not become a projectile in a collision.

Margin Notes

Stand-Alone Screens and Tablets

The following considerations describe installation considerations when utilizing a tablet-based or stand-alone video screen placed somewhere in the front of the vehicle. This includes screens that are permanently mounted, as well as those with quick-release mounting.

An attractive feature of a tablet or removable standalone screen in the vehicle is its portability; however, ensuring a secure installation is essential.

- A safe mounting method such as a pedestal or bracket installed into the vehicle is preferred to reduce the chance of the screen becoming a projectile in a sudden stop or accident.
- Powering a removable/carry-in screen is an additional consideration. A clean, hardwired power plug-in may be preferred and that requires more labor time and cost than connecting to an existing power point, such as a cigarette lighter adapter.
- Review the tablets and stand-alone screen sections of Chapter 1 for a detailed overview of some more labor-intensive installation possibilities if a more integrated look is preferred. Consult the installation technician for additional guidance on labor and any parts/materials charges before developing a final quote to the customer.
- The installation should consider whether the vehicle can easily be returned to factory-like condition.

In-Dash or "Driver Viewable" Video Installation Considerations

The video screen viewable to a driver generally has a specific purpose other than entertainment, such as controls for the audio system, GPS navigation or reverse camera images. It's important that a Mobile Product Specialist know the laws in their state(s) where "video entertainment screens in view of the driver" are concerned. Many states prohibit this type of use.

CTA recommended practice is **no moving video images in view of the driver while the vehicle is in motion** except for infotainment system controls, GPS navigation and safety cameras (reverse cam, front IR cam, front DVR dash cam, etc.).

- CTA recommended practice is no moving video images in view of the driver while the vehicle is in motion except for infotainment system controls, GPS navigation and safety cameras (reverse cam, front IR cam, front DVR dash cam, etc.).

Margin Notes

- In-dash mobile video entertainment systems and other devices carrying video signals (such as movies, TV shows, streaming videos, etc.) that are potentially in view of the driver should be installed to manufacturer specifications using safety connections such as parking brake inputs, vehicle-in-motion sensing, etc.

VEHICLE SECURITY AND/OR REMOTE STARTER SYSTEM INSTALLATION CONSIDERATIONS

Availability of Data Interface

Modern vehicles are a complicated network of computer modules that typically require a **data integration module** to allow a remote starter or security system to function properly without the loss of any existing vehicle electronic functions. It's important to consider the use (and extra sale) of a data integration module because it reduces installation time and complexity. In many cases, it's simply not possible to successfully install a remote starter and/or security system in a modern vehicle without one.

Consumers may be enticed by a low-priced advertisement for a remote starter or security system, but there is often fine print that necessitates extra cost. Data integration module(s) required to complete the job safely and successfully are commonly not part of low advertised prices since they are specific to the vehicle and vary in cost/complexity. Be aware when customers assume a low advertised price is all-inclusive because it seldom is that way.

Data integration modules can be very simple or highly complex.

- An example of simple is a data transponder emulator. This is a module to replicate the transponder chipped key used in most new vehicles so that the vehicle "thinks" an authorized key is in the ignition cylinder.

- An example of highly complex data integration is a module that completely controls the ignition and starting timing of the remote start sequence.

Even when selling a security system, an integration module is required on most modern vehicles to control functions such as the central locking system, or to recognize door and trunk triggers out of the vehicle's data bus signals.

Data interface manufacturers have excellent web-based application guides. This allows both a product specialist and technician to easily research what is required for each model of vehicle. Knowing the year of the vehicle is important as vehicle manufacturers can change vehicle systems in as little as two model years. Going out to the customer's vehicle to verify the vehicle model year by referencing the 10th character in the Vehicle Identification Number (VIN) and which type of starting system is present represents the most accurate way to utilize application guides with the best accuracy.

Margin Notes

Some companies manufacture vehicle security and remote starter systems with the integration module built into one unit. This has both advantages and disadvantages. One of the biggest advantages is a streamlined installation as it no longer requires technicians to wire two separate units together to make the system(s) function. This allows technicians to be more efficient at their job and allows sales of more units to install. The only major drawback is conditional to the vehicle. If the installation does not require any sort of data interface because the vehicle doesn't require it, using this type of 'everything-in-one system' increases hardware cost because it contains functionality not required to successfully complete the installation.

While rare, some vehicles without a commercially available interface solution may require the client to sacrifice a valid transponder key to allow their remote starter to function. This typically applies to European vehicles, but it is best to consult with the installation technician as to the availability of a data module available for a specific year/make/model of European vehicle. European vehicles such as Audi, Mercedes-Benz, Volkswagen, Porsche and others often present a challenge for data and transponder interface manufacturers to bring a solution to market.

Wire-to-Wire (Analog) Connections

When it comes to selling security and/or remote starting systems, it's important to know the brands and models sold in your store and whether those brands are capable of being used with the integration module you have available. Many security and/or remote starter units have a "data port" plug-in connection to interface with the integration module's communication port. This is known as a data-to-data connection. There are scenarios where the two units won't be compatible through the data port connections and must be wired in a method called "wire-to-wire" or "analog" connections. This can increase labor time required for the technician to complete the installation and should be considered when planning the system installation and cost for the customer. Wire-to-wire allows the technician to troubleshoot a data-to-data issue quickly by having access to analog inputs and outputs for testing, but the cost of that access means connecting several individual wires between the security/remote starter and the integration module rather than plugging in a data port connection.

When using wire-to-wire connections in a vehicle security system, it's important to know the different types of electrical signals that used in a vehicle for various circuits monitored by the security system such as the passenger compartment (doors), hood and trunk, etc. This is critical to ensure the correct product or installation type is used and the correct integration method is part of the labor cost (when additional labor is required).

These are common 'analog' trigger inputs/outputs:

- **Negative Trigger** – A negative trigger provides a ground output when the entry point is opened or device (such as a sensor) is triggered. This is a simple

Margin Notes

trigger and all security systems can directly connect to this type of trigger without any special accessories or additional wiring.

- **Positive Trigger** – A positive trigger provides a positive output when the entry point is opened. This is also a simple trigger and all security systems can directly connect to this type of trigger without any special accessories or additional wiring.
- **Normally Closed Trigger** – A normally closed trigger provides a negative or positive output when the entry point is closed and an open circuit when the entry point is open. A normally closed circuit presents a greater challenge to integrate with and only a few security systems can directly connect to this type of trigger without any special accessories, modules or additional wiring. For the other security/RS systems that do not support a direct connection, additional wiring, parts (such as diodes and resistors) and labor are required. Ford and Lincoln vehicles tend to use normally closed circuits. Check with the specific manufacturer of the product, as well as a technician to ensure compatibility if 'wire-to-wire' connections are part of the installation plan.

T-Harnesses (Plug and Play)

Along with 'everything-in-one systems' where the security/remote starter and the integration module is a single unit is the ability to connect it all to the vehicle using a plug and play integration harness. This is also known as a "T-Harness." The biggest advantage to using a plug and play integration harness is the installation becomes much less intrusive to the vehicle's electrical system and greatly decreases the time it takes to complete the installation. This allows more sales and more installation of security/remote starter systems overall. These harnesses minimize or eliminate any hard-wired connection required for the vehicle's wiring. In turn, that reduces the probability of any issues that may arise from new car dealerships blaming the security/remote starter system on other vehicle issues.

Location of Components for Security Purposes

Vehicles are one of the harshest environments for electronics. Products are expected to perform in a high-vibration environment, withstand wide temperature variances, and be able to work with voltages that can range from below 10 volts up to spikes of 15 volts or more. The location of components is critical to keep moisture out and vibration minimized, all while considering the safety and serviceability of the existing vehicle components. These are general guidelines that a Mobile Product Specialist should convey to the client about the importance of professional installation:

- Control modules for any security and/or remote starter system are to be securely mounted inside the vehicle away from any moving parts such as steering components, HVAC ventilation actuators, as well as control pedals.
- Add-on sensors for security systems should be mounted in accordance with the manufacturer's instructions for the best performance.
- Valet or auxiliary disarm switches should be placed where a client can access them but not easily found by a thief.
- Under hood components such as sirens and pin switches should not interfere with any wiring or access to components under the hood.

Margin Notes

- The main power source(s) should always be fused properly so, in the event of any electrical issues, they serve their intended purpose to protect the vehicle. Making sure customers understand how these components will be installed in the vehicle can help sell your company and technicians' skills.

Location of Transmitter/Receivers and Antennas for Optimum Signal/Range
External antennas for security/remote starter systems should be installed in accordance with the manufacturer's recommendation. This is almost always affixed to the inside of the windshield, away from any metallic tint or defroster lines and out of direct view of the driver. Antenna performance is affected by the location of the antenna as well as metallic tint or electronics built into the glass (such as defrost/heated windows or embedded radio antennas). Going out to a client's vehicle can help determine if there are going to be any issues with interference from window tint or electronics in the windshield.

Installation-Related Safety Considerations Specific to Remote Start
Special installation-related considerations must be applied when it comes to installing remote starters into vehicles equipped with a Smart Key starting system (also called "Push-to-Start" or "PTS" vehicles). To remote start many of these vehicles, the normal starting procedure is out of order or different than "key start" vehicles. In addition, the act of "takeover" where the remote starter electronically hands off control to the vehicle's normal electrical functionality is different.

In a Smart Key system, vehicle circuits need to be powered up without necessarily turning a physical key switch. In some cases, the vehicle will be required to shut off, then be restarted with the normal push button sequence before being able to drive it after it was originally remote started. There are a few reasons for this. The main reason is hidden diagnostic codes may be present during the remote start sequence. Diagnostic codes present while remote starting and left powered on in a takeover could trigger dash warning lights or other diagnostic trouble codes (DTCs).

In some cases, when a technician must emulate the factory remote starter, the vehicle's remote starter system shuts the vehicle down regardless. In this case, there is no choice but to first turn off remote start, then restart the vehicle through the normal push button sequence. When takeover is available, it is important that the system allows for a secure takeover from remote start.

For secure takeover that appears seamless, here's how it works (electronically):

1. Once the unlock button is pressed on the key fob (or is activated by a proximity remote), a 45 second timer is activated.

2. Inside that 45 second window, the remote starter should sense electrical triggers of the door open and then closing (confirming someone has entered), and the brake depressed (confirming a person is seated in the driver's seat).

3. In some cases, the vehicle takeover will only occur if a valid proximity key is in the vehicle, further enhancing the secure takeover.

Margin Notes

Forty-five seconds is a typical range of time and is chosen to allow just enough time for the authorized user of the vehicle to unlock, enter the vehicle, and depress the brake to allow successful takeover from remote start. This is not a concern on most key start vehicles as the key needs to be physically turned to keep the ignition on and unlock the steering column to drive away.

INSTALLATION CONSIDERATIONS OF IN VEHICLE COMMUNICATION, DRIVER SAFETY AND AWARENESS DEVICES

GPS Navigation and Tracking

The following items are important to consider when selling labor and planning an installation that involves GPS navigation or tracking:

GPS Antenna Considerations

- When mounting the GPS antenna, select a position where it has a clear line-of-sight to the sky in order to receive a signal from GPS satellites. This is critical for proper operation.
- The antenna must not be mounted under metal, a plastic or fiberglass panel that has foil-backed sound damping material, or paint with heavy metallic content (metal flake, etc.).
- The antenna does not need to be mounted on a flat plane but it is recommended. The closer to flat it can be mounted the higher the accuracy will be for the device. Modern vehicles have numerous areas under the dashboard or under windshield cowl that provide a suitable mounting spot and provide moderate protection from damage or weather.
- Most devices are GPS (Global Positioning System) compatible, but some newer devices are also GLONASS (GLObal NAvigation Satellite System) compatible. GPS is a U.S.- based system, and GLONASS is a Russian- based system, but both have numerous satellites that provide similar data to effectively pinpoint the location of a device. A device that supports GPS alone is adequate for most applications, but a device that supports both GPS and GLONASS has a higher probability of acquiring a signal, and typically the signal acquisition is faster.

Vehicle Speed Sense Wire (VSS)

- Very few aftermarket navigation devices utilize a physical connection to a vehicle speed sense wire (also called VSS or speed pulse). The VSS connection is normally used to provide an analog or digital signal to give the device a hard-wired speed reference. The accuracy provided by coordinates from the GPS satellite signals and triangulation processing can very closely estimate vehicle speed. This method is how a mapping app on a smartphone can estimate your arrival time with great accuracy.
- If a VSS connection is required or recommended, some vehicles may require an adapter, typically provided in the radio harness, to provide the signal easily. Be sure to inquire about the output capability of the harness module to ensure it matches the input needed for the device being installed.
- If no adapter or harness is available, most vehicle Engine Control Modules or

Powertrain Control Modules have one or more wires that have the VSS signal present and can be used to provide a wired input to the device. Other places that the VSS signal could be found is at the Antilock Braking System Module, factory audio amplifier or at the gauge cluster.

Margin Notes

BLUETOOTH HANDS-FREE

Microphone Placement vs. Speaker (where voice is heard)

The placement of an aftermarket Bluetooth microphone is important to the user experience and call quality for both people on a call. Since most modern vehicles have Bluetooth hands-free as standard or optional equipment from the factory, it is recommended to use the factory location if possible, or to place the microphone close to this location. The vehicle engineers have placed it there to avoid feedback and excessive noise, so it makes sense to use the same location if possible.

Other general installation considerations include:

- The microphone should not be placed near a speaker that will be playing the voice of the other person on the call inside the car. A microphone close to the speaker can cause an echo or feedback (high-pitched whine or whistles).
- The microphone head should not face any speaker directly, regardless of the distance, as it will be more prone to pick up the voice of the other caller and could produce an echo effect.

INSTALLATION CONSIDERATIONS OF ADAS DEVICES

Advanced driver assistance systems (ADAS) enhance safety and awareness in the driving process. When designed with a safe human-machine interface, they should increase safety behind the wheel and more generally overall road safety.

Reverse Cameras and Parking Sensors

Installation Considerations of a Wire Run

When installing a reverse camera or back-up (parking) sensors, all wires and cables should be run near or with factory harnesses that run from the rear of the vehicle to the module or head unit. This provides the best chance of avoiding moving parts, heat and moisture as factory wiring is typically routed to stay a safe distance away from those hazards.

Here are some additional considerations:

- Any holes drilled or cut in the rear of the vehicle should be far from engine exhaust outlets and sealed to prevent noxious gases or water from entering the vehicle.
- Removal of interior panels such as door sill plates, kick panels and A-pillars is commonplace. This is not unlike any other installation task where wires must run from the front to the back of the vehicle.
- Removal body panels such as bumpers and fenders, or vehicle parts like wheels or trunk liners may be required to properly install the camera or sensors and run the wires and cables. This may necessitate allocating additional installation

Margin Notes

labor charges. When the work takes place, the technician should note how each panel or part is attached to the vehicle, and to reattach them with the same method and specifications for the safety of the occupants and the integrity of the vehicle's performance and crash worthiness. Therefore, added labor costs are often warranted.

- It is important to keep all wiring that is run on outside of the interior away from areas that could interfere with the system performance and/or cause damage to the wiring (i.e., exhaust pipes, cv axles, motorized spoilers, etc.). This is the main reason most technicians choose to run all cables inside the vehicle for the duration of the wire run, or minimize any wiring outside of the vehicle.
- Wireless cameras that employ a transmitter in (or near) the camera and a receiver in (or near) the display or head unit must be mounted in a way that provides consistent transmission success without interruption to ensure delay or loss of signal does not induce a collision.

How the Rear View Camera is Viewed

The screen for a rear camera system must be mounted in view for the driver. Dash-mounted screens, rear view mirror replacements with LCD screen and aftermarket head units are all ways to view the image from a rear camera system. The type of vehicle needs to play a part in how the viewing of the rear view camera image is decided. For instance, convertibles are not a desirable choice for aftermarket rear view mirror screens as the image may be washed out when the top is down. Large dash-mounted screens may not work well with some vehicles depending on dashboard shape, etc. Some vehicles may not be able to have the OEM head unit replaced with an aftermarket Double-DIN head unit with a screen. All this must be considered when choosing the way to view the rear camera image.

There are numerous types of cameras with different mounting types and capabilities, so choosing the appropriate one for the vehicle can impact the ability to properly view behind the vehicle during operation. The type of camera chosen to install can dictate where or how it is mounted.

- A narrow field of vision means the camera will likely need to be close to the center of the vehicle, whereas a wide-angle camera could be mounted slightly off-center. This is important to consider when choosing initial placement with the customer.
- Some cameras offer a mirror-image or reversed view of the image provided, but these settings are often configured during the installation (such as on an aftermarket head unit or rear view mirror with LCD screen).
- Some cameras require cutting a wire or connecting a wire during installation to get the desired effect on the screen image orientation.

Be sure the planned installation accommodates the type of camera selected and how the intended image will be viewed for the best results.

Margin Notes

Use of a Factory Rear View Camera

When replacing a factory head unit or display with an aftermarket one, it is possible in some vehicles to retain the factory reverse camera. This camera would then be intended to display an image on a new aftermarket head unit or other screen when the factory screen has been removed or disabled.

Retaining the use of a factory camera or screen requires knowing the type of video signal and operating voltage. Many OEM cameras use +6 volts for power, rather than +12 volts. When the customer wishes to retain a factory camera that uses 6 volts for power and connect to with an aftermarket head unit that provides a +12 Volt reverse trigger output, a 6-volt step down in voltage must be implemented or damage to the camera may occur. Some integration devices and wiring harness adaptors may already accommodate that step-down voltage requirement. If directly powering the factory camera from an aftermarket head unit, be sure the technician verifies the operating voltage of the factory rear view camera before removal of the factory head unit.

The second integration concern for a factory rear view camera is the video output signal. Factory rear view camera systems do not typically, if ever, utilize aftermarket-typical composite video (yellow RCA) connections for video transmission from the factory camera to the display or head unit. Therefore, the technician must interface with the existing rear view camera signal in one of the following ways:

- Using the existing composite video signal by splicing into existing wires in the vehicle or using an aftermarket harness to integrate with them at the head unit or display harness.
- Using an aftermarket module to integrate with existing digital video signals (such as LVDS or GVIF) that require processing or conversion to a typical composite type video signal input on the aftermarket head unit or display.

Verify the video signal type during the sale to prevent missing an important adapter or module that is needed, and so the installation can take place without damage to either factory or aftermarket components that are hooked up incorrectly.

Installation of Parking/Distance Sensors

Front and rear parking sensors (also called distance sensors) can be installed in most vehicles. There are generally two different types to suit the style of bumper or bumper fascia on the vehicle. Both types include the use of an audible beeper and/or visual aide (LED) that the driver should be able to hear and see:

1. The first type requires holes drilled into the rear bumper fascia/cover to place the sensors (one hole per sensor). The layout of the parking/distance sensors should be evenly spaced and parallel to the ground at roughly 15-18" off the ground. These sensor types are flush mounted and can be paint-matched to the vehicle if they do not already come painted to match. They must not be directly mounted into steel bumpers without special isolation spacers/rings or

Margin Notes

the unit may give false readings. When determining general placement, some vehicle bumper covers may be marked on the back side where the vehicle manufacturer would place factory-installed sensors if the vehicle had that option. Check with the technician to see if that's the case. Even with the bumper cover still on the vehicle, visually potential locations to identify areas lacking the available space for the sensor to occupy due to body lines, other components occupying an area, etc.

2. The second type of rear sensor uses ultrasonic (microwave) frequency to detect objects and can be placed behind the rear bumper fascia/cover. While this is invisible and does not require any paint matching or holes to be drilled into the vehicle, the accuracy may be less than that of dedicated sensors installed into the bumper fascia/cover.

   Plastic bumper covers are most common, but occasionally a steel bumper will be encountered on a vehicle. Steel or other ferrous or metallic materials can impact the effectiveness of sensors designed for plastic bumpers, so the technician should be sure the sensors being used are appropriate for the application.

   Some sensors can be painted, but this should be verified during the sales process and before installation. Sensors that can be painted to match factory paint typically have certain procedures that must be followed to prepare the sensor for the application of paint and may require certain types of paint to function properly. Color matching of sensors would typically need additional installation time for the vehicle to be at the shop or be done ahead of time before the installation begins.

Installation Considerations for Lane Departure Warning Systems

Aftermarket Lane Departure Warning (LDW) systems warn the driver with audible beeps if the vehicle leaves its lane without signaling. These systems use sophisticated optical sensors installed near the rear view mirror and watch the painted lines and road reflectors to determine if the vehicle has left its lane. When installing Lane Departure Warning systems, wiring must remain away from anything that can damage the wires, either from moving parts or excessive heat.

Optical sensors (which are special cameras) are critical to the performance of the system. It is important that the technician install the sensor unit in accordance with the manufacturer's specifications. In most cases, a point on the inside of the windshield that is at or near the center of the vehicle, with no obstruction to the forward view is recommended for the optical sensor camera. The area of glass where the optical sensor views the road should be an area that is cleared by the windshield wipers and is high enough to have a clear view of the front of the vehicle.

Since most aftermarket LDW optical sensor units are applied to the interior of the windshield on the glass, it is imperative that the installation technician use the

Margin Notes

appropriate 3M VHB adhesive tape. This adhesive tape will withstand moisture, heat and the mild expansion and contraction of the glass panel during hot and chilly days. Proper preparation of the glass, including cleaning solutions and scrubbing, should be done by the installation technician thoroughly prior to the application of the adhesive to promote long life of the bond.

Since the optical sensor unit is typically installed near the center of the top of the windshield, it is important to note the following when discussing mounting the unit with the customer and how the routing of the wire harnesses will be done:

- The unit should not be in the driver's line of sight and no portion of it should impede vision at any angle through any window.
- The unit should be mounted in a way that prevents it from falling off the windshield due to impacts to the vehicle such as potholes or other vehicle driving scenarios. This could cause the driver to panic or impede operation of the vehicle.
- The harness should be routed in a path that does not obstruct vision through the windshield.
- The harness should be routed across the headliner and down any pillars or panels in the vehicle that does not affect the function of any safety devices such as airbags, air curtains or breakaway mirrors.
- Any display panel or screen used by the device to convey information to the driver should be mounted within the driver's main vision area, so attention is not taken away from the road when LDW alerts occur. It should be mounted using the same applicable guidelines as the sensor unit if mounted on or near the windshield.

Many aftermarket LDW units require calibration so the sensor and processing unit can properly judge distance, vehicle width and other vehicle characteristics. This will directly impact the measurement accuracy of the unit and ultimately the customer's satisfaction with the product. Some units must be driven on different road or traffic conditions to calibrate properly, so be sure to communicate this to the customer before work begins.

Installation Considerations for Forward Collision Avoidance Systems

Forward Collision Avoidance (FCA) systems use optical sensors (cameras), laser and/or radar frequencies to warn the driver of hazards in front of the vehicle. Aftermarket systems do not have the ability to alter the vehicle's path or speed like OEM systems do and are mainly audible and/or visual aids. Proper install methods include wire routing away from excessive heat, moving components and a clear line of site to the road.

Several types of sensors, including optical, are critical to the performance of the system. It is important that the technician install all the sensors in accordance with the manufacturer's specifications. In most cases, a central optical sensor camera is mounted to a point on the inside of the windshield that is at or near the center of the vehicle, where there is no obstruction to the forward view. The area of glass that

Margin Notes

the camera views the road should be an area that is cleared by the windshield wipers and is high enough to have a clear view of the front of the vehicle.

Since most aftermarket FCA units are applied to the interior of the windshield on the glass, it is imperative that the installation technician use the appropriate 3M VHB adhesive tape. This adhesive tape will withstand moisture, heat and the mild expansion and contraction of the glass panel during hot and chilly days. Proper preparation of the glass, including cleaning solutions and scrubbing, should be done by the installation technician thoroughly prior to the application of the adhesive to promote long life of the bond.

Since the optical sensor unit is typically installed near the center of the top of the windshield, it is important to note the following when discussing mounting the unit with the customer and how the routing of the wire harnesses will be done:

- The unit itself should not be in the line of site of the driver when scanning from one side to the other through the windshield. No portion of it should impede vision at any angle through the window.
- The unit should be mounted in a way that prevents it from falling off the windshield due to impacts to the vehicle such as potholes or other vehicle driving scenarios. This could cause the driver to panic or impede operation of the vehicle.
- The harness should be routed in a path that does not obstruct vision through the windshield.
- The harness should be routed across the headliner and down any pillars or panels in the vehicle that does not affect the function of any safety devices such as airbags, air curtains or breakaway mirrors.
- Any display panel or screen used by the device to convey information to the driver should be mounted within the driver's main vision area, so attention is not taken away from the road when alerts occur. It should be mounted using the same applicable guidelines as the sensor unit if mounted on or near the windshield.

Other sensors such as radar or laser sensors may be placed in the front bumper or in the front grille of the vehicle. Care should be taken to mount them in a way that avoids damage from car washes, road debris and inclement weather. Be sure the installation technician knows to route cables and harnesses to the sensors so that vehicle serviceability and functionality is not negatively affected.

Many aftermarket FCA units require calibration of some sort so the sensor and processing unit can properly judge distance, vehicle width and other vehicle characteristics. This will directly impact the measurement accuracy of the unit, and ultimately the customer's satisfaction with the product. Some units must be driven on different road or traffic conditions to calibrate properly, so be sure to communicate this to the customer before work begins.

Installation Considerations for Blind Spot Detection Systems

Blind Spot Detection (BSD) systems use various forms radar and radio frequencies to warn the driver of hazards approaching from either side near the rear quarter

Margin Notes

of the vehicle, or in the "blind spot." Aftermarket systems are mainly visual and audible warnings and can range from a warning tone when the blinker is turned on and an object is detected on that side, to a system that shows a persistent marker on the A-pillar or in the side view mirrors when an object is detected on that side of the vehicle.

Some units use cameras installed in the passenger side mirror, or one in both side mirrors, to either detect a moving object or to give a video feed of that side of the vehicle when changing lanes. Units that provide a video feed need to be connected to a screen of some sort, whether it is an existing OEM screen, a rearview mirror or an aftermarket head unit.

Other types utilize a small radar sensor installed in the rear quarter panel of both sides of the vehicle to monitor an area near the rear of the vehicle and signal the driver when an object is detected. These must be calibrated to the vehicle and position they are mounted in to give proper feedback to the driver. These types of units are not applicable in some vehicles that do not offer the appropriate mounting area or body panel structure to accommodate mounting them or calibrating them.

Regardless of the type of Blind Spot Detection system installed, it is important to discuss the system with the customer, so they have the appropriate expectations. It is also important to find out what types of driving or parking they perform, such as trailering. In some types of driving, these units may fail or provide incorrect feedback causing over-correction or panic by the driver, resulting in an accident.

RADAR/LASER DETECTOR INSTALLATION CONSIDERATIONS

What to consider in a Radar and Laser Detector Installation

This content covers the finer points of installation considerations related radar and laser detectors used in vehicles to alert the driver of law enforcement's speed detection device use. This section is not testable on the Mobile Product Specialist exam because of regional limitations in some U.S. states and Canadian provinces. However, it is helpful to understand the category.

Topics covered in this section:

- Installation considerations of dash-mounted detectors.
- Installation considerations of remote-mounted detectors.

Dash-Mounted Detector System Installation Considerations

Installing a dash-mounted detector typically consists of two simple things: correct placement of the device and powering it. Based in the relative simplicity, many customers feel confident doing it themselves; however, more complex mounting (especially where local laws prohibit certain locations) and hard wiring the power may lead a customer to elect for professional installation.

Placement of a Dash-Mounted Radar Detector

Typical placement of dash-mounted radar detectors is on or above the dashboard

Margin Notes

facing forward so that the radar detector has a clear line of sight out of the front window. Most dash-mounted radar detectors come with mounting brackets that have suction cups, so the unit can be easily mounted and dismounted from the dashboard or front window.

Rear view mirror mounting is an option. Installation typically involves installing a kit onto the rear view mirror stem to which the detector attaches. The detector can then be easily removed from the mount when the customer leaves the vehicle.

U.S. States like Minnesota and California have specific vehicle code provisions that prohibit the use of any devices attached to the front window. It's important to ensure the customer is aware of their optimum placement and where it's legal.

There is an opportunity to sell and install a remote-mounted (hidden) radar detector system. Remote-mounted systems can have significantly improved performance without any of the visual distraction in a dash-mounted device. Only a small display/ control panel is necessary and those can easily be custom-mounted in just about any location the customer wishes.

Generally, the guidelines for placement of dash-mounted detectors are as follows:

- For detection of **radar**, the higher the better (such as below the rear view mirror or on the visor).
- For detection of **laser**, the lower the better (such as on the dash board). The sun visor where some DIY customers would choose to place it is the least effective position for laser detection.
- If a compromise is required, **choose the lower positioning for detectors that do both types** because laser is more difficult to detect than radar and needs the optimum placement.
- Ensure a clear field of view in both the front and rear. Any obstructions in the rear window will limit the effective range of rear coverage on detectors which have that feature.
- Customers in Minnesota and California should be advised that installation (if they plan to do it themselves) of a windshield mount is a violation of the vehicle code in those states. Encourage them to consider lower mounting positions rather than up high if the dash-mounted device does both radar and laser detection. Most people's second choice for mounting is instinctively up high on the sun visor and that should be avoided any time the unit has laser capabilities. Rear view mirror semi-permanent mounts, such as Blendmount rear view mirror mount kits, are another option and are often used in conjunction with a hard-wired power connection (instead of a coiled lighter power cord).
- Avoid placing the dash-mounted detector behind parking stickers, electronic toll transponders, windshield wiper blades or anything similar that will obstruct the detector's window or lens.
- Window tint can obstruct the effective range of dash-mounted radar detection. This is another good reason not to place the detector on the visor or high up as many windshields have a factory tint. Metallic or "hybrid" window films on

rear and side windows will also limit the effective range of rear coverage on detectors which have that feature.

Margin Notes

Powering the Dash-Mounted Radar Detector

Powering the dash-mounted radar detector is typically accomplished by one of two methods: either it is connected to a cigarette lighter adapter plug (included with the unit) or it can be "hard wired" into the vehicle's fuse panel so there are no messy cords running down around the dash panels. Either way, the radar detector installation is relatively simple and can be accomplished by most Do-it-Yourself (DIY) customers who are willing to read the directions included with the unit.

There is a third method that some radar detectors offer, batteries. These will usually be multiple AA or AAA batteries but offer an alternative to having coiled power cords running around the dashboard. It is important to note that a detector that runs on batteries offers less performance than a similarly priced corded detector. Be sure that customers know that before making final choices.

- Cigarette lighter power cord is generally standard with dash-mounted detectors and okay for a DIY customer.
- Hard-wired installations can usually be done with additional custom labor. Provide an option for the installation technician to handle the wired connections for a reasonable fee (especially if other installation work is being done). This can be one of several approaches:
    - o Rear view mirror: a short power cable that connects the detector to a vehicle's powered rear view mirror connector. May not apply to all vehicles and mirrors.
    - o Fuse box or under-dash: a long power cable that connects the detector to an ignition-switched +12 Volt line in the vehicle's fuse box or under-dash wiring. This is the most common hard-wired type of power cable installation.

Some detectors with hard-wire options in a kit form may include a remote module for muting the detector and displaying power and alert status to further enhance the ease-of-use for the driver.

Remote-Mounted Detector System Installation Considerations

Before the installation of a remote-mounted (hidden) system takes place, there are a few things a technician should do to ensure a trouble-free outcome. These considerations are important for a Mobile Product Specialist to know, both the sales process In describing the unit's function performance, as well as when quoting the installation in their specific vehicle.

Bench Testing

It is highly recommended to bench test the entire remote-mounted system before installation. This is accomplished by connecting all the components, connecting the system to a +12VDC power and powering the system on to ensure no error codes are displayed. Checking for system updates is recommended at this time according to the manufacturer's recommended procedure.

Margin Notes

Software Updates

The most feature-rich systems will require software updates from time to time, such as updates to a speed and red-light camera database. One of the most common update methods is via USB connection to a computer. Ensure the USB jack is easily accessible for the customer to perform system updates. If software updates are available the technician, he or she should perform them while the system is on the bench.

Hardware Installation Details

Next, these are the installation-related details that influence a successful remote-mounted detector job:

- **Radar Sensors** – Radar sensors are mounted in the front of the vehicle. Some systems also offer a rear radar sensor that is mounted in the back of the vehicle, facing rearward. These sensors are weatherproof and designed to be mounted outside of the vehicle. While a clear view of the road offers the best performance, radar sensors can be mounted behind plastic (such as a bumper fascia) with minor impact on performance. Radar sensors should not be mounted behind any metallic objects. Connection to the system's interface typically involves routing the sensor wiring through the vehicle's firewall.
- **Laser Sensors** – Laser sensors require a clear view of the road. Laser sensors must also be mounted level and facing forward (or rearward in the case of rear-mounted sensors). Many laser sensor installation kits include bubble levels to set the sensor exactly level with the ground. Connection to the system's interface typically involves routing the sensor wiring through the vehicle's firewall.
- **Interface** – The interface module (the component to which sensors, displays, power/ground, etc., connect) is typically mounted inside the vehicle's cabin, out of sight. Under or behind an area of the dash is a common location, but the presence of a USB port for software updates may necessitate a hidden, but accessible location.
- **Display** – The system's display should be mounted where the driver can easily see it without being distracted. The technician and product specialist should consult with the customer for preferred mounting locations. Some systems also include optional discrete alert displays consisting of a single LED light. These are typically installed directly into the vehicle's instrument panel cluster (IPC).
- **Controller** – The controller oversees the settings of the system and is typically mounted in the dash or console. Some are wired and some wireless. Be sure to consult with the customer for preferred mounting locations and convey those preferences to the technician installing the system. Ease of access to all the buttons on the controller is an important consideration.
- **GPS Receiver** – Many systems incorporate a GPS receiver. Most GPS receivers can be installed inside or outside the vehicle, some may require extra effort to seal the antenna from moisture if mounted externally. GPS antennas can cause interference with some sensitive electronics such as adaptive cruise control systems, so precaution should be taken to stay clear of these items when planning the installation. The GPS receiver can be mounted behind plastic out of sight, such as below the vehicle's rear parcel shelf, which may be preferable to the

customer. Do not cover a GPS receiver with metal. It should have a 'line of sight' to the open sky, very similar to the requirements of a GPS navigation antenna.

Margin Notes

To accomplish a successful remote-mounted radar/laser detector system, removal of body panels such as bumpers and fenders, or vehicle parts like wheels or trunk liners may be required to properly install the remote-mounted sensors and run the wiring to the control unit inside the vehicle. Additionally, some units will have front and rear sensors, plus front (possibly also rear) laser shifters/transceivers. Multiple front and rear sensors/transceivers add complexity to finding secure but effective mounting locations for each component to do its job. All these factors necessitate allocating additional installation labor charges that are specific to the work involved, so always consult an experienced technician for guidance.

When the work takes place, the technician should note how each panel or part is attached to the vehicle, and to reattach them with the same method and specifications for the safety of the occupants and the integrity of the vehicle's performance and crash worthiness. Therefore, added labor costs are often warranted for remote-mounted radar/laser systems. It provides the technician with the time to do the job properly.

5

CUSTOMER-FACING ETIQUETTE AND RECOMMENDED PRACTICE

CUSTOMER-FACING ETIQUETTE AND RECOMMENDED PRACTICE

Margin Notes

The MECP Mobile Product Specialist position is a critical component of a productive retail operation. Aftermarket automotive electronics are full of new and exciting technologies, and it's the role of the Mobile Product Specialist to apply those technologies to a broad range of customers and vehicles. The specialist must communicate effectively with both the retail shop's installation technicians as well as its clients.

Client-Facing Practices

Although the technician will install the products and technologies into a client's vehicle, the MECP Mobile Product Specialist matches the client's needs with the products that will work best in their vehicle. This improves customer loyalty and overall satisfaction with their aftermarket automotive electronics purchases.

Outreach and Greeting

This section provides some well-accepted, MECP-recommended practices to help you develop rapport, convey your professionalism, and inspire confidence in your and your store's expertise in aftermarket automotive electronics.

Before Customers Visit the Store

- **Phone Etiquette**

  Getting telephone customers into the store allows you to demonstrate your professionalism. Invite prospective customers to visit the store for a tour, an evaluation of their vehicle, and to experience your products hands-on. This invitation gives you a better chance to get to know the customer and identify their needs, plus go over their vehicle with them in person.

  Some retail stores have policies on telephone price quotes; however creating interest over the phone then extending an offer of an in-person vehicle evaluation and shop tour may be a more effective strategy to lure a prospective customer into the store. Set an appointment so the phone prospect has a reasonable expectation they will be talking to a product specialist within a short time upon their arrival. This shows good organization as well as respect for a prospective customer's time.

- **Social Media Etiquette**

  Social media is one of the strongest ways to advertise to prospective customers and entice them to your store. Aftermarket in-vehicle technology products, professional installation and innovative integration techniques resonate with quality-minded consumers so it's important to stay up to date with social media content. Interactive posts designed to get responses or shares work best. Be positive and avoid negative or disparaging commentary. Stay neutral to current events and stick to topics that relate to the store (holiday sales, car show events, etc.).

  Be sure to maintain a balance between promotional posts such as a brand arrival or a sale on a particular item and technology-based information, which suggests the shop has deep expertise in a category.

Margin Notes

The technology-based post can be about Bluetooth, remote starters, Hi-Res audio, or the importance of a safety camera that has great optics in direct sunlight or dark surroundings. Be creative. The idea is to use social media to promote your store in more ways than simply pushing products.

- **Email Etiquette**
  Reaching out via email is another way to communicate the latest product innovations, services you provide and sales promotions to current and prospective customers. From safety to convenience features, most consumers have in-vehicle technology needs either for themselves or for others as a gift, so it's a good idea to map out a calendar of email outreach that coincides with common promotional times of the year such as:

  - New Year's Day
  - Valentine's Day
  - St. Patrick's Day
  - Spring Break
  - Mother's Day
  - Memorial Day
  - Graduation (High School, College, Trade Schools)
  - Father's Day
  - Beginning of Summer
  - Fourth of July
  - End of Summer/Back to School
  - U.S. Labor Day
  - Beginning of Remote Start Season
  - Halloween
  - Thanksgiving/Black Friday in the United States
  - Small Business Saturday (following Thanksgiving in the United States)
  - Cyber Monday (following Thanksgiving in the United States)
  - Pre-Holiday December
  - Christmas/Hanukah Holiday Season

  If your shop interacts with Canadian customers, holidays may (depending on the province) include:

  - National Flag of Canada Day
  - Family Day
  - Islander Day
  - Nova Scotia Heritage Day
  - Luis Riel Day
  - Yukon Heritage Day
  - Commonwealth Day
  - Easter Sunday or Monday
  - Vimy Ridge Day
  - St. George's Day
  - Victoria Day
  - National Patriots' Day

Margin Notes

- National Aboriginal Day
- St. Jean Baptiste Day
- Discovery Day
- Canada Day
- Orangemen's Day
- Heritage Day in Alberta
- Civic/Provincial Day
- Terry Fox Day
- New Brunswick Day
- British Columbia Day
- Natal Day
- Canadian Labour Day
- Canadian Thanksgiving Day
- Boxing Day

The frequency of email outreach is different for each store and clientele; however, avoid over saturating inboxes with too many emails. When email messages are sent, make them count. Ensure correct spelling and, if possible, visual interest from well done graphics. For stores with a website, it's helpful if the email outreach has links to web site so that the click-through rates (CTRs) can be tracked to gauge effectiveness. Email marketing is a very economical way to drive more customers through the door to stir the next sale or promotion.

Tracking the emails that are opened and where those recipients click allows refinement of subsequent email marketing efforts because the approaches that work well can be repeated whereas efforts that don't have healthy engagement can be revised to a better strategy.

Customer Visits to the Store

- **Recommended General Dress Code**
  Maintaining a clean and professional dress code is smart and helps prospective customers with the buying process. Knowing who is (and is not) an employee on the sales floor can be accomplished with uniforms. Front-of-house sales staff have different needs of professionalism and durability of uniforms compared with installation technicians, but that doesn't mean you can't have style. A classic approach will garner the best results from consumer responses rather than fashion fads and trends.

- **Recommended Store Cleanliness Guidelines**
  Remember that customers are entrusting their vehicles to your shop, so a clean and presentable sales floor conveys professionalism. Waiting areas, bathrooms and any space to which the consumer has immediate access should be neat and uncluttered all the time. The rewards will be closing more sales because these areas aren't cluttered or filthy and the potential buyer will stay in the store longer. Keep the store and floor clean, bathrooms hygienic and safe for employees and customers.

Margin Notes

- **Timely Greeting of Customers**
  All prospective customers want to be acknowledged and welcomed, even if the sales floor staffing is with another guest. Use the 10/10 rule; this means 10 feet into the store or 10 seconds after entering the store you should acknowledge a guest, even with a simple statement like "Welcome to *XYZ Audio*, we will be right with you." This simple contact buys time to finish with current clients to whom you are attending or allows enough time for another product specialist to assist that new guest. Ignoring guests who've made the effort to visit your store is unacceptable.

Qualifying the Customer

Part of being an excellent product specialist is to gather specific information upon the customer's visit to the store, both about their reason for coming in and about their vehicle.

- **Identify Reason for Visit (Products/Categories if Interest)**
  There are many reasons why a prospective customer may visit your store. It may be for smartphone connectivity, sound system upgrades, safety add-ons, rear seat entertainment or additional vehicle security. The principal objective is to ask qualifying questions to determine the area(s) of interest. Recommendations in the sales process should always consider:
  - The vehicle and its complexity or limitations (if any)
  - Availability of the product(s)
  - Budget
  - Delivery timelines

  Oftentimes, what a prospective customer came in for can be a great opportunity to qualify interests. In-store and in-vehicle demonstrations can expand their knowledge and increase the sales ticket.

  A good example is someone who inquires about a new in-dash head unit. If the Mobile Product Specialist asks what their current sound system lacks, they may respond with, "It does not sound good." If their overall goal is improving the sound, replacing the in-dash head unit may not be the ideal path to pursue. Rather, adding a subwoofer and amplification to the system, perhaps even a digital signal processor (DSP) to help with tailoring the sound system's sonic attributes is a better way to accomplish their goals. A few polite and inquisitive questions early in the process can help define their overall goals and how best to accomplish those goals with a combination of aftermarket products and installation services.

- **Look at the Vehicle Together**
  Looking at the prospective customer's vehicle together gives them peace-of-mind that the Mobile Product Specialist is making a valid effort to understand their needs. While it's not possible in every scenario because of sales floor

Margin Notes

location, weather, staffing limitations, etc., it's an excellent policy to implement where possible and allows the product specialist to see firsthand what the customer's vehicle contains as well initially evaluate its condition. This can steer product recommendations as well as what labor procedures are required to accomplish the installation.

In the process of inspecting that prospective customer's vehicle, the Mobile Product Specialist has the added opportunity to create excitement and additional rapport. Cataloging pictures of previous installations in the same (or similar) vehicles reinforces knowledge of the vehicle and that the store is able to handle installation of that type confidently and competently.

- **Validate Year/Make/Model/Trim Level**
  Gathering valid information about the vehicle make, model, production year and trim level expedites the qualification process. Accurate information about the vehicle identifies products or processes that are important due to varying product sizes such as speakers, data bus protocols or other subtle differences even with the same year/make/model, but different trim level. Create a quote sheet or electronic file with the customer's contact info and vehicle info. This will help in the bidding process and allow notes of changes to be easily documented.

  - **10th Character of VIN Number**
    Determining the model year of the vehicle is identifiable from the 10th character of the VIN number. Use the graph as a reference. This is also easily located online search terms such as "VIN Model Year" or "10th Digit VIN."
  - **Owned or Leased**
    Knowing if the customer owns or leases the vehicle helps in the process of determining how permanent the installed items are. The difference of owning versus leasing may also influence budgets, particularly if the

A **1980**	L **1990**	Y **2000**	A **2010**
B 1981	M 1991	1 2002	B 2011
C 1982	N 1992	2 2002	C 2012
D 1983	P 1993	3 2003	D 2013
E 1984	R 1994	4 2004	E 2014
F 1985	S 1995	5 2005	F 2015
G 1986	T 1996	6 2006	G 2016
H 1987	V 1997	7 2007	H 2017
J 1988	W 1998	8 2008	J 2018
K 1989	X 1999	9 2009	K 2019

customer plans to return the vehicle in a few years. A leased vehicle may need be returned in the original condition (including preserving whatever electronics are removed until reinstallation), and the product specialist can relieve the client's concerns about aftermarket electronics. It's an easy question to ask and goes a long way to help with installation planning.

Margin Notes

- **Evaluate Existing Equipment**
  Adding or using existing equipment can present challenges. It's important to establish whether the equipment functions properly and what lifespan it has left. Older electronics can be incompatible with newer technologies. Speakers are exposed to UV rays, moisture, and uncalibrated amplifier power can have an increased potential for failure.

  When a shop has a fully outfitted test bench, this helps validate customer-supplied equipment. Many shops charge a small fee to test each customer-supplied item, and if they check out, the shop can deduct that fee from the installation cost. This includes testing of speakers, amplifiers, head units, video products and more. Testing existing equipment allows the technician to see firsthand the condition of the equipment on the bench and if it is worth the labor of installing. Inform the consumer that warranty on labor for customer-supplied equipment may be different (or none at all). Be upfront about all practices and policies related to customer-supplied equipment. Expectations and conditions of the customer-owned equipment should be clarified prior to committing to the job. This minimizes surprises when changes need to be made.

  It's also important to establish the State of Health (SoH) of the vehicle's battery and charging system. A Mobile Product Specialist should visually inspect the condition of the vehicle battery. If there is visible corrosion or the vehicle is difficult to start, ask a technician to perform the MECP recommended State of Health charging system test as outlined in the MECP Advanced Installation Technician study guide. Establishing the health of the vehicle's charging system is important, particularly for audio installations using power amplifiers and security/remote starter systems where a dead battery is often mistakenly blamed on the aftermarket equipment. Having a documented State of Health for the vehicle battery and charging system at the beginning of the sales process allows the Mobile Product Specialist to identify any vehicle electrical repairs the customer may consider before having any aftermarket equipment installed, such as replacing the battery or alternator if a charging system problem is identified.

- **Ask What They Don't Like About the Current Configuration/Features**
  Ask what the customer likes and dislikes about a technology or what they feel their vehicle lacks. Be sure to take notes as this will give you direct bullet point goals to achieve with the service or product you will recommend. Such

Margin Notes

qualifying questions provide a solution-based approach rather than clerking a sale. When asked, many customers will openly share what they dislike about their vehicle's electronics (or sound system) and speak about the objective of why they visited store.

Recommendations Based on Accurate Information

Whatever a Mobile Product Specialist recommends for a customer, it must be appropriate to suit the vehicle, the needs the customer wishes to address and (preferably) provide a clear solution-based approach. This often requires some initial research and planning based in application guides, inventory, warranties and whether or not the customer is going to have professional installation services, or they will install the equipment themselves.

- **Online Application Guides**

  Many manufacturers of aftermarket electronics and speakers have online application guides or OS-specific apps (Android, iOS) that help narrow down products by providing the vehicle's year/make/model. This information may influence applicable head unit size, dash kits or interfaces needed, what size speakers and locations apply or if a data interface module is necessary to complete the job. It is important to find these answers before settling on specific main products (such as a head unit, certain sized speaker or remote starter), because the integration accessory may not be available or even been engineered yet.

  Alternatively, the inclusion of a required integration accessory may push the customer's budget out of range. For instance, an entry-level in-dash single-DIN head unit may require hundreds of dollars in a dash kit, wiring harness, antenna adaptor and steering wheel control interface if the vehicle is a new model. Utilizing online manufacturer application guides and apps is required to quote the job with a complete picture of what necessary products, installation accessories and time is needed to complete the installation successfully.

- **Evaluate Condition/Safety of Existing Installed Products**

  Presuming the any existing equipment has been validated/tested for operation, it's also important to ensure the equipment is safely installed. This includes:

  - Proper mounting/fit of in-dash electronics (head units, video monitors, etc.).
  - Proper mounting of speakers.
  - Proper mounting of subwoofer enclosures.
  - Proper circuit protection on electronics, particularly high current (amplifiers, lighting).
  - Proper mounting of electronics exposed to weather (pin switches, sirens, reverse cameras, etc.).
  - Proper calibration of amplifier outputs.
  - Proper electrical wiring connections, particularly any data-bus connections.

Margin Notes

Where safe mounting, correct circuit protection, safe wiring and connection practices or weatherization of equipment is lacking, the equipment should be reinstalled correctly if the items being added to the vehicle will depend on the existing equipment. Ignoring this will only create problems when the new equipment is installed and does not function as intended due to the dependence on the existing equipment. When in doubt, ask an installation technician to provide their expert opinion to the customer. Most customers appreciate the analysis and advice that comes from a professional, even if the result is an unexpected safety concern.

- **What's Available (In Stock or via Suppliers)**
  It's often said that in sales, the best item to sell is the one in stock. This statement may not always be the case as modern vehicles are considerably more specialized with what installation accessory or additional labor is required, even for the simplest add-on item. Using online manufacturer application guides or apps for specifics and knowing what suppliers carry (including lead time for shipping) is crucial to getting the sale right. Knowing this information determines if the time line works for the customer's expectations and if expediting the item is necessary. If products do not need to be ordered, knowing this timeline will help installation scheduling.

- **Product Warranty**
  Many customers appreciate and expect peace-of-mind when it comes to product warranty. Some manufacturers offer short, over-the-counter warranties that may not include considerations about professional installation. Other product warranties are longer if they are professionally installed by authorized dealers that have firsthand knowledge of the product and how it applies. Some stores offer, in addition to the manufacturer's warranty, an optional extended warranty. Depending on the replacement cost/complexity of the product, extended warranties can provide a tangible value to the consumer and add to the profitability to the sale. Whatever the store's offerings and policies about product warranties, it's important to know this information as part of the sales process so that you convey accurate information and create realistic expectations. Be sure to give the original product packaging to the customer for their own safe keeping in case of a warrantable event.

  A Mobile Product Specialist must also clarify the warranty on labor. Shops that offer an extended-term labor warranty or lifetime labor warranty can use this as a selling tool when closing a sale. The added peace-of-mind that a comprehensive labor warranty provides is important. Some shops limit a comprehensive labor warranty to equipment they sell and install. Customer-supplied equipment (whether used or purchased from another source) may carry exclusions or different conditions of warranty. Every shop has differing policies and procedures on the installation labor warranty, but it's important to be crystal clear about what is offered in the shop.

Margin Notes

- **Do-it-Yourself (DIY) or Do-it-for-Me (DIFM) Customer**
  Making Do-it-Yourself (DIY) sales to customers that decide to perform a given installation themselves does happen, whether they have experience or not. DIY enthusiasts have different reasons for why they wish to perform an installation on their own, including budget reasons, suggested ease by a friend or family member, or feeling empowered from an online video on the topic (You Tube, etc.). It's fair to say vehicles aren't getting easier to work if you're not a professional in the field. Issues tend to arise a lot faster with DIY customers because newer vehicles are inclusive of sophisticated electronics and data bus systems of which a DIY customer may know very little. As the specialist, inform them of vehicle complexities to try to influence the DIY to choose professional installation instead. If they still insist on doing the install themselves, don't push too hard. Chances are good that they will come back to the shop to get the job done right.

  The Do-it-for-Me (DIFM) customer is broader ranging than a DIY. This customer requires some or all of the process done by a professional. Ideal DIFM customers visit the store, purchase products, then have them professionally installed. Sometimes, the DIFM customer can separate the process into two segments: purchase of the product(s) and the labor to install the product(s). The internet drives product research, purchase interest and sales of electronics, including car electronics and accessories. Consumers often do basic research, gather information and look for a deal when surfing the internet. While gathering information, they may be unaware of product reliability or brand concerns, or gather references of product pricing that do not reflect what brand/current models are sold in your store. DIFM consumers may also focus on a specific product online, such as a head unit or amplifier, and omit purchasing the important installation accessories (or even consider the added costs, regardless of labor). These are all opportunities for a shop with a good web presence and qualified Mobile Product Specialists to win over prospective customers. Combined with professional installation, it's the best-case scenario to ensure customers have a positive experience with their in-vehicle technology purchase and installation.

Magnuson-Moss Warranty Act

The Magnuson-Moss Act is a term often discussed among industry colleagues. It's most often brought up when, after installing some type of aftermarket equipment in a customer's car, something else goes wrong, and the vehicle manufacturer/dealership refuses to warranty anything on the vehicle because of the aftermarket equipment. What exactly is the Magnuson-Moss act and how does it relate to the aftermarket car electronics industry and an MECP Mobile Product Specialist?

The Legal Jargon

The Magnuson-Moss Warranty Act is a United States federal law that was enacted in 1975 that governs warranties on consumer products. It was brought about to fix

Margin Notes

problems created from manufacturers using disclaimers on warranties in an unfair or misleading manner. The act was sponsored by Sens. Warren G. Magnuson and Frank E. Moss. This act was the first federal statute to address the law of warranty, and the act's overall purpose was to improve the information available to consumers, prevent deception and improve competition in the marketing of consumer products, which are defined as property distributed in commerce and used for personal, family or household purposes.

The Magnuson- Moss act mandates that if a written warranty is provided on any consumer product, it must completely and conspicuously disclose, in easily understood words, the terms and conditions of the warranty. The law does not require that all products sold have a warranty (they may be sold "as is"), but if a product does have a warranty, the warranty must comply with this law. In addition, according to the act, a written warranty on a consumer product that costs more than $10, must be clearly labeled as "full" or "limited." A full warranty means that whoever promises to fix the item must do so in cases of defect or where the item does not conform to the warranty. This action must be done within a reasonable time and without charge. A limited warranty can contain reasonable restrictions regarding the responsibilities of the manufacturer or seller for the repair or replacement of the item.

What the Magnuson-Moss Act Requires

In passing the Magnuson-Moss Warranty Act, Congress specified many requirements that warrantors must meet. Congress also directed the Federal Trade Commission (FTC) to adopt rules to cover other requirements. The FTC adopted three rules under the Act, the Rule on Disclosure of Written Consumer Product Warranty Terms and Conditions (the Disclosure Rule), the Rule on Pre-Sale Availability of Written Warranty Terms (the Pre-Sale Availability Rule) and the Rule on Informal Dispute Settlement Procedures (the Dispute Resolution Rule). In addition, the FTC has issued an interpretive rule that clarifies certain terms and explains some of the provisions of the Act.

The Act and the rules establish three basic requirements:

1. As a warrantor, a company must designate, or title, their written warranty as either "full" or "limited."
2. As a warrantor, a company must state certain specified information about the coverage of their warranty in a single, clear and easy-to read document.
3. As a warrantor or a seller, a company must ensure that warranties are available where their warrantied consumer products are sold so that consumers can read them before buying.

The titling requirement, established by the Act, applies to all written warranties on consumer products costing more than $10. However, the disclosure and pre-sale availability requirements, established by FTC Rules, apply to all written warranties on consumer products costing more than $15.

Margin Notes

What the Magnuson-Moss Act Does Not Require

The Act does not require that any company provide a written warranty. The Act allows companies to determine whether or not to warranty their products in writing. However, once a company decides to offer a written warranty on a consumer product, it must comply with the Magnuson-Moss Act.

The Act does not apply to oral warranties. Only written warranties are covered.

The Act does not apply to warranties on services. Only warranties on goods are covered. However, if a warranty covers both the parts provided for a repair and the workmanship in making that repair, the Act does apply to it.

The Act does not apply to warranties on products sold for resale or for commercial purposes. The Act covers only warranties on consumer products. This means that only warranties on tangible property normally used for personal, family or household purposes are covered. This includes property attached to or installed on real property.

What the Magnuson-Moss Act Does Not Allow

There are three prohibitions under the Magnuson-Moss Act. They involve implied warranties, so-called "tie-in sales" provisions and deceptive or misleading warranty terms.

1. **Disclaimer or Modification of Implied Warranties** – The Act prohibits anyone who offers a written warranty from disclaiming or modifying implied warranties. This means that no matter how broad or narrow the written warranty is, the customers always will receive the basic protection of the implied warranty of merchantability.

   There is one permissible modification of implied warranties, however. If a company offers a "limited" written warranty, the law allows them to include a provision that restricts the duration of implied warranties to the duration of the limited warranty. For example, if a company offers a two-year limited warranty, they can limit implied warranties to two years. However, if they offer a "full" written warranty, they cannot limit the duration of implied warranties.

2. **"Tie-In Sales" Provisions** – Generally speaking, tie-in sales provisions are not allowed. Such a provision would require the purchaser of a warrantied product to buy an item or service from a particular company to use with the warrantied product in order to be eligible to receive said warranty. This is an example of prohibited tie-in sales provisions:

   In order to keep your new ABC Brand Vacuum Cleaner warranty in effect, you must use genuine ABC Brand vacuum cleaner bags. Failure to have scheduled maintenance performed, at your expense, by the ABC Maintenance Company Inc., voids this warranty.

   While a company cannot use a tie-in sales provision, the warranty need not cover use of replacement parts, repairs or maintenance that is inappropriate

Margin Notes

for the product. This is an example of a permissible provision that excludes coverage of such things:

While necessary maintenance or repairs on your ABC Vacuum Cleaner can be performed by any company, we recommend that you use only authorized ABC dealers. Improper or incorrectly performed maintenance or repair voids this warranty.

Although tie-in sales provisions generally are not allowed, companies can include such a provision in their warranty if they can demonstrate to the satisfaction of the FTC that their product will not work properly without a specified item or service.

3. **Deceptive Warranty Terms** – Obviously, warranties must not contain deceptive or misleading terms. You cannot offer a warranty that appears to provide coverage but, in fact, provides none. For example, a warranty covering only "moving parts" on an electronic product that has no moving parts would be deceptive and unlawful. Similarly, a warranty that promised service that the warrantor had no intention of providing or could not provide would be deceptive and unlawful.

What Does It All Mean?

What the Magnuson-Moss Act means for the MECP Mobile Product Specialist is this: **modifying a customer's vehicle will not void its warranty (if it has one). No modification can legally void a warranty in whole**. That said, if a part fails on a customer's vehicle after work was performed and it was directly caused by the work that took place, the shop who sold/installed the aftermarket equipment is responsible for that repair.

If an aftermarket amplifier was installed and suddenly the vehicle's BCM or Telematics module starts acting up, the installing shop is not responsible. If a high-powered aftermarket amplifier was installed in a vehicle and put so much power that the factory speakers were blown as a result, that would absolutely void the warranty of the factory speakers. The reason for this is obvious; the amount of power installed was far more than the factory speakers could handle and this was the direct cause of the failure. Thus, it makes sense the customer no longer has a factory warranty on the OEM speakers. If a wheel bearing fails or a fan belt snaps and an aftermarket exhaust had just been installed, the manufacturer would have to prove the exhaust system caused the bearing failure or the belt to snap in order to deny a warranty claim. Remember, the warrantor is responsible for proving that the failure was directly caused by the modification, and that had the modification not been performed, the failure wouldn't have happened.

If the customer needs to go to a dealership for any type of warranty issue, help them choose the dealership wisely, as they will vary greatly in how they handle warranty claims. Check credible websites for reviews to see how the dealership handles problems. If the customer has modified their vehicle with aftermarket equipment and/or performance parts, it's always best to work with a dealer that

Margin Notes

is familiar with these attributes and that acceptance of aftermarket parts by the dealership can vary widely.

In rural areas, there may not be a choice of dealerships, but rest assured that the customer with the aftermarket equipment is still protected by the law. Be well armed with the knowledge contained in this section, ensure the customer is equally well-informed and prepare to visit the dealership with a smile. No service department at a dealership wants to deal with (or help) an irate customer, just like 12 Volt retailers don't. If they don't want to cover the claim, simply ask them to prove what caused the failure and get it in writing. Remember, legally, the customer with the aftermarket equipment is protected under the Magnuson-Moss Act.

Secondly, what the Act means for the retailer, is that if you a consumer is sold a product with a written warranty from the product manufacturer, but it is not warrantied in writing, the retailer can disclaim the implied warranties. (These are the implied warranties under which the seller, not the manufacturer, would otherwise be responsible.) But, regardless of whether the retailer warranties the products they sell, as the seller, retailers must give their customers copies of any written warranties from product manufacturers. These are always included in the packages of the products. Therefore, it's good practice to always give the customer all of the packaging and documentation that came with the products they are sold.

Document Location(s) of Equipment for Service

Whenever aftermarket equipment installations take place at a 12 Volt retailer, it's important to note the locations of any new components that will either need to be accessible for service or troubleshooting of any kind. This includes fuse holders, main control units, antennas and/or RF receivers. Be sure to document the location of user-accessed items like any knobs, buttons or switches that are part of the installation so those aren't overlooked. This documentation allows the customer to be more informed on the installation as well as provide a record of service should the vehicle ever come back to your shop or need to be remotely diagnosed, such as if the customer experiences an issue on a road trip and another shop has to check it out. This is covered in greater detail later in the chapter under recommendations for delivering the vehicle.

Document Customer Preferences and Settings

It's also important, both when checking in and releasing a customer's vehicle, to make sure certain features and preferences are recorded and or enabled. This cuts down on customer confusion which can lead to frustration. Since they will already have to familiarize themselves with a new piece of equipment, make that transition as smooth as possible.

Make sure when a customer's vehicle enters the shop for any installation or service work, record the customer's personal vehicle settings like: seat position, mirror position and radio presets. These settings can (and should) be documented on a check-in sheet. The check-in is best done with the customer present, so they

Margin Notes

can see the inspection of the vehicle and sign off on the sheet when completed. A good check-in sheet is a must in any installation shop, period. The effort to complete and protection provided by the check-in process far outweighs any perceived inconvenience and assures that the employees and the business are not unreasonably blamed for anything that might have been wrong with the vehicle when it arrived. See the example of a check-in sheet in the Appendix.

After all of the work has been performed by the installation technicians, it is also important to take the time to set up and review the features of the customer's new equipment. If a new head unit has just been installed, for example, store all of the previously recorded AM/FM/Satellite Radio presets that were present on the factory radio (refer to the check-in sheet for this info. Set the clock, adjust the audio settings to a somewhat neutral level (until the customer learns how to do it themselves) and finally, pair the customer's phone and test the Bluetooth features before releasing the vehicle. This will ensure that the customer has a pleasant experience and will not have to return to the shop due to a simple problem that could have been avoided. It also provides an opportunity to become familiar with the equipment, which helps when you are demonstrating the installation for the customer. References to the information on a vehicle check-in sheet are covered the next section under recommendations for delivering the vehicle and setting (or resetting) customer settings.

Delivering the Vehicle

Customers have many options when they bring their business to a qualified retail store with knowledgeable MECP Mobile Product Specialists and Installation Technicians on staff. When it's time to deliver their vehicle with a completed installation, that's the ideal opportunity to solidify that the customer made the right choice. Delivering the vehicle to the customer can be one of the most powerful tools in a retailer's arsenal and can make the difference between an average experience and one with which they will leave feeling confident about their decision and eager to share their experience with others.

10 Recommended Value-Added Steps:

Here are 10 key components to consider implementing or addressing with each and every vehicle to ensure customers get the extra value they expect from doing business with MECP Mobile Product Specialists and Installation Technicians:

1. **Set Clock, Radio Station Presets, and Illumination Colors** – As mentioned in the documentation and customer preferences section earlier in this chapter, set all clock functions such as the time, date and time zone if applicable. Don't forget about the AM or PM for head units that make the distinction, or to ask if customers with an international background or in the military would prefer the 24-hour clock format. It's good practice to ask the customer what time is on their watch or phone and set their radio to match, including the format (AM/PM or 24-hour time). Sometimes customers may want the time set ahead of the actual time to keep from being late. Whatever the request, set it up exactly how the customer wishes and show them how to make the adjustment as well.

Margin Notes

If the vehicle check-in sheet has a spot to enter a customer's existing radio presets, use it to store the same stations on the same presets as what they had with their previous radio (before the old radio gets disconnected and removed, of course). Remember to also set up any other source presets such as satellite radio. Many manufacturers of OEM and aftermarket head units allow for mixed presets such as having FM and Satellite radio presets saved within the same band. If this feature is available, be sure to discuss it with the customer and demonstrate how to save their favorite stations.

2. **Initiate Subscription-Based Services (Satellite Radio, Smartphone Control of RS, etc.)** – Nothing is more aggravating than getting a new piece of technology and not being able to enjoy it right away. Be sure that the customer experiences no such aggravation by making all necessary activations and/or connections to any subscription-based services and functions before they leave the shop. If they have a satellite radio tuner, help them choose a package and activate their new subscription. Give them a printed channel lineup so they can familiarize themselves with available content. Satellite radios need to be turned on for a period of time during the activation process so that the channel information may download to the receiver. Take the time to make sure the unit is fully functional while the customer is still at the shop.

   If the customer purchased a remote start and/or security system that will be controlled by an app from their phone, walk them through the process of downloading the app and activating the service. Always try to have the customer download the respective app for their new system prior to picking up their vehicle. This will save time during the delivery process and will give the customer a chance to become familiar with the app and its features. This way, if questions arise, they can be answered before the customer begins using their new technology and the experience will be far more aggravation-free.

3. **Pair the customer's smartphone and demonstrate Bluetooth functions** – Most aftermarket head units are compatible with smartphones via Bluetooth wireless connection and require the initial introduction of the head unit to the phone via the process called "pairing." Go over the pairing process with your customer and get their phone connected to their new head unit. If the aftermarket head unit allows for streaming Bluetooth audio (A2DP support), make sure the audio setting for Bluetooth audio is set for "all speakers" (or similar) so music from all speakers is audible when using the phone as the media source. Make a test phone call using the customer's phone and show them how it works.

   Demonstrate how to answer, end or reject an incoming call. Also demonstrate how to switch between the vehicle's Bluetooth and the handset in the case there are passengers in the car who want to have a private conversation. Finally, demonstrate how to initiate a call using the phone-related buttons on the head unit so the customer keeps their eyes on the road and not on their phone. Many aftermarket multimedia head units support some amount of voice-control for outbound dialing. Most modern vehicles have steering wheel controls that, when connected to the new head unit, allow the functionality necessary to do some telephone functions if those features were present with the factory radio. All of those efforts help the customer enjoy the technology in a safe manner.

Margin Notes

4. **Provide an Audio System Performance Worksheet (RTA/SPL measurements, etc.)** – Many shops record the state of the audio system prior to doing any upgrades, and then compare that to the outcome after upgrades are completed. This is a great way to give the customer tangible evidence of why they should feel good about their decision to invest in their new sound system. Show the customer reading/measurements taken prior to the new equipment being installed, then show the readings/measurements after the installation is completed. Explain what the differences are, how they were accomplished using the new equipment and why each is important.

   - For example: If the job was adding a subwoofer to enhance an OEM audio system, the technician may have taken a reading with a real time analyzer (RTA) to show the frequency response of the factory system using pink noise, presumably with notable weakness in the low frequency (20-100Hz) region. When compared to a reading taken after the subwoofer is installed, it will clearly show a boost in the low frequencies which demonstrates the effective outcome of adding a subwoofer in an objective way. In addition to the RTA reading, the sound pressure level (SPL) of the vehicle can be measured before and after and then explain the difference to the customer. Pictures of the RTA during such readings are a great tool to help the customer understand why their system sounds better after the upgrade and gives tangible (objective) proof of the differences.

5. **Vacuum Interior** – Everyone likes getting into a clean car. This is probably the most overlooked, detail and one of the easiest things to ensure a customer is pleased they chose you to work on their vehicle. No matter what the job was, always take a couple of minutes to vacuum the floors, seats, and cargo areas of the vehicle. It's also a great touch to clean their windshield and rear view mirrors. The installation technician probably never even touched them, but the customer is going to be looking at their mirrors and through their windshield for the entire ride home from your shop. Providing a clean view and a clean place to sit for that ride is the kind of detail that keeps customers coming back. They will notice that you took the time to do something extra and that will go a long way towards earning more business from them in the future.

6. **Wash/Detail Vehicle for Long-Term Installations** – Work areas get dusty over long periods of time. For larger, more time-consuming projects, wash the vehicle prior to delivery. If the retailer does not have the facilities to wash cars, make arrangements with a local detail service to come to the

Margin Notes

shop and wash the vehicle onsite. As with any project, return the customer's vehicle in equal or better condition than it was when it was dropped off for the installation. There are always exceptions. For example, if the vehicle has an extremely expensive paint job or graphics the customer may ask that the vehicle not be washed due to the liability of damaging it during cleanup. It's a good practice to check with the customer ahead of time. Always use quality cleaning products to avoid issues with damage to paint or other materials on vehicles and be sure they are recommended for use in each particular application.

7. **Demonstrate Features/Functions Directly to Customer** – With modern technology and in-vehicle electronics, the list of features and functions can be quite overwhelming. Imagine how a customer feels if they aren't properly instructed on how to use their new equipment. This can be true for even technology-savvy customers because every piece of aftermarket equipment is different and requires some learning before a comfort level is achieved. Start out by demonstrating how to operate the basic functions of their new equipment. Here are a few examples:

   - The aftermarket head unit "walk through" – This is an overview of the need-to-know functions of a given device with which the customer will interact. With a new head unit walk through, show the customer the basics of how to turn the unit on and off, change source inputs, change and save radio stations using the auto and manual seek functions, adjust volume, adjust subwoofer volume, change tracks, fast forward/rewind and load/eject media be it a disc, flash drive or other media connected to or inserted into the head unit. Then have the customer go through the functions while watching and assisting if they get stumped. Once the basics are covered, proceed to the more advanced functions such as setting the color of the display and/or buttons to match their OEM instrument panel lighting color scheme, making sound adjustments (equalizer or tone controls, crossovers, etc.), display content, clock setup, source level adjustments, etc. When complete, ask the customer if they feel comfortable operating the head unit. Ask them if they have any questions and if anything you have covered doesn't make sense. This gives you the opportunity to review it again if there is any confusion.

   - In the case of a new audio DSP signal processor device installed, show the customer how to change the presets that were configured by the installation technician, adjust the volume and note what is a safe level of operation, access an auxiliary input (if equipped), make changes to the subwoofer level, and any other functions the DSP device may offer. For advanced users only, a Mobile Product Specialist can bring a tablet or laptop into the car and show customers how to access the detailed adjustments available with the DSP. Keep in mind, however, your technician is trained in how the system should be set up and detailed adjustments should be made with relative caution. Sometimes it may be to your

Margin Notes

advantage to only show the user features (and not the more advanced tuning features/software) if you feel the customer is not likely to make useful changes in the tuning software.

- Perhaps the customer purchased a lighting system with RGB color options. Help them download the app on their phone (if applicable) or give them their IR or RF remote control and show them how to operate the functions such as strobe or fading patterns, color changes, brightness, music sync, etc.

- If a new amplifier was installed to power existing speakers, play the customer's favorite music tracks and talk to them about how the additional power the amplifier is providing is allowing the speakers to achieve clarity at a higher volume level than without the amplifier present. Explain to them that the amplifier has been precisely calibrated by an experienced MECP certified technician to deliver peak performance. Show the customer the maximum volume limit determined by the technician. Remind the customer that the maximum recommended volume limit ensures the best performance, which means going beyond the maximum recommended level may cause damage to their speakers and create unwanted distortion. In an ideal calibration, this probability of damaging speakers and exhibiting distortion is minimal in the hands of an experienced technician because the technician would always strive to adjust the processor to have only the range of adjustment that is safe.

  These are just a few examples of different products that you will be demonstrating to customers. Whatever the product may be, make sure to go over all of its features until the customer understands how to operate and have a great experience with their new technologies.

8. **Provide All Owner's Manuals for Equipment** – Owner's or operator's manuals usually contain operation instructions, warranty information and product specifications. Provide all applicable product manuals to the customer. This is simply good practice but also a necessary component of written manufacturer warranties as described in the Magnusson-Moss Act described earlier in this section.

   To keep all the manuals, warranties and other paperwork together, make an envelope or packet with those manuals and provide to the customer after demonstrating their new equipment. It's also good practice to include a business card with the store's contact information in case the customer runs in to any confusion operating the equipment in the future. This makes it quick and easy for customers to contact the shop (or the Mobile Product Specialist directly) first for help.

9. **Provide Explanation of Equipment Warranty and Labor Warranty Policies** – The warranty policy for each piece of aftermarket is most likely included in

Margin Notes

the owner's manual or a separate written document. This is referenced in the previous Magnusson-Moss Act section earlier in the chapter. Take time to inform the customer duration of the manufacturer's warranty, what is covered and what is not, what to do in case of a potential issue, who to contact and what the process will be if warranty repair or replacement is needed. If the store has a specific warranty policy, written or verbal, deliver it to the customer respectively and separate of the product warranty. Remember that written warranties are enforceable under the Magnusson-Moss Act so don't be ambiguous about stating and showing warranty policies of the shop that cover labor, diagnostics, removal/replacement, etc., and are separate warranties/policies from the product manufacturer's warranty. Ask the customer if they have any questions about the warranties and review any necessary information. If optional extended warranties on either product or labor are offered, this is a good time to discuss the merits of those additional warranties because the customer should understand where the inclusive warranties begin and end.

10. **Provide Contact Information for Questions/Issues Post-Sale** – Always provide customers after-the-sale contact information to quickly address any issues that may arise. There are typically three principal instances where a customer may need to contact someone with a question or an issue pertaining to their installation and/or equipment.

    a) **Instances where an equipment-related issue is identified** (remote not working, battery draining unexplained, etc.) - When delivering the vehicle to the customer, show them all areas where new equipment installation may need periodic service. These areas include but are not limited to:

    - Batteries in remote controls for security/remote start systems, head unit remotes, radar detector controllers, rear seat entertainment system remotes, wireless headphones, wireless radar detectors, etc. Demonstrate how to access the battery in the device, tell them which battery size it is (such as AA, CR2032, etc.) and how to replace it. Better yet, invite customers to return to the store and offer to do it for them.

    - How to set the clock in a new head unit (long after leaving the store). Unless the clock is automatically updated via GPS or RDS, this is a something that customers who purchase anything with a clock in it will need do twice a year in most states or provinces that observe Daylight Saving Time (DST). Offering to reset the customer's clock for DST is a great service to offer and provides an opportunity invite them back to the store to check out new products and technologies. Early November is a great time to talk about a remote start system and March is the perfect time to install a rear seat entertainment or radar detection system before vacation and summer road trips. This approach provides the opportunity to do both while resetting their clocks.

Margin Notes

- Fuse location for the equipment as previously stated in the documentation of important components as part of the installation work. Although the customer should be told to always return to the store for diagnostics in the event of a blown fuse, they need to be aware of where the fuse is and how to disconnect or remove it in case the need arises. Explain to them that the fuse is a protection device for its respective part of the circuit and if the fuse blows, that is indicative of an issue that needs to be addressed by a professional technician at your shop prior to replacing it with another fuse. Without first determining the cause of the blown fuse, simply replacing it will not necessarily fix the root cause of the problem. Also, address that the fuse should never be replaced with any type or amperage rating other than the size installed.

- Reset instructions where applicable. Ever had to power off/reset a cell phone because it got stuck on an app or stopped functioning properly? What about a computer? Ever pressed "control, alt, delete"? Of course. The aftermarket car electronics industry offers a wide variety of integration devices such as radio replacement modules, steering wheel control interfaces, auxiliary interface devices and video input modules just to name a few. The one thing most of these have in common is they rely on embedded operating software (called firmware) to work properly. Just like a cell phone or computer, these types of devices have the potential to stop working properly and may only need a simple reset or off/on power cycle in order to get them working again. Don't let a customer be surprised by something like this. Let them know, up front, that the device they've had installed (whatever it might be) is very high tech and that if there ever is an issue with its functionality, it will be taken care of promptly and they will be back up and running quickly – typically at no charge. The key is for the customer not to panic and simply contact the shop first thing when an issue is noticed.

  It's worth noting that even OEM features such as Apple CarPlay®, Android Auto™, USB connectivity, voice control and other infotainment/hands-free features also do not work as intended 100 percent of the time. The best thing to offer the customer is to be their technology ambassador so that when they encounter an issue known to be firmware-related, they need only contact the shop using the contact info previously provided to help with the remedy.

- Hood pin replacement. Mechanical hood pin switches don't last forever. Regions where snow and rain are excessive only shorten the longevity of a hood pin switch. Hood pins used on security systems provide an entry point trigger and on remote starters provide a very necessary safety input (providing status to the remote starter of whether the hood is open or closed), so having it in working order is very important. This

Margin Notes

would be a great item to have the customer bring their vehicle in for an annual or bi-annual "check-up" to be sure the hood pin is operating properly and in good condition.

- Firmware updates. With equipment utilizing firmware, updates may be necessary to keep the equipment functioning with newer technology such as a new phone or updated portable device operating system. This may also be necessary if a vehicle has visited a dealership for service and had factory-specified vehicle computer updates, something a customer may not think to mention when all of the sudden something your shop installed stops working as it did before. This is different than resetting procedures (turning something off and back on to "reset"). Be sure to instruct the customer to come back to the store to have the firmware updated in the event they change phones or other peripheral device or have had the vehicle serviced with an on-board computer update, and the product installed ceases to operate properly after such upgrade or update of the peripheral device.

- Navigation updates. Most in-dash navigation units provide periodic updates to their mapping software to give the customer the most up-to-date information on new routes, points of interest, speed limits, interchanges, etc. Some of these are provided for a fee and some of them are at no cost to the customer. In either case, be sure to inform the customer how to go about getting the updates and how to load the updates into their system. Often this will be via disc or media card but can also be USB or via Wi-Fi if the head unit is so enabled. If your store installs navigation updates as a service, familiarize them with the process so they will know what to do when the update time arrives.

b) **Instances of Car Dealership Conflicts (dealership quickly blames aftermarket equipment)** – First, familiarize yourself with the Magnuson-Moss Warranty Act covered in detail earlier in the chapter Mobile Product Specialists need to know about the Magnusson-Moss Warranty Act. Most dealerships, service advisors or mechanics are unaware of the Magnuson-Moss Warranty Act or of the protection it provides the consumer. Customers need to be confident that adding aftermarket equipment to their vehicle is perfectly safe and will not void their warranty when installed correctly.

Many dealerships and mechanics are unfamiliar with aftermarket technologies. Although some car dealerships have aftermarket products available through their parts counter or through an expediter, much of the electronics are already "baked in" to the vehicle when it hits the car lot.

Some aftermarket electronics unfamiliar to a new car dealership include remote start systems, head units, amplifiers, auxiliary input devices, radar

Margin Notes

systems, blind spot detection, interlock devices, aftermarket lighting and any kind of interface device that connects into the vehicle's CAN-Bus or MOST infotainment system. Unfamiliarity with these types of products may lead dealerships to make a premature determination or assumption that such equipment is the cause of an issue with the vehicle without first following proper diagnostic protocols. This can be the source of much aggravation for customers if they are not properly informed on how to handle the situation. Let the customer know that although rare, should this type of situation present itself, they should contact the shop immediately.

Inform the customer that the shop will communicate with the dealership or mechanic on their behalf to ensure the dealership or mechanic is able to do their job and eliminate your equipment as a cause of any issue with the vehicle. Also, offer to look over their vehicle at no charge before the customer takes it to a dealership for routine maintenance or a repair. This provides an opportunity to identify any issue with the installed aftermarket equipment (if there is one) and save the customer the frustration of spending more time in the mechanic's shop or at a dealership. It's all too often that a customer's equipment is removed from their car by the mechanic on the assumption that it is causing a problem, only to discover removing or disabling the equipment did not solve the problem. You can avoid problems by educating customers before they have a chance to find themselves in this situation. It earns customer trust and exhibits professionalism.

A useful tool in these situations is a custom printed door jamb decal. This is a small decal that can be placed in the door jamb of the car that has your store's logo and contact information. These decals are a great way for a mechanic or anyone else working on the car to know who performed the installation of aftermarket equipment. The decal provides contact information in the event there is a question or issue related to the equipment. A short instruction such as "Before service work, please call 555-5555" or "Upgrades performed by (store name)" can also be included on the decal. These decals can also be placed directly on aftermarket equipment such as remote start system modules, amplifiers, radio replacement interface modules or any other piece of aftermarket equipment that another service center may come across after a customer's vehicle leaves the shop.

c) **Instances Where Service is Required and Customer is Out of the Area (traveling)** – Sometimes a customer may experience an issue when on vacation, a business trip or may have moved to a different part of the country. Whatever the store's policy is, explain it to the customer in detail, including who to contact in the case of such an event. Some manufacturers have nationwide warranty policies that allow the consumer to receive service at authorized dealers other than where the equipment was originally purchased and installed. The details of such policies vary and should be

Margin Notes

described in the written warranty statement provided by the manufacturer. A retailer should have their own specific policy on how this will be handled. It may define who will be responsible for different costs associated with services performed by other shops when the customer is not able to bring the vehicle back for such service. Whatever the case, provide the customer with instructions on contacting the installing shop first and then there is an opportunity to handle the situation for them and put them in contact with the right person or facility. There's a very good possibility that one retailer may know someone in the business who is nearby the customer's location that wouldn't mind helping out if needed.

Customer Follow-Up

Every retailer offering aftermarket car electronics and professional installation should have a series of efforts that focus on customer retention. If the shop provided a great experience in the sale and installation of aftermarket car electronics technology, keep those customers happy and put the retailer top of mind for their next purchase, referrals or simply feeling comfortable to contact the retailer with questions that arise.

Courtesy Calls

Use a calendar to schedule reminders. Each day, call everyone from the same day of the week from the previous week, month, year, etc. Know the purpose of the call and what the expected accomplishment is. Take notes. Address any issues and show appreciation.

Making courtesy calls can be a very powerful tool in your arsenal for many reasons:

- People like to feel appreciated. The fact that a Mobile Product Specialist took the time out of their day to pick up the phone and make a personal call to them will speak highly of a commitment to serving customers after the sale.
- A follow up call can gather valuable feedback that may not otherwise been known. This is especially valuable in the case that the customer had some sort of an issue during or after the job was completed. Now you have the opportunity to offer to make it right and keep them happy.
- When calling customers, there is an opportunity to offer those services that may enhance their purchase and bring them back in to the store. If they purchased a new amplifier, talk to them about the latest speakers that would make their vehicle sound even better. Did the customer have a remote starter system installed? Remind the customer that the shop can install an add-on device that will allow them to start their vehicle from their smart phone. Perhaps they just had a brand-new head unit installed and didn't purchase the optional back-up camera. Let them know about the upcoming sale or "demo day" the store is having on cameras and safety equipment and invite them back for a visit.

Know what the objective is **before** picking up the phone. Be prepared to answer any questions the customer may have or address concerns if they arise. Tell them how much you appreciate them choosing to do business with the shop and that help or further assistance is always a phone call or a visit away if they need anything at all or just want to come see what's new. This is the perfect time to ask them to share their experience with others by submitting a positive online review for your store!

Margin Notes

Thank You Cards or Emails
Hand-written thank you cards or letters can be a very powerful tool for a Mobile Product Specialist's career. Think of the last time you received a hand-written thank you card from a business. It's safe to say you remember from which business it originated. Be sure to use proper grammar and spelling and that the handwriting is neat and clearly legible. Have some stationery printed up with the store's logo and contact information at the top or bottom and then use the body to hand-write the message. This can be on letter size paper or even as postcards to save postage on a tight budget but be sure to use the store's branding in all communications with customers.

Pre-printed cards or letters are the next best thing and can be done and mailed in a matter of seconds at very little cost. Simply hand write the customer's name at the top and sign at the bottom. Pre-printed cards provide a nice touch to handwrite a short, quick message at the bottom such as "The audio system turned out great!" or "Hope you're enjoying the warm car!" or "No more sore neck muscles with that new back-up camera!" Whatever the message, think of a way to personalize it and positive responses will result from those happy customers.

This is also another great opportunity to ask that existing customers to refer their friends to the shop. It could go something like:

- "Our main source of new customers is from referrals. If we've done a great job, please tell your friends and family of your experience and invite them to stop in for a visit to our store."
- "We love our friends! And we love your friends too! Tell them to come see us and we'll give you 10 percent off your next visit just for spreading the word! Come by or call me for details."
- "You know what sounds even better than your new audio system? Your friends and family telling you how great it sounds! When they do, please let them know we hooked you up! We appreciate referrals!"
- "Want to get rewarded for spreading the word about the great service at XYZ Car Audio? Refer a friend and get a free XYZ T-shirt next time you come in."

Don't forget to include a couple of your own business cards in the thank you letter so customers can give them to their friends and family. Referrals are very powerful and help future customers feel confident in choosing the store to do their business.

Email Follow-Up
There are countless services and software packages available to make follow up contact with your customers. This software or functionality is known as Customer

Margin Notes

Relationship Management (CRM) software. Some CRM software is industry-specific and some are customizable for multiple applications. All of these types of software and services rely on the customers' email address being correctly entered into your point-of-sale software in order to work. If a shop wishes to use a service for email newsletters or other targeted customer communication via email, an email address must be captured and documented for **each and every customer or prospective customer**. This is one of the least expensive ways of following up with customers or prospects and works great as long as the front-end work is completed. This also allows the company to reach out to customers or prospects in the future with emails advertising sales, car shows, new products, new team members, appointment reminders, warranty expirations and much more. For resources on companies to contact for such services, a simple web search of "retail CRM providers" or "email marketing service providers" returns quite a number of results.

Text Message Follow-Up

Text message follow-up can be a useful tool to send appointment reminders, status updates of a special order or in-process installation or that the vehicle work is complete. The software to support text messaging for specific reminders can be an add-on to an existing point of sale system, or a separate service integrated with the database of customer information. It's another very convenient method of customer communication for very specific things like appointment reminders and status updates related to **existing appointments or transactions**. Don't use text messaging as a marketing tool for closing sales, announcing events or store news. As a general rule, the rate of opens and clicks on links in a text message can't be tracked like an email.

Request Positive Online Reviews

The Internet has many positive effects on small businesses, particularly with the ability to see how customers like or dislike a given company or their services. Simply type in a company's name and read user reviews on sites such as Google®, Yelp, Facebook, Yahoo, Bing, and many more. Start each day with a personal goal to give such great service to customers that they will choose, when asked, to leave you the best review possible. A study by an Internet search marketing agency shows that 84% of potential customers trust an online review as much as a personal recommendation and that if asked, 70% of customers will leave an online review. What does it mean to a Mobile Product Specialist? It means that customer-facing professionals should be very aware of how important previous customer's reviews are to future customers.

Treat each and every customer with an experience they will not forget. Ask them if they need a place to sit while waiting on their vehicle or for a particular staff member to help them. Ask if they'd like a bottle of water or coffee. Arrange for them a ride to or from work, etc. Be sure all the things covered earlier in "delivering the vehicle" were done and remember, they are ultimately the source of employee paychecks at a retailer no matter what role each employee plays in the business.

Margin Notes

It can go something like this when invoicing their ticket begins: *"This will only take a few moments. While you're waiting, would you mind sharing your experience with an online review?"*

When the customer says "yes" or "sure", send them a link to the shop's review site or provide detailed instructions on how to do a review online. Customers are much more likely to do it while they are standing there in the shop in-person rather than remembering to do it after they leave.

Another, more detailed approach might be: *"Mr. Customer, it looks like we've gotten your vehicle completed just the way you wanted it. I'll just be a few moments putting your ticket into the computer. If I may ask a favor of you, would you mind giving us some feedback on (name of review site)? The majority of our business comes from referrals and most of our customers say they chose us because of our 5-star (name of site) reviews. It also helps us, the staff, earn promotions and raises. If you're 100 percent satisfied and don't mind doing it for me, I can send an easy-to-use link to your mobile phone and you can do it while I'm getting your invoice finalized."*

Some retailers provide customers a tablet where they can login and do a review. If customers are asked every time, online reviews will escalate in no time and the shop's staff start to see an influx in customers coming because of those reviews. Online reviews can be pulled up and used as part of the sales process with prospective customers.

There are companies that offer services directed specifically at getting more positive online reviews. These are typically monthly subscription type services. One benefit to services like these is that they may allow "less than great" reviews to be identified before they actually get posted to an online site, giving the opportunity to contact the customer, handle their issue and make them happy. Some additional study-related details that suggest the importance online reviews play:

- 84 percent of people trust online reviews as much as a personal recommendation.
- 70 percent of consumers will leave a review for a business if they're asked to.
- 90 percent of consumers read less than 10 reviews before forming an opinion about a business.
- 54 percent of people will visit the website after reading positive reviews.
- 73 percent of consumers think that reviews older than three months are no longer relevant.
- 74 percent of consumers say that positive reviews make them trust a local business more.
- 58 percent of consumers say that the star rating of a business is most important.

Source: www.brightlocal.com

Margin Notes

Additional customer satisfaction statistics:

- A dissatisfied customer will tell between 9-15 people about their experience. (source - White House Office of Consumer Affairs)
- Around 13 percent of dissatisfied customers will tell 20 people or more. (source - White House Office of Consumer Affairs)
- 78 percent of surveyed customers say that competent customer service reps are most responsible for a happy customer experience. (source - Genesys Global Survey)
- 83 percent of complainants that received a reply on social media liked or loved the fact that the company responded. (source - Bain & Co.)
- 88 percent of consumers are less likely to buy from companies that leave complaints on social media unanswered. (source - Conversocial)

VIP Customer Reminders

A great way to keep customers coming back is to keep them informed of the "latest and greatest" the industry has to offer. A "product spotlight" email or a flyer in the mail can be the seed that spikes their interest enough to get them to come by the store and check it out. Even if they aren't in the market for the product at the moment, they'll know that it's available at the store and can inquire when the need arises. A personal phone call can also be a very effective means to getting the customer excited about a new technology or product.

The customer's contact information is the single most valuable follow-up item to acquire. Without it, contact with the customer via email, postal mail or telephone can't occur. If an estimate for a prospective customer is completed, be sure to enter their information into the shop's point of sale system so that it may be retrieved later should they decide to go forward with the estimate. It's also very important to update information for current customers each time they make a purchase or come into the store to look around.

It goes like this: *"Mr. Customer, are you still at 123 Main Street? Is your email still customer@....com? And I have 555-555-1212 for your phone number. Is that still current? Great! Thanks for the update."* The ownership and management of a successful retailer places a huge importance on acquiring customer's contact information. Do it every time and make sure it is complete and accurate.

APPENDIX

INSTALLATION TECHNICIAN:

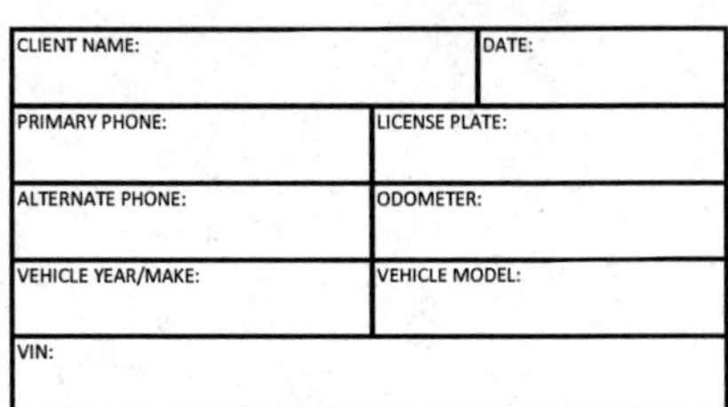

CLIENT NAME:	DATE:
PRIMARY PHONE:	LICENSE PLATE:
ALTERNATE PHONE:	ODOMETER:
VEHICLE YEAR/MAKE:	VEHICLE MODEL:
VIN:	

Car Stereo Shop

VEHICLE CHECKLIST			PRE-CHECKLIST COMPLETED BY:			POST-CHECKLIST COMLPETED BY:		
O = Operational X = Non-Operational	Pre-Check	Post-Check	O = Operational X = Non-Operational	Pre-Check	Post-Check	O = Operational X = Non-Operational	Pre-Check	Post-Check
Interior Lights			Front Wipers			Alarm		
Dash Lights			Rear Wipers			Power Antenna		
Parking Lights			Rear Defroster			Power Locks		
Headlights			Climate Control Fan			Power Windows		
Turn Signals			Air Conditioner			Power Mirrors		
Hazard Lights			Heater			Power Trunk Release		
Brake Lights			Radio			Power Sunroof		
Cigarette Lighter			Front Speakers			Power Seats		
Horn			Rear Speakers			Heated/Cooled Seats		
Gauges			Clock			Other		

Comments:

Interior Comments:

Exterior Comments:

Radio Presets
1) 2) 3) 4) 5) 6)

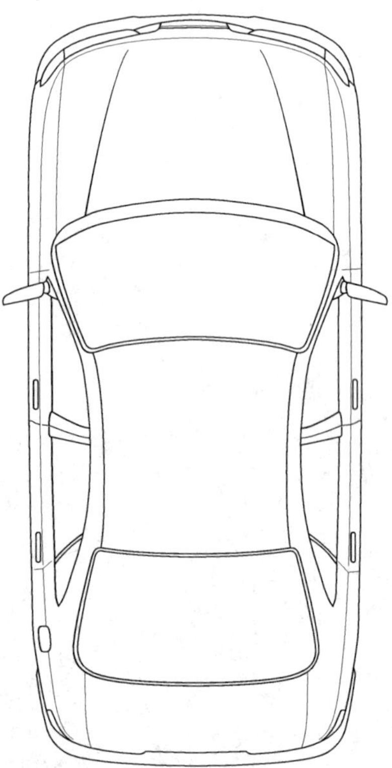

MODEL #	ID#	INSTALLATION DESCRIPTION	V.I.P. $
		TOTAL	

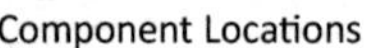

Component Locations

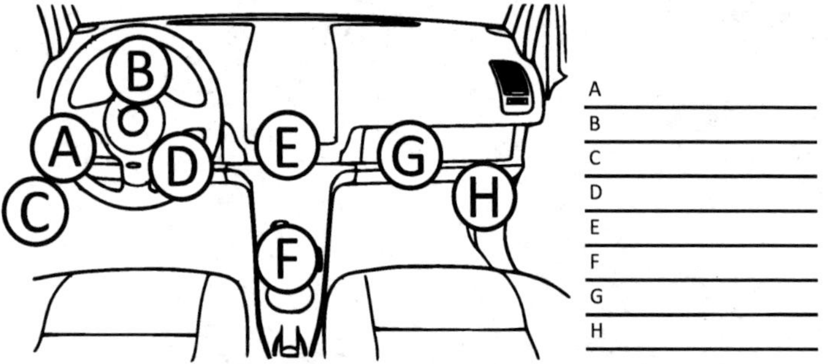

A ______
B ______
C ______
D ______
E ______
F ______
G ______
H ______

Connected Options:		Aux or Output
Power Locks		
Power Trunk Release		
Power Window Control		
Remote Start		
Turbo/Temp/Timer		
Domelight Supervision		
Defogger		
Headlights		
Horn Honk		
Starter Kill		
Other:		

Notes:

I authorize the listed work to be performed. / I have inspected and approve of the listed work performed. All of the features and functions of the installed components have been demonstrated to me. I have inspected the vehicle and it is to my satisfaction, both functionally and cosmetically.

PRE-INSTALL SIGNATURE:	DATE:
POST-INSTALL SIGNATURE:	DATE:

OHM'S LAW

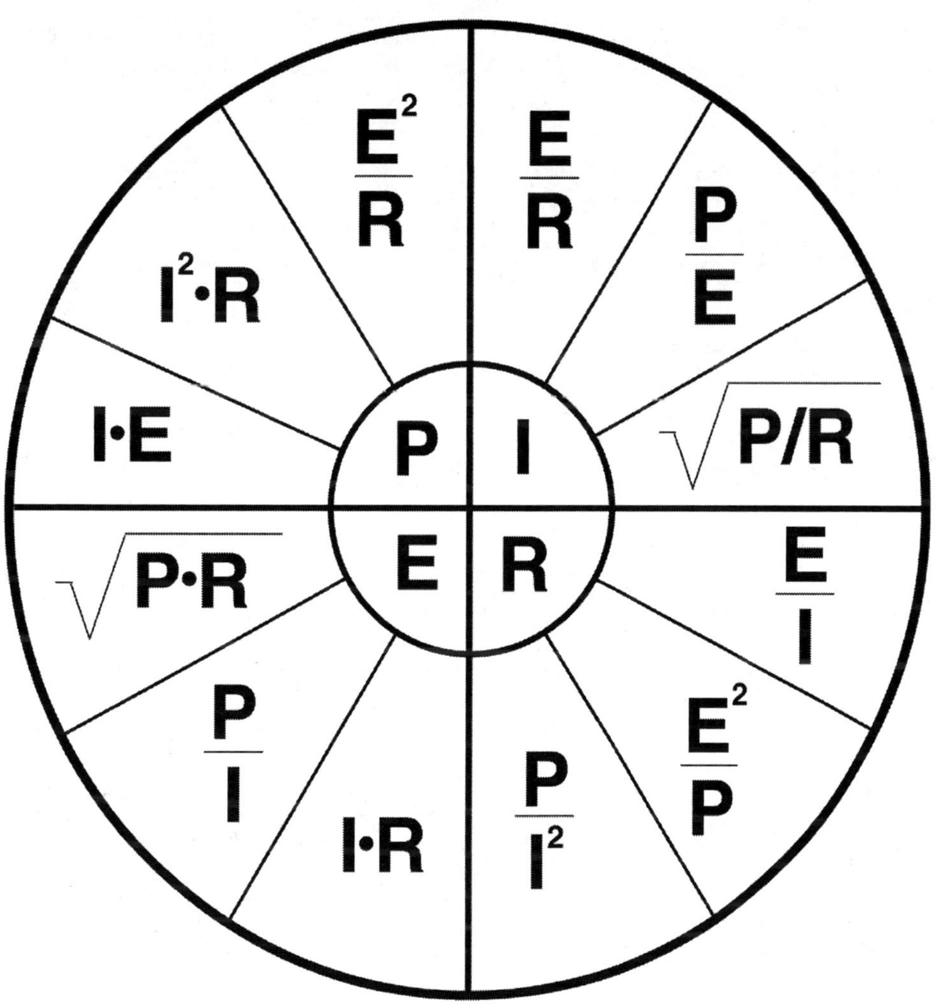

P = Watts **E = Volts**

I = Amps **R = Resistance**

Quick Reference Subwoofer Wiring Configuration Chart

Use this quick reference subwoofer wiring configuration chart when wiring multiple voice coils and/or multiple subwoofers. The number of voice coils to use as a reference could be either multiple single voice coil (SVC) subwoofers, or one or more dual voice coil (DVC) subwoofers.

Series-Parallel

Series-parallel combinations require an even number of voice coils (4 or more). That could be two DVC subwoofers or four SVC subwoofers, or any combination of multiples of voice coils as long it is an even number.

Results in WHITE (Possible Choice)	Results in GRAY (Not Recommended)
These results indicate a compatible wiring configuration only <u>if the amplifier supports it.</u>	These results indicate the wiring configuration in the cell is **<u>NOT</u> recommended.**

2 Voice Coils = 2 SVC or 1 DVC Subwoofer

Voice Coil (Ohms)	Wired in Series (Ohm Load)	Wired in Parallel (Ohm Load)	Series-Parallel (Ohm Load)
1 Ω ea.	**2 Ω**	0.5 Ω	N/A
2 Ω ea.	**4 Ω**	**1 Ω**	N/A
3 Ω ea.	**6 Ω**	**1.5 Ω**	N/A
4 Ω ea.	**8 Ω**	**2 Ω**	N/A
6 Ω ea.	12 Ω	**3 Ω**	N/A
8 Ω ea.	16 Ω	**4 Ω**	N/A
12 Ω ea.	24 Ω	**6 Ω**	N/A

3 Voice Coils = 3 SVC Subwoofers

Voice Coil (Ohms)	Wired in Series (Ohm Load)	Wired in Parallel (Ohm Load)	Series-Parallel (Ohm Load)
1 Ω ea.	**3 Ω**	0.33 Ω	N/A
2 Ω ea.	**6 Ω**	0.66 Ω	N/A
3 Ω ea.	9 Ω	0.99 Ω	N/A
4 Ω ea.	12 Ω	**1.33 Ω**	N/A
6 Ω ea.	18 Ω	**2 Ω**	N/A
8 Ω ea.	24 Ω	**2.66 Ω**	N/A
12 Ω ea.	36 Ω	**4 Ω**	N/A

4 Voice Coils = 4 SVC or 2 DVC Subwoofers

Voice Coil (Ohms)	Wired in Series (Ohm Load)	Wired in Parallel (Ohm Load)	Series-Parallel (Ohm Load)
1 Ω ea.	**4 Ω**	0.25 Ω	**1 Ω**
2 Ω ea.	**8 Ω**	0.5 Ω	**2 Ω**
3 Ω ea.	12 Ω	0.75 Ω	**3 Ω**
4 Ω ea.	16 Ω	**1 Ω**	**4 Ω**
6 Ω ea.	24 Ω	**1.5 Ω**	**6 Ω**
8 Ω ea.	32 Ω	**2 Ω**	**8 Ω**
12 Ω ea.	48 Ω	**3 Ω**	12 Ω

6 Voice Coils = 6 SVC or 3 DVC Subwoofers

Voice Coil (Ohms)	Wired in Series (Ohm Load)	Wired in Parallel (Ohm Load)	Series-Parallel (Ohm Load)
1 Ω ea.	**6 Ω**	0.16 Ω	0.66 Ω
2 Ω ea.	12 Ω	0.33 Ω	**1.33 Ω**
3 Ω ea.	18 Ω	0.5 Ω	**2 Ω**
4 Ω ea.	24 Ω	0.66 Ω	**2.66 Ω**
6 Ω ea.	36 Ω	**1 Ω**	**4 Ω**
8 Ω ea.	48 Ω	**1.33 Ω**	**5.33 Ω**
12 Ω ea.	72 Ω	**2 Ω**	**8 Ω**

Additional Resources

Additional wiring resources for multiple SVC or DVC subwoofers are also available at many manufacturers' websites.

GLOSSARY

GLOSSARY

NUMERIC ENTRIES

3G – Third Generation. A general term that refers to wireless air interface technologies offering increased capacity and capabilities delivered over the original 1G and 2G digital wireless networks. 3G network standards describe minimum peak speeds of at least 200kbits/s, but many of the implementations of 3G air interfaces are much faster than that (in the low 10-20Mbit/s range).

4G – Fourth Generation. A general term that refers to wireless air interface technologies offering increased capacity and capabilities above 3G digital wireless networks. 4G network standards describe peak speeds of 100Mbit/s for high mobility communication (such as moving cars) or 1Gbit/s for stationary users.

802.11 – IEEE 802.11 is a set of standards for implementing wireless local area network (WLAN) device communication in the 2.4, 3.6 and 5 GHz frequency bands. The 802.11 family consists of a series of over-the-air modulation techniques that use the same basic protocol. The protocols a, b, g, n, etc. are often simply generalized as 802.11xx indicating multiple compatibility. Wireless access using the 802.11 protocols is commonly called "WiFi" by consumers and consumer products. (See also "WiFi")

A

A2DP – Advanced Audio Distribution Profile – A Bluetooth profile for streaming 2 channels of 20Hz-20kHz audio from one Bluetooth device to another.

AAC – Advanced Audio Compression. An encoding and variable compression scheme for digital music. AAC is the default compression scheme for iTunes® when "ripping" music to the program or purchased music from the iTunes service.

AC (Alternating Current) – Energy that alternates back and forth at a certain frequency changing polarity as it alternates. The frequency is measured in Hertz (Hz). In automobiles, AC is produced internally in the alternator and then rectified to DC. Audio signals are also AC.

Accessories – Comfort, convenience and safety products not essential to the performance of a vehicle, such as audio, security products, floor mats and seat covers. In the business of automotive, anything not supplied with the basic vehicle in all instances for a given trim level or package is an accessory. Those accessories can be available from the vehicle manufacturer (OEM), from the vehicle dealer or from aftermarket suppliers and retailers. (See also "OEM" and "Automotive Aftermarket")

Accessory Power – Refers to a source of power in the vehicle (controlled by a positive switching, non MUX ignition switch) that has +12VDC on it when the ignition key is in the ACC and RUN positions, but has no power in the START position. (See also "Ignition #1" and "Ignition #2")

Acoustical Energy – Energy consisting of fluctuating waves of pressure called sound waves.

Acoustics – A science dealing with the production, effects, and transmission of sound waves through various mediums. In the case of mobile audio, it's sound through air in the space of the vehicle interior.

Active Arming – A method for arming a security system that requires some action by the operator. This action could include pressing a button on a remote transmitter or entering a code on a keypad. (See also "Passive Arming")

ADAS (Advanced driver-assistance systems) – Systems in a vehicle intended to help the driver in the driving process to increase both car and road safety. Examples include Lane Departure Warning (LDW), Forward Collision Warning (FCW), blind spot monitoring, parking sensors, tire pressure monitoring sensors (TPMS) and much more.

AGM – Absorbed Glass Mat. A type of lead-acid automotive battery where the electrolyte is held in glass mats, as opposed to freely flooding the plates. The plates in an AGM battery may be any shape. Some are flat, others are bent or rolled.

Air Horns – A type of horn that uses compressed air instead of an electric diaphragm or voice coil to produce sound. These horns are usually driven by an electric air pump that receives its trigger from a host security system.

Air Interface – The operating system of a wireless network. Underlying technologies include AMPS, TDMA, CDMA, GSM and iDEN with a host of derivatives built on the basis of those technologies. The air interface type(s) are often one or the other based on the service provider.

Alarm Reset – The property of an alarm system that resets the alarm to an alarmed state after a preset period of time. (See also "Auto Reset")

Alternator – A mechanically driven automotive device that generates AC electricity and is rectified into pulsed DC to power the electrical accessories in the vehicle and charge the starting battery. The alternator is the primary source of vehicle power while the engine is running.

Alternator Whine – A siren-like whining that occurs when engine RPM's increase. The noise is often the result of a voltage differential created by more than one ground path between the audio system components or fatigued charging system components such as the alternator or battery.

Ambience Synthesizer – A unit that produces an artificial ambience pattern; one that is used to create the impression of the listener and/or performer being in a particular performance space. Also known as an "effects processor."

Ammeter – An instrument used for measuring the amount of current flowing in a circuit.

Amperage – A unit of electrical current; the force through which the energy is pushed through a conductor. Measured in Amperes ("Amps" for short); Ohm's Law symbol for Amperes is "I".

Ampere – The unit of measurement used to determine the quantity of electricity flowing through a circuit. One ampere flows through a 1 Ohm resistance when a potential 1 Volt is applied.

Amplification – An increase in signal level, amplitude, or magnitude.

Amplitude – The measure of how much signal is contained in an alternating signal. Amplitude is typically expressed in units of Volts or decibels (dB).

Amplitude Modulation (AM) – A method of modulation in which the amplitude of the carrier voltage is varied in proportion to the changing frequency value of an applied (audio) voltage. (See also "Frequency Modulation")

Analog – An electrical signal in which the frequency and level vary continuously in direct relationship to the original acoustical sound waves. Analog may also refer to a control or circuit which continuously changes the level of a signal in a direct relationship to the control setting.

Antenna – A mechanical device such as a rod or wire that picks up a received signal or radiates a transmitted signal.

Antenna Adaptor – An accessory intended to adapt one type of antenna connector to another type, typically used when adapting a vehicle's proprietary AM/FM antenna connection to work with the Motorola-style connector on an aftermarket head unit.

Arm – The term used to describe the act of causing a security system to reach a state in which it will protect the vehicle.

Arming Delay – A term used to describe the elapsed time between the moment a security system is first told to arm and the moment it is actually armed. This normally applies only to systems that are passively armed, but it can apply to actively armed systems, as well.

Atom – A unit of matter, the smallest unit of an element, having all the characteristics of that element and consisting of a dense, central, positively charged nucleus surrounded by a system of electrons. The entire structure has an approximate diameter of 10-8 centimeter and characteristically remains undivided in chemical reactions except for limited removal, transfer, or exchange of certain electrons. Atoms with 1-3 electrons on the outer "shell" are considered conductors when the electrons break free.

Atomic Nucleus – See "Nucleus"

Attenuate – To lessen the amount of force, magnitude, or value of something.

Audio Frequency Spectrum – The band of frequencies extending roughly from 20 Hz to 20 kHz.

Audio Oscillator – A device that produces tones at specific frequencies for testing either equipment or entire systems.

Audio Signal – An electrical representation of a sound wave in the form of alternating current (AC) or voltage.

Auto Electric – Automotive repair businesses specializing in electrical and lighting products for commercial and passenger vehicles, as well as in the repair/replacement of failing electrical parts. Many retailers selling and installing car audio & security products can also perform these Auto Electric services because of their ability to troubleshoot vehicle electrical systems.

Auto Reset – The ability of a security system to automatically reset itself after being triggered. (See also "Alarm Reset")

Automotive Aftermarket – Replacement or add-on purchases for a vehicle after its original sale, including parts, accessories, lubricants, fuel, appearance products and repairs. The Mobile Electronics Aftermarket (also called "Car Electronics" or "In-Vehicle Electronics") is but one segment of the larger overall Automotive Aftermarket industry.

B

Back-up Battery – A separate battery added to the security system as an alternate power supply to serve as a backup in case the vehicle's main battery is disabled by a thief. Back-up batteries are typically the lead-acid gel cell type and are most effective when hidden from detection.

Balanced (Audio Input or Output) – An audio signal transfer scheme in which the positive and negative signal leads have a mirror image opposite signal between them to increase the noise immunity of unwanted electrical interference. To operate as a true balanced system of signal transfer, both the source and the next component downstream must be capable of configurations in a balanced mode of operation. A single ended head unit (for example) will not transmit a balanced signal to an amplifier featuring balanced inputs. (See also "Single Ended")

Bandpass Filter – A device which incorporates both high-pass and low-pass filters in order to limit and attenuate both ends of the frequency range.

Bandwidth – Refers to the "space" in the frequency response of a device through which audio and/or data signals can pass (between lower and upper frequency limits; in audio applications those points where the signal level has rolled off 3 dB).

Bass – The low audio frequency range, normally considered to be below 125Hz.

Bass Reflex – a vented enclosure that allows control of rear radiated sound waves through a tuned vent opening. The area and length of the opening(s) are critical to optimum low frequency performance.

Battery – A device that stores electrical energy. A battery makes direct current through a collection of individual cells. Most automotive batteries contain six 2.11-Volt cells to create a 12.66-Volt battery. (See also "Cell")

BCM – Body Control Module.

Bias – An unbalanced sound level, often used in the term "side biased" where the left and right channels are not equally perceived by the listener (usually because they sit closer to one side or the other in the car).

Bluetooth – A short-range protocol that allows wireless connections in the 2.4GHz spectrum between compatible devices with a range of 30 feet. While it's often associated with hands-free mobile phone usage, depending on the Bluetooth profiles of two devices, the applications can extend to virtually any kind of data or command exchanges wirelessly.

Bluetooth Profile – The specific operational characteristic intended to provide the scope of how a Bluetooth device behaves. Two Bluetooth devices must support compatible profiles to be able to connect (also called "Pair").

Bojo Tools – A brand name of fiberglass reinforced plastic (FRP) pry tools that are "non-marring" to sensitive vehicle panels and surfaces.

Boomy – Usually refers to excessive bass response, or a peak in the bass response of a recording, playback, or sound reinforcement system.

Bridging – Bridging combines left and right channels of an amplifier into a single, more powerful L+R mono channel by using the full voltage rail of one channel as the "positive" output and the full voltage rail of the other channel as the "negative" output. Bridging is common when using an amplifier for a subwoofer application.

Brain – The common term used to refer to the main control unit of a security system or other types of complex systems. (See also "Control Unit")

Butterworth Filter – A filter used in audio crossovers with -3dB attenuation at the cutoff frequency. The pass-band in a Butterworth filter exhibits flat response and a more linear phase response compared to other filter types, but sacrifices some steepness in attenuation in doing so. (See also "Chebyshev Filter" and "Linkwitz-Riley Filter")

Buying Group – Consortium of businesses that buys in large quantities at discount prices.

C

CAN – Controller Area Network. Also called "CAN-Bus." Originally developed by the Robert Bosch Company to provide a cost-effective communications bus for in-car electronics. There are several CAN Bus derivatives in use for automotive applications, both two and single wire implementations. (See also "HS CAN", "MS CAN", "SW CAN" and "LSFT CAN")

Capacitance – The property exhibited by two conductors separated by a dielectric, where an electric charge becomes stored between the conductors. (Also see Farad.)

Capacitor (Non-Polar) – An electronic device that stores energy and releases it when needed based on the frequency of the signal. Used in passive crossover audio filtering applications. Non-polar capacitors do not have specific terminals for positive and negative connections. Rated in Farads. (See also "Electrolytic Capacitor")

Capacitor (Polarized) – An electronic device that stores energy and releases it when needed. Used in power supply applications. Polarized capacitors have specific terminals for positive and negative connections. Rated in Farads. (See also "Electrolytic Capacitor")

Cell (Energy Storage) – A single unit for producing DC electricity by electrochemical or biochemical action. A common 12.66-Volt vehicle battery is composed of a number of individual cells connected together. Each cell is typically rated at 2.11-Volts; a common automotive battery is composed of six separate two-volt cells.

Cell (Wireless Communications) – The basic geographic unit of wireless coverage. Also, shorthand for generic industry term "cellular." A region is divided into smaller "cells," each equipped with a low-powered radio transmitter/receiver. The radio frequencies assigned to one cell can be limited to the boundaries of that cell. As a wireless call moves from one cell to another, a computer at the Mobile Telephone Switching

Office (MTSO) monitors the call and at the proper time, transfers the phone call to the new cell and new radio frequency. The handoff is performed so quickly that it's not noticeable to the callers.

Cell Site – The location where a wireless antenna and network communications equipment is placed in order to provide wireless service in a geographic area.

Channel (Audio) – The term used to describe a specific output or input in an audio system, usually as simple as "Left Channel" or "Right Channel" in stereo signals. Depending on the device (such as a signal processor or multi-channel source), there may be further designations of center, rear or low frequency channels.

Channel (Security) – The term used to describe the number of different functions possible for manipulating the buttons on a remote control transmitter.

Channel (Wireless Communication) – A frequency or band of frequencies assigned to a station or communications system. Also, a sub-circuit of a larger system (e.g., voice channel, control channel, paging channel).

Chassis – The metal frame of the vehicle.

Chebyshev Filter – A filter that has some ripple in the pass-band but has an initial attenuation slope which is steeper than a Butterworth filter. (See also "Butterworth Filter" and "Linkwitz-Riley Filter")

Chirp – The term used to describe the brief sounding of a security system's siren designed to indicate the state of arm of the system.

Circuit – A closed circular path through which current flows from a voltage source, through various components, and back to the voltage source.

Circuit Breaker – An electromechanical device designed to quickly break the electrical connection should a short circuit or overload occur. A circuit breaker is similar to a fuse, except it will reset itself or can be manually reset, and will again conduct electricity.

Clipping – Distortion that occurs when a power amplifier is overdriven. This can be seen visually on an oscilloscope, when the peaks of a waveform are flattened, or "clipped off," at the signal's ceiling.

Closed Circuit – A continuous unbroken circuit in which current can flow without interruption. Also known as a closed loop.

Closed Loop – A feedback path in a self-regulating control system. Unlike a standard open state trigger that needs to have a connection established to serve as a trigger, a closed loop trigger will act to trigger a security system when its loop (connection) is broken.

Coaxial Speaker – A coaxial speaker has a large cone for the low range and a smaller tweeter for the high spectrum. There is a crossover network that divides and routes the signal to the correct driver. Named for two speakers sharing a single axis.

Compliance – The measurement in liters or cubic feet of the volume of air that is equal to the compliance of a speaker's total suspension.

Cone – The most common shape for the radiating surface of a loudspeaker. Also called a "diaphragm', it is the part of the speaker that moves air. (See also "Diaphragm")

Constant Output – An output of a security system that provides a constant or continuous output to drive a device. Often used for sirens and engine interrupts.

Control Unit – The central processor for a security system or other vehicle functions. (See also "Brain" or "ECU")

Coulomb – (pronounced koo-loam) – An amount of electrical charge which contains 6.24 x 1018 (6,240,000,000,000,000,000) electrons. One coulomb per second past a given point is equal to 1 ampere of current flowing.

Crossover – A device that separates the different frequency bands and redirects them to different components. A crossover can be active (electronic) or passive (inductors, capacitors, and resistors)

Crossover Frequencies – The frequencies at which a passive or active (electronic) crossover network divides the audio signals, which are then routed to the appropriate speakers.

Crossover Network – A unit that divides the audio spectrum into two or more frequency bands.

Current – The rate of electrical or electron flow through a conductor between objects of opposite charge. Symbol is "I" or "A", measured in Amperes or "Amps".

Current Sensing – A name given to a form of alarm system trigger that relies on sensing a change in the power supply of the vehicle. More accurately called voltage sensing, this feature is found only on inexpensive alarms, if at all anymore.

D

Damping (not DampENing) – The reduction of the magnitude of resonance by the use of some type of material, typically achieved by adding mass to an object. The damping material converts the energy of unwanted resonant vibrations into heat.

dB/SPL – Indicates the relative intensity of sound. The implied reference level is the threshold of human hearing, commonly called the "auditory threshold" referenced to 1kHz @ 0dB/SPL.

dBV – Decibel Volts is a method of expressing a ratio of voltage "amplification" or "attenuation" in the circuit or device.

dBmW – Decibel milliwatts is a method of expressing a ratio of RF signal power "gain" or "loss" in the circuit or device.

DC – Direct Current. A flow of electrons that travels only in one direction.

Decibel (dB) – Named for Alexander Graham Bell, a decibel is a tenth of a bel, and is used as an expression of power. A decibel isn't really a measure of anything, rather it is a ratio of two power levels – a reference (either specified or implied) and then something measured.

Dedicated Fuse – A fuse designated to supply power and protection for one particular circuit only.

Delay (Audio Signal Processing) – The practice of delaying one or more audio channels to create the illusion the speakers are further away from the listener, thereby making the true furthest distance speaker more evenly matched with others in delivery of sound to the listener's ear. Delay is intended to only to provide one seat in the vehicle for optimized listening. (See also "Channel Delay", "Digital Delay", and "Signal Delay")

Destructive Interference – A phenomenon that occurs when speakers are 180 degrees out of phase. For example, what one speaker is trying to produce, the other speaker is fighting to cancel. One speaker's wave is in the positive phase (pressure), while the other speaker's wave is in the negative phase (rarefaction).

Diaphragm – A thin metal or dielectric disc used as the vibrating member in high frequency loudspeakers; also known as the "cone" in traditional loudspeakers.

Digital Delay – An audio signal delay for one or more channels completed in the digital domain of a head unit, signal processor or amplifier. (See also "Channel Delay", "Delay", and "Signal Delay")

Difference of Potential – The total numeric value measured between two points of different electrical potential. Difference of potential is commonly called "Voltage".

DIFM – "Do-It-For-Me" refers to consumers who use professionals to perform maintenance and repair work on their vehicles, including installation of their mobile electronic products (audio, security, convenience, safety, etc.).

Diode – A two-electrode (two-terminal) semiconductor device that allows a voltage to pass through it in one direction only. The direction of the diode terminals based on the polarity of the electrical circuit is how it determines passing or blocking.

DIN – Deutsche Industrie Normen. DIN refers to industrial standards that are used in the manufacture of many goods used in Europe, especially German made OEM automotive parts. In mobile audio, DIN refers to a standard head unit dimension of approximately 7" wide x 2" high.

Disarm – The opposite of arm, or the term used to describe the action of placing a security system in an inactive or standby mode.

Distortion – Sound that is modified or changed in some way. In a speaker, distortion is produced by several factors, many of which are related to poor construction. Voice coil rubbing (caused by being overdriven) is the most common cause of distortion.

DIY – "Do-It-Yourself" refers to consumers who perform maintenance and repair work on their own vehicles, including installing their own mobile electronic equipment.

DMM – Digital Multimeter. A digital meter that gives a precise reading of voltage, current, or ohms. This type of meter "samples" the input and feeds it to a digital readout and provides the technician with a numeric result by which they can make easy decisions about whether the circuit or device is operating as intended.

Dome Light – The common term used to describe the overhead (or headliner) mounted interior courtesy light. This circuit is often a connection point for vehicle security systems to monitor any entry into the passenger compartment.

Door Lock Solenoid – The proper name for the electric bi-directional actuator used to provide powered control of vehicle door locks. Also called a Door Lock Actuator.

Doppler Sensor – Another name for a spatial type sensor typically used in vehicle security systems or ADAS products, also commonly called a radar sensor.

DPDT – Double Pole Double Throw. A term used to describe a switch or relay that has two separate poles or contacts and can throw or make electrical contact with two separate stationary contacts simultaneously.

Driver – Another term for a loudspeaker. This term is often used when the loudspeaker is coupled with a horn for increased output and controlled dispersion of sound.

DSP – Digital Signal Processing (or Processor). A type of processing accomplished by a micro-computer chip specifically designed for signal manipulation, or a component using such processing. The term is often misused as a synonym for ambience synthesizer; however, DSP can do much more than sound field creation. Very often DSP-based audio devices utilize setup routines and controls that require a computer or smartphone app connecting to the device to set the operating parameters.

DTC – Diagnostic Trouble Code. A five character code generated by the on board diagnostics (OBD-II) system in 1996 and later vehicles indicating the nature of a malfunction or problem condition.

Duty Cycle – An engineering term used to describe the actual time (or frequency) that a circuit or device operates. A pulsing alarm output that is on for seven-tenths of a second and off for three-tenths of a second would have a 70% duty cycle.

DVC – Dual Voice Coil. A speaker with two voice coils. Many subwoofers have dual voice coils to increase the power handling and flexibility to load the amplifier for increased power output. (See also "Voice Coil" and "SVC")

Dynamic Range – The range difference between the quietest and the loudest passages of the musical selection or program signal being played.

E

Earth – European terminology often given to the electrical ground or chassis ground potential. (See also "Ground")

ECM – Electronic Control Module.

ECU – Electronic Control Unit.

Efficiency – The measurement of a loudspeaker or amplifier's ability to convert input power to output power (work). Formula: Efficiency = (power out/power in) x 100. Efficiency is always expressed as a percentage.

Electrolyte – The name for the mixture of diluted sulfuric acid found in standard lead-acid vehicle storage batteries.

Electrolytic Capacitor – A capacitor with a negative and a positive terminal that passes only alternating current. Electrolytics are available in polarized and non-polarized configurations. Non-polarized (NP) capacitors are useful as inexpensive crossovers, blocking low frequencies from passing through to mid- or high-frequency speakers. Polarized capacitors have specific positive and negative poles. Polarized capacitors are used for storing and releasing energy.

Electron – An electron is a negatively charged component of an atom. Electrons exist outside of and surrounding the atom nucleus. Each electron carries one unit of negative charge and has a very small mass as compared with that of a neutron or proton.

Emergency Override – A button or switch installed in the vehicle is used specifically to override or disarm a security system in the event that the primary means is unavailable or disabled.

EMR Detector – A tool used to find the source of low-frequency electromagnetic interference known as electromagnetic radiation, or EMR.

Engine Disable – A means, either electrical or mechanical, of preventing the vehicle's engine from either starting or running. The most common variety of engine disable uses a simple automotive relay to inhibit either the starter or the ignition.

Entry Delay – The time interval a security system waits before sounding the alarm after a vehicle's door has been opened.

Equal Loudness Contours – See "Fletcher-Munson Curves."

Exit Delay – The name given to the amount of time a security system waits once it's given a command to arm. Exit delays are usually found on non-remote security systems that rely on keypads or the ignition switch to arm. This delay gives the operator time to exit the vehicle before the system arms.

F

Farad (F) – The basic unit of capacitance. A capacitor has a capacitance of 1 Farad when a charge of 1 volt across the capacitor produces a current of 1 ampere through it. Named after Michael Faraday. There one million microfarads in 1 Farad.

FCC – Federal Communications Commission. The U.S. government agency that oversees and regulates electronic communications.

Fidelity – A term used to describe the accuracy of recording, reproduction, or general quality of audio processing.

Flashing Lights – A term used to describe interfacing the vehicle's parking lights, dome light, emergency lights, etc., with a security system so that the lights flash by the command of the security system.

Flat Response – An output signal in which fundamental frequencies and harmonics are in the same proportion as those of the input signal being amplified. A flat frequency response would exhibit relatively equal response to all fixed-point frequencies within a given spectrum.

Fletcher-Munson Curves – A set of curves that depict the uneven frequency response of human hearing that are extremely dependent upon relative loudness. The curves show the human ear to be most sensitive to sounds in the 2 kHz to 4 kHz area. This means sounds above and below 2-4 kHz must be louder in order to be heard just as loud. For this reason, the Fletcher-Munson curves are referred to as "equal loudness contours."

FM – See "Frequency Modulation."

Free Air Resonance – The frequency at which a speaker will naturally resonate.

Frequency – The term in physics that refers to a number of vibrations or cycles that occur within a given time.

Frequency Counter – A device that assists in speaker parameter testing, as well as identifying the frequency of specific tones or electrical signals.

Frequency Modulation (FM) – A method of modulation in which the frequency of the carrier voltage is varied with frequency of the modulating voltage (See also "Amplitude Modulation")

Frequency Response – A term that describes the relationship between a component's input and output with regard to signal frequency and amplitude.

Fundamental Frequency – The original frequency component of a harmonic series.

Fuse – A device designed to provide protection for a given circuit or device by physically opening the circuit. Fuses are rated by their amperage and are designed to blow or open when the current being drawn through it exceeds its design rating.

Fusible Link – Designed to perform the same task as a fuse, but resembles a wire. Fusible links are commonly used in ignition switches and other high-current circuits.

G

Gain – The degree of signal amplification, typically expressed in voltage or dB units.

Gain Control – The input sensitivity (level matching) control on an amplifier that allows the input section to be matched to the incoming signal voltage. The gain control is not a volume control.

GEM – Generic Electronic (Control) Module.

Generator – A rotating machine that produces DC electricity. Also an electronic device used for converting DC voltage into AC of a given frequency and wave shape.

Glass Sensor – A device designed to detect the sound of breaking glass or metal to- glass contact, thus triggering a security system. Also called sound sensors, glass-breaking sensors, or sound discriminators.

GLONASS – GLObal Navigation Satellite System (GLONASS). A network of 24 satellites developed and maintained by the Russian Federal Space Agency. These satellites relay similar information to receivers in a similar method to GPS. Some location-based consumer electronics devices can receive both GPS and GLONASS satellite signals. (See also "GPS")

GPRS – General Packet Radio Service. A packet technology approach that enables high-speed wireless Internet and other GSM-based data communications. It makes very efficient use of available radio spectrum for transmission of data.

GPS – Global Positioning System. A system of 24 satellites maintained by the US government orbiting the earth that each broadcast unique position data to compatible GPS receivers. Data from at least three satellites must be received to triangulate the exact longitude and latitude (X-Y) location of the GPS device. A fourth GPS satellite is necessary to accurately determine elevation/altitude (Z). (See also "GLONASS")

Ground – The term given to anything that has an electrical potential of zero. Most modern vehicles are designed around a negative ground system, with the metal frame being the vehicle's ground (electrically also called "chassis" or "chassis ground").

Ground Loop – The condition that occurs when a voltage potential exists between two separate ground points and they are not electrically equal.

GSM – Global System for Mobile Communication. The United States offers GSM in the 1800 MHz bandwidth. Many network providers use GSM. See also "CDMA" (the competing wireless communication phone protocol to GSM).

Gross Vehicle Weight (GVW) – The total weight of the loaded vehicle, including chassis, body and payload. Also known as Gross Vehicle Weight Rating (GVWR).

GVIF – Gigabit Video Interface. A type of digital video signal, originally developed by Sony that is used between devices such as navigation systems and an in-dash video screen.

H

Harmonic – The overtones and undertones that define the acoustic difference between two sounds with the same fundamental frequency.

Harness – The universal name for a bundle or loom of wires that compose the wiring for a system. (See also "Wiring Harness")

Headroom – The difference between the highest level present in an audio signal and the maximum level an audio device can handle without noticeable distortion. A greater amount of headroom reduces the chances for unwanted distortion in an audio system.

Hertz (Hz) – The unit of frequency within a specific period, such as alternating or pulsating current; 1 Hz = 1 cycle per second.

High Frequency – Refers to radio frequencies in the 3-30 MHz band. In audio it usually refers to frequencies in the 5-10 kHz band.

High-Pass Filter – A network of components which attenuate all frequencies below a predetermined frequency selected by the designer. Frequencies above cut-off are passed without any effect.

Horn (Audio) – Refers to a loading device when part of a bass enclosure, or a directional device when used with a high-frequency driver or compression driver.

Horn (Security) – Refers to the built-in factory horn in the vehicle. Factory horns can be of the diaphragm type, voice coil type, or air-pump driven type (air horn). All types of horns can be interfaced to a security system.

Horsepower – A unit that is used to measure the power of engines and motors. One unit of horsepower is equal to the power needed to lift 550 pounds one foot in one second. This unit has been widely replaced by the watt in scientific usage; one horsepower is equal to 746 watts.

HPSA+ – Evolved High-Speed Packet Access. A CDMA based air interface in late 3G / early 4G applications. HPSA+ also uses MIMO multi-antenna transmission technology.

HRTF – Head Related Transfer Function describes how sound from a specific location arrives at each ear and how that effect places the perception of the sound source spatially in three dimensions, including above, below, to the side of and behind the listener.

HS CAN – An acronym for High Speed CAN Bus.

HVLP – High Volume Low Pressure. Environmentally friendly pneumatic spray equipment that transfers a high degree of material with minimal air pressure

I

iDEN – Integrated Digital Enhanced Network. A specialized mobile technology that combines two-way radio, telephone, text messaging and data transmission into one digital network. Introduced by Motorola and used by AirTel Montana, Nextel Communications, Nextel Partners, and Southern LINC Wireless, among others.

Ignition Kill – A device designed to prevent the vehicle's ignition circuit from operating. An ignition kill device can work by either interrupting one or both of the primary wires leading to the ignition coil or by shorting out (grounding) the ignition coil's positive primary wire. Also called "Ignition Disable".

Ignition #1 Power – Refers to a source of power in the vehicle (controlled by a positive switching, non MUX ignition switch) that has +12VDC on it when the ignition key is in the RUN position and START positions, but has no power in the ACC position.

Ignition #2 Power – Refers to a source of power in the vehicle (controlled by a positive switching, non MUX ignition switch) that has +12VDC on it when the ignition key is in the RUN position, but has no power in the ACC or START positions.

> **Note:** *Do not confuse the Ignition #2 electrical function of the ignition switch with terminology many remote starter instructions use to describe their second, sometimes third primary ignition switch connections. In most cases, from a remote starter standpoint – the Ignition #2 and ACC wiring from the vehicle both get connected to the remote starter's "Accessory" outputs because they don't need to stay powered while the vehicle starts (whereas Ignition #1 circuits do) and that's often the only differentiation the remote starter makes with the way it's output wiring is labeled.*

ILD – Interaural Level Difference. The differences of levels in a sound between two ears caused by 'shadowing' of the head that help humans localize the source of the sound. At 1600Hz and up, most localization of sound is ILD related. (See also "ITD")

Imaging – The width and definition of a sound stage. Instruments should appear to be coming from their correct positions, relative to recording.

Impact Sensor – A sensor designated to detect various degrees of impact or vibration applied to the vehicle and then produce an output to trigger a security system.

Impedance (Audio) – A measurement of the resistance to the audio current by the voice coil of the speaker. (See also "Nominal Impedance")

Impedance (Electrical) – The dynamic resistive opposition offered by a device or circuit to the flow of alternating current (AC).

Inductive Coupling – Radiated noise that is transmitted through a magnetic field to surrounding lines.

Inductor – An electrical component in which impedance increases as the frequency of the AC increases; also known as "coils" that are used in passive crossovers. Inductors are rated in Henries.

Infinite Baffle – A loudspeaker baffle of (theoretically) infinite space that has no openings for the passage of sound from the front to the back of the speaker.

Infrared Sensor – A type of spatial sensor that uses infrared energy to detect an object (a hand, arm, or body) entering a protected area. (See also "Spatial Sensors")

Infrasonic – Refers to sounds or signals whose frequencies are below the normal human hearing range, generally considered to be 20 Hertz.

Input (Audio) – Speaker-level or preamp-level (RCA) signal connections that run into one audio component from another audio component's output. Speaker-level inputs are commonly called "High Level" and preamp-level inputs are commonly called "Low Level."

Input (Security) – Any wire on a security system or remote starter designed to accept a signal from some outside source such as the vehicle's wiring. Door trigger, hood trigger, trunk trigger, foot brake trigger and sensor trigger wires are all inputs.

Instant Trigger – The term used to describe any trigger input on a security system that is designated to cause the system to respond instantly when triggered.

Integrity – The expected durability or sturdiness of an installed component or connection.

Inventory Turns/Turnover – The number of times inventory is replenished within a particular time, calculated by dividing the cost of goods sold by the average inventory for the period.
ITD – Interaural Time Difference. The differences of arrival time of a sound between two ears that help humans localize the source of the sound. At 800Hz and below, most localization of sound is ITD related. (See also "ILD")

J

Joule – A unit of electrical energy equal to the work done when a current of one ampere passes through a resistance of one ohm for one second. Named after James P. Joule.

Jump – To provide a temporary circuit around a component or other circuit.

K

Keysense Wire – The wire or circuit in the vehicle providing an electrical output to signify the key is placed in the ignition cylinder or, in push-to-start vehicles, the key fob transponder is in close enough proximity to allow the vehicle to start.

Kirchhoff's Current Law (KCL) – A law stating that the total current entering a point or junction in a circuit must equal the sum of the current leaving that point or junction.

Kirchhoff's Voltage Law (KVL) – A law stating that the voltage supplied to a DC circuit must equal the sum of the voltage drops within the circuit.

kHz – Abbreviation for kilohertz, or 1000 cycles per second.

L

Last Door Arming – A feature found on some security systems that enables the system to suspend itself from arming until the last door of the vehicle has been secured.

LCD – Liquid Crystal Display.

LED – Light Emitting Diode. A form of diode that sheds light when connected in a forward biased condition. LED lighting is used in many applications for status indicator purposes as well as an alternative to incandescent lighting. LED technology is also used in video display screens.

Lexan® – A brand name of acrylic plastic. Commonly used in optically clear and translucent colors for custom installation applications.

Linkwitz-Riley Filter – A filter used in audio crossovers that has a steeper -6dB attenuation at the cutoff frequency than 'normal' -3dB Butterworth filter characteristics. Also called a "Butterworth Squared" filter or "L-R Filter". (See also "Butterworth Filter" and "Chebyshev Filter")

Load – any electrical component that is connected to a circuit that consumes electricity. Typical loads in automotive electrical systems include light bulbs, electrical motors, amplifiers, electronic fuel pumps, control modules, etc.

Loudspeaker – An electro-acoustic transducer that converts electrical audio signals at its input to audible sound waves at its output.

Low Frequency – Refers to radio frequencies within the 30 -300 kHz band. In audio it usually refers to frequencies in the 40-160 Hz band.

Low-Pass Filter – A network of components which attenuate all frequencies above a predetermined frequency selected by the designer. Frequencies below cut-off are passed without any effect.

LSFT CAN – An acronym for Low Speed, Fault Tolerant CAN Bus.

LTE – Long Term Evolution. An air interface standard of high speed wireless data transmission used 4G wireless data communications. LTE is based on the GSM/EDGE and UTMS/HPSA network technologies, although LTE is incompatible with 2G and 3G air interface networks so it must be operated in a separate wireless spectrum.

LVDS – Low Voltage Differential Signaling. A type of digital video interface format used in some automotive applications in which a digital video signal is transferred from one or more devices to a screen in the dash over twisted pairs of copper cables. Commonly used for navigation or rear view cameras in modern OE automotive applications.

M

Magnet – A device that can attract or repel pieces of iron or other magnetic material. Speaker magnets provide a stationary magnetic field so that when the coil produces magnetic energy, it is either repelled or attracted by the stationary magnet.

Matrix Processing – A signal processing scheme in which standard 2-channel audio is processed with proprietary methods to derive a multi-channel output to achieve the effect of surround sound. Dolby Pro Logic (II, IIx, IIz etc.), DTS (Neo:6 and Neural), Harman (Logic7 and QLS) and Bose Centerpoint are examples of branded and proprietary matrix processing schemes. (See also "Upmixer")

MDF – Medium Density Fiberboard. MDF is an engineered wood product made from mechanically refined wood fibers combined with resin, which are bonded together under heat and pressure. Subwoofer enclosures are often constructed from MDF.

MEKP – Methyl Ethel Ketone Peroxide. The chemical used to accelerate curing of Polyester Resin.

Memory – The word most commonly used to refer to a system's ability to retain specific information.

MHz – Abbreviation for Megahertz, or 1,000,000 (1 million) cycles per second. Wireless mobile communications within North America generally occur in the 800 MHz, 900MHz and 1900MHz spectrum frequency bands.

Microprocessor – A semiconductor that can be programmed to perform a variety of tasks in many different electronic applications.

Midrange Driver – A loudspeaker specifically designed to reproduce the frequency in the middle of the audible bandwidth. Most musical energy lies in the midrange band.

MIL – Malfunction Indicator Light. A dash mounted indicator of a re-occurring DTC in a vehicle with OBD-II. Also called the "Check Engine" light. (See also "DTC" and "OBD-II")

Milliamps (mA) – A unit of measurement of electrical current equal to 1/1000th of an ampere (0.001 amperes). The milliampere is the most common unit used when measuring quiescent (or "standby") current drain.

MIMO – Multiple Input, Multiple Output. The use of multiple antennas at both the transmitter and receiver to improve communication performance. It is one of several forms of smart antenna technology. Note that the terms input and output refer to the radio channel carrying the signal, not to the consumer devices having antennas.

MIN/MAX – A feature of a DMM in which the highest (MAX) or lowest (MIN) recorded value over the measurement period is displayed.

Module – A term commonly used to describe a self-contained part or device that can perform a specific function.

Monitor (Security System) – A security system input that awaits a trigger or command from a sensor or vehicle electrical circuit.

Monitor (Video) – The video display device(s) used to view the video output generated by the video source. Typically an LCD screen in a mobile application.

Motion Sensors – A sensor specifically designed to detect a gentle or sharp up and down or side-to-side motion of the vehicle. This is sometimes called a tilt sensor in reference to a thief jacking the vehicle up to remove wheels.

MOSFET – Metal Oxide Semiconductor Field Effect Transistor.

M.O.S.T. (MOST) – Media Oriented Systems Transport. A data transfer infotainment system, either over optical or copper connections (depending on the generation), engineered for the automotive applications since 2002. Generations include MOST 25, MOST 50 and MOST 150.

MP3 (MPEG 1, Audio Layer 3) – A popular encoding and variable compression scheme for digital music. Must have a device with MP3 decoding for playback.

MPEG – Moving Picture Experts Group.

MS CAN – An acronym for Medium Speed CAN Bus.

MSDS – Material Safety Data Sheet. The technical and safety information for any specific chemical(s) that OSHA requires a business to have on file in an accessible location.

Multimeter – A common term used to describe a Volt-Ohm-Meter, or VOM. A Multimeter usually can measure volts, ohms, and amperes or milliamperes. A Digital Multimeter is often called simply "DMM", sometimes also called a DVOM. (See also "DMM")

Multiplex – see "MUX"

Multi-Source – An audio/video system featuring multiple source units (see Source Unit).

Multi-Zone – An audio/video system with multiple locations to listen and view the A/V entertainment.

MUX – A low current, multi function circuit found on many newer vehicles used in a variety of functions previously supported by dedicated wires for each discrete function. MUX circuits use variable voltages or data messages on a single wire (or pair of wires) between a controller and a receiving device (such as a BCM) to command multiple functions depending on the position of the controller and the other conditions. The goal is weight and cost savings for vehicle manufacturing. These systems are often low voltage (less than battery voltage) depending on the function tested. Also called "Multiplex" or "Variable Voltage" circuits.

N

Navigation System – See "PND" and "Route Guidance System"

Negative Door Switches – A door switch circuit that provides the negative polarity trigger for the factory interior lights, key buzzer, factory alarm, BCM, etc.

Negative Lead – The lead or line connected to the negative terminal of a current, voltage, or power source.

Neutrons – Neutrons are part of the nucleus of all atoms (except hydrogen) and are electrically neutral in their charge. Neutrons have about equal mass to a proton, which is the positively charged part of the nucleus.

NHTSA – National Highway Traffic Safety Administration. The agency that develops and administers educational, engineering, and enforcement programs for safe vehicle use and cost-effective highway travel.

Noise Floor – The noise power generated by an audio device in the absence of any input signal. It is generally measure in decibels.

Nominal Impedance – The minimum impedance a loudspeaker presents to an amplifier, directly related to the power the speaker applied to the speaker. Actual impedance varies with the frequency applied.

Normally Closed – Refers to the electrical state in which a switch may rest. Its contacts are held together or closed so that current is allowed to flow through its contacts.

Normally Open – Refers to the electrical state in which a switch may rest. Its contacts are held apart or open so that no current flows through its contacts.

NTSB – National Transportation Safety Board. An independent agency charged with determining the probable cause of transportation accidents and promoting transportation safety.

NTSC – National Television System Committee. The analog color television broadcast standard used in North America and Japan, though also a video transfer standard between compatible devices through the composite video (yellow RCA) connection on video devices.

Nucleus – The positively charged center of an atom, made of protons and neutrons, around which electrons orbit.

O

OBD – On Board Diagnostics System.

OBD-II – Second Generation OBD Systems, present on all vehicles sold in the US since 1996.

Octave – A measured musical interval between two tones when the ratio between the frequencies of the tone is 2:1 (double or half of the other). "Oct" is a prefix meaning "eight". In music, there are 8 steps, tones or "notes" within an octave. For notes spaced an octave apart, human ear hears them as being essentially the same. That's why, in music, notes spaced an octave apart have the same name; "A", "B", "C", etc.

Ohm – The unit of measurement for electrical resistance. Named after Georg Simon Ohm.

Ohm's Law – The statement of the relationship between current, voltage, and resistance. Where I = Current, E = Voltage, and R = Resistance, I=E/R, E=I*R, and R=E/I.

OE – Original Equipment. Parts and components supplied to manufacturers for motor vehicle production.

OEM – Original Equipment Manufacturer. A company that supplies parts and components for the production of motor vehicles (such as Ford, GM, BMW, Toyota, Mercedes-Benz, Hyundai, Honda, etc.).

Open Circuit – A circuit containing a switch, filament, voice coil, etc., which is not intact and current cannot flow through.

Optical Input – A digital input that receives pulses of light transmitted through an optically conductive cable from a compatible Optical Output.

Optical Output – A digital output that transmits pulses of light through an optically conductive cable to a compatible Optical Input.

Oscillator – A device that produces an alternating current or pulsating current or voltage electronically.

Oscilloscope – A measurement tool that can display a signal waveform while simultaneously measuring the frequency and voltage of the signal. Among other uses, this tool is very useful in setting up the gain position on amplifiers to avoid prematurely clipping the waveform coming out of the amplifier.

OSHA – Occupational Safety and Health Administration. The U.S. government agency that regulates workplace safety and health.

Output (Audio) – Speaker-level or preamp-level (RCA) signal connections sent from one audio system component's output to another component's input or the audio signal from an amplifier to the system speakers. Speaker-level outputs are commonly called "High Level" and preamp-level outputs are commonly called "Low Level."

Output (Security) – Any wire on a security system designed to produce a signal intended to be wired to some outside circuit or device. Siren wires, flashing light wires, and door locks are all outputs.

Override Switch – A switch that provides a secondary means to disarm or override a security system in the event the primary means is unavailable. This switch is also often used for valet or other security programming functions. (See also "Emergency Override")

P

Pain Generator(s) – A name given to a type of siren that is specifically designed to produce a sound of the proper volume and pitch so as to cause physical pain to a thief's ears.

Pair (or Pairing) – The term used to describe wirelessly connecting two or more compatible Bluetooth devices to one another. Where numeric keypads are present on one (or both) devices, often a code is required for first time pairing. Once paired, the devices can operate with one another using their established Bluetooth profile(s). See also "Bluetooth Profiles".

PAL – Phase Alteration Line is the analog color television broadcast standard used in many Western European countries (except France), the Middle East, and parts of Africa and South America.

Panic – The name given to the feature of a security system that provides the ability to the operator to cause the system's siren to sound at will. The panic feature is typically initiated either by pressing a button or buttons on the remote control transmitter by keypad command, by push button, or by toggle switch.

Parallel Wiring – A circuit in which two or more devices are connected to the same source of voltage, sharing a common positive and negative point, so that each device receives the full applied voltage.

Parasitic Current Draw– A term that describes the amount of current consumed by a circuit when it is not performing any work or otherwise "at rest". Also referred to as "standby" current draw or "quiescent current."

Passive Arming – The ability of some security systems to arm without requiring any direct action from the operator of the vehicle. Passive arming is usually accomplished when the operator exits the vehicle in the normal fashion. (See also "Last Door Arming")

Passive Crossover – An electrical circuit consisting of capacitors, inductors, and resistors designed to separate an audio signal into specific frequency ranges.

Passive Repeater Antenna – A non-permanently installed, glass-mount antenna that is without physical connection to the cellular telephone, but is intended to enhance the reception of signal within the confines of the vehicle.

PCM (OEM Vehicle Electronics) – Powertrain Control Module.

PCM (Digital Audio) – Pulse Code Modulation.

Peak – An emphasis over a frequency range not greater than one octave.

Perceptual Coding – A technique used in recording to minimize the size of digital files with little or no audible degradation upon playback. Most all compressed audio files (AAC, WMA®, MP3, etc.) use some algorithm of perceptual coding to achieve smaller file sizes.

Period – The amount of time required for a single cycle of a sound wave.

Phase – The timing of a sound wave that is measured in degrees from 0 to 360.

Phase Shift (Audio Filtering) – Frequency interaction in the crossover region of passive or active crossovers, or in the center frequencies of other overlapping audio filters, that can cause some frequencies to be delayed with respect to frequencies not in the signal path of the filter(s).

Plexiglas® – A brand name of acrylic plastic. Commonly used in optically clear and translucent colors for custom installation applications.

Piezo – The name usually given to piezo electric drivers. This type of driver has no voice coil or magnetic assembly. Instead, piezo electric material expands and contracts when voltage is applied. The material vibrates and either radiates sound directly or drives a diaphragm. They can be used effectively only on high frequencies.

Piezo Sensors – A type of shock or impact sensor that utilizes the properties of the piezo electric effect inherent in some materials. A piezo sensor typically uses a piezo electric element to sense impacts or vibrations applied to a vehicle.

Pin Switch – A simple, spring-loaded mechanical switch, used in many different vehicles, that's designed to turn on interior lights when doors are opened. Pin switches are also used in the installation of most security systems in the hood or trunk/hatch as a means of triggering the system if such points are opened.

Pink Noise – Random noise with equal energy per octave covering 20Hz-20kHz used as a test signal. Human ears perceive this as sounding relatively "flat" in frequency response (since pink noise is based on octaves rather than individual frequencies, there is no increase in energy in the high octaves). Because of this, and because Real Time Analyzers (RTA) tend to look at octave or 1/3 octave ranges, pink noise is very useful for measuring the frequency response of audio equipment, as well as for determining in-vehicle response for car audio system design and tuning applications.

PND – An acronym for Personal Navigation Device, which is a hand held route guidance systems using GPS receivers and integrated maps, often with touch screen control. These are mistakenly sometimes simply called a "GPS", which is a misnomer because GPS is only the positioning data from the satellites, but not the mapping or navigational directions.

Pneumatic – Operated or powered by compressed air. Pneumatic tools are also called "air tools."

POF – Plastic Optical Fiber.

POI – Point of Interest. A term used to describe locations of business, landmarks, or emergency services stored in the digital map of a Route Guidance System.

Point of Entry – The term used to describe the doors, hood, trunk/hatch, windows, sunroof, or any other point through which a thief can gain entry into a vehicle.

Polarity – In electricity, refers to the condition of being either positive or negative.

Polarity Reversal (Circuit Operation) – A Single DPDT switch (or two SPDT switches) connected between a pair of DC input terminals so that the polarity of a pair of output terminals can be reversed or switched.

Positive Door Switches – A door switch circuit that provides the positive polarity trigger for the factory interior lights, key buzzer, factory alarm, BCM, etc.

Positive Lead – The lead or line connected to the positive terminal of a current, voltage, or power source.

Potential – The electrical charge that allows work to be done in a circuit. Potential is commonly called Voltage. A circuit must have an electrical potential for electrons to flow.

Potentiometer – A variable resistor made with either carbon or wire wound material that attenuates (adds resistance) to a signal.

Power – The amount of energy (in joules) that a device delivers or consumes divided by the time (in seconds) that the device is operating.

Power Door Locks – The feature where door locking and unlocking is performed by some mechanical means other than human power. Power door locks may be electric, vacuum, or a combination of the two.

Power Line Noise – A varying AC ripple that is found riding on a DC voltage. It is recognized by a whining that varies with engine speed.

Power Windows – The feature where the opening and closing of the vehicle's windows is performed by some mechanical means other than human power. Power windows are typically operated by electric motors.

Power Supply Capacitor – A polarized, large value capacitor specifically intended to stabilize supply voltage during periods of peak current demand. Also called a "Stiffening Capacitor."

Preamp – A circuit unit that takes a small signal and amplifies it sufficiently to be fed into the power amplifier for further amplification. A pre-amp includes all of the controls for regulating tone, volume, and channel balance.

Protons – Protons make up part of the nucleus of all atoms except hydrogen, whose nucleus consists of a single proton. In neutral atoms, the number of protons is the same as the number of electrons. In positively charged atoms (as in electrically conductive materials), the number of protons is greater than the number of electrons, and in negatively charged atoms (as in insulator materials) electrons outnumber protons.

Proximity Sensor – A common term for a spatial-type sensor that can be either the radar, ultrasonic, or infrared type. (See also "Spatial Sensor")

Pulsed Output (Security) – An output of a security system usually used to flash parking lights or honk horns; it is pulsed or turned on and off by the security system. In some cases an output may be programmable to behave this way when activated.

PVA – Poly Vinyl Alcohol is a mold release spray used in fiberglass fabrication.

PWM – Pulse Width Modulation is an electrical behavior that allows short bursts of electrical pulses to power a circuit or device.

Q

Quiescent Current – A term that describes the amount of current consumed by a circuit when it is not performing any work or otherwise "at rest". Also referred to as "standby" or "parasitic" current draw.

Qtc – Measurement of a speaker and enclosure working together as one.

Qts – The measurement of the speaker as a motor, taking into consideration all mechanical and electrical losses.

R

Radar Sensor – A common name for a type of spatial sensor used in automotive security systems to protect/monitor open areas (such as convertibles, truck beds, etc.). Radar sensors are also sometimes used in ADAS products, such as parking sensors or blind spot monitoring.

Range (Audio) – Usually described as frequency range, this is a system's frequency response, beyond which the frequency is attenuated below a specified tolerance. Also, the frequency band or bands within which a receiver or component is designed to operate.

Range (Security) – The maximum operating distance that can exist between a vehicle and the remote control transmitter expressed in feet, meters, yards or fractions of miles or kilometers.

Rarefaction – A state or region of minimum pressure in a medium traversed by compression waves (sound waves). Speakers rarefy air when they move inward.

RDS (Radio Data System) – RDS scrolls text on the head unit display to help sort broadcasts by type (talk, sports, etc.) and provide drive-time warnings of accidents.

Real-Time Analyzer (RTA) – A spectrum analyzer that measures the amplitude versus frequency (X vs. Y plot) of a 20Hz-20kHz audio signal bandwidth while in real time.

Receiver – A device designed to receive a signal or command from a source such as a transmitter.

Rectification – The process of turning AC into (pulsing) DC. Modern alternators use a process called Full Wave Rectification with a minimum of 6 diodes.

Relay – An electromagnet switch that allows small, relatively low-level signals to operate higher amperage devices. Also used when polarity reversal is necessary.

Remote (Security) – The remote control transmitter used with an RF-based remote security system.

Remote Turn-On – the discrete turn-on circuit in most mobile electronic audio products. Head units typically have a remote turn-on output whereas preamp level processors and amplifiers typically have a remote turn-on input. Where a remote turn-on trigger is lacking, signal sensing may be an alternative method of turning on a processor or amplifier. (See also "Signal Sensing")

Remote Start – The feature where a security system or accessory module allows the vehicle operator to start the engine using a remote transmitter without actually being inside the vehicle.

Reset (Security) – The ability of a security system to automatically stop sounding the siren and return to an armed state after being triggered, as long as no further trigger conditions are present.

Resistance – The electrical term used to describe the property that various materials possess to restrict or inhibit the flow of electricity. Electrical resistance is relatively low in most metals and relatively high in most nonmetallic substances. Electrical resistance is measured in Ohms.

Resonance – The tendency of objects to vibrate or become 'excited' at certain frequencies. This can be a useful or undesirable effect, as in planned enclosure or driver resonance, or as in unplanned enclosure resonance or vibrating panel resonance.

Retriggering – See "Alarm Retriggering."

Reverb – The remainder of sound that exists in a listening space after the source of the sound has stopped. Reverb is sometimes mistakenly called echo (which is an entirely different sounding phenomenon). Common reverb can be heard with activity like clapping hands (or bouncing a basketball) in a large enclosed space (like a gym). All spaces have some reverberation, though cars have shorter times in which that reverberation is heard. In some cases, if the reverberation is low enough in volume and short enough in duration from the original sound, the human ear may not notice it and perceive it as a separate sound. (See also "RT60")

RF – Radio Frequency. An AC frequency that is higher than the highest audio frequency.

RGB – Red/Green/Blue. An acronym used to describe analog video signal transfer where the primary colors of red, green and blue each have their own conductor. RGB signals in automotive applications have three different variations: RGBS, RGBHV, and RGsB. The main differences are how the conductor that controls picture information synchronizing is implemented.

Ripple (Acoustic Response) – The deviation from a flat response in the pass band, generally used to describe vented subwoofer enclosure characteristics.

Ripple (Charging System) – The amount of Alternating Current (AC) present on a DC circuit's power line.

RPM – Revolutions per Minute. Refers to a vehicle's engine revolutions.

RMS – Root Mean Square. The equivalent thermal DC value of an AC signal. An AC RMS value represents the same degree of thermal quantity as a constant DC value.

Roll-Off – Relates to the attenuation of frequencies, above or below a given point, at a specific rate.

Roof-Mount Antenna – A permanently-installed antenna located on the vehicle's roof. Communication antennas are commonly roof mount applications (except for convertibles).

Route Guidance System – A GPS based, electronic guidance system installed into vehicles using digital mapping and point of interest information to facilitate getting from a location to the desired destination with precise directions. This is generally an installed item whereas a handheld (portable) navigation system is often called a PND. (See also "PND")

RT-60 – An abbreviation for the specification of Reverb Time -60dB. It is an expression used to more specifically state what a given reverb time is. The purpose of the RT60 specification is to provide an objective measure of reverb time. The spec says that reverb time is defined as the time it takes the reverb to go down in volume by 60 dB, or to 1 millionth of the original volume.

S

Scanning – The popular term given to the way a thief breaks into a remote security system by quickly and sequentially transmitting all the possible security codes of a victim's security system.

Seat Sensor – A pressure-activated switch designed specifically for use in detecting any pressure applied to vehicle's seat.

Sensitivity (Audio) – The rating of a loudspeaker that indicates the level of sound intensity the speaker produces (in dB) at a distance of one meter when it receives one watt of input power.

Sensitivity (Security) – The relative adjustment of a particular sensor with regard to how easy or difficult it is to trigger by its intended purpose. Very often the cause of unintended "false alarms" is due to overly sensitive security sensors that react to wind, loud noises, or otherwise normal circumstances.

Sensor (Security) – A device designed to detect or sense an intrusion or attack upon a vehicle by monitoring such things as motion, vibration, impact, sound, or the presence of a foreign mass.

Sensor (Safety) – A device designed to detect or sense the presence of a safety concern, such as vehicles in a driver's blind spot or obstacles encountered while parking. These types of sensors are used throughout many ADAS-based products and systems. (See also "ADAS")

Sensor Bypass – The ability of a security system to automatically or manually delete or bypass the triggers from all or some of the sensors tied into the security system.

Shock Sensor – A sensor that is specifically designed to detect a shock or impact applied to the vehicle.

Short Circuit – The condition that occurs when a circuit path is created between the positive and negative poles of a battery, power supply, or circuit. A short circuit will bypass any resistance in a circuit and cause it not to operate.

Shrink – Polyester resin that has been mixed with excessive amounts of MEKP and is prone to cracking upon becoming cured.

Signal Delay (Audio) – See "Delay" and "Digital Delay."

Signal-to-Noise Ratio – The s/n ratio indicates how much audio signal there is in relation to noise, or a specified noise floor.

Signal Sensing (Audio) – A method of turning on a signal processor or amplifier when a dedicated remote turn-on signal is not present. Signal sensing works when the circuit senses an audio signal and provides a command (or output trigger) to activate the device(s) requiring a turn-on signal. (See also "Remote Turn-On)

Single-Ended (Audio Input or Output) – An audio signal transfer scheme in which the outer shield of the 2 conductor cable is electrically common with BOTH left and right channels and only the center conductors differ in signal content. Most RCA input and outputs on mobile electronic equipment are single-ended type.

Siren – Any kind of device, mechanical or electronic, that is designed to produce a loud warning sound when triggered by a security system.

SI Unit – Systeme International d'Unites. A complete metric system of units of measurement for scientists; fundamental quantities are length (meter), mass (kilogram), time (second), electric current (ampere), temperature (kelvin), amount of matter (mole) and luminous intensity (candela); The United States is the only country in the world not using only SI units.

SKU – Stock Keeping Unit. Refers to each single item carried by a retailer. Every color, style and item having its own vendor or vendee number has its own SKU.

Sound – A type of physical kinetic energy called acoustical energy. (See also "Acoustical Energy")

Sound Discriminator – A device designed to listen to, evaluate, and discriminate between the sounds that may be heard within the interior of a vehicle, and then trigger the security system if the sound fits within the parameters of what the sensor is designated to react to. A glass break sensor is a common use of a sound discriminator.

Sound Pressure Level (SPL) – An acoustic measurement for the ratios of sound energy. Rated in decibels (dBA and dBC "weighting" are common for replication of human hearing curves).

Sound Waves – Fluctuating waves of pressure traveling through a physical medium such as air. Acoustic waves alternate compressions (pressure) and rarefactions (vacuum) in air.

Source Unit – The unit in which the audio (or video) program material originates. Source units may feature playback of multiple source material formats. The most common form of source unit is the in-dash head unit and source formats include digital audio media, video, navigation, auxiliary inputs, etc.

Spatial Sensors – Devices specifically designed to monitor the space in and around the vehicle. When used in vehicle security systems, these detect intrusions into or around the vehicle. When used in ADAS (driver safety) systems, these detect the presence of other vehicles, pedestrians or hazards. These sensors work on a variety of different principles, including ultrasonics, radar, radio frequency, and infrared.

SPDT – Single Pole Double Throw. A switch or relay that has only one pole or contact but whose contact can throw or make electrical contact with two separate stationary contacts. This is the most commonly used relay in the mobile electronics industry.

Spider – A flat, round, springy device that holds the vibrating cone of a dynamic loudspeaker. The spider is where the diaphragm meets the voice coil.

Spike Suppression – The process of using a diode across the coil terminals of an electromechanical relay to suppress or "quench" any back EMF generated by the current exiting the magnetic field of the coil.

SPST – Single Pole Single Throw. A switch or relay that has only one pole or contact and can only throw or make electrical contact with one stationary contact.

Staging – The accuracy with which an audio system conveys audible information about the size, shape, and acoustical characteristics of the original recording space and the placement of the artists within it.

Standby Current Draw – A term that describes the amount of current consumed by a circuit when it is not performing any work or otherwise "at rest". Also referred to as "parasitic" current draw or "quiescent current."

Starter Disable – Any circuit or device used alone or in conjunction with a security system that is designed to prevent the vehicle's starter from operating.

Status – The state a system is in at any given time, typically used in describing security and remote starter systems.

Stiffening Capacitor – The unofficial name given to a polarized, large value capacitor specifically intended to stabilize supply voltage during periods of peak current demand. This term was coined by industry technical experts Richard Clark and David Navone. Also called a "Power Supply Capacitor."

Subwoofer – A loudspeaker made specifically to reproduce frequencies below 125 Hz.

SVC – Single Voice Coil. A speaker with only one voice coil. (See also "Voice Coil" and "DVC")

Switch – A switch is any form of mechanical, electronic, electromechanical, magnetic, or mercury device that either opens or closes a circuit.

Switch Sensing – Refers to the inputs on a security system designed to detect a switch closure from such triggers as a door, hood, or trunk/hatch pin switches.

System Reset – See "Reset" and "Alarm Reset."

T

Tach Wire – An electrical input on a remote starter system that monitors the engine speed and shuts the vehicle down when a predetermined threshold is exceeded.

TDMA – Time division multiple access. A digital communications scheme used in some air interface technologies by dividing calls into time slots, each one lasting only a fraction of a second. Each call is assigned a specific portion of time on a designated channel. By dividing each call into timed 'packets,' a single channel can carry many calls at once. GSM is based on TDMA technology.

Thermal – The property of temperature considered in the performance characteristic of a device.

Time Alignment™ – A trademarked term for delaying one or more audio signals coined by E.M. Long, the developer of UREI 813 Studio Monitors which used analog all-pass delays used to align the outputs of the high and low frequency drivers in the monitors. Today, time alignment is a common term used to describe signal delay of multiple channels in digital signal processors, even though the original use was in the analog domain. (See also "Delay")

Tolerance Rating – The rating (expressed as a percentage) given to an electronic component's measured value compared against its rated value. Greater tolerance numbers indicate the measured value may be further away from the rated value.

Total Harmonic Distortion (THD) – Given as a percentage, a measurement of how much a device may distort a signal. Figures below 0.1% are considered to be inaudible with test tones. Figures below 1% are actually very difficult to hear with music program material, hence the standard THD testing level of power amplifiers at 1%.

TosLink – A proprietary connector style developed by Toshiba used in optical connections on consumer digital audio products.

TPS – Throttle Position Sensor.

Transponder Key – A proprietary (electronically coded) key used in an OEM anti-theft system. The transponder key must correctly "communicate" the appropriate code to allow the vehicle to start and run normally.

Transceiver – A combination radio transmitter/receiver usually installed in a single housing and sharing some components. (See also "Transmitter" and "Receiver")

Transducer – Any device that converts energy from one form to another, e.g., electrical to acoustic or vice versa. Loudspeakers and microphones are two types of transducers.

Transfer Function (Subwoofer) – The change in the low end of a low frequency system brought on by loading the device into the cabin of a vehicle.

Transmitter (Security) – The hand-held remote control used to arm/disarm and perform accessory functions on a vehicle security system. More commonly called a remote.

Transmitter (Subscriber or Radio Services) – A land based tower or device that transmits signals to compatible devices that are intended to receive those signals such as mobile phones, GPS navigation systems receiving real time traffic data over an RF network, satellite radio repeaters, and even non-subscriber AM/FM radio.

Trigger – The common name for any type of stimulus that will cause a security system to produce an alarm. A trigger could come from a pin switch, a sensor, or a direct command from a transmitter or accessory button.

Troubleshooting – The practice by which problems are identified and repaired by process of elimination.

Trunk Release – A feature that enables the release of the trunk/hatch by remote control.

Tuner Selectivity – The ability of and AM/FM tuner to discriminate between two signals very close to each other in frequency. This is important in major metropolitan areas. Lower numbers are more preferable.

Tuner Stereo Separation – The ability of an FM tuner to accurately separate the left and right channel information of a stereo broadcast. Measured in decibels (dB), higher numbers are more preferable.

Tweeter – A small loudspeaker or driver meant to reproduce high frequencies, typically 2kHz and above.

U

Ultrasonic Sensor – A form of spatial sensor typically used in vehicle security applications designed to detect an intrusion into a vehicle by monitoring the interior space with ultrasonic energy.

Unfused Wire – Any section of wire between the power supply and a load that does not include the protection of a fuse or circuit breaker.

Uni-Body Chassis – A vehicle chassis design where the frame and main body cavity are integrated into a single structure.

Universal Product Code (UPC) – Also known as "bar code." Numbers printed on product package that can be electronically scanned for information such as brand, manufacturer and price.

Upmixer (or Upmixng) – A signal processing scheme wherein a two channels of audio information using matrix processing creates multiple channels (including center and rear) to simulate a discrete (5.1 type) sound effect. This is often helpful to include attributes from the original recording not easily replicated in a car or small listening space. Many 'premium' OEM audio systems such as Bose Centerpoint, Harman Logic7 or QTS and Dolby Pro Logic II derivatives employ upmixers and dedicated channels in the factory amplifier or sound system electronics. (See also "Matrix Processing")

V

V2I – Vehicle to Infrastructure. The communication element of a vehicle communication system that "talks" to roadway infrastructure. A V2I roadway is often referred to as "smart road" or "smart highway" when describing how it would provide added safety and efficiency for vehicles traveling on that V2I roadway.

V2V – Vehicle-to-Vehicle is an automobile technology designed to allow automobiles to "talk" to each other. V2V communications form a wireless ad hoc network on the roads. In North America V2V systems use a region of the 5.9 GHz band, a frequency also used by WiFi.

V2X – Vehicle-to-Everything is a communication system concept that passes information from a vehicle to any entity that may affect the vehicle, and vice versa. It is a vehicular communication system that incorporates other more specific types of communication as V2I (Vehicle-to-Infrastructure), V2V (Vehicle-to-Vehicle), V2P (Vehicle-to-Pedestrian), V2D (Vehicle-to-Device) and V2G (Vehicle-to-Grid for electric and alternative fuel vehicles). The overall concept for V2X is safety, with energy savings also being important.

Valence Electron – a negatively charged electron in the outer shell of an atom which can combine with other atoms to form molecules and electrical current flow. It is when negatively charged valence electrons leave conductive material atoms that they become "free electrons" and are attracted to the opposite polarity creating current flow.

Valet – A term used to describe the state in which a security system may be placed so that it would be prevented form arming passively and/or actively.

Valet Switch – The switch designed to provide the control to place the security system into or bring the system out of the valet state.

Variable Voltage Circuit – see "MUX"

Vas – Mechanical compliance. A measurement in liters or cubic feet of the volume of air that is equal to the compliance of the speaker's total suspension.

Vehicle Speed Sensor (VSS) – A discrete sensor on the vehicle that reports vehicle speed to the vehicle's computer(s) and other speed dependent devices.

Voice Coil – A single coil of wire that takes in the electrical energy coming from the amplifier and converts it into acoustic energy or mechanical motion by attaching to the speaker's cone. This is known as a single voice coil (SVC). Many subwoofers have dual voice coils (or DVC) to increase the power handling and flexibility to load the amplifier for increased power output. (See also "SVC" and "DVC").

Volt – The term used to refer to the property of electrical pressure through a circuit.

Voltage – The electrical pressure required to do electrical work. Voltage is also caked potential. Voltage must be present for electrical current to flow within a closed circuit.

Voltage Drop – The amount of energy consumed when a device has resistance in its circuit. The voltage (E) measured across a resistance (R) carrying a current (I). E= I x R. (See also "Volt")

Voltage Sensing – A name given to a form of vehicle security system trigger or remote starter input that relies on sensing a change in the voltage of the vehicle. Some remote starter systems rely on voltage sensing as an alternative to a tachometer input, for example.

VOM – Volt-Ohm-Meter, sometimes called a Volt-Ohm-Millimeter. A Multimeter that measures voltage, ohms, and milliamperes.

VSS – Vehicle Speed Sensor. This is an electrical connection often required for many route guidance systems installed in a vehicle.

W

WAAS – Wide Area Augmentation System. An air navigation aid in the US developed by the Federal Aviation Administration to augment the Global Positioning System (GPS), with the goal of improving its accuracy, integrity, and availability. Originally intended for use by aircraft, WAAS is also available in many consumer GPS devices, including in-vehicle navigation systems.

Watt – The basic practical unit of measure for electrical or acoustical power.

Wattage – Electrical power.

Watt's Law – Similar to Ohm's Law, it demonstrates the relationships between Voltage (E) and Current (I) to represent a quantity of Power (P). With the Watt's Law formula, knowing two elements can mathematically compute the third element.

Wave – A single oscillation in matter (e.g., a sound wave). Waves move outward from a point of disturbance, propagate through a medium, and grow weaker as they travel farther. Wave motion is associated with mechanical vibration, sound, heat, light, etc.

Waveform – The shape of a wave, typically viewed on an oscilloscope. (See also "oscilloscope" and "clipping")

Wavelength – The length of distance a single cycle or complete sound wave travels.

White Noise – Random noise with equal energy per

frequency covering 20Hz-20kHz. This differs from Pink Noise as pink noise has equal energy per octave (rather than frequency). Based on how humans perceived the differences in sound from octave to octave, pink noise – rather than white noise – is the preferred test signal for frequency related measurements in mobile audio systems. (See also "Pink Noise")

WiFi – WiFi provides wireless connectivity over unlicensed spectrum (using the IEEE 802.11xx standards), generally in the 2.4, 3.6 and 5 GHz radio bands. WiFi offers local area connectivity to WiFi-enabled devices. (See also "802.11")

Window Roll-up – The term used for the feature that causes the window(s) on a vehicle to close upon arming, or open and close as part of a convenience feature of a security system. Also called "Window Closure."

Wi-Max – A wireless technology based on the IEEE 802.16 standard providing metropolitan area network connectivity for fixed wireless access at broadband speeds.

Wiring Harness – A specific application of wires and proprietary connectors to facilitate connection of electronic components in multiple locations.

Wiring Harness Adaptor – A wiring harness adaptor is utilized to adapt replacement components into OEM applications for "plug in" compatibility, such as installing an aftermarket head unit to replace a factory head unit.

WMA (Windows Media Audio) – An encoding and variable compression scheme for digital music. Must have a device with WMA decoding for playback.

WMV® (Windows Media Video) – An encoding and variable compression scheme for digital video. Must have a device with WMV decoding for playback.

Woofer – A large dynamic loudspeaker that is well suited for reproducing bass frequencies, typically 6-18 inches in diameter when used in car audio applications.

WOT – Wide Open Throttle; The electrical condition present whenever the TPS is fully engaged. (See also "TPS")

X

Xmax (Electrical) – The distance a speaker cone can travel before the magnetic gap loses control over the voice coil.

Xmax (Mechanical) – Also known as Xmech. The distance a speaker cone can move before the suspension physically reaches maximum travel.

Z

Zero Output – The absence of output signal or output power.

Zobel Network – A type of filter used to make the impedance a loudspeaker presents to its amplifier output appear as a steady resistance. This is beneficial to the amplifier performance. The impedance of a loudspeaker is partly resistive.

Zone – The specific area of a security system's coverage, or a term used to describe a specific trigger input such as "door zone" or "sensor zone."

INDEX

INDEX

NOTES